The essence of ultimate decision remains impenetrable to the observer — often, indeed, to the decider himself. . . . There will always be the dark and tangled stretches in the decision-making process — mysterious even to those who may be most intimately involved.

John Fitzgerald Kennedy

I have come across men of letters who have written history without taking part in public affairs, and politicians who have concerned themselves with producing events without thinking about them. I have observed that the first are always inclined to find general causes, whereas the second, living in the midst of disconnected daily facts, are prone to imagine that everything is attributable to particular incidents, and that the wires they pull are the same as those that move the world. It is to be presumed that both are equally deceived.

Alexis de Tocqueville

Written under the auspices of
The Faculty Seminar on Bureaucracy, Politics, and Policy
of the Institute of Politics,
John Fitzgerald Kennedy School of Government,
Harvard University

ESSENCE OF DECISION
Explaining the Cuban Missile Crisis

Graham T. Allison

Harvard University

Little, Brown and Company

Boston

To my mother and father

Acknowledgments

Quotation from the following works was made possible by the kind permission of the publishers.

Elie Abel, *The Missile Crisis.* Quoted material (© 1966 by Elie Abel) is
used by permission of J. B. Lippincott Company; Paul R. Reynolds, Inc.;
and MacGibbon & Kee Limited.

Arnold Horelick and Myron Rush, *Strategic Power and Soviet Foreign
Policy.* Quoted material (© 1965, 1966 by The Rand Corporation) is used
by permission of The University of Chicago Press and The Rand Corporation.

Robert F. Kennedy, *Thirteen Days: A Memoir of the Cuban Missile Crisis.*
Quoted material is used by permission of W. W. Norton & Company, Inc.;
and Macmillian of London and Basingstoke.

Richard Neustadt, *Presidential Power.* Quoted material is used by permission of John Wiley & Sons, Inc., Publishers.

Theodore C. Sorensen, *Kennedy.* Quoted material (© 1965 by Theodore C.
Sorensen) is used by permission of Harper & Row, Publishers, Inc.; and
and Hodder and Stoughton Limited.

Preface

My aims in this book are two. On the one hand, I examine the central puzzles of the Cuban missile crisis. Several participants in this nuclear confrontation have already told the story, each from his own point of view. None of these accounts directly addresses the major questions of the crisis. I try to in this book.

On the other hand, I explore the influence of unrecognized assumptions upon our thinking about events like the missile crisis. Answers to questions like why the Soviet Union tried to sneak strategic offensive missiles into Cuba must be affected by basic assumptions we make, categories we use, our angle of vision. But what kind of assumptions do we tend to make? How do these assumptions channel our thinking? What alternative perspectives are available? This study identifies the basic frame of reference used by most people when thinking about foreign affairs. Furthermore, it outlines two alternative frameworks. Each frame of reference is, in effect, a "conceptual lens." By comparing and contrasting the three frameworks, we see what each magnifies, highlights, and reveals as well as what each blurs or neglects.

The structure of this book reflects my dual objectives. Three conceptual chapters sketch three rough-cut frames of reference. These chapters are separated by three case studies, each of which uses one of the frames of reference in searching for answers to the major questions of the Cuban missile crisis. By addressing central issues of the crisis first from one perspective, then from a second, and finally from a third, these chapters not only probe more deeply into the event, uncovering additional insights; they also demonstrate how alternative conceptual lenses lead one to see, emphasize, and worry about quite different aspects of events like the missile crisis.

On the one hand, substantive instance; on the other, conceptual argument. Today I must confess that I am no longer certain where one ends and the other begins, or, indeed, which is the head and which the tail of my own dog. But I am certain about the impulse that led me to pursue these two aims jointly.

This book attempts to address the entire community of foreign policy observers, which comprises both "artists" and "scientists." For the artists, the appeal of the conceptual chapters may be minimal. As "spinach and calisthenics," they will be palatable to the extent they stimulate new insight into old problems, clearer perception of additional facets, and better substantive studies. But for the scientists, the theoretical chapters constitute the contribution: pointing out the existence of implicit conceptual frameworks within which investigations proceed and spelling out some of the systematic implications of alternative models. In attempting to address both audiences simultaneously, I open myself to the objection that the cases lack the subtlety and craft of "art," whereas the theoretical chapters display little of the system and rigor of "science." How justifiable such criticism may be is left to the reader's judgment. But there should be no ambiguity about the reasons for my attempt.

If a common ground exists between the artists and the scientists, that ground is explanation. Neither art's appreciation of the uniqueness of occurrences nor science's grasp of occurrences as mere instances of more general propositions is limited to explanation. But central to both enterprises is an attempt to understand and explain why events occurred. The artist may appear (to the scientist) overly fascinated with nuance and randomness that would be better treated as extraneous fluff around common, recurring elements. The scientist may seem (to the artist) to ride roughshod over relevant, particular details in the quest for generality. But the achievement of neither group in the foreign policy community justifies arrogance toward, or neglect of, the other's work. Thus, my attempt to produce explanations and, in the same book, to formulate systematically the concepts and propositions in terms of which the explanations are produced, seems appropriate.

However wide the gulf between artists and scientists, in the end both must be mellowed by awareness of the insight expressed in the epigraph: *"The essence of ultimate decision remains impenetrable to the observer — often, indeed, to the decider himself. . . . There will always be the dark and tangled stretches in the decision-making process — mysterious even to those who may be most intimately involved."*[1]

A Reader's Guide. My argument in this book has been percolating for more than five years. Drafts of pieces of the argument have circulated since the summer of 1967. But when I finally decided to sit down and write the book, a colleague offered me some advice. Rather than stumbling around thinking about a general unknown reader, or trying to write for everyman, he suggested instead that I choose four or five real people and let them stand for the circle of readers to whom I was writing. I found the advice quite helpful. And it may be instructive to identify these individuals — in general terms — and to state, briefly, my hopes in writing for each.

The first two "representative readers" are a colleague and a student. The colleague is a professional analyst of foreign policy and international relations; the student, a bright college sophomore. For the colleague the chapters on the missile crisis should provide new material, a fresh look at the central issues, and an illustration of the general argument. More ambitiously, the conceptual chapters try to (1) provide a comprehensive overview of the product of analysis in various areas of foreign policy and international relations; (2) present a set of categories which can be used in judging that product; (3) undermine prevailing assumptions both about the nontheoretical nature of foreign policy analysis and about the rampant disjointedness of efforts in various substantive areas of foreign policy; (4) challenge the basic categories and assumptions within which most analysts think about problems of foreign policy; and (5) sketch two sharp, provocative alternative conceptual frameworks. The basic outline of the general argument can stand on its own feet. (Indeed, a number of other scholars are using the alternative models in their own studies.[2]) But, strictly speaking, the argument is unfinished. It stands as an invitation to my colleague, and to the reader: please join the discussion.

For the student, the chapters on the missile crisis are meant to make persuasive an unhappy, troubling, but unavoidable fact about this world. No event demonstrates more clearly than the missile crisis that with respect to nuclear war there is an awesome crack between *unlikelihood* and *impossibility*. The theoretical chapters, especially the summaries of various areas of the literature, should acquaint him with what serious analysts do and with what their analyses have produced. But the chief attraction will, I hope, be the speed at which the interested student is brought to the frontiers of analysis of foreign policy, and indeed of all public policy.

Third and fourth are a layman who is a regular reader of foreign policy articles in *The New York Times*, and a serious journalist. As I pondered their interests and tastes, I found less difference between these two individuals and the first two readers than I had first imagined. Thus I hope that both the layman and the journalist will find the entire study relevant, for some of the same reasons. But they, or some people like them, may be bored by the summaries of the literature and the more formal considerations in each of the conceptual chapters. If so, they can omit the conceptual chapters, except for the statements of each paradigm.

Fifth, is the wife of one of my colleagues, an intelligent person not especially interested in foreign affairs, and thus a good stand-in for "general readers." After reading an earlier draft of the manuscript, this colleague recommended it to his wife with the advice, "Read the introduction and then just read the alternate chapters on the missile crisis." These chapters can be read simply as an unfolding of the evidence about this crucial event from three alternative vantage points. The general reader should be forewarned, however, that this path will not leave him with a confident account of "what really happened." Indeed, if I had been successful, it should lead him to become interested in the issues to which the conceptual chapters are addressed.

A Note on Sources. As John F. Kennedy warned with explicit reference to the Cuban missile crisis, "Any historian who walks through this mine field of charges and countercharges should proceed with some care." My discussion of the missile crisis makes use of all information in the published record. As the footnotes attest, the amount of information available in public primary sources is extraordinary. I have also been privileged to have interviews and conversations with most of the high-level participants in the crisis. Moreover, I have the benefit of extended and repeated conversations with many individuals who have spent time reminiscing with the central participants. And, finally, I have interviewed a large number of people who were involved in the lower-level operations of the U.S. government during the crisis. These individuals provided a valuable guide through the maze of public material. For their patience and consideration, as well as their information, I am most grateful. Some of my sources insisted on anonymity. Others were promised an opportunity to review any manuscript that quoted them directly. My aspiration here is not to write a definitive history but rather to demonstrate the possibility and utility of alternative approaches to events of this sort (given the information available in public sources). Therefore, the three stories of the missile crisis in this book are documented entirely from the public record.

Acknowledgments. The origins of this book go back at least to the spring of 1966 when several Harvard faculty members began meeting to discuss the impact of "bureaucracy" on "policy" — the gap between the intentions of the actors and the results of governmental action. The "May Group," as we came to be known after our chairman, Ernest R. May, included Morton H. Halperin, Fred C. Iklé, William W. Kaufmann, Andrew W. Marshall, Richard E. Neustadt, Don K. Price, Harry S. Rowen, and myself as *rapporteur*. That group hooked me on the problem, supplied me with more ideas than I could assimilate, and criticized every successive attempt to formulate what became the general argument of this book. Indeed, the book represents to a large extent the most recent but still unfinished "Evolving Paper" of that group — though, obviously, none of them can be saddled with responsibility for any of the faults in this statement of the argument. Today the group meets as the Research Seminar on Bureaucracy, Politics, and Policy of the Institute of Politics in the John F. Kennedy School of Government at Harvard. Over these five years, membership in the group has included Francis M. Bator, Joseph L. Bower, William C. Capron, Michel Crozier, Philip B. Heymann, Albert O. Hirschman, Stanley Hoffmann, Henry D. Jacoby, Doris H. Kearns, Lance Liebman, David S. Mundel, Edwin O. Reischauer, Thomas C. Schelling, James Q. Wilson, Samuel L. Williamson, and Adam Yarmolinsky. To this group, and to each of the members individually, I am most grateful.

Since this book has been so long in the making, drafts of the manuscript, or pieces thereof, have circulated in various forms. In addition to members of the May Group, a large number of other readers have offered pertinent criticisms and suggestions. For services beyond any call of duty or responsibility, I want to thank Alexander L. George, William R. Harris, Roger Hilsman, Theodore R. Marmor, Warner C. Schilling, Leon V. Sigal, Harrison Wellford, Martin S. Wishnatsky, Albert Wohlstetter, Roberta Wohlstetter, and Charles Wolf, Jr.

Several institutions have supported my research and writing. The Institute of Politics served as catalyst for the original May

Group and as patron in a variety of ways ever since. The Rand Corporation gave me spare time during two summers in a critical, stimulating environment. An early draft was revised while I was a Research Associate at the Center for International Affairs at Harvard. An International Affairs Fellowship from the Council on Foreign Relations allowed me to complete the manuscript and to begin pushing further some of its implications.

Final preparation of the manuscript was greatly aided by Janet Shur's excellent research assistance, Joan Wyatt's service not only as typist but also as copy editor, and Susan Elliott's chasing of references.

Four individuals deserve special note for the intellectual and personal debt I have incurred. The influence of Thomas C. Schelling will be obvious in my chapter on Model I. The impact of ideas that Andrew W. Marshall has been propagating for a decade is marked, especially in my chapter on Model II. My heaviest debt, which is clearest in my chapter on Model III, is to Richard E. Neustadt. To each of these men I am deeply grateful. Elisabeth K. M. Allison, my wife, pushed me at the beginning, served as an indefatigable research assistant during the long haul, and nudged me across the finish line by sweetly, but not infrequently, inquiring, "When are you going to be through?"

Contents

ESSENCE OF DECISION

OCTOBER 1962

SUN	MON	TUE	WED	THU	FRI	SAT
	1	2	3	4	5	6
7	8	9	10	11	12	13
14	15	**16**	**17**	**18**	**19**	**20**
21	**22**	**23**	**24**	**25**	**26**	**27**
28	29	30	31			

Introduction

The Cuban missile crisis was a seminal event. History offers no parallel to those thirteen days of October 1962, when the United States and the Soviet Union paused at the nuclear precipice. Never before had there been such a high probability that so many lives would end suddenly. Had war come, it could have meant the death of 100 million Americans, more than 100 million Russians, as well as millions of Europeans.[1] Beside it, the natural calamities and inhumanities of earlier history would have faded into insignificance. Given the odds on disaster — which President Kennedy estimated as "between one out of three and even" — our escape seems awesome.[2] This event symbolizes a central, if only partially "thinkable," fact about our existence.

Although several excellent accounts are now available, the missile crisis remains, as Harold Macmillan has observed, a "strange and still scarcely explicable affair."[3] Even the central questions have eluded satisfactory answers:

Why did the Soviet Union place strategic offensive missiles in Cuba? For what purpose did the Russians undertake such a drastic, risky departure from their traditional policy? Given the repeated American warnings that such an act would not be tolerated, how could Khrushchev have made such a major miscalculation?

Why did the United States respond with a naval quarantine of Soviet shipments to Cuba? Was it necessary for the United States to force a public nuclear confrontation? What alternatives were really available? What danger did the Soviet missiles in Cuba pose for the United States? Did this threat justify the President's choice of a course of action that he believed entailed a 33 to 50 percent chance of disaster? Did that threat require more immediate action to disable the Soviet missiles in Cuba before they became operational?

Why were the missiles withdrawn? What would have happened if, instead of withdrawing the missiles, Khrushchev had announced that the operational Soviet missiles would fire if fired upon? Did the "blockade" work, or was there an "ultimatum" or perhaps some "deal"? Why did the Soviets remove the missiles rather than retaliate at other equally sensitive points — Berlin, for example?

What are the "lessons" of the missile crisis? What does this event teach us about nuclear confrontations? What does it imply about crisis management and government coordination? Is this a model of how to deal with the Soviet Union?

Satisfactory answers to these questions await information that has not yet come to light and more penetrating analysis of available evidence. This study provides new information about the missile crisis and a more powerful analysis of some aspects of it. But the missile crisis also serves here as grist in a more general investigation. This study proceeds from the premise that satisfactory answers to questions about the missile crisis wait for more than information and analysis. Real improvement in our answers to questions of this sort depends on greater awareness of what we (both laymen and professional analysts) bring to the analysis. When answering questions like "Why did the Soviet Union place missiles in Cuba?" what we see and judge to be important and accept as adequate depends not only on the evidence but also on the "conceptual lenses" through which we look at the evidence. Another purpose of this study is therefore to explore some of the fundamental yet often unnoticed choices among the categories and assumptions that channel our thinking about problems like the Cuban missile crisis.

The General Argument

When we are puzzled by a happening in foreign affairs, the source of our puzzlement is typically a particular *outcome:* the Soviet emplacement of missiles in Cuba, the movement of U.S. troops across the narrow neck of the Korean peninsula, the Japanese attack on Pearl Harbor.* These occurrences raise obvious questions: *Why* did the Soviet Union place missiles in Cuba? *Why* did U.S. troops fail to stop at the narrow neck in their march up Korea? *Why* did Japan attack the American fleet at Pearl Harbor? In pursuing the answers to these questions, the serious analyst seeks to discover why one specific state of the world came about — rather than some other.

In searching for an explanation, one typically puts himself in the place of the nation, or national government, confronting a problem of foreign affairs, and tries to figure out why he might have chosen the action in question. Thus, analysts have explained the Soviet missiles in Cuba as a probe of American intentions. U.S. troops marched across the narrow neck in Korea because American objectives had escalated as a consequence of easy victories in the South. The attack on Pearl Harbor is explained as Japan's solution to the strategic problem posed by U.S. pressure in the Far East.

In offering (or accepting) these explanations, we are assuming governmental behavior can be most satisfactorily understood by analogy with the purposive acts of individuals. In many cases this is a fruitful assumption. Treating national governments as if they were centrally coordinated, purposive individuals provides a useful shorthand for understanding problems of policy. But this simplification — like all simplifications — obscures as well as reveals. In particular, it obscures the persistently neglected fact of bureaucracy: the "maker" of government policy is not one calculating decisionmaker but is rather a conglomerate of large organizations and political actors. What this fact implies for analysts of events like the Cuban missile crisis is no simple matter: its implications concern the basic categories and assumptions with which we approach events.

More rigorously, the *argument* developed in the body of this study can be summarized in three propositions:

1. *Professional analysts of foreign affairs (as well as ordinary laymen) think about problems of foreign and military policy*

---

*The term *outcome* is introduced here as a technical concept meaning a selectively delimited state of the real world importantly affected by the action of a government. The assertion is that in thinking about problems of foreign affairs, what most participants and analysts are really interested in are outcomes and the specific actions governments take that affect outcomes.

*in terms of largely implicit conceptual models that have signi-
ficant consequences for the content of their thought.*[4]

In thinking about problems of foreign affairs, professional
analysts as well as ordinary laymen proceed in a straightforward, informal, nontheoretical fashion. Careful examination of
explanations of events like the Soviet installation of missiles in
Cuba, however, reveals a more complex theoretical substructure.
Explanations by particular analysts show regular and predictable
characteristics, which reflect unrecognized assumptions about
the character of puzzles, the categories in which problems should
be considered, the types of evidence that are relevant, and the
determinants of occurrences. The first proposition is that bundles of such related assumptions constitute basic frames of
reference or conceptual models in terms of which analysts and
ordinary laymen ask and answer the questions: What happened?
Why did it happen? What will happen?* Assumptions like
these are central to the activities of explanation and prediction.
In attempting to explain a particular event, the analyst cannot
simply describe the full state of the world leading up to that
event. The logic of explanation requires that he single out the
relevant, important determinants of the occurrence.[5] Moreover,
as the logic of prediction underscores, he must summarize the
various factors as they bear on the occurrence. Conceptual
models not only fix the mesh of the nets that the analyst drags
through the material in order to explain a particular action; they
also direct him to cast his nets in select ponds, at certain depths,
in order to catch the fish he is after.

2. *Most analysts explain (and predict) the behavior of national
   governments in terms of one basic conceptual model, here
   entitled Rational Actor or "Classical" Model (Model I).*[6]

In spite of significant differences in interest and focus, most
analysts and ordinary laymen attempt to understand happenings in foreign affairs as the more or less purposive acts of

---

*In arguing that explanations proceed in terms of implicit conceptual
models, this essay makes no claim that foreign policy analysts have
developed any satisfactory, empirically tested theory. In this study
the term *model* without qualifiers should be read "conceptual
scheme or framework."

unified national governments. Laymen personify rational actors and speak of their aims and choices. Theorists of international relations focus on problems between nations in accounting for the choices of unitary rational actors. Strategic analysts concentrate on the logic of action in the absence of an actor. For each of these groups, the point of an explanation is to show how the nation or government could have chosen to act as it did, given the strategic problems it faced. For example, in confronting the problem posed by the Soviet installation of strategic missiles in Cuba, the Model I analyst frames the puzzle: Why did the Soviet Union decide to install missiles in Cuba? He then fixes the unit of analysis: governmental choice. Next, he focuses attention on certain concepts: goals and objectives of the nation or government. And finally, he invokes certain patterns of inference: if the nation performed an action of this sort, it must have had a goal of this type. The analyst has "explained" this event when he can show how placing missiles in Cuba was a reasonable action, given Soviet strategic objectives. Predictions about what a nation will do or would have done are generated by calculating the rational thing to do in a certain situation, given specified objectives.

3. *Two alternative conceptual models, here labeled an Organizational Process Model (Model II) and a Governmental (Bureaucratic) Politics Model (Model III),* provide a base for improved explanations and predictions.*[7]

Although the Rational Actor Model has proved useful for many purposes, there is powerful evidence that it must be supplemented, if not supplanted, by frames of reference that focus on the governmental machine — the organizations and political actors involved in the policy process. Model I's implication that important events have important causes, i.e., that monoliths perform large actions for large reasons, must be balanced by the appreciation that (1) monoliths are black boxes covering various gears and levers in a highly differentiated decisionmak-

---

*Earlier drafts of this argument have generated heated discussion about proper names for the models. To choose names from ordinary language is to promote familiarity and to court confusion. Perhaps it is best to think of these models simply as Model I, Model II, and Model III.

ing structure and (2) large acts result from innumerable and often conflicting smaller actions by individuals at various levels of bureaucratic organizations in the service of a variety of only partially compatible conceptions of national goals, organizational goals, and political objectives. Model I's grasp of national purposes and of the pressures created by problems in *inter*-national relations must confront the *intra*-national mechanisms from which governmental actions emerge.

Recent developments in organization theory provide the foundation for the second model, which emphasizes the processes and procedures of the large organizations that constitute a government. According to this Organizational Process Model, what Model I analysts characterize as "acts" and "choices" are thought of instead as *outputs* of large organizations functioning according to regular patterns of behavior. Faced with the problem of Soviet missiles in Cuba, a Model II analyst frames the puzzle: From what organizational context and pressures did this decision emerge? He then fixes the unit of analysis: organizational output. Next, he focuses attention on certain concepts: the strength, standard operating procedures, and repertoires of organizations. And finally, he invokes certain patterns of inference: if organizations produced an output of this kind today, that behavior resulted from existing organizational features, procedures, and repertoires. A Model II analyst has "explained" the event when he has identified the relevant Soviet organizations and displayed the patterns of organizational behavior from which the action emerged. Predictions identify trends that reflect established organizations and their fixed procedures and programs.

The third model focuses on the politics of a government. Events in foreign affairs are understood, according to this model, neither as choices nor as outputs. Rather, what happens is characterized as a *resultant* of various bargaining games among players in the national government. In confronting the problem posed by Soviet missiles in Cuba, a Model III analyst frames the puzzle: Which results of what kinds of bargaining among which players yielded the critical decisions and actions? He then fixes the unit of analysis: political resultant. Next, he focuses attention on certain concepts: the perceptions, motivations, positions, power, and maneuvers of the players. And finally, he invokes certain patterns of inference: if a government performed an action, that action was the resultant of bargaining among players in games. A Model III analyst has "explained" this event when he has discovered who did what to whom that yielded the action in question. Predictions are generated by identifying the game in which an issue will arise, the relevant players, and their relative power and skill.[8]

A central metaphor illuminates the differences among these models. Foreign policy has often been compared to moves and sequences of moves in the game of chess. Imagine a chess game in which the observer could see only a screen upon which moves in the game were projected, with no information about how the pieces came to be moved. Initially, most observers would assume — as Model I does — that an individual chess player was moving the pieces with reference to plans and tactics toward the goal of winning the game. But a pattern of moves can be imagined that would lead some observers, after watching several games, to consider a Model II assumption: the chess player might not be a single individual but rather a loose alliance of semi-independent organizations, each of which moved its set of pieces according to standard operating procedures. For example, movement of separate sets of pieces might proceed in turn, each according to a routine, the king's rook, bishop, and their pawns repeatedly attacking the opponent according to a fixed plan. It is conceivable, furthermore, that the pattern of play might suggest to an observer a Model III assumption: a number of distinct players, with distinct objectives but shared power over the pieces, could be determining the moves as the resultant of collegial bargaining. For example, the black rook's move might contribute to the loss of a black knight with no comparable gains for the black team, but with the black rook becoming the principal guardian of the palace on that side of the board.

Some Reservations

This bald summary conveys none of my reservations about the persuasiveness of the argument in its present form. To make these points fully convincing would require greater length than seems reasonable here, and more success than I have had in coming to grips with several hard problems. First, the argument that most analysts tend to rely on a single conceptual model sounds crudely reductionist. In spite of my recognition and description of several variants of Model I, my insistence on their logical similarity may, nonetheless, seem procrustean. Second, because explanation and prediction of international events are not developed theoretical enterprises, few analysts proceed exclusively and single-mindedly within a pure conceptual model. Instead, they think predominantly in terms of one model, occasionally shifting from one variant of it to another and sometimes appropriating material that lies entirely outside the boundaries of the model. These first two problems give rise to a third. When examining uses of the Rational Actor Model, and especially when considering to what extent one has been relying upon some variant of this model, one can always find that it does not really capture *all* of his analytical activity. Fourth, the richness of variations on the classical theme makes a clearly specified account of the model seem little more than a caricature or a strawman. Fifth, the alternative models are not fully developed. Finally, since the body of literature applying these alternative models to problems of foreign affairs is quite small, my applications of them are simply initial, tentative efforts.

In spite of my limited success in dealing with these difficult problems, many readers have found the general argument a suggestive contribution not only to discussion of the missile crisis but also to general thought about governmental behavior, especially in foreign and military affairs. Consequently, I have been persuaded to set these ideas down as the beginning, not the end, of an extended argument. In part, my compliance stems from the fact that defense of the stated propositions requires more than theoretical argument. The proof of the pudding is in the demonstration that the frameworks produce different explanations. The burden of the argument in this study is shared — some will insist carried — by three case studies that display the products of the conceptual models as each is applied in turn to the same problem: the central puzzles of the Cuban missile crisis. While differences among the conceptual models are examined systematically in the concluding chapter, these alternative explanations of the same happening are more revealing about the character of those differences — by showing the models at work.

A single case can do no more than suggest the kinds of differences among explanations produced by the three models. But the Cuban missile crisis is especially appropriate for the purposes of this study. In the context of ultimate danger to the nation, a small group of men, unhitched from the bureaucracy, weighed the options and decided. Such central, high-level, crisis decisions would seem to be the type of outcome for which Model I analysis is most suited. Model II and Model III are forced to compete on Model I's home ground. The dimensions and factors uncovered by Model II and Model III in this case will therefore be particularly suggestive.

1

Model I: The Rational Actor

When confronted by a puzzling international event, how does one proceed? Let the reader consider, for example, how he would respond to the assignment "Explain the Soviet installation of missiles in Cuba." The typical analyst or layman begins by considering various aims that the Soviets might have had in mind — for example, to probe American intentions, to defend Cuba, or to improve their bargaining position. By examining the problems the Soviets faced and the character of the action they chose, the analyst eliminates some of these aims as implausible. When he is able to construct a calculation that shows how, in a particular situation, with certain objectives, he could have chosen to place missiles in Cuba, the analyst has explained the action. (Indeed, the statement "I can't understand [or explain] why the Soviets did such and such" points to an inability to balance an action with a plausible calculation.) The attempt to explain international events by recounting the aims and calculations of nations or governments is the trademark of the Rational Actor Model.

As it is exemplified in academic literature, policy papers, the press, and informal conversations, most contemporary thought about foreign policy proceeds within this conceptual model. Consider several brief examples. The most widely cited explanation of the Soviet emplacement of missiles in Cuba has been produced by two Rand sovietologists, Arnold Horelick and Myron Rush.[1] They conclude that "the introduction of strategic missiles into Cuba was motivated chiefly by the Soviet leaders' desire to overcome . . . the existing large margin of United States strategic superiority."[2] How do they reach this conclusion? In

Sherlock Holmes style, they magnify several salient characteristics of the action and use these features as criteria against which to test alternative hypotheses about Soviet objectives. For example, the size of the Soviet deployment and the simultaneous emplacement of more expensive, more visible intermediate-range missiles as well as medium-range missiles, they argue, exclude an explanation of the action in terms of Cuban defense — since that objective could have been secured with a much smaller number of medium-range missiles alone. Their explanation presents an argument for one objective that permits interpretation of the details of Soviet behavior as a value-maximizing choice.

What is the point of the puzzle raised by *The New York Times* reporters over Soviet deployment of an antiballistic missile system?[3] The question, as the *Times* states it, concerns the Soviet Union's objective in allocating such large sums of money for this weapon system while at the same time seeming to pursue a policy of increasing detente. In former President Johnson's words, "The paradox is that this [Soviet deployment of an antiballistic missile system] should be happening at a time when there is abundant evidence that our mutual antagonism is beginning to ease."[4] This development is troubling because the juxtaposition of Soviet antiballistic missile deployment and evidence of Soviet actions toward detente poses an apparent contradiction. Toward what objective could the Soviet government have rationally chosen to pursue these two courses of action simultaneously? This question arises only when the analyst attempts to structure events as purposive choices of consistent actors.

How do analysts explain the coming of the First World War? According to Hans Morgenthau, "The first World War had its origins exclusively in the fear of a disturbance of the European balance of power."[5] In the pre–World War I period, the Triple Entente was a delicate counterweight to the Triple Alliance. If either bloc could have gained a decisive advantage in the Balkans, it would have achieved a decisive advantage in the balance of power. "It was this fear," Morgenthau says, "that motivated Austria in July 1914 to settle its accounts with Serbia once and for all, and that induced Germany to support Austria unconditionally. It was the same fear that brought Russia to the support of Serbia, and France to the support of Russia."[6] How is Morgenthau able to resolve this problem so confidently? By imposing on the data a "rational outline."[7] The value of this method, according to Morgenthau, is that "it provides for rational discipline in action and creates that astounding continuity in foreign policy which makes American, British, or Russian foreign policy appear as an intelligible, rational continuum . . . regardless of the different motives, preferences, and intellectual and moral qualities of successive statesmen."[8]

Stanley Hoffmann's essay "Restraints and Choices in American Foreign Policy" concentrates, characteristically, on "deep forces" — the international system, ideology, and national character — which constitute restraints, limits, and blinders.[9] When he explains particular occurrences, however, though emphasizing relevant constraints, he focuses on choices of nations. American behavior in Southeast Asia is explained as a reasonable choice of "downgrading this particular alliance [SEATO] in favor of direct United States involvement," given the constraint that "one is bound by one's commitments; one is committed even by one's mistakes."[10] More frequently, Hoffmann uncovers confusion or contradiction in a nation's choice. For example, U.S. policy toward underdeveloped countries is explained as "schizophrenic."[11] The method Hoffmann employs in explaining national behavior as rational decision (or departure from this norm), he calls "imaginative reconstruction."[12]

Deterrence is the cardinal issue of contemporary strategic literature. Thomas Schelling's *Strategy of Conflict* formulates a number of propositions focused upon the dynamics of deterrence in the nuclear age. One of the major propositions concerns the stability of the balance of terror: in a situation of mutual deterrence, the probability of nuclear war is reduced not by the "balance" (the sheer equality of the situation) but rather by the *stability* of the balance, i.e., the fact that neither opponent in striking first can destroy the other's ability to strike back.[13] How does Schelling support this proposition? His confidence in it derives not from an inductive canvass of a large number of previous cases, but instead from two calculations. In a situation of "balance" but vulnerability, there are values for which a rational opponent could choose to strike first, e.g., to destroy enemy retaliatory capabilities. In a "stable balance," however, each can respond to a first strike by inflicting unacceptable damage. This capability guarantees deterrence since no rational agent could choose a course of action effectively equivalent to national suicide. Whereas most contemporary strategic thinking is driven *implicitly* by the motor upon which this calculation depends,

Schelling explicitly recognizes that strategic theory does assume a model. The foundation is, he asserts, "the assumption of rational behavior — not just of intelligent behavior, but of behavior motivated by a conscious calculation of advantages, a calculation that in turn is based on an explicit and internally consistent value system."[14]

What is striking about these examples from the literature of foreign policy and international relations are the similarities among analysts of various styles when they are called upon to produce explanations. Each assumes that what must be explained is an action, i.e., behavior that reflects purpose or intention. Each assumes that the actor is a national government. Each assumes that the action is chosen as a calculated solution to a strategic problem. For each, explanation consists of showing what goal the government was pursuing when it acted and how the action was a reasonable choice, given the nation's objective. This cluster of assumptions characterizes the Rational Actor Model. In most respects, contrasts in the thinking of Morgenthau, Hoffmann, and Schelling could not be more pointed. Recognition of the extent to which each employs Model I, however, highlights basic similarities among Morgenthau's method of "rational reenactment," Hoffmann's "imaginative reconstruction," and Schelling's "vicarious problem solving," and family resemblances among Morgenthau's "rational statesman," Hoffmann's "roulette player," and Schelling's "game theorist."[15]

In spite of considerable differences in emphasis and focus, most contemporary analysts (as well as laymen) proceed *predominantly* — albeit most often implicitly — in terms of this framework when trying to explain international events. Indeed, the assumption that occurrences in foreign affairs are the *acts of nations* has been so fundamental to thinking about such problems that the underlying model has rarely been recognized: to explain an occurrence in foreign policy simply means to show how the government could have rationally chosen that action.[16] In this sense, the frame of reference can be called the "classical" model.

To prove that most analysts think largely in terms of the classical model is not my purpose. Rather, this chapter attempts to convey to the reader a grasp of the model and a challenge: let the reader examine the literature with which he is most familiar and make his own judgment. The first section of this chapter consists of a rapid tour of major works in a number of areas central to the study of foreign policy and international relations. The second section attempts to clarify the concept of rational action — the essence of this conceptual model — by considering briefly the more rigorous theoretical models of action used in economic, game, and decisionmaking theory. This section is necessarily more technical. Some readers will prefer simply to think of this model as an attempt to understand the behavior of governments by analogy with the behavior of individuals making calculated, rational choices, and will thus prefer to skim this section. The third section formalizes this conceptual model as a paradigm and outlines several variants of the basic paradigm.

The Classical Model Illustrated

Diplomatic History

Consider the problem of the cause of the First World War. This chestnut has attracted the attention of the finest diplomatic historians for half a century, though debate on the fiftieth anniversary of that war's conclusion was hardly less vigorous than on the first. The two classic contributions to this scholarly debate review the same documents but come to diametrically opposed conclusions about the issue. On the one hand, Bernadotte Schmitt concludes that German determination caused the war: "The conciliatory reply of Serbia to the Austrian ultimatum was brushed aside because the ruling clique was determined on war."[17] On the other hand, Sidney Fay finds: "It was the hasty Russian general mobilization . . . while Germany was still trying to bring Austria to accept mediation proposals, which finally rendered European war inevitable."[18] The difficulty raised by these contrary conclusions is nowhere expressed more clearly than by Schmitt, in his autobiographical essay, "Fifty Years of Exploring History":

> Fay's *Origins of the World War*, published in 1928, took a lenient view of Germany's responsibility, whereas my book, *The Coming of the War 1914* (1930), laid the chief burden on Germany. This has always troubled me. We had both taken advanced degrees at eminent universities. . . . We used the same documents and read the same biographies and memoirs in preparing our respective books — and came up with quite different interpretations. It is sometimes asserted that we are both pre-

judiced because Fay studied in Germany and I in England, but surely there is more involved than that. Is there something wrong with our methods of historical study and training when two scholars draw such conflicting conclusions from the same evidence?[19]

Though Schmitt raises a number of complex questions about historical methods, the central dispute arises only within a special set of assumptions about the attribution of cause. Their argument about *the* cause of the war turns on judgments about the decisions, actions, and attitudes of nations. Identification of these decisions, acts, and attitudes requires that the various activities and thoughts of individuals within each of the relevant governments be neatly summarized. This instance of what Arthur Schlesinger, Jr., has called "the passion for tidiness [which] is the historian's occupational disease" is suggestive of the basic frame of reference employed by most diplomatic historians.[20]

Strategy

In explaining occurrences in foreign affairs, diplomatic historians reflect the intuitions and expectations of educated laymen, albeit in a more elaborate and consistent form.[21] Contemporary strategists refine these instincts. Thus the literature of contemporary strategy is especially instructive for our purpose. *The Strategy of Conflict* stands unchallenged as the finest formulation of the principles of contemporary strategic thinking. According to its author, Thomas Schelling, strategy analyzes and explains the maze of national actions and reactions as more or less advantageous moves in a game of interdependent conflict. Nations act in situations of tempered antagonism and precarious partnership, each nation's best choice depending on what it expects the other to do. Strategic behavior influences an actor's choice by working on his expectations of how his behavior is related to his adversary's.[22]

Schelling's discussion of deterrence was noted at the outset of this chapter. Here we must limit our attention to two further problems of contemporary strategy: limited war and signaling. About these issues, Schelling sets forth the following propositions. First: all kinds of limited war become more probable as the impossibility of all-out surprise attack becomes evident.[23] Second: limited war requires limits — i.e., mutual recognition of restraints. These tacit agreements, arrived at through partial or haphazard negotiations, require terms that are qualitatively distinguishable from the alternatives and cannot simply be a matter of degree. For example, in the Korean War the 38th parallel was a powerful focus for a stalemate, and the main alternative, the "narrow waist," was a strong candidate not just because it provided a shorter defense line but because it would have been clear to both sides that an advance to the waist did not necessarily signal a determination to advance farther and that a retreat to the waist did not telegraph any intention to retreat farther.[24] Third: the explicit statements and the tactical moves of nations constitute strategic signals. Adversaries watch and interpret each other's behavior, each aware that his own actions are being interpreted and each acting with a consciousness of the expectations he creates.

What evidence is adduced to support these propositions? The assertion that limited wars are more likely to occur when the balance of strategic capabilities is stable is supported by a chain of reasoning. In an unstable strategic context, a rational opponent might initiate a nuclear war rather than accept the loss of a limited war. An adversary who might be tempted to initiate a limited war must therefore proceed cautiously. In a stable strategic context, however, nuclear war means *mutual* annihilation; and, therefore, adventurous nations can instigate limited wars with less fear of all-out retaliation. Confidence in the second proposition — limited wars will be limited only at points that enjoy a certain saliency — springs not from scrutiny of history's limited wars but rather from thinking about the inability of rational antagonists in certain gaming situations to come to an agreement at any other point. The third proposition — a conception of international politics as "essentially bargaining situations" in which alert, intelligent, coordinated nations speak and move in order to influence other nations by changing their expected payoffs — constitutes a highly refined instance of the Rational Actor Model.[25]

Herman Kahn's most recent strategic study, *On Escalation,* takes as its explicit point of departure Schelling's notion of a "competition in risk-taking."[26] Kahn concentrates on the coercive aspects of national behavior in international politics, which involve *"instrumental* motivation — narrow considerations of profit and loss."[27] He tries to formulate "relatively general principles, more or less true for all the interaction of escalation and negotiation in which a fear of further escalation and a desire not to set undesirable precedents or to weaken desirable restraints are present."[28] With this focus, Kahn stretches a ladder of six thresholds and forty-four rungs that provides a backdrop for explaining various occurrences and playing out numerous scenarios. Both the explanations and the predictive scenarios unfold sequences of events. But what governs the movement from one frame of the scenario to the next? Plausible constructions of what unitary, value-maximizing actors would do pull the reader from frame to frame.

The character of Kahn's thought process is perhaps most clear in his discussion of how the United States would actually fight a central war, i.e., a war involving major nuclear attacks on the homelands of both superpowers. Fears that a "fog of war" would accompany nuclear attacks on the antagonists' homelands have led some analysts to believe that mutual miscalculation and bureaucratic momentum would create chaos. But Kahn maintains that "there has been a systematic overestimation of the importance of the so-called 'fog of war' — the inevitable uncertainties, misinformation, disorganization, or even breakdown of organized units — that must be expected to influence central war operations."[29] His expectations about central war stem from his confidence in *dead reckoning*. This term, borrowed from navigation, refers to the ability of a pilot or captain, by knowing his ship's starting point and environment and by reading its internal instruments, to determine where he is purely by mathematical calculation.[30]

> The commander or decision-maker may know a good deal about how the war started and the basic conditions existing at the outbreak; or information may become available specifiying these reasonably well, even though this information was not known before the war's outbreak. From this point forward, even though he is completely cut off from all information external to his own organization and forces, and perhaps even from much of that, he may still have enough of an idea of events and their timetable, at least in outline, and a sufficient judgment of what the other side is trying to accomplish (through knowledge of its logistics, forces, doctrines, and other constraints) to "play" both sides hypothetically by dead reckoning.[31]

In a central nuclear war, the United States would play out both its own and the antagonist's hand by calculating what rational actors would do at each point. Moreover, the application of this concept of dead reckoning is not limited to hypothetical central wars. Indeed, Kahn, who has observed military decisionmaking much more closely than most civilian analysts, maintains that "What I am talking about really is one basic mode — perhaps *the basic mode* — of decisionmaking in any military head-quarters."[32] At a minimum, it is the motor that moves Herman Kahn's thinking.

The "scenario" and the "war game" stand as emblems of contemporary strategic thinking. They also epitomize the classical model. The eminent American military strategist, Albert Wohlstetter, characterizes the method and scope of Rand's use of one gaming technique:

> RAND analysts, in conducting map exercises to determine the performance of alternative defenses, typically try some defense tactics and then attempt to figure the best means the enemy has available for countering this tactic; then they try another tactic, examine the possible countermoves again, and so on. In this way each strike calculated is actually the result of a rather extensive canvass not only of our tactics but also of enemy reactions. Matching best enemy countermoves to our own choices was also an important part of RAND's work on air base choice. This sort of matching is one kind of "minimax" analysis. Precisely the same sort of matching of move and countermove is relevant in designing and evaluating bilateral arms control arrangements which should not be taken as a matter of simple faith.[33]

What is distinctive about this approach? In Wohlstetter's words, it "attempts to introduce the enemy by letting him, in his *best interest,* do his worst to our forces and then seeing which of our forces accomplishes the job most effectively in the face of this best enemy attempt."[34] The question of what the enemy will do is answered by considering the question of what a rational, unitary genie would do.

Contemporary strategists' refined version of the standard frame of reference has considerable appeal to policy makers who must make decisions on the basis of partly read, partially digested, uncertain information. The Rational Actor Model permits a brief summary of the relevant aspects of a problem, in terms that are familiar from ordinary language. Consider, for example, how government officials estimate the likely effects of American military deployments on the behavior of other nations. In the early 1960s, the Defense Department concluded that the

United States should press for a significant build-up of NATO conventional forces. The chain of reasoning was stated clearly by the then (1961) Assistant Secretary of Defense Paul Nitze:

> If you were sitting in the Kremlin, which situation [first, a NATO armed with nuclear weapons alone, or second, a NATO armed both with nuclear and a significant conventional capability] would be considered most likely to bring you face to face with nuclear war if you persisted in a train of actions violating what the West takes to be its vital interests? To me, the answer is clear. If I were in the Kremlin I would be much more concerned in the second situation; I would consider it much more likely that the West would find it politically possible to initiate action in defense of the Berlin access routes from the second posture than from the first.[35]

For every analyst, enemy reactions constitute a critical but elusive factor. One advantage of the Rational Actor Model is that it provides an inexpensive approximation by letting the analyst think about what he would do if he were the enemy. As Schelling has stated in another context, "You can sit in your armchair and try to predict how people will behave by asking how you would behave if you had your wits about you. You get, free of charge, a lot of vicarious, empirical behavior."[36]

No recent policy maker has had greater impact on strategic thinking within the U.S. government than former Secretary of Defense Robert McNamara. One of his most important policy addresses, the speech at Ann Arbor in 1962, was designed "to expose his audience to the way in which the United States planned its nuclear operations, explain the problems raised by the existence of other national nuclear capabilities, and underscore the vital but limited role in deterrence played by strategic nuclear forces."[37] That speech is therefore an important source of clues to the thinking of policy makers.

After rehearsing a series of fallacies, McNamara turned to the problems of surprise attacks and escalation: "Let us look at the situation today [1962]. First, given the current balance of nuclear power, which we confidently expect to maintain in the years ahead, a surprise nuclear attack is *simply not a rational act* for any enemy. Nor would it be *rational* for an enemy to take the initiative in the use of nuclear weapons as an outgrowth of a limited engagement in Europe or elsewhere. I think we are entitled to conclude that either of these actions has been made highly *unlikely*."[38]

Of what does McNamara's confidence in the asserted unlikelihood of surprise attack or expansion to nuclear war consist? The argument proceeds in three steps. From a fact about
the physical world — the United States has strategic superiority
over the Soviet Union — the former Secretary moves to a theoretical assertion within the model: given a standard rational calculus, a major element in which is enemy awareness of American
nuclear superiority, there is little an enemy could hope to
achieve by surprise attack or escalation. On the basis of this
assertion, he draws an inference about the probability of an
occurrence in this world, namely enemy warheads exploding on
U.S. or European territory as a result of a surprise attack or
escalation.

Sovietology

Strategic Power and Soviet Foreign Policy, by Arnold Horelick and Myron Rush, analyzes Soviet foreign policy from 1957
to 1965. The authors unravel the most tangled Russian actions
as calculated decisions by the Soviet leaders. The seemingly un-
yielding facts of Soviet strategic purchases throughout this
period are turned round and round until they fit comfortably
into a larger, purposeful picture. This analysis resolves the
mysteries of Soviet foreign policy and strategic posture in terms
of four types of pieces: (1) the foreign policy objectives of the
contending powers, (2) the means available to them for pursuing their objectives, (3) the principles that guide their employment of these means and their distinctive styles of political
warfare, and (4) the constraints under which they operate in
conducting the struggle.[39]

The famed "missile gap" is unveiled as a myth fostered by
Khrushchev to fuel the Soviet political offensive against West
Berlin of 1958–1962. Exposure of the myth of Soviet intercontinental ballistic missile (ICBM) superiority forced the Soviet
leadership to seek to regain the initiative by moving missiles to
Cuba. The relative quiescence of Soviet foreign policy since the
missile crisis follows from their strategic inferiority.

For Horelick and Rush, an understanding of these years of
Soviet foreign policy requires insight into the Soviet failure to
capitalize on their technological advantage in 1958 by constructing a large intercontinental missile fleet.[40] Their explanation
focuses on Soviet calculations:

A decision to procure a large number of first-generation, or even second-generation, ICBM's entailed a certain risk that the force might have serious technical deficiencies and, further, might be considerably degraded within a few years by the opponent's countermeasures. New systems already under development probably promised to be superior. In view of the great demands on Soviet resources, the leaders doubtless hesitated to expend the large amount of funds needed, especially to procure a force that was subject to early obsolescence.[41]

But this calculation does not constitute a sufficient explanation. As the authors willingly acknowledge, "whatever the limitations on Soviet resources and capacities, however, the USSR has spent huge sums on air defense and on acquiring an 'overkill' capability against Western Europe."[42] Though some analysts attempt to explain this disparity between the extraordinarily large purchase of shorter-range ballistic missiles and the incredibly small purchase of ICBMs in terms of the greater technological uncertainty surrounding the ICBMs, Horelick and Rush are not tempted by that escape. As they recognize: "Technical uncertainties as to how the Soviet ICBM would perform were in some degree matched by similar uncertainties about the shorter-range ballistic missiles, which were nevertheless deployed in large numbers."[43] How, then, is this seemingly intractable configuration of facts about Soviet behavior understood?

Horelick and Rush infer that the Soviet leaders must have been virtually certain that a U.S. attack upon the Soviet Union would not occur:

Had there been serious doubt on this score, ordinary prudence would have required the procurement of a sizeable force without much delay. Such a force would have been needed to reinforce deterrence of a United States attack and, in the event deterrence failed, to provide a more adequate capability to fight a war. Instead, because of his assurance that there would be no American attack, Krushchev chose to procure a small force at a slow pace.[44]

The inference is from a physical fact — the Soviet failure to acquire a substantial first-generation or second-generation ICBM force — to what they "must have believed." *Must,* since if they had believed otherwise, their chosen course of action would simply not have been rational.[45]

Sinology

Communist China's entry into the Korean War in November 1950 caught most of Washington entirely off guard. Indeed, this event so surprised Douglas MacArthur, the American military commander in Korea, that U.S. troops were forced to make "the longest retreat in American military history." The problem of Chinese intervention in the Korean War has thus been a central issue for scholars of Chinese Communist behavior. Allen Whiting's *China Crosses the Yalu* is the most noted examination of this problem. By scrutinizing the Chinese Communist press for clues on strategy and tactics during 1950, he is able to construct an explanation of Chinese behavior. Why did China enter the war?

> In sum, it was not the particular problems of safeguarding electric power supplies in North Korea or the industrial base in Manchuria that aroused Peking to military action. Instead, the final step seems to have been prompted in part by general concern over the range of opportunities within China that might be exploited by a determined, powerful enemy on China's doorstep. At the least, a military response might deter the enemy from further adventures. At the most, it might succeed in inflicting sufficient damage to force the enemy to compromise his objectives and to accede to some of Peking's demands. Contrary to some belief, the Chinese Communist leadership did not enter the Korean War either full of self-assertive confidence or for primarily expansionist goals.[46]

Whiting spells out the objectives and plans that led to Chinese entrance into the war. But as Whiting — one of the most careful sinologists — is quick to acknowledge, he has no access to the internal thoughts of Peking. His analysis depends on more than careful examination of the available facts: "Basic to such evaluation is an assumption of *rational decision-making* in Peking. This posits decisions as resulting from a logical assessment of desired goals and available means and as being implemented in a manner calculated to make the gains outweigh the costs."[47] This assumption — which is central to the classical model — provides a path through what would otherwise seem an incomprehensible swamp.

Having adopted this frame of reference, the analyst can use Chinese actions as evidence about Chinese goals and objectives.

Whiting instructs the reader concerning the use of his method of analysis: "Actual decisions may be inferred from negative as well as positive evidence."[48] For example, many analysts have argued that the main reason China entered the Korean War was to protect Manchurian industry, which was dependent on supplies from North Korea. At the time, this belief prompted Western spokesmen to make repeated statements about "China's legitimate interest" near the border. But Whiting discounts this explanation on the grounds that "Peking ignored this issue completely in its domestic as well as its foreign communications. The absence of propaganda about protection of the hydroelectric installations, despite the need to maximize popular response to mobilization of 'volunteers,' suggests that this consideration played little if any role in motivating Chinese Communist intervention."[49]

Communist China and Arms Control, by Morton H. Halperin and Dwight Perkins, examines a second important problem in Sinology.[50] In analyzing Chinese policy on arms control, they seek to explain the acts and decisions as means calculated to achieve two classes of goals: (1) Chinese national interests and (2) Marxist-Leninist goals.[51] Chinese national interests account for the Sino-American conflict, efforts to remove the influence and power of the United States from Southeast Asia, and the invasion of Tibet. On the other hand, "China's behavior in the Sino-Soviet dispute and in some of the issues surrounding it is most easily explained by a genuine and substantial interest by the Chinese leadership in the fortunes of the world Communist revolution, a revolution that may not always be the surest way of promoting the security and development of the Chinese state."[52] What underlies the attempt to explain Chinese decisions and acts in terms of such abstract goals is a basic assumption of the model: "The Chinese Communist leadership pursues its objectives in a systematic and logical way, given its perception of the world."[53]

Military Force Posture

What determines a nation's military force posture? That is, at any point in time, why does the Soviet Union or the United States have one particular configuration of military hardware and weapons systems rather than some other? Most analysts attempt to understand a nation's force posture as the chosen means of implementing strategic objectives and military doctrine. In fact, military analysts, both within the American intelligence community and without, typically expend considerable effort in balancing statements about a nation's strategic objectives with evidence about that nation's actual hardware and systems. Thus they construct a coherent picture in which force posture follows as a more or less logical deduction from objectives and doctrines. For example, in the late 1950s H. S. Dinerstein examined published Soviet doctrines announcing a strategy of destroying the enemy military forces before those forces could destroy Soviet citizens and inferred that the Soviets must have been maintaining "a (strategic) striking force able to hit with considerable precision."[54]

The less the information about the internal affairs of a nation or government, the greater the tendency to rely on the classical model. But this framework is not uncommon in American analysts' explanations of U.S. force posture. Participants in the U.S. weapons procurement process can usually relate an infinitely untidy history of any particular action with which they are familiar, but the mass of disjointed detail creates an impression of randomness. There seems to be no satisfactory way of packaging these details. Consequently, both academic observers and participants (when they stand back from a particular incident) tend to offer explanations and predictions by reference to the value-maximizing choices of the nation or national government. For example, a major study of the determinants of U.S. force posture, *The Weapons Acquisition Process* by Peck and Scherer (published in 1962 after many man-years of research and more than twenty case studies by a Harvard Business School project), proceeds in these terms.[55] While Peck and Scherer are more concerned with an economic analysis of outcomes than they are with the process by which the outcomes are produced, they nevertheless conclude that "weapons systems program decisions" are to be explained as "attempts to maximize some function such as the surplus of expected military value (from the military value functions) over development cost (from the development possibility curves)."[56] Using these functions, they predict which weapons the United States will develop. "If a nation's aggregate weapons development budget is limited, only those programs with the highest surpluses of expected military value over development cost will be pursued."[57] This framework leads them to isolate "technical and scientific ideas" as the principal determinants of innovations in the force posture, like the Atlas ICBM and the F4H interceptor.[58]

American Foreign Policy

For perceptive, influential interpretation and criticism of American foreign policy, Henry Kissinger's works are unparalleled. His style of analysis, however, is representative of a broad stream of scholarship concerned with the foreign and military policy of the United States and other countries. Kissinger focuses primarily on national character, psychology, and preconceptions in explaining failures of American foreign policy. For example, his first widely publicized book, *Nuclear Weapons and Foreign Policy,* explains the general American postwar failure "to prevent a hostile power from expanding its orbit and developing a capability to inflict a mortal blow on the United States" as a consequence of our ill-conceived strategic doctrine.[59] "We added the atomic bomb to our arsenal without integrating its implications into our thinking."[60] We failed to get "clear about what strategic transformations we are prepared to resist."[61] "Our notion of aggression as an unambiguous act and our concept of war as inevitably an all-out struggle have made it difficult to come to grips with our perils."[62] More specifically, Kissinger explains our failure at the end of the Korean War to "push back the Chinese armies even to the narrow neck of the Korean peninsula, [thereby] administering a setback to Communist power in its first trial at arms with the free world" as a result of "our strategic doctrine [that] made it very difficult . . . to think of the possibility of intermediary transformations [between imposed unconditional surrender and a return to the status quo]."[63] Similarly *The Necessity for Choice* identifies the "lack of a strategic doctrine and a coherent military policy" as the cause of the "deterioration of our position in the world . . . we have experienced since World War II."[64]

The "we" and "our" that Kissinger refers to are the U.S. government and the American foreign policy community. It is these actors whose psychology and preconceptions Kissinger uncovers and whose doctrines and actions he criticizes as unsatisfactory approximations to his high standard of a rational strategic doctrine. Indeed, no strand is more stark in Kissinger's work than his persistent prescription: we must develop a strategic doctrine that will "define what objectives are worth contending for and determine the degree of force appropriate for achieving them."[65] We must "define for ourselves the nature of a peace consistent with our values and adequate for our security."[66]

Theory with a Capital "T"

It is easier to name the major theorists of international relations than to define their field. In spite of considerable differences among such scholars as Hans Morgenthau, Arnold Wolfers, Raymond Aron, and the "frontiersmen" of international relations theory, when they are producing explanations, all reflect to some degree the basic classical model.

The dean of postwar international relations theorists is Hans Morgenthau. The introduction to his major work *Politics Among Nations* emphasizes the necessity of employing a framework when studying foreign policy. He states clearly the frame of reference upon which he relies: "To give meaning to the factual raw material of foreign policy, we must approach political reality with a kind of *rational outline,* a map that suggests to us the possible meanings of foreign policy."[67] To explain national action in specific situations, the analyst must rethink the nation's problem and reenact the leaders' choice. Morgenthau provides explicit instructions.

> We put ourselves in the position of a statesman who must meet a certain problem of foreign policy under certain circumstances, and we ask ourselves what the rational alternatives are from which a statesman may choose who must meet this problem under these circumstances (*presuming always that he acts in a rational manner),* and which of these rational alternatives this particular statesman, acting under these circumstances, is likely to choose.[68]

In a brilliant essay entitled "The Actors in International Politics," Arnold Wolfers observes: "Until quite recently, the 'states-as-the-sole-actors' approach to international politics was so firmly entrenched that it may be called the traditional approach."[69] He examines two more recent strands in the literature, the "minds of men" theory and the "decision-making" approach and argues that these new frames of reference amount to a rather meager departure from the traditional approach.

While accepting contributions from these strands, Wolfers defends the traditional "state-as-actor" model as the "standard on which to base our expectations of state behavior and deviations."[70] It establishes "the 'normal' actions and reactions of states in various international situations."[71]

International Politics and Foreign Policy, edited by James Rosenau, contains the most extensive collection of selections from contemporary international relations theorists.[72] Fifty-five selections from the works of what Rosenau calls "frontiersmen" are distinguished primarily by their concern with theory and method as opposed to history or policy.[73] In an introductory note Rosenau sensitively delineates common characteristics of the majority of these works: "Most observers . . . [posit] a state-as-decision-maker model of the actors who comprise the international system. That is, action in the international system is ordinarily attributed to states, but these states are recognized to be a complex of governmental officials who act on behalf of and in response to their national societies."[74] Rosenau recognizes that "to speak of Germany wanting this, or France avoiding that, is to run the risk of oversimplifying, of ascribing human characteristics to nonhuman, abstract entities."[75] He, nevertheless, defends this approach as a necessary abbreviation.[76]

Raymond Aron's monumental *Peace and War: A Theory of International Relations* encompasses so wide a range of subjects and reveals such diverse interests that one hesitates to use it as an illustration. Nevertheless, it can be noted that much of his theory is dependent on the assumption of a rational, unified, national actor. *"The theory of international relations starts from the plurality of autonomous centers of decision* [national governments], *hence from the risk of war and from this risk it deduces the necessity of the calculation of means."*[77] Criticizing the attempts of theorists such as Morgenthau to explain national action by reference to a single goal, Aron argues that governments pursue a spectrum of goals, tempered by "the risk of war [that] obliges it [the government] to calculate forces or means."[78] His theory explores (1) the sociological influences on "the stakes of the conflicts among states, [and] the goals which the participants choose," (2) the international systems or diplomatic constellations in which states pursue these goals, and (3.) the historical characteristics of the present international system.[79] But the actor whose goals are sociologically determined and who must act in a particular international system is a rational, calculating national government. When explaining national actions, Aron focuses on the calculations of this actor, on "the logic of the conduct of international relations."[80]

A Rigorous Model of Action

The preceding tour begins to suggest the breadth of the influence of Model I in the literature of foreign affairs. To see how deeply this framework is engrained in our thinking, it is useful to consider the language used in writing or speaking about international events. We speak of occurrences not as unstructured happenings but rather as "the Soviet *decision* to abstain from attack," "the Chinese *policy* concerning defense of the mainland," and "Japanese *action* in surrendering." To summarize the relevant aspects of a state of the world as a nation's "decision" or "policy" is — at least implicitly — to slip into the rational actor framework. These terms derive their meaning from a conceptual web, the major strands of which constitute the classical model.[81] *Decision* presupposes a decider and a choice among alternatives with reference to some goal. *Policy* means the realization in a number of particular instances of some agent's objectives. These concepts identify phenomena as actions performed by purposeful agents. This identification involves a simple extension of the pervasive everyday assumption that what human beings do is at least "intendedly rational," an assumption fundamental to most understanding of human behavior.[82]

This everyday assumption of human purposiveness has a counterpart that plays a central role in the social sciences. One strand of social science concentrates on the reactive aspects of human behavior, specifying regularities of behavior in certain typical situations. But the central tradition in the social sciences examines the purposive, calculated, and planned aspects of human behavior.[83] Thus economics, political science, and to a large extent sociology and psychology study human behavior as purposive, goal-directed activity.

But what does it mean to conceive of behavior as "action"? When one thinks of activity as "intendedly rational" or studies behavior as goal-directed, what do these notions entail? A rigorous model of this concept of action has been formulated in economics, decision, and game theory. The model's rigor stems from its assumption that action constitutes more than simple purposive choice of a unitary agent. What rationality adds to the concept of purpose is *consistency:* consistency among goals and objectives relative to a particular action; consistency in the application of principles in order to select the optimal alternative. Von Neuman and Morgenstern's last work on rationality has not been superseded: "It may safely be stated that there exists, at present, no satisfactory treatment of the question of rational behavior."[84] Nevertheless, these theories have developed an important ideal type.

Classical "economic man" and the rational man of modern statistical decision theory and game theory make optimal choices in narrowly constrained, neatly defined situations. In these situations rationality refers to an essentially Hobbesian notion of consistent, value-maximizing *reckoning* or adaptation within specified constraints.[85] In economics, to choose rationally is to select the most efficient alternative, that is, the alternative that maximizes output for a given input or minimizes input for a given output. Rational consumers purchase the amount of goods, A, B, and C, etc., that maximizes their utility (by choosing a basket of goods on the highest possible indifference curve.) Rational firms produce at a point that maximizes profits (by setting marginal costs equal to marginal revenue). In modern statistical decision theory and game theory, the rational decision problem is reduced to a simple matter of selecting among a set of given alternatives, each of which has a given set of consequences: the agent selects the alternative whose consequences are preferred in terms of the agent's utility function which ranks each set of consequences in order of preference.

The basic concepts of these models of rational action are:

1. GOALS AND OBJECTIVES. The goals and objectives of the agent are translated into a "payoff" or "utility" or "preference" function, which represents the "value" or "utility" of alternative sets of consequences. At the outset of the decision problem the agent has a payoff function which ranks all possible sets of consequences in terms of his values and objectives. Each bundle of consequences will contain a number of side effects. Nevertheless, at a minimum, the agent must be able to rank in order of preference each possible set of consequences that might result from a particular action. (Many theories imply stronger integral or ratio scales.)[86]

2. ALTERNATIVES. The rational agent must choose among a set of alternatives displayed before him in a particular situation. In decision theory these alternatives are represented as a

decision tree. The alternative courses of action may include more than a simple act, but the specification of a course of action must be sufficiently precise to differentiate it from other alternatives.

3. CONSEQUENCES. To each alternative is attached a set of consequences or outcomes of choice that will ensue if that particular alternative is chosen. Variations are generated at this point by making different assumptions about the accuracy of the decisionmaker's knowledge of the consequences that follow from the choice of each alternative.

4. CHOICE. Rational choice consists simply of selecting that alternative whose consequences rank highest in the decision-maker's payoff function.[87]

These categories formalize the concept of rational action that underpins economics, decision, and game theory, as well as the less structured notion that underlies our everyday assumption of human purposiveness both in individual behavior and in national foreign policy. *Rationality refers to consistent, value-maximizing choice within specified constraints.* Applications of this model of purposive action are considerable and instructive. The model permits decision and game theorists to structure problems of choice. In the most advanced social science, this model constitutes the fundamental assumption of consumer theory and the theory of the firm. Indeed, though Anthony Downs overstates the point, he is largely accurate in asserting that "economic theorists have nearly always looked at decisions as though they were made by rational minds. . . . Economic theory has been erected upon the supposition that conscious rationality prevails."[88] The implications he draws from this assertion are directly on target: "The traditional [economic] methods of prediction and analysis are applicable. . . . If a theorist knows the ends of some decision-maker, he can predict what actions will be taken to achieve them as follows: (1) he calculates the most reasonable way for the decision-maker to reach his goals, and (2) he assumes this way will actually be chosen because the decision-maker is rational."[89] In addition, the assumption of rationality provides impressive explanatory power. As John Harsanyi, one of the most insightful theorists of rationality, has stated: "The concept of rational behavior is often a very powerful explanatory principle because it can account for a large number of empirical facts about people's behavior in terms of a few simple assumptions about the goals (or ends) people are trying to achieve."[90] How does the social scientist apply this concept? Again to quote Harsanyi:

> From the point of view of a social scientist trying to explain and predict human behavior, the concept of rationality is important mainly because, if a person acts rationally, his behavior can be *fully explained* in terms of the goals he is trying to achieve. When we say that Napoleon's strategy in a particular battle was rational, this means that his strategy choice can be explained essentially by pointing out that this was the best strategy for him to choose in terms of his military objectives at the time.[91]

Nevertheless, the power of the theory of rational action derives from its rigor — rigor purchased at the price of assumptions too heroic for many empirically oriented social scientists. The rigorous model of rational action maintains that rational choice consists of value-maximizing adaptation within the context of a *given* payoff function, *fixed* alternatives, and consequences that are *known* (in one of the three senses corresponding to certainty, risk, and uncertainty). But what guarantees that value-maximizing behavior within these parameters will in fact maximize the agent's values?[92] Obviously it would not, if the set of alternatives failed to include an option whose consequence ranked higher than any of the stated alternatives.

In order to maintain claims concerning "optimal choice," theorists are forced to retreat to one of two defenses (though they often fail to recognize this necessity and thus blur their chosen defense). On the one hand, the theorist can make the assumption of *comprehensive rationality,* according to which "*the* payoff function" means an accurate mapping of all consequences in terms of all the agent's values; "*the* alternatives" means "*all* alternatives"; and "*the* consequences" means "*all* consequences" that will result from the choice of any alternative. For example, the problem of rational choice in a game of chess is the problem of selecting the move that leads to the most preferred outcome, i.e., the one move that will bring the player the most advantageous consequences according to his payoff function.

On the other hand, the more common — and more satisfactory — defense is to make an assumption of *limited rationality* and to restrict claims concerning "optimal choice" accordingly.

By assuming an *economic definition of the situation,* economists impose a bench-mark that stipulates the content of the "values," "alternatives," and "consequences" in the rigorous model. This leads many economists to overlook a wide range of values and consequences that are important to students of political, psychological, and sociological behavior. But within these stipulated bounds, they can identify value-maximizing activity.[93]

A Rational Actor Paradigm

By using the concepts of the more rigorous models of action, we can sharpen the general characterization of Model I that emerged from our examination of the literature. Formulation of Model I as an "analytic paradigm" — in the technical sense of that term developed by Robert K. Merton for sociological analyses — highlights the distinctive thrust of this style of analysis.[94] According to Merton, a paradigm is a systematic statement of the basic assumptions, concepts, and propositions employed by a school of analysis. The components of the paradigms formulated in this study include the basic unit of analysis, the organizing concepts, the dominant inference pattern, and, simply for illustrative purposes, several of the propositions suggested by the paradigm. Considerably weaker than any satisfactory theoretical model, these paradigms nevertheless represent a short step in that direction from looser, implicit conceptual models. To articulate a largely implicit framework as an explicit paradigm is, of necessity, to caricature. But caricature can be instructive.

I. *Basic Unit of Analysis: Governmental Action as Choice.* Happenings in foreign affairs are conceived as actions chosen by the nation or national government.[95] Governments select the action that will maximize strategic goals and objectives. The "solutions" to strategic problems are the fundamental categories in terms of which the analyst perceives what is to be explained.

II. *Organizing Concepts*
  A. *National Actor.* The nation or government, conceived as a rational, unitary decisionmaker, is the agent. This actor has *one* set of specified goals (the equivalent of a consistent utility function), *one* set of perceived options,

and a *single* estimate of the consequences that follow
from each alternative.

B. *The Problem.*   Action is chosen in response to the strategic problem the nation faces. Threats and opportunities
   arising in the international strategic "marketplace" move
   the nation to act.

C. *Static Selection.*   The sum of activity of representatives
   of the government relevant to a problem constitutes what
   the nation has chosen as its "solution." Thus the action
   is conceived as a steady-state choice among alternative
   outcomes (rather than, for example, a large number of
   partial choices in a dynamic stream).

D. *Action as Rational Choice.*[96]   The components include:

   1. *Goals and Objectives.*   National security and na-
      tional interests are the principal categories in which
      strategic goals are conceived. Nations seek security
      and a range of other objectives. (Analysts rarely trans-
      late strategic goals and objectives into an explicit
      utility function; nevertheless, analysts do focus on
      major goals and objectives and trade off side effects
      in an intuitive fashion.)

   2. *Options.*   Various courses of action relevant to a
      strategic problem provide the spectrum of options.

   3. *Consequences.*   Enactment of each alternative course
      of action will produce a series of consequences. The
      relevant consequences constitute benefits and costs
      in terms of strategic goals and objectives.

   4. *Choice.*   Rational choice is value-maximizing. The
      rational agent selects the alternative whose conse-
      quences rank highest in terms of his goals and
      objectives.

III. *Dominant Inference Pattern.*   If a nation performed a
     particular action, that nation must have had ends toward
     which the action constituted a maximizing means. The Ra-
     tional Actor Model's explanatory power stems from this
     inference pattern. The puzzle is solved by finding the pur-
     posive pattern within which the occurrence can be located
     as a value-maximizing means.

IV. *General Propositions.*   The disgrace of foreign policy studies
    is the infrequency with which propositions of any generality

are formulated and tested. In arguing for explicitness about the categories in which analysis proceeds, this study emphasizes the importance of being serious about the logic of explanation. Consequently, the propositions upon which explanations depend need to be formulated clearly. To illustrate the kind of propositions on which analysts who employ this model rely, several are formulated.

The basic assumption of value-maximizing behavior produces propositions central to most explanations. The general principle can be formulated as follows: the likelihood of any particular action results from a combination of the nation's (1) relevant values and objectives, (2) perceived alternative courses of action, (3) estimates of various sets of consequences (which will follow from each alternative), and (4) net valuation of each set of consequences. This yields two propositions.

A. An increase in the costs of an alternative (a reduction in the value of the set of consequences that will follow from an action, or a reduction in the probability of attaining fixed consequences) reduces the likelihood of that action's being chosen.

B. A decrease in the costs of an alternative (an increase in the value of the set of consequences that will follow from an action, or an increase in the probability of attaining fixed consequences) increases the likelihood of that action's being chosen.[97]

V. *Specific Propositions*

   A. *Deterrence.* The likelihood of successful deterrence is a function of the factors specified in the general proposition. Combined with various assertions, this general proposition yields the propositions of the theory of deterrence.

     1. A stable nuclear balance reduces the likelihood of nuclear attack. This proposition is derived from the general proposition, plus the asserted fact that a second-strike capability affects the potential attacker's calculations by increasing the likelihood and the costs of one particular set of consequences that might follow from attack — namely, retaliation.

     2. A stable nuclear balance increases the probability of limited war. This proposition is derived from the gen-

eral proposition, plus the asserted fact that, though increasing the costs of a nuclear exchange, a stable nuclear balance nevertheless produces a more significant reduction in the probability that such consequences would be chosen in response to a limited war. Thus this set of consequences weighs less heavily in the calculus.

B. *Soviet Force Posture.* Soviet force posture (i.e., weapons and their deployment) constitutes a value-maximizing means of implementing Soviet strategic objectives and military doctrine. A proposition of this sort underlies Secretary of Defense Laird's leap from the fact of two hundred SS-9s (large intercontinental missiles) to the assertion that "the Soviets are going for a first-strike capability, and there's no question about it."[98]

VI. *Evidence.* The fundamental method employed in rational actor analysis is what Schelling has called "vicarious problem solving." Faced with a puzzling occurrence, the analyst puts himself in the place of the nation or government. Examination of the strategic characteristics of the problem permits the analyst to use principles of rational action to sift through both commissions and omissions. Evidence about details of behavior, statements of government officials, and government papers are then marshaled in such a way that a coherent picture of the value-maximizing choice (from the point of view of the nation) emerges.

It must be noted, however, that an imaginative analyst can construct an account of value-maximizing choice for any action or set of actions performed by a government. Putting the point more formally, if somewhat facetiously, we can state a "Rationality Theorem": there exists no pattern of activity for which an imaginative analyst cannot write a large number of objective functions such that the pattern of activity maximizes each function. The problem for the good Model I analyst is therefore not simply to find an objective or cluster of objectives around which a story of value-maximizing choice can be constructed, but to insist on rules of evidence for making assertions about governmental objectives, options, and consequences that permit him to distinguish among the various accounts.

Variants of the Classical Model

This paradigm exhibits the basic logic of a cluster of approaches that we have labeled the classical or Rational Actor Model. Analysts who think in these categories package the activities of various officials of a national government as actions chosen by a unified actor, strongly analogous to an individual human being. An action is explained by reference to the aims of the unitary, national actor. The explanation permits the reader to understand why the event occurred by redoing the calculation and thereby discovering how, in the given context with certain objectives, the actor came to choose the action in question.

But as our examination of various uses of this approach suggests, its basic logic is found in a number of interestingly different variants. The point of each is in one sense the same: to place the action within the purposive framework of a unified actor. But differences among these approaches are also important. Indeed, in emphasizing the similarities in basic logic rather than various differences, this account may be misleading. A further study, now in progress, focuses on the differences among the various approaches now lumped together under one general rubric.[99] But here it may be helpful to identify, if only tentatively, several variants of this approach, each of which might be exhibited similarly as a paradigm.

The preceding paradigm reflects the most refined version of the model found in the literature of modern strategy. Analysts like Schelling and Wohlstetter state propositions about the reactions of nation A to nation B, such as the proposition about the stability of the balance of terror. Problems and pressures in the international strategic marketplace yield probabilities of occurrence. The international actor, which could be any nation, is simply a value-maximizing mechanism for getting from the strategic problem to the logical solution.

A second type of analysis focuses not upon nations in general, but rather upon a nation or national government with a particular character. Characteristics of this actor limit the goals, options, and consequences of the basic paradigm. Thus (1) propensities or personality traits or psychological tendencies of the nation or government, (2) values shared by the nation or government, or (3) special principles of action change the "goals" or narrow the "alternatives" and "consequences" considered. In contrast to the first variant's concentration on the nation's strategic goals and objectives, this variant emphasizes a government's more specialized objectives, including its own perpetuation. For example, whereas an analyst using the first variant might attempt to explain the United Arab Republic's recent actions by reference to strategic objectives and fears, an analyst employing this second variant would refer to the particular objectives and fears of the present government. Similarly, explanations of the Soviet deployment of ABMs by reference to the Soviets' "defense-mindedness" reflect this variant.

A related, but nevertheless different, type of analysis focuses explicitly on an individual leader or leadership clique as the actor whose preference function is maximized and whose personal (or group) characteristics are allowed to modify the basic concepts of the paradigm. This individual's weighting of goals and objectives, tendencies to perceive (and to exclude) particular ranges of alternatives, and principles employed in estimating the consequences that follow from each alternative serve as the basic framework within which the choice must be located.[100] For example, the actor in Whiting's analysis is not "any nation" or "any China." Rather, as Whiting states, "Alternative courses of action open to the Chinese [are] derived from the frame of reference within which the *new regime* evaluated events, alternative political goals, and the available means of promoting policy."[101] Nathan Leites' analysis of Soviet behavior constructs an "operational code of the Bolsheviks."[102] These principles of action rather than general principles of rational action are then used to explain purposive activity of the Soviet government.

A more complex variant of the basic model recognizes the existence of several actors within a government — for example, hawks and doves or military and civilians — but still attempts to explain (or predict) an occurrence by reconstructing the calculations of the victorious actor. Thus, for example, some revisionist histories of the Cold War recognize the forces of light and the forces of darkness within the U.S. government but explain American actions as a result of goals and perceptions of the victorious forces of darkness. This variant obviously includes some conspiracy theorists.[103]

Some analysts employ the basic model (in one of its forms) essentially as a *norm*. Actual events are then explained (and criticized) as approximations to choices expected by the classical model. Kissinger, Kennan, and to some extent Hoffmann rely on this variant.[104] This variant suggests the relations among uses of the classical model for (1) explanation, i.e., answering the question of why X rather than Y happened; (2) problem solving, i.e., answering the question of what is the preferred way for a national government to achieve certain goals; and (3) evaluating, i.e., determining what grade a nation's performance deserves, given certain criteria. Uses of this model for purposes other than explanation will be considered in the final chapter.

Each of these forms of the basic paradigm constitutes a formalization of what analysts typically rely upon implicitly. In the transition from implicit conceptual model to explicit paradigm, much of the richness of the best employments of this model has been lost. But the purpose in raising loose, implicit conceptual models to an explicit level is to reveal the basic logic of an analyst's activity. Perhaps some of the remaining artificiality that surrounds the statement of the paradigm can be diluted by noting a number of the standard additions and modifications used by analysts who proceed *predominantly* within the Rational Actor Model. First, in the course of a document, analysts shift from one variant of the basic model to another, occasionally appropriating in an *ad hoc* fashion aspects of a situation that are logically incompatible with the basic model. Second, in the course of explaining a number of occurrences, analysts sometimes pause over a particular event about which they have a great deal of information and unfold it in such detail that they create an impression of randomness. Third, having employed other assumptions and categories in deriving an explanation or prediction, analysts will present their product in a neat, convincing rational policy package. This accommodation is a favorite of members of the intelligence community who are often very familiar with the details of a process but who feel that by putting an occurrence in a larger rational framework they make it more comprehensible to their audience. Fourth, in attempting to offer an explanation — particularly in cases where a prediction derived from the basic model has failed — the notion of the actor's "mistake" is invoked. Thus, the inaccurate prediction of a "missile gap" is written off as a Soviet mistake in not taking advantage of an opportunity. Both these and other modifications permit Model I analysts considerably more leeway than the paradigm might suggest. But such accommodations are essentially appendages to the basic logic of these analyses.

2

Cuba II: A First Cut

The "missiles of October" offer a fascinating set of puzzles for any analyst.[1] For thirteen days in October 1962, the United States and the Soviet Union stood "eyeball to eyeball," each with the power of mutual annihilation in hand. The United States was firm but forebearing. The Soviet Union looked hard, blinked twice, and then withdrew without humiliation. Here is one of the finest examples of diplomatic prudence, and perhaps the finest hour of John F. Kennedy's Presidency.

In retrospect, this crisis seems to have been a major watershed in the Cold War. Having peered over the edge of the nuclear precipice, both nations edged backward toward detente. An understanding of this crisis is thus essential for every serious student of foreign affairs.

To understand how — at a time when war could have meant the destruction of both societies — these superpowers moved to the brink of nuclear war, and, having got there, how they managed to retreat, it is necessary to answer three central questions. Why did the Soviet Union attempt to place offensive missiles in Cuba? Why did the United States choose to respond to the Soviet missile emplacement with a blockade of Cuba? Why did the Soviet Union decide to withdraw the missiles? Fortunately, the openness of the crisis makes it possible to reconstruct the calculations of both nations with a certain amount of confidence.[2]

Why Did the Soviet Union Decide to Place Offensive Missiles in Cuba?

The Soviet Union had never before stationed strategic nuclear weapons outside its own territorial borders — either in the Communist nations of Eastern Europe or in Red China.[3] On September 11, 1962, the Soviet government authorized Tass to reiterate the government's policy on the transfer of nuclear weapons to third nations:

> The Government of the Soviet Union authorized *Tass* to state that there is no need for the Soviet Union to shift its weapons for the repulsion of aggression, for a retaliatory blow, to any other country, *for instance Cuba.* Our nuclear weapons are so powerful in their explosive force and the Soviet Union has such powerful rockets to carry these nuclear warheads, that there is no need to search for sites for them beyond the boundaries of the Soviet Union.[4]

Through the most confidential channels of communication, at the highest levels, the Soviet Union sought to assure the United States concerning this policy. On September 4, Soviet Ambassador Dobrynin called on Attorney General Robert Kennedy with a confidential message from Chairman Khrushchev.[5] In that message Khrushchev promised that the Soviet Union would create no trouble for the United States during the election campaign. To minimize the chance of any misunderstanding — especially since some Congressmen were pointing to Soviet activity in Cuba — the President responded that very day with a firm warning: the introduction of offensive missiles into Cuba would raise the gravest issue.[6] On September 6, Dobrynin urgently requested a meeting with Special Counsel to the President Theodore Sorensen. At that meeting he delivered a second personal message from Chairman Khrushchev to President Kennedy: "Nothing will be undertaken before the American Congressional elections that could complicate the international situation or aggravate the tension in the relations between our two countries. . . . The Chairman does not wish to become involved in your internal affairs."[7] Sorensen challenged the sincerity of the Chairman's wishes, pointing out that the late summer shipments of Soviet personnel, arms, and equipment into Cuba were already generating international tensions and aggravating American domestic politics. But Dobrynin reiterated his assertion that the Soviets were doing nothing new in Cuba: the steps taken were entirely defensive.[8] Georgi Bolshakov, a Soviet official who had established a working relationship with several New Frontiersmen, including Robert Kennedy (and through whom Khrushchev's personal letters to the President had first arrived) relayed a message from Khrushchev and Mikoyan: "No missile capable of reaching the United States would be placed in Cuba."[9] On October 13, in response to questioning by Chester Bowles about the presence of Soviet "offensive weapons" in Cuba, Dobrynin emphatically and convincingly denied any such possibility.[10] The Soviet signal was clear.

Nor was the American warning faint. Through private channels, Robert Kennedy warned Dobrynin that the United States would not tolerate offensive weapons in Cuba; Sorensen emphasized the message to Dobrynin on September 6; Bowles reiterated it. The United States staked its public prestige on the warning. In response to Khrushchev's private note, the President's public statement of September 4 drew a distinction between "offensive" and "defensive" weapons. The President acknowledged that there was no evidence of Soviet offensive weapons in Cuba but warned: "Were it to be otherwise, the gravest issues would arise."[11] On September 7, Congress granted the President standby authority to call up additional reservists.[12] On September 13, the President made a major public statement on the Communist build-up in Cuba. If Cuba should "become an offensive military base of significant capacity for the Soviet Union," he proclaimed, "then this country will do whatever must be done to protect its own security and that of its allies."[13]

Some analysts have suggested that though loud, the warning was nevertheless vague, since the distinction between "offensive" and "defensive" could be a matter of intent or purpose as well as of capability.[14] (Indeed, in the midst of the crisis, Khrushchev claimed that the missiles stationed in Cuba were "defensive in purpose."[15]) But the record demonstrates that the American warning was explicit and that the Soviets understood it. The President's September 4 statement not only drew the distinction between offensive and defensive weapons. It specified the meaning of *offensive* — "offensive ground-to-ground missiles" — and it warned that "the *presence* of offensive ground-to-ground missiles or of other significant offensive capability either in Cuban hands or under Soviet direction and guidance" would be a sufficient condition for U.S. action.[16] The Soviets could not have misunderstood this warning. They repeatedly assured the United States, both privately and publicly, that no missile capable of reaching the United States would be stationed in Cuba.

These moves and countermoves seem like a textbook case of responsible diplomacy. The United States formulated a policy stating precisely "what strategic transformations we [were] prepared to resist."[17] The Soviet Union acknowledged these vital interests and announced a strategy that entailed no basic conflict. This would also seem to be a model case of communication, or signaling, between the superpowers. By private messages and public statements, the United States committed itself to action should the Soviets cross an unambiguous line (by placing offensive missiles in Cuba). All responses indicated that the Soviets understood the signal and accepted the message.[18]

Flowing from these warnings, promises, and assurances, U.S. expectations converged in the now notorious "September estimate."[19] Approved by the United States Intelligence Board (USIB) on September 19, this National Intelligence Estimate concluded that Soviet emplacement of offensive missiles in Cuba was highly unlikely.[20] When, on October 14, the United States discovered Soviet offensive missiles in Cuba, the U.S. government was shocked. What President Kennedy's announcement of the crisis called "this secret, swift and extraordinary build-up of Communist missiles . . . this sudden, clandestine decision to station strategic weapons for the first time outside of Soviet soil," posed for the policy makers — and poses for any analyst — a troubling question.[21] Why did the Soviet Union undertake such a reckless move? What objective could the Soviets have had that would have justified a course of action which entailed a high probability of nuclear confrontation? What was the Soviet intention in placing offensive missiles in Cuba?

These questions were the first to be considered at the initial meeting of the Executive Committee of the National Security Council (ExCom), which convened at 11:45 A.M. on Tuesday, October 16. Discussion at that meeting generated five alternative hypotheses, which were more precisely defined in the days that followed. Subsequent analyses have typically emphasized one or another of these alternatives. Careful examination of the details of Soviet action should allow us to distinguish among the hypotheses more clearly than the policy makers could in the heat of the crisis, and perhaps to understand more accurately what the Soviet Union really had in mind.

Hypothesis One: Bargaining Barter

Khrushchev installed missiles in Cuba with the intent of using them as a bargaining counter in a summit or U.N. confrontation with Kennedy. Withdrawal of Soviet missiles in Cuba would be traded for withdrawal of U.S. missile bases in Turkey. On Thursday, October 25, this analogy provided the pivot of Walter Lippmann's column in *The Washington Post*. How could this crisis be peacefully resolved? According to Lippmann:

> The way is to try to negotiate a face-saving agreement. The only place that is truly comparable with Cuba is Turkey. This is the only place where there are strategic weapons right on the frontier of the Soviet Union. . . . There is another important similarity between Cuba and Turkey. The Soviet missile base in Cuba, like the U.S.-NATO base in Turkey, is of little military value. . . . The two bases could be dismantled without altering the world balance of power.[22]

Similar proposals were made by members of the European press and by a number of U.N. delegates from nonaligned nations.

The Soviet statements and behavior also point toward a hypothesis of this sort. The encirclement of the Soviet Union by American bases, especially missile bases, constituted a long-standing and serious threat. The Soviet statement on September 11, which declared that the Soviet Union had no need to station offensive missiles in any other country, zeroed in on U.S. missile bases.

> The whole world knows that the United States of America has ringed the Soviet Union and other Socialist countries with bases. What have they stationed there — tractors? . . . No, they have brought armaments there in their ships, and these armaments stationed along the frontier of the Soviet Union — in Turkey, Iran, Greece, Italy, Britain, Holland, Pakistan, and other countries belonging to the military blocs of NATO, CENTO, and SEATO — are said to be there lawfully, by right. They consider this their right! But to others the U.S. does not permit this even for defense, and when measures are nevertheless taken to strengthen the defenses of this or that country, the U.S. raises an outcry and declares that an attack, if you please, is being prepared against them. What conceit! . . . Equal rights and equal opportunities must be recognized for all countries of the world.[23]

On the very day that the President first learned of the missiles, Khrushchev stressed this point in a conversation with the new

American Ambassador to Moscow, Foy Kohler. As Sorensen sum-
marizes the memorandum of conversation: "The one ominous
note in that otherwise genial conversation had been a sharp
reference to the U.S. Jupiter bases in Turkey and Italy."[24] During
the crisis, Soviet delegates at the United Nations proposed a
mutual withdrawal of missiles from Cuba and Turkey; Soviet
contacts in Britain made this proposal; the head of Soviet intelligence (KGB) in Washington pressed it in private conversations.
Indeed, the Saturday (October 27) letter from Khrushchev to the
President focused on this analogy, pointing out that the United
States had "stationed devastating rocket weapons, which *you*
call *offensive,* in Turkey literally right next to us."[25] A number of
analysts have therefore concluded that the Soviet action must
have been designed as a counter to U.S. missiles in Turkey.

Careful examination of the details of the Soviet operation
casts doubt upon this hypothesis. First, whether the Soviets
would have accepted the cost and risk of this operation merely
to provide an exchange for U.S. missiles in Turkey is questionable. The United States was already committed to withdrawal of
the missiles in Turkey — without any *quid pro quo.*[26] In fact,
President Kennedy was greatly perturbed when he learned that
the United States still had missiles in Turkey. On two previous
occasions he had directed that they be removed.[27] While it might
be argued that the Soviets could not be sure of U.S. intentions,
the fact that American Thor missile installations in England
were in the process of being dismantled was certainly suggestive.[28] Second, a Cuban base for Soviet missiles would be incom-
parably more valuable to the Soviet Union's nuclear delivery
capability than the Turkish missile bases were to U.S. strategic
forces: Turkish missiles constituted less than 3 percent of the
United States' overwhelming capability to deliver first-strike nuclear payloads on Soviet territory and were virtually useless for a
second strike because of their extreme vulnerability. Conversely,
the missiles under construction in Cuba would have doubled the
Soviet Union's first-strike nuclear delivery capability against the
United States. Third, the magnitude and character of the Soviet
strategic weapon deployment in Cuba is disproportionate to the
hypothesis that the Soviets intended simply to buy a bargaining
counter. The United States had only one squadron of Jupiters
(fifteen missiles) deployed in Turkey.[29] How could a trade have
possibly embraced the forty-two medium-range ballistic missiles
(MRBMs) and twenty-four to thirty-two intermediate-range ballistic missiles (IRBMs), which the Soviets were installing?

Finally, the costly and essentially unsalvageable sites being prepared for IRBMs seem superfluous for any Cuban-Turkish missile base exchange, since the United States had no equivalent missiles in Turkey.

The evidence is compatible with the hypothesis that, after the crisis erupted, the Soviet Union seized on a Cuba-Turkey bargain as the best hope in a bad situation. But the characteristics of the operation cannot sustain the claim that the Soviets made the initial move with this in mind.[30]

A stronger version of the hypothesis maintains that the trade envisaged included other U.S. bases around Russian borders (missiles in Italy and bases in Iran) and even in Berlin.[31] While these stakes more adequately balance the character of the Soviet action and the risks involved, this version of the hypothesis still does not adequately explain the facts. First is the size of the Soviet missile deployment: given the American commitment to act against any installation of offensive missiles, a smaller number of MRBMs alone would have provided a sufficient agenda for action. Second, if the intention had been to withdraw the missiles, the expense of permanent IRBM sites should have been avoided. Third, Khrushchev had earlier found the American commitment to Berlin unshakable. He had been, and presumably continued to be, unwilling to act in Berlin for fear that an American response would mean war. The proximity of the United States to Cuba and promises to act to prevent Cuba from becoming a Soviet offensive missile base were unambiguous. Thus, the Russians had more reason to believe that the United States would demand withdrawal of the Soviet missiles without yielding in Berlin (as in fact happened), or that war would come, than that the United States would trade for Berlin.

If Khrushchev had succeeded in completing the offensive missiles and springing on the United States a *fait accompli,* it is conceivable that the President would have wobbled. In that case, the shakiness of political will itself, rather than any explicit deal, would have provided the opportunity for eventual Soviet action in Berlin and elsewhere. That, however, is an alternative hypothesis.[32]

Hypothesis Two: Diverting Trap

Berlin was the linchpin of a second hypothesis, according to which the Soviets intended the missiles in Cuba to stand as a lightning rod. If the United States responded by striking "little

Cuba," NATO would be split and the world horrified. Such an act would fuel anti-Americanism in Latin America for years to come. It would prove to Soviet Stalinists and to the Chinese as well that the United States was no paper tiger. While the U.S. government was distracted by adverse public opinion at home and abroad, the occasion would be ripe for a strong Soviet move against Berlin. Another "Suez" would trap the United States in confusion, while Khrushchev moved in a second "Hungary."

This hypothesis can account for a number of the aspects of Soviet behavior that otherwise seem inexplicable. Why did the Soviet Union move in the face of the American President's unmistakable warnings? To make the United States act. Why were the Soviets seemingly sloppy in their coordination of the constructing of missiles in Cuba and the camouflage of the missiles at the sites? Because they wanted the United States to discover their activity. In the ExCom, advocates of this hypothesis argued that even the substantial presence of Soviet troops might be a crude, but nonetheless realistic, effort to construct a mirror image of Berlin. Finally, this hypothesis certainly answers the persistently bothersome question: Why Cuba *instead* of Berlin?

In spite of these merits, however, this hypothesis about Soviet plans is not tenable. Nothing could have been calculated to make an American strike against the missiles less attractive than the presence of over ten thousand Russian military personnel near the missile sites. A surprise attack on the missiles could not have avoided killing large numbers of Soviet citizens. If the Soviets' objective had been to dangle irresistible bait, they could have turned over a smaller number of missiles to the Cubans and let it be known that they would not respond to a U.S. attack. But the notion of trading thousands of Soviet lives in Cuba for the lives of thousands of American soldiers in Berlin, without further repercussions, is mad. Second, this hypothesis is not consistent with actual Soviet behavior. Khrushchev withdrew the missiles before an American attack. Had the Soviets wanted an American strike on their missiles in Cuba, they could simply have prolonged the crisis for several more days. (The United States was prepared for an attack on October 30, if the Soviet Union had not announced withdrawal of the missiles on the twenty-eighth.) Third, because of the strength of the American commitment, and the presence of American troops, the analogy between Berlin and Hungary is very weak. A Soviet move against Berlin would almost automatically have meant a major war.

Hypothesis Three: Cuban Defense

Though the Bay of Pigs (Cuba I) was a rather frail effort, the Soviet Union had substantial reason to believe that the United States might attempt to do the job right. The Bay of Pigs demonstrated that the United States could act. Hawkish congressional speeches, the words and actions of Cuban refugee groups, and exaggerated reports of CIA activities reaching Moscow from Havana supported this fear. Moreover, the United States had permitted some publicity about a military exercise called Philbriglex–62, which was to take place in the Caribbean in the fall of 1962. The exercise called for a force of 7,500 Marines, supported by four aircraft carriers, twenty destroyers, and fifteen troop carriers, to storm the coral beaches of Vieques Island, off the southeast coast of Puerto Rico. The announced purpose of the exercise was to liberate a mythical Republic of Vieques from the tyranny of a mythical dictator named Ortsac — a name, which, spelled backward . . .[33]

If the Marines attacked, Castro's defeat was certain. The Soviet Union could not provide enough conventional support to make a difference in such a distant war. In the battle, which might last several weeks, the Soviet Union would be forced to sit idly by: a Hungary in reverse. Rattling their missiles, which, as the Soviets now knew, the United States had discovered were few, held little promise. If there was a significant probability of U.S. action against Cuba, the Soviets had to act first in order to deter it. The decision to send missiles to Cuba came in answer to this threat.

Khrushchev explained Soviet action in just these terms. His letter of October 28, which announced that the missiles would be dismantled and withdrawn, stated the purpose for which they had been installed. In the face of the threat of U.S. invasion, "The Soviet government decided to render assistance to Cuba with means of defense against aggression — only with means for defense purposes. . . . We supplied them to prevent an attack on Cuba — to prevent rash acts."[34]

In reporting to the Supreme Soviet in December 1962, Khrushchev asserted: "At the request of the Cuban government we shipped arms there. . . . Our purpose was only the defense of Cuba."[35] Weeks after the crisis, Mikoyan insisted in an informal conversation with the President that these weapons were purely defensive and that they were justified, given the threat posed by former Vice-President Richard Nixon and certain Pentagon generals.[36]

The temptation to dismiss these statements lightly should be resisted.[37] There is powerful evidence that, from the Soviet point of view, Cuban defense was not a negligible matter. Though a self-proclaimed socialist state, Cuba nonetheless stood as the Communists' only showcase in the Western world. By the summer of 1962, the Soviet Union had given Castro $750 million in aid as well as large amounts of military equipment. Prior to the summer build-up, Soviet military supplies included jet fighters, military boats, and approximately 100,000 tons of ground weapons and equipment, which made the Cuban army the best equipped in Latin America. The summer build-up of weapons preceding the installation of missiles involved large amounts of expensive, essentially irretrievable, first-line defensive equipment. In addition to more modern infantry armaments, the Soviets sent modern supersonic MIG-21 fighters, coastal defense cruise missiles, surface-to-air missiles (SAMs) and large quantities of transportation, electronic, communications, radar, and construction equipment.

Events in Cuba also support the hypothesis that Moscow provided the missiles for Cuban defense. Since 1960, Moscow had resisted Cuban demands for specific military-security guarantees. Even after the Bay of Pigs, Soviet spokesmen were careful to refer to the Soviet *capability*, rather than to commitment, to come to Castro's defense. But Castro's demands, combined with an internal Cuban struggle between Communists and Castroites, created tensions that severely strained Cuban-Soviet relations through the spring of 1962. This dispute peaked at the end of March with Castro's purge of Annibal Escalenté, the man who had been organizing the Communist Party cadres around him. In the late spring, there was a shift in Soviet policy. Cuba's position in the 1962 May Day slogans was improved.[38] In a speech to a group of Cubans in Moscow, Khrushchev stated for the first time publicly that the Soviet Union was providing weapons to Cuba.[39] Castro made a strange apology to a group of Soviet technicians for the "poor treatment" they had received in Cuba.[40] In July a steady stream of ships bearing Soviet arms began to flow to Cuba.[41] In late July, on returning from a visit to the Soviet Union, Raul Castro (Fidel's brother) boasted that the only serious threat to Cuba was an American invasion, which "we can now repel."[42]

If Cuban defense was the Soviet objective, the adventure succeeded. The President's pledge that Cuba would not be invaded — either by the United States or by any other nation in the Western Hemisphere — removed the threat that the Soviet missiles were sent to deter. Thus, the missiles could be withdrawn.[43]

Though persuasive, this account of Soviet motives will not withstand careful examination. If deterrence of an American attack on Cuba had been the Soviet's primary objective, they had no need to install MRBMs in Cuba. The equipment they supplied to the Cuban Army certainly precluded an American attempt to destroy Castro discreetly — without a major attack. No amount of conventional arms in Cuban hands could defeat a major American attack on Cuba. If deterrence of a major attack had been their problem, the presence of a sizeable contingent of Soviet troops would have been the solution. As a deterrent, the value of Soviet troops in Cuba would be roughly equivalent to that of American troops in Berlin. This line of reasoning might seem to neglect the very expensive nature of troop commitments — as the Soviets had learned in East Germany. But in fact the Soviet deployment of nuclear-tipped missiles included 22,000 Soviet personnel, nearly 10,000 of whom were there to guard the offensive weapons.[44]

A second objection to the Cuban-defense hypothesis centers on the nuclear question. If for some reason the Soviets felt a nuclear deterrent was necessary, tactical nuclear weapons could have been emplaced more quickly, at less cost, and with considerably less likelihood of being discovered. Moreover, this deterrent came complete with an established principle of limited war justifying its employment: the right to strike bases from which an attack is launched. (In the Korean War the United States had maintained this right of reprisal against airfields used by planes bombing South Korea.)[45] Third, if for some reason strategic rockets were thought necessary, a much smaller number of MRBMs, with none of the more expensive and more easily detectable IRBMs, would have sufficed. Indeed, it is difficult to conceive of a Soviet deployment of weapons less suited to the purpose of Cuban defense than the one the Soviets made. Finally, by moving offensive strategic missiles into Cuba, in the face of the President's firm warning and the Soviets' solemn promises, the Soviet Union assumed risks manifestly out of proportion to the objective of Cuban defense. In undertaking a course of action that in Gromyko's words "brought the world one step, perhaps only a half step, from an abyss," the Soviets had to be fishing for something much larger.[46] Cuban defense might have been a subsidiary effect of the Soviet gamble, but not its overriding objective.

Hypothesis Four: Cold War Politics

The magnitude of the risk assumed by the Soviet Union has provided the most compelling argument for a fourth hypothesis. Believing, as he told the poet Robert Frost several months earlier, that the American people were "too liberal to fight," Khrushchev embarked on "the supreme Soviet probe of American intentions."[47] Undertaken in secrecy, sustained by duplicity, the success of Khrushchev's plan required a *fait accompli*. Confronted with operational missiles, the United States would react indecisively. Protests through diplomatic channels or in the United Nations would simply advertise the hollowness of the Monroe Doctrine, the Rio Treaty, and, most important, the President's own word. By unmasking an irresolute America, the Soviet Union would drastically reduce the credibility of U.S. commitments to other nations. After the failure to act here, who could expect the United States to act elsewhere? European suspicions of America's willingness to fulfill its pledges would multiply. Potential Castros in Latin America and other parts of the world would be encouraged. More aggressive Communists in China would see the real effectiveness of Soviet leadership. Though obviously risky, a victory in this case would demonstrate that the tide in the Cold War had turned. This hypothesis was put most forcefully in an early ExCom meeting by Ambassador Charles Bohlen's quotation of a Lenin adage comparing national expansion to a bayonet thrust: "If you strike steel, pull back; if you strike mush, keep going."[48]

President Kennedy accepted this hypothesis, acted on the basis of it in choosing the blockade, and, in retrospect, explained the Soviet action in these terms.[49] On Sunday, October 21, in response to a question by Arthur Schlesinger, Jr., concerning why the Soviets might have done such an amazing thing, Kennedy pointed to the potential Soviet political gains in (1) drawing Russia and China closer together, or at least strengthening the Soviet position in the Communist world by showing that Moscow was capable of bold action in support of a Communist revolution, (2) radically redefining the setting in which the Berlin problem could be reopened after the election, and (3) dealing the United States a tremendous political blow.[50] His announcement of the presence of Soviet missiles in Cuba to the nation and the world underlined this hypothesis. Kennedy argued that the clandestine attempt to station strategic weapons for the first time outside the Soviet Union constituted a deliberate, provocative, and unjustified change in "the status quo, which cannot be accepted by this country if our courage and our commitment are ever to be trusted again by either friend or foe. The 1930s taught us a clear lesson: aggressive conduct, if allowed to go unchecked and unchallenged, ultimately leads to war."[51] At the end of 1962, when called upon to interpret these events, he emphasized the importance of *appearance* of change in the balance of power: "It [the Soviet emplacement of missiles in Cuba] would have politically changed the balance of power. It would have appeared to, and appearances contribute to reality."[52]

This hypothesis represents the most widely accepted explanation of the Soviet move. The central phrase of Schlesinger's account has already been quoted: "the supreme Soviet probe of American intentions."[53] Sorensen accepts the President's choice of this hypothesis.[54] And there can be no doubt that political advantages would have accrued to the Soviet Union if the United States had acquiesced in the accomplished fact with protest alone.[55]

Indeed, of even greater importance would be the fact that in placing missiles in Cuba the Soviet Union flew in the face of hard words from the President about the grave consequences that such an action would set in motion. In the statements of September 4 and 13 the President drew a clear line between the defensive weapons already in Cuba (which the United States was presumably willing to tolerate) and weapons with offensive capability — specifically ground-to-ground missiles — that would constitute a direct threat to the United States. At the second press conference he reiterated his previous warning, stating specifically that U.S. action would not await an overt act but would occur if Cuba should "become an offensive military base of significant capacity for the Soviet Union."[56] Therefore, the first explicit statement on surface-to-surface missiles appeared several days before the first arrival of Soviet missiles and equipment. The second — again warning of action in response to mere presence, even without overt action — preceded the initiation of site construction and deployment. Before its plan to emplace strategic missiles in Cuba entered its final and decisive stage, then, the Soviet Union had two opportunities to reconsider its action. This blatant challenge to the American President's explicit, solemn announcements to his constituents and the world had to be primarily a political probe.

In spite of the persuasiveness of these arguments, it is necessary to consider several salient aspects of the situation that this hypothesis ignores. First, as Robert McNamara, former Secretary of Defense and an advocate of this hypothesis, has wondered publicly on several occasions, why did the Soviet Union need to probe the firmness of American intentions any further after the strong American stand in Berlin in 1961? The initial Soviet decision to send nuclear missiles to Cuba must have been made soon after the United States had refused to flinch at Khrushchev's Berlin ultimatum, forcing him to back down. Certainly the evidence suggests that, during the Berlin campaign, "the Soviet leaders became sufficiently convinced of the quality of the West's will to resist."[57] But why, then, another test? Second, the size and character of the Soviet weapon deployment was asymmetric with a mere political probe. To challenge American intentions and firmness, even a few MRBMs, threatening the entire southeastern United States (including Washington) should suffice. What could the IRBMs possibly add to the achievement of this objective? Finally, why choose Cuba as the location for a probe? At no point on the globe outside the continental United States were the Soviets so militarily disadvantaged vis-à-vis the United States as in the Caribbean. As President Kennedy, an advocate of the hypothesis, put the difficulty: "If they doubted our guts, why didn't they take Berlin?"[58]

Hypothesis Five: Missile Power

Having been tried and found wanting in the missile gap game, the Soviets faced two quandaries. In the short run, they seemed doomed to a paralyzing strategic inferiority. In the long run, the gap could be closed, but at considerable cost. The purchase of ICBMs and submarine-based missiles would require a sizeable allocation of scarce Soviet resources. If Cuba could be converted into a missile launcher, the Soviets might escape both problems. MRBMs and IRBMs based in Cuba would provide a swift, significant, and comparatively inexpensive addition to the

Soviet capability to strike the United States. Over the longer haul, this "unsinkable carrier" promised more rumble for the ruble. The Cuban missile deployment was thus a bold effort to alter the unhappy strategic environment in which the Soviet Union found itself in 1962.

Having failed twice in his offensives against Berlin — to some extent because of the adverse strategic balance — Khrushchev required some "chips" as a prerequisite to any further political initiatives. After the United States announced its awareness of the marked Soviet nuclear delivery inferiority, Khrushchev must certainly have been concerned about the weakness of his base for international moves. Indeed, he may well have worried lest the American superiority tempt the United States to more provocative uses of its power. The Cuban missile base afforded a significant opportunity.

Though Castro's statements about this issue have displayed a characteristic lack of consistency, a number of his remarks to friendly inquiries support this hypothesis. Claude Julien quotes him: "They explained to us that in accepting them [the missiles] we would be reinforcing the socialist camp the world over, and because we had received important aid from the socialist camp, we estimated that we could not decline."[59]

But what was the *military worth* of the Cuban missile base? As Albert and Roberta Wohlstetter state in their incisive analysis of these events, the beginning of wisdom on questions of this sort is a recognition that "it is not very sensible to talk with great confidence on these subjects."[60] Responsible judgment is difficult, even with complete access to privileged information. The classified data are uncertain, the public data still more so, and few of the commentators have looked carefully at the quantitative implications of even the public data.[61] Nevertheless, several tentative points are clear. What the Soviet Union could hope to achieve in terms of missile power is sensitive to a number of calculations. First, the performance of an offensive missile varies with distance, improving significantly with proximity. Guidance accuracy is especially affected by distance. Second, in the short run, the only choice open to the Soviet leaders confronting an awesome missile inferiority was a move of this sort. The missiles sent to Cuba represented a marked addition to Soviet forces capable of reaching the United States, since the United States was outside the range of MRBMs and IRBMs that were based in the Soviet Union. Moreover, the Soviet Cuban deployment — forty-eight

MRBMs and twenty-four IRBMs — amounted to a doubling of Soviet first-strike capabilities.[62] Third, there is no reason to believe that the Russian build-up would stop with seventy-two missiles. The Soviet Union had numerous MRBMs, which, if transported to Cuba, could provide additional capability to strike the United States. If the United States offered no interference, further installations at a similarly impressive speed might have reversed the Soviet Union's position of missile inferiority. Fourth, attacks from Cuba would outflank the U.S. Ballistic Missile Early Warning System (BMEWS). These missiles could cover virtually the entire United States before an effective warning could be sounded. American strategic bombers, which were on a fifteen-minute alert, would become extremely vulnerable. Though the Soviet missiles could be destroyed by a U.S. first strike, they would provide the Soviet Union with a significant first-strike capability. Finally the Cuban missile base offered the Soviet Union the opportunity to acquire missiles capable of striking the United States by buying the cheaper MRBMs and IRBMs rather than the more expensive ICBMs. The serious Soviet resource constraint, which had hindered their development as a first-rate missile power, could thus have been overcome.

According to this hypothesis, the Cuban missile episode was an attempt to achieve missile power parity by doubling the Soviet missile capability against the United States. The introduction of IRBMs — which is not explained by any of the other hypotheses — can be understood as a way of targeting strategic bomber and missile bases in the United States that could not be reached by MRBMs. That this strategic power might have been utilized later for political capital need not be denied. The act of missile emplacement, however, was not a political probe, but rather was a necessary prerequisite to any successful political move.[63]

Arthur Schlesinger, Jr., dismisses this hypothesis in favor of the political-probe theory, maintaining that the missiles shipped to Cuba, though representing a doubling of the Soviet strategic capability against the United States, still left the United States with a substantial superiority: "Since this would still leave the United States with at least a 2 to 1 superiority in nuclear power targeted against the Soviet Union, the shift in the military balance of power would be less crucial than that in the political balance."[64] This assertion depends on the assumption that the missiles that arrived constituted the entire Soviet program. Schlesinger offers no argument to support this assumption and there seem to be no grounds for it. Moreover, even if the Soviet build-up had ended with a two-to-one Soviet inferiority, this amounted to an order-of-magnitude improvement in the Soviet position: from a dangerous inferiority they could restore a credible balance of terror at a single stroke.

The missile power hypothesis thus offers the most satisfactory explanation of the thinking behind the Soviet move. It incorporates more of the critical details about the characteristics of the Soviet action. It molds these facts into the most plausible account of the Soviet choice. It permits an understanding of the Cuban venture as another application of the strategy that the Soviets had been pursuing for the previous five years: the strategy of bluff and deception designed to rectify the adverse strategic balance.[65] But it must be acknowledged that this hypothesis, as well as the other four, is subject to another class of difficulties.

First, each of the five hypotheses assumes that a Soviet decision to emplace missiles led to a developed plan for implementing that decision.

> Moscow evidently saw the operation in two stages — first, the augmentation of Cuban defensive capabilities by bringing in surface-to-air anti-aircraft (SAM) missiles and MIG-21 fighters; then, as soon as the SAMs were in place to protect the bases and deter photographic reconnaissance (a SAM had brought down the U-2 over Russia in 1960), sending in offensive weapons, both ballistic missiles and Ilyushin-28 jet aircraft able to deliver nuclear bombs.[66]

But Soviet actions are not entirely compatible with this reconstructed plan. MRBMs were installed *before* the SAM covers were completed. Sorensen expresses forcefully the bewilderment of both the President and the intelligence community over this fact: "Why the Soviets failed to coordinate this timing is still inexplicable."[67]

Khrushchev's grand plan for unveiling his *fait accompli* presents a second difficulty. He had announced privately his intention to visit the United Nations in the second half of November.[68] His message of September 6 (delivered via Dobrynin and Sorensen) stated that such a trip, if it proved necessary, "would be possible only in the second half of November. The Chairman does not wish to become involved in your internal affairs."[69] The Soviet Central Committee Plenary session was set for November 19–23.[70] If he could come to that session fresh from a major international victory, he would have the initiative. But that would necessitate a visit to the United Nations, unveiling of the missiles, and return to Moscow between November 15 and 19. On the other hand, if he postponed his U.N. display until after the Central Committee meetings, he would visit the United Nations between November 23 and 31. In either case, one major fact fails to fit. The *fait accompli* gambit required that the missile installation be completed. But even on the round-the-clock schedule adopted after the U.S. announcement that the missiles had been discovered, the IRBM complexes would not have achieved operational readiness until after the fifteenth of December.[71] This further failure of coordination is difficult to understand.[72]

A third puzzle arises about the Soviet omission of camouflage at the missile sites. Immediately after the crisis, commentators speculated at great length about the Soviet plan for the United States to discover the missiles during construction. How else can one explain the fact that the SAMs were constructed in the standard four-slice pattern for the protection of strategic missiles, a pattern with which U.S. intelligence men had become familiar from interpreting U-2 films of construction sites within the Soviet Union?[73] But a Soviet desire to be found out hardly squares with the clandestine fashion in which the missiles were transported to Cuba and from the docks to the sites.

Fourth, why did the Soviet Union fail to take into account the American U-2 flights over Cuba?[74] The Soviets certainly knew about the U-2s and their capabilities, having captured the U-2 in which Gary Powers was downed over the Soviet Union. They should have known about the semimonthly overflights of Cuba by U-2s. But if they did, how could they expect the United States not to discover their missiles in the process of construction?

Finally, why did the Soviet Union persist in the face of the President's repeated warnings? Was the signal not heard? Was the warning not credible? How could the Soviets have believed that President Kennedy would not react to their move?

Why Did the United States Respond to the Missile Deployment with a Blockade?

U.S. response to the Soviet Union's emplacement of missiles in Cuba must be understood in strategic terms as simple value-maximizing escalation. American nuclear superiority could be counted on to paralyze Soviet nuclear power. Soviet transgression of the nuclear threshold in response to an American use of lower levels of violence would be wildly irrational, since it would mean virtual destruction of the Soviet Communist system and the Russian nation. American local superiority was overwhelming: it could be initiated at a low level while threatening, with high credibility, an ascending sequence of steps short of the nuclear threshold. All that was required was for the United States to bring to bear its strategic and local superiority in a way that demonstrated American determination to see the missiles removed, while at the same time allowing Moscow time and room to retreat without humiliation. The naval blockade (euphemistically called a quarantine to circumvent the niceties of international law) did just that.[75]

The process by which the U.S. government selected the blockade exemplified this logic. Informed of the presence of Soviet offensive missiles in Cuba, the President assembled his most trusted advisers. The principal members of this group, which was later christened the Executive Committee of the National Security Council (ExCom), included Attorney General Robert Kennedy, Secretary of State Dean Rusk, Secretary of Defense Robert McNamara, Director of the Central Intelligence Agency John McCone, Secretary of the Treasury Douglas Dillon, Special Assistant for National Security Affairs McGeorge Bundy, Special Counsel Theodore Sorensen, Undersecretary of State George Ball, Deputy Undersecretary of State U. Alexis Johnson, Assistant Secretary of State Edwin Martin, Soviet expert Llewellyn Thompson, Deputy Secretary of Defense Roswell Gilpatric, Assistant Secretary of Defense Paul Nitze, and Chairman of the Joint Chiefs of Staff Maxwell Taylor.[76] The President charged this group to "set aside all other tasks to make a prompt and intensive survey of the dangers and *all possible courses of action.*"[77] The group functioned as "fifteen individuals on our own, representing the President and not different departments."[78] As one of the participants recalls, "The remarkable aspect of those meetings was a sense of complete equality. Protocol mattered little when the nation's life was at stake. Experience mattered little in a crisis which had no precedent. Even rank mattered little when secrecy prevented staff support."[79] Most of the following week was spent canvassing all the possible tracks and weighing the arguments for and against each. Six major categories of action were considered.

1. DO NOTHING.   American vulnerability to Soviet missiles was not new. Since the United States already lived under the gun of missiles based in Russia, a Soviet capability to strike the United States from Cuba too made little real difference. Indeed, the real danger was that the United States might over-react to this Soviet move. The Soviet action would be announced by the United States in such a calm, casual manner that it would deflate whatever political capital Khrushchev hoped to make of the missiles.

This proposal fails on two counts. First, it grossly underestimates the military importance of the Soviet move. Not only would the Soviet Union's missile capability have been instantly doubled and the U.S. early warning system outflanked but the Soviet Union would have had an opportunity to reverse the strategic balance by further installations and, indeed, in the longer run, to invest in cheaper, shorter-range, rather than more expensive longer-range, missiles. Second, the political importance of the Soviet move was undeniable: it challenged the American President's solemn warning. If the United States failed to respond, no American commitment would be credible.

2. DIPLOMATIC PRESSURES.   Several forms were considered: an appeal to the United Nations or Organization of American States for an inspection team, a secret approach to Khrushchev, and a direct approach to Khrushchev — perhaps at a summit meeting. The United States would demand that the missiles be removed, but the final settlement might include neutralization of Cuba, with U.S. withdrawal from the Guantánamo base or withdrawal of U.S. Jupiters from Turkey or Italy.

Each form of the diplomatic approach had its particular drawbacks. To arraign the Soviet Union before the U.N. Security Council held little promise since the Russians could veto any proposed action. (Zorin of the Soviet Union happened to be chairman of the Council for October.) While the diplomats argued, the missiles would become operational. To send a secret emissary to Khrushchev demanding that the missiles be withdrawn would pose untenable alternatives. On the one hand, this would invite Khrushchev to seize the diplomatic initiative, perhaps committing him to strategic retaliation in response to an attack on tiny Cuba, while waiting for left-wing opinion in the United States and overseas to force a conference à la Munich. On the other hand, this would tender an ultimatum that no great power could accept. To confront Khrushchev at a summit would guarantee demands for U.S. concessions, and the similarity between U.S. missiles in Turkey and Russian missiles in Cuba could not be ignored.

But why not trade the Jupiters in Turkey and Italy for the missiles in Cuba? The United States had already chosen to withdraw these missiles (in order to replace them with superior, less vulnerable Polaris submarines in the Mediterranean). The middle of a crisis, however, was no time for concessions. The offer of such a deal might confirm suspicions that the West would yield and thus tempt the Soviets to demand more. It would undoubtedly confirm European suspicions about American willingness to sacrifice European interests when the chips were down. Finally, the basic issue had to be kept clear. As the President stated in reply to Bertrand Russell's plea for concessions, "I think your attention might well be directed to the burglars rather than to those who have caught the burglars."[80]

3. A SECRET APPROACH TO CASTRO.   The crisis provided an opportunity to divorce Cuba from Soviet Communism by offering Castro the alternatives: "split or fall." This approach had a formidable drawback: the missiles belonged to the Soviet Union. Soviet troops transported, constructed, guarded, and controlled the missiles. Their removal would thus depend on a Soviet decision.

4. INVASION.   The United States could take this occasion not only to remove the missiles but also to rid itself of Castro. A Navy exercise had long been scheduled in which Marines would liberate the imprisoned island of Vieques.[81] Why not simply shift the point of disembarkation? (The Pentagon's foresight in planning this operation would be an appropriate antidote to the CIA's Bay of Pigs.)

Preparations were made for an invasion, but only as a last resort. An invasion would force American troops to confront 20,000 Soviets in the Cold War's first case of direct contact between troops of the superpowers. Such brinksmanship courted nuclear disaster, practically guaranteeing an equivalent Soviet move against Berlin.

5. SURGICAL AIR STRIKE.   The missile sites should be removed by a clean, swift, conventional air attack. This was the firm, effective counter-action that the attempted deception deserved. A surgical strike would remove the missiles and thus eliminate both the danger that the missiles might become operational and the fear that the Soviets would realize the American

discovery and act first. Preceded by Presidential announcement of the missiles' presence on Saturday and accompanied by an explanatory address, increased surveillance of the island to prevent further installations, and a call for a summit, this would settle the matter.

Several difficulties blunted this alternative's initial appeal. First, could the strike really be "surgical"? Even if the missile sites could have been destroyed, the Soviet MIGs and IL-28 bombers might attack Guantánamo or the southeastern United States. Moreover, as the Air Force warned, destruction of all the missiles could not be guaranteed.[82] Some might be fired during the attack; some might not yet have been pin-pointed. To assure destruction of Soviet and Cuban means of retaliation, what was required was not a surgical but rather a massive attack — of at least 500 sorties. This might result in chaos and political collapse, eventually necessitating a U.S. invasion. Second, a surprise air attack would of course kill Russians at the missile sites — and elsewhere, if the attack were more massive. An attack on the military troops and citizens of a superpower could not be regarded lightly. Pressures on the Soviet Union to retaliate would be so strong that an attack on Berlin or Turkey was highly probable. Third, the chief flaw in this track stemmed from the question of advance warning. Could the President of the United States, with his memory of Pearl Harbor and his vision of future U.S. responsibility, order a "Pearl Harbor in reverse"? For 175 years, unannounced Sunday-morning attacks had been an anathema to U.S. tradition.[83] The United States could not betray its heritage. No way could be found to solve the problem of advance warning. To attack without warning was no live option. A warning would give the Soviets the opportunity to commit themselves publicly to a response, to hide the missiles — in short, to tie us in knots.[84]

6. BLOCKADE. Indirect military action in the form of some type of blockade became more attractive as the ExCom dissected the other alternatives. An embargo on military shipments to Cuba enforced by a naval blockade was not, however, without its own problems. Even the term presented a formidable difficulty. Vice-President Johnson had recently maintained that a blockade was "an act of war."[85] A blockade would deny the traditional freedom of the seas demanded by several of our close allies and might be held illegal, in violation of the U.N. Charter and international

law, unless the United States could obtain a two-thirds vote in the OAS.

Second, could the United States blockade Cuba without inviting Soviet reprisal in Berlin? Joint blockades would probably result in the lifting of both, bringing the United States back to the present point and allowing the Soviets additional time to complete the missiles. Third, the possible consequences of the blockade resembled those that ruled out the air strike. If Soviet ships did not stop, the United States would be forced to fire the first shot, inviting retaliation. Moreover, Castro might attack American ships blockading his island. Finally, how could a blockade be related to the problem: namely, the existence of missiles already on the island of Cuba and approaching operational readiness daily? A blockade offered the Soviets a spectrum of delaying tactics with which to buy time to complete the missile installations. Did this situation not call for an American *fait accompli*?

In spite of these enormous difficulties the blockade had comparative advantages: (1) It was a middle course between inaction and attack, aggressive enough to communicate firmness of intention, but still not so precipitous as a strike. (2) It placed on Khrushchev the burden of choice for the next step. He could avoid a direct military clash by keeping his ships away. His was the last clear chance. (3) No possible military confrontation could be more acceptable to the United States than a naval engagement in the Caribbean. At our doorstep, a naval blockade was invincible. (4) This move permitted the United States, by flexing its conventional muscles, to exploit the threat of subsequent non-nuclear steps in each of which the United States would enjoy significant superiority.[86]

Particular arguments about advantages and disadvantages were powerful. An explanation of the American choice of the blockade, however, must take into account more general principles. As President Kennedy stated in drawing the moral of the crisis:

> Above all, while defending our own vital interests, nuclear powers must avert those confrontations which bring an adversary to the choice of either a humiliating defeat or a nuclear war. To adopt that kind of course in the nuclear age would be evidence only of the bankruptcy of our policy — or of a collective deathwish for the world.[87]

Considered in this light, the blockade was the only real option.

Why Did the Soviet Union Withdraw the Missiles?

On Sunday morning, October 28, the Soviets broadcast the message that ended the critical phase of the crisis. Khrushchev announced the Soviet decision to "dismantle the arms which you describe as offensive and to crate and return them to the Soviet Union."[88] The American objective was achieved. Obviously the United States had done something right. The reason the Soviet Union decided to withdraw the missiles is, however, not so obvious.

To many analysts of the crisis — particularly to analysts within the American military establishment — the answer is simple.[89] The United States possessed overwhelming strategic and tactical superiority. Tactically, American ships, planes, and manpower were sufficient for any possible action in the Caribbean. Strategically, U.S. capability could pose a credible threat of nuclear holocaust to the Soviet Union. Because of this overwhelming strategic and tactical superiority, once the United States credibly communicated its determination to have the missiles withdrawn, the outcome was certain. The President's statement on October 22 and the blockade set in boldface the firm American commitment to force withdrawal of the missiles. All that remained was for the Soviet Union to calculate its only remaining move and withdraw. As the major U.S. government postmortem on the crisis — written by Walt Rostow and Paul Nitze in February 1963 — reportedly concluded: the principal error of Kennedy and his advisers was that they laid

> too much stress upon the danger of nuclear war. . . . This exaggerated concern had prompted consideration of improvident actions (an air strike by American bombers to take out all the missile installations) and counseled hesitations where none were necessary. Since the United States could get its way without involving nuclear weapons, the burden of choice rested entirely on the Soviets.[90]

As Weintal and Bartlett report, "In the aftermath, it seemed clear to the planners that a Soviet nuclear initiative was a negligible prospect throughout the crisis because its consequences would have been suicidal to the Soviet Union."[91]

This explanation has been refined by a number of strategic analysts of the Soviet withdrawal. Herman Kahn analyzes the events as a "traditional crisis" in which U.S. "preemptive escalation" in surprising the Soviet Union with a blockade saddled the Soviets with the choice between withdrawal and puncture of a provisional threshold.[92] Thomas Schelling's analysis of these events singles out the blockade as a successful "compellant threat," after earlier "deterrent threats" had failed to prevent Soviet nuclearization of Cuba.[93] Perhaps the most careful, sustained strategic analysis is provided by the Wohlstetters:

> What was threatened was a local non-nuclear action, a measure of very limited violence, only the boarding of ships. On the staircase of ascending steps in the use of force, there would have been many landings, many decision points, at which either side could choose between climbing higher or moving down. The United States nuclear retaliatory force would have made a Soviet missile strike against the United States catastrophic for Russia.[94]

Why did the Soviet Union withdraw the missiles? *"Chairman Khrushchev stepped down to avoid a clash of conventional forces in which he would have lost. To avoid this level of loss, he would have had irresponsibly to risk very much higher levels."*[95]

The major problem with this explanation of Soviet withdrawal of the missiles lies in its focus on the *blockade* as the sufficient demonstration of U.S. determination. Did the blockade work? Or was it rather the case that the blockade failed in just the way that many of its opponents had predicted? For, after all, what did the blockade have to do with the missiles already on the island of Cuba and rapidly approaching operational readiness? The blockade exhibited U.S. willingness to escalate this crisis to the point of risking a local, non-nuclear naval encounter — with all the possible diplomatic ramifications of such a confrontation. It forced Khrushchev to choose among three alternatives: (1) avoid a showdown by keeping Soviet vessels out of the area, (2) submit to the quarantine by permitting ships to be stopped and searched, and (3) provoke the United States to a first use of force by violating the quarantine. But if he chose the first, why could he not also proceed to complete the forty-two missiles already present?

Indeed, this is precisely what happened. The Soviet tanker *Bucharest,* which obviously could not be carrying outlawed contraband, was allowed to cross the blockade after identifying herself.[96] A Soviet-chartered, Panamanian-owned, American-built liberty ship of Lebanese registry, the *Marcula,* which carried only trucks, sulfur, and spare parts, submitted to being stopped and searched.[97] Sixteen of the eighteen Soviet dry-cargo ships steaming toward Cuba, including five with large hatches, came to a halt well outside the perimeter of the blockade.[98] Construction of the missiles in Cuba rushed feverishly toward completion.[99] The facts would seem to belie explanation of Soviet missile withdrawal in terms of the blockade alone.

President Kennedy's announcement of the blockade emphasized that it was an *initial* step. No attempt was made to disguise the massive build-up of over 200,000 invasion troops in Florida.[100] Squadrons of U.S. tactical fighters moved to airports within easy striking distance of targets in Cuba. The State Department press officer, in making an announcement on Friday, referred reporters to a passage in the President's Monday night speech that read, "Further action will be justified if work on the missiles continues."[101] At 9 P.M. Saturday, Defense Secretary McNamara called to active duty twenty-four troop-carrier squadrons of the Air Force Reserve, approximately 14,000 men.[102] Thus the blockade was but the first step in a series of moves that *implicitly* threatened air strike or invasion. The blockade allowed Khrushchev time to adjust to the American discovery of his bold attempt before it became an accomplished fact. It added firmness to the initial commitment of the United States to see the missiles withdrawn. The alert of American forces around the globe articulated U.S. intention to act elsewhere if necessary. But what forced stoppage of the construction of the missiles — work that proceeded rapidly up until Khrushchev's Sunday morning announcement — was the threat of further local steps posed by the extraordinary build-up and readiness of American air-strike and invasion forces.[103] The blockade constituted an effective and wise initial step. But only when coupled with the implicit threat of further action — action in the form of alternatives rejected during the first week for reasons that have already been discussed — did it succeed in forcing Soviet withdrawal of the missiles. Without the implicit threat of air strike or invasion, the blockade alone could have prevented Soviet ships from bringing additional missiles to Cuba, but would not have forced the removal of the missiles already present.

Khrushchev's report of this crisis to the Supreme Soviet attributed even greater importance to the threat of air strike or invasion: "We received information from Cuban comrades and from other sources on the morning of October 27th *directly stating* that this attack would be carried out in the next two or three days. We interpreted these cables as an *extremely alarming warning signal.*"[104] Khrushchev's report maintains that the threat was not left to the Soviet imagination or to its interpretation of the American military build-up. He asserted that the threat was "explicitly stated" and there is considerable evidence to suggest that in this he spoke accurately.[105]

On the final Saturday, after the U.S. government had hammered out its reply to the Soviet letters, the President's brother, at the request of the President, delivered a copy of this public letter to the Soviet Ambassador. The public reply contained no explicit threat. But Robert Kennedy warned the Soviet Ambassador that "the point of escalation was at hand," that the United States would take "strong and overwhelming retaliatory action . . . unless [the President] received immediate notification that the missiles would be withdrawn."[106] As Robert Kennedy himself recalled:

> Saturday, October 27 was the most serious time. A note was sent to Mr. Khrushchev on Saturday night saying that President Kennedy and the U.S. government would have to receive notification by the next day that the missiles were going to be withdrawn or the consequences would be extremely grave for the Soviet Union.[107]

Testifying before a subcommittee of the House Committee on Appropriations in February 1963, Secretary of Defense McNamara confirmed the fact that the threat of air strike or invasion was not left implicit:

> We had a force of several hundred thousand men ready to invade Cuba. . . . Khrushchev knew without any question whatsoever that he faced the full military power of the United States, including its nuclear weapons. . . . We faced that night the possibility of launching nuclear weapons. . . *and that is the reason, and the only reason, why he withdrew those weapons.*[108]

Khrushchev withdrew the Soviet missiles not because of the blockade, not because of the implicit threat of "further action," but because of an *explicit* threat of air strike or invasion on Tuesday — unless he served immediate notice that the missiles would be withdrawn. The middle road — i.e., the blockade — may have provided time for Soviet adjustment to the fact of American commitment to withdrawal of the missiles, but it also left room for the Soviet Union to bring the missiles to operational readiness. What narrowed that room was no pantomime.

Though the U.S. build-up in Florida may have been required to convince the Soviet Union of U.S. ability to move up the ladder of escalation, the Soviets were not left to guess what the next step would be or when it would come. Rather, an explicit threat, with a specific time limit, was conveyed by Robert Kennedy to Dobrynin and through him to Chairman Khrushchev.

3

Model II: Organizational Process

For some purposes, governmental behavior can be usefully summarized as action chosen by a unitary, rational decisionmaker: centrally controlled, completely informed, and value maximizing. But this simplification must not be allowed to conceal the fact that a government consists of a conglomerate of semi-feudal, loosely allied organizations, each with a substantial life of its own. Government leaders do sit formally and, to some extent, in fact, on top of this conglomerate. But governments perceive problems through organizational sensors. Governments define alternatives and estimate consequences as their component organizations process information; governments act as these organizations enact routines. Governmental behavior can therefore be understood, according to a second conceptual model, less as deliberate choices and more as *outputs* of large organizations functioning according to standard patterns of behavior.

To be responsive to a wide spectrum of problems, governments consist of large organizations, among which primary responsibility for particular tasks is divided. Each organization attends to a special set of problems and acts in quasi-independence on these problems. But few important issues fall exclusively within the domain of a single organization. Thus government behavior relevant to any important problem reflects the independent output of several organizations, partially coordinated by government leaders. Government leaders can substantially disturb, but not substantially control, the behavior of these organizations.

To perform complex routines, the behavior of large numbers of individuals must be coordinated. Coordination requires standard operating procedures: rules according to which things are done. Reliable performance of action that depends upon the behavior of hundreds of persons requires established "programs." Indeed, if the eleven members of a football team are to perform adequately on any particular down, each man must not "do what he thinks needs to be done" or "do what the quarterback tells him to do." Rather, each player must perform the maneuvers specified by a previously established play, which the quarterback has simply called in this situation.

At any given time, a government consists of *existing* organizations, each with a *fixed* set of standard operating procedures and programs. The behavior of these organizations — and consequently of the government — relevant to an issue in any particular instance is, therefore, determined primarily by routines established in these organizations prior to that instance. Explanation of a government action starts from this base line, noting incremental deviations. But organizations do change. Learning occurs gradually, over time. Dramatic organizational change occurs in response to major disasters. Both learning and change are influenced by existing organizational capabilities and procedures.

Borrowed from studies of organizations, these loosely formulated propositions amount simply to *tendencies*. Each must be hedged by modifiers like "other things being equal" and "under certain conditions." In particular instances, tendencies hold — more or less. In specific situations, the relevant question is: more or less? But this is as it should be. For "organizations" are no more homogeneous a class than "solids." When scientists tried to generalize about "solids," they achieved similar results. Solids tend to expand when heated, but some do and some don't. More adequate categorization of the various elements now lumped under the rubric "organizations" is thus required. Moreover, the behavior of particular organizations seems considerably more complex than the behavior of solids. Additional information about a given organization is required for further specification of the tendency statements. In spite of these two caveats, the characterization of government action as organizational output differs sharply from Model I. Attempts to understand problems of foreign affairs in terms of this frame of reference should produce quite different explanations.

Studies of organizations have had little influence upon the

existing literature of international affairs.[1] Few specialists in international politics have studied organization theory. It is only recently that organization theorists have come to study organizations as decisionmakers; behavioral studies of foreign policy organizations from the decisionmaking perspective have not yet been produced. It seems unlikely, however, that these gaps will remain unfilled. Considerable progress has been made in the study of the business firm as a decisionmaking organization. Scholars have begun applying similar insights to situations in which the decisionmaker is a government organization rather than a firm. And interest in an organizational perspective is spreading rapidly among institutions and individuals concerned with actual government operations.

Organizational Theory and Economics

One venerable tradition in the social sciences permits the expression of personal discoveries in an individually tailored vocabulary. Unfortunately, this encourages much repackaging of existing theories and not a little confusion. Avoiding that pitfall, the present chapter makes maximum use of terms and concepts developed by organization theorists and economists. This approach acknowledges the model's intellectual debt while making explicit the relation between the Organizational Process Paradigm for international politics and models of other types of organizations.

It can be reasonably claimed that organization theory is a young science.[2] James March dates the origin of contemporary, cumulative studies of organizations: "The field as a more or less identifiable cluster of research interests within a number of social sciences dates for most purposes from a group of books written between 1937 and 1947 — Barnard, Roethlisberger and Dickson, and Simon."[3] Thus Chester Barnard's *The Function of the Executive* and Herbert Simon's *Administrative Behavior* mark the beginning and the end of the decade of definition of organization theory as a semi-discipline. The second decade witnessed an enormous increase in effort devoted to the systematic study of organizations. Many of the "discoveries" of that decade (and of earlier periods) are summarized in a logically ordered, propositional form by March and Simon in their path-breaking book, *Organizations,* published in 1958.[4] March and Simon formulated three central problems with the "state of the art" as it stood at the end of the second decade: (1) "The literature leaves one with the impression that after all *not a great deal has been said* about organizations"; (2) "but it has been said over and over in a variety of languages. Consequently, we require a serious effort toward the construction of a *common language*"; (3) "There is in the literature a *great disparity between hypotheses and evidence.*"[5]

The third decade of organization theory's short life — which observed another exponential leap in resources devoted to the examination of organizational behavior — was capped by the publication of the monumental *Handbook of Organizations* in 1965.[6] As its introduction modestly states, the *Handbook* attempts to "summarize and report the present state of knowledge about organizations."[7] Contributions to the volume came from four political scientists, five economists, five psychologists, six students of business and industrial organizations, and ten sociologists; yet the editor found it unnecessary either to provide a glossary or to identify the contributors by discipline. Thus some progress has been made in coming to grips with the problem of a common vocabulary. The *Handbook's* 1,247 double-columned pages suggest that considerably more has now been said about organizations. The sophistication of some of the articles indicates that even the third problem may not prove entirely intractable: the study of organizations has acquired considerable momentum as the result of inputs from so many disciplines. As James March, the editor of the *Handbook*, states in the introduction:

> The vitality represented by the contributors to the *Handbook*, and by contemporary organizations, suggests that it [the study of organizations] is going somewhere. There is commitment by first-class scholars. There is a set of interesting theoretical ideas. There is an involvement in empirical research. There is a large, mostly untouched, and usually cooperative group of organizations for study. There is widespread recognition of the significance of organizational behavior both as a factor in the analysis of complex social systems and as an important special case of human activities.[8]

The *Handbook's* chapter headings indicate the range of subjects studied by organizational theorists: management theory; economic theories of organization; organizational growth and development; communications in organizations; organizational decisionmaking; interpersonal relations in organizations;

organizational control structures; the comparative analysis of organizations.[9] Obviously an attempt to summarize this literature is beyond the scope of the present study. Indeed, the *Handbook* itself is the summary to which the interested reader is referred. It should be useful, nevertheless, to indicate the strand of organization theory upon which Model II is most dependent.

The branch of organization theory that takes as its focus the decisionmaking process in organizations affords the richest source of insights for the paradigm developed in this chapter.[10] For two decades, the seminal figure in this area has been Herbert Simon. Simon's work is motivated by the attempt to understand the basic features of organizational structure and function as they derive from the characteristics of human problem-solving and rational choice.[11]

Most theories of individual and organizational choice employ a concept of "comprehensive rationality," according to which individuals and organizations choose the best alternative, taking account of consequences, their probabilities, and utilities. But, as we have observed in Chapter 1, such choices require: (1) the generation of all possible alternatives, (2) assessment of the probabilities of all consequences of each, and (3) evaluation of each set of consequences for all relevant goals. These requirements are, in Simon's words, "powers of prescience and capacities for computation resembling those we usually attribute to God."[12] By focusing on the limits of human capacity in comparison with the complexities of the problems that individuals in organizations must face, Simon develops the concept of "bounded rationality." The physical and psychological limits of man's capacity as alternative generator, information processor, and problem solver constrain the decisionmaking processes of individuals and organizations. Because of these bounds, intendedly rational action requires simplified models that extract the main features of a problem without capturing all of its complexity.

Simon's work finds five characteristic deviations from comprehensive rationality that are displayed by the simplifications of human problem solvers:

1. FACTORED PROBLEMS. Problems are so complex that only a limited number of aspects of each problem can be attended to at a time. Thus individuals factor (split up) problems into quasi-independent parts and deal with the parts one by one.

Organizations factor complex problems into a number of roughly independent parts which are parceled out to various organizational units. Ideally problems are factored by a means-end analysis, which assigns separable pieces of a problem to organizational subunits as subgoals. The structure of an organization thus reflects the problems that its subunits factor. (Roles consist of specified subsets of premises that guide actions in a particular subunit.)[13]

2. SATISFICING. Maximization or optimization is replaced by satisficing. In choosing, human beings do not consider all alternatives and pick the action with the best consequences. Instead, they find a course of action that is "good enough" — that satisfies. Organizations are happy to find a needle in the haystack rather than searching for the sharpest needle in the haystack.[14]

3. SEARCH. Comprehensive rationality requires consideration of all alternatives, thus making the problem of search trivial. Where satisficing is the rule — stopping with the first alternative that is good enough — the order in which alternatives are turned up is critical. Organizations generate alternatives by relatively stable, sequential search processes. As a result, the menu is severely limited.[15]

4. UNCERTAINTY AVOIDANCE. Comprehensively rational agents deal with alternate consequences of action by estimating probabilities of possible outcomes. People in organizations are quite reluctant to base actions on estimates of an uncertain future. Thus choice procedures that emphasize short-run feedback are developed. Organizations, like house thermostats, rely on relatively prompt corrective action to eliminate deviations between actual and desired temperatures, rather than accurate prediction of next month's temperature.[16]

5. REPERTOIRES. Repertoires of action programs are developed by organizations and individuals. These constitute the range of effective choice in recurring situations.[17]

In economics, recent developments in the theory of the business firm recapitulate the growth of organization theory. The traditional theory of the firm treats the business firm as a unitary agent — an instance of that infamous abstraction *homo economicus*. The theory assumes that: (1) firms seek to maximize profits; (2) firms operate with perfect knowledge. With no further assumptions about the psychological characteristics of economic man, the theory then explains the firm's behavior in terms of forces outside the firm. The entrepreneur, faced with a determinate supply schedule for factors of production, a given price for his product, and a technologically determined production function, is a predictable animal: profit is maximized when marginal cost is equal to the price that equals marginal revenue; the marginal rate of substitution between products and between factors of production equals their price ratio; equilibrium is achieved at the point of optimal use of inputs and outputs.

The propositions yielded by this theory have been formulated precisely:[18]

1. A number of equations n may be derived and solved for the optimal quantities of the firm's n commodities (both inputs and outputs).

2. At equilibrium, the marginal rate of substitution between two products, or between two factors, is equal to the ratio of their prices.

3. The marginal physical productivity of a factor with respect to a product (the rate of change of the amount of the factor used with respect to the product's output) is equal to their price ratio.

4. The quantity of a good produced is selected so that its marginal cost (with respect to this product) is equal to its (given) price.

5. A price increase for a product raises its supply; a price increase for a factor reduces its demand.

6. "Cross" price effects are symmetric. That is, the rate of change of a first commodity with respect to the price of a second commodity is equal to the rate of change of the second with respect to the price of the first.

7. A price increase of a good tends to affect the other commodities by decreasing the outputs of products and increasing the inputs of factors.

A prominent feature of this theory is the assumption of a perfectly competitive environment. But imperfect factor markets and imperfect product markets have been treated as extensions of this case.[19] Theories of imperfect competition essentially hold the basic theory of the firm constant while changing market assumptions. This attempted extension of the theory of the firm has produced a number of targets for critics. First, the assumption of profit maximization has been challenged. Second, the assumption of certainty or knowledge of the probability distribution of future events has been questioned. Third, divergence between theoretical firms and real world firms has been noted.

Critics of the assumption that firms maximize profits challenge two discrete aspects of this assumption. One cluster of critics accepts the notion of "maximization" but attacks the assumption that "profits" are what is maximized. Rothschild substitutes survival for profits; Baumol maintains that sales subject to a profit constraint is the objective.[20] Others claim that firms maximize not a single goal but rather a series of goals: profits, sales, survival, maintenance of a share of the market, liquidity, managerial comfort.[21] Papandreou attempts to sum up a number of goals in a "general preference function" which itself is what the firm maximizes.[22] A second cluster of critics challenges the notion of "maximization." Simon's critique of this concept, and his suggestion of satisficing as a substitute, has been noted. Gordon, Margolis, and others argue that maximization should be replaced by a concept of goals as constraints that must be satisfied.[23]

Critics of the assumption of "perfect information" also come in two stripes. As we have noted, Simon and the Carnegie School focus on the bounded character of human capabilities. Firms are physically unable to possess full information, generate all alternatives, and calculate all consequences in terms of all values. Thus they arrange a negotiated environment and adopt rules of thumb for choice and search. March and Simon develop the principle of sequential search and spell out its implications for the theory of choice.[24] The second group focuses on the cost of information and calculation in a world of uncertainty. Additional information is always available — at a cost. Further calculation can always be done — if someone is paid to do it. Thus the simplifications, which determine choices, utilize considerably less information and calculation than the human beings involved are capable of assimilating.

The debate about the gap between the firm of economic theory and what observers of actual businesses call firms has produced not a little methodological confusion. Invoking empirical observation, critics point out that the firm of economic theory is in fact an organization. Its acts are not those of a unitary, rational, perfectly informed entrepreneur but of an organization. Goals grow out of the interaction among various participants in the organization.[25] Prices are set by the full cost (or markup) method.[26] Inventory turnover is used as a surrogate for demand estimates;[27] cost calculations are done in standard rather than marginal terms;[28] all actions are governed by standard business procedures and shortcuts.[29] These would seem to be straightforward factual propositions about which there need be no debate. But the traditional theory of the firm persists, and not without defenders. In defense of the classic consensus, Milton Friedman accepts each of the propositions about the way firms actually operate but challenges their implications.[30] What these points show is that the theory of the firm meets the test of *"descriptive inaccuracy,"* which, according to Friedman, is a mark of all powerful theory. The criterion by which the theory must be tested is its predictive power. Friedman argues that, on these grounds, the theory is acceptable — though he cites little evidence for his claim about its predictive powers.[31]

The utility of Friedman's point turns on the purpose for which the theory of the firm is constructed. Cyert and March are undoubtedly correct in their suggestion that "much of the controversy is based on a misunderstanding of the questions the conventional theory of the firm was designed to answer."[32] If the theory of the firm is restricted exclusively to aggregate level explanations of resource allocation by a price system, its predictions about these outcomes are a key criterion of its success. But the classical theory of the firm is also employed to answer questions about the internal allocations of resources and the process of price and output decisions as well. For this task the theory's performance as a predictor is not impressive. The prudent path for the development of a theory of micro-behavior would seem to require micro-assumptions more similar to observed characteristics of an actual firm.[33]

The first milestone along this road was set by an insufficiently heralded book, *A Behavioral Theory of the Firm,* by Richard Cyert and James March, published in 1963.[34] Proceeding from a careful catalogue of challenges to the classical theory of the firm and a survey of the literature of organization theory, Cyert and March make a new departure. In contrast to traditional theories that explain the firm's behavior in terms of market factors, Cyert and March focus — as organization theory would suggest — on the effect of organizational structure and conventional practice upon the development of goals, the formulation of expectations, and the execution of choice.[35]

This product of the Carnegie School represents an extension of Simon's concern with problem-solving under conditions of bounded rationality. Cyert and March attempt to understand organizational decision as choice made in terms of goals, on the basis of expectations. Thus the framework of the analysis is fixed by three categories: (1) organizational goals, (2) organizational expectations, and (3) organizational choice. Following Barnard, Cyert and March view the organization as a coalition of participants (some of whom are not necessarily on its payroll, e.g., suppliers and customers) with disparate demands, changing focuses of attention, and limited ability to attend to all problems simultaneously. Bargaining among potential coalition members produces a series of *de facto* agreements that impose constraints on the organization. The list of these more or less independent constraints, imperfectly rationalized in terms of more general purposes, constitute an organization's goals.[36] Organizational expectations arise from inferences drawn from available information. Organizational choice emerges as the selection of the first alternative that expectations identify as acceptable in terms of goals.

At the core of this theory are four concepts that relate variables affecting the three major categories (goals, expectations, and choice).

1. QUASI-RESOLUTION OF CONFLICT.   There is no internal consensus within a firm at the level of operational goals. Nevertheless, organizations thrive with considerable latent goal conflict. The prevailing coalition imposes on the organization a series of independent, aspiration-level constraints. In their price and output model of the business firm, Cyert and March postulate a profit goal, a sales goal, a market share goal, an inventory goal, and a production goal. Individual subunits of the organization handle pieces of the firm's separated problem in relative independence. The sales department is responsible for sales goals and strategy, the production department for production. Inconsistency that occurs as a result of this "local rationality" is absorbed by "organizational slack." Conflicts among goals are resolved by sequential attention to goals. Conflicting pressures to "smooth production" and to "satisfy customers" are typically resolved by doing first one and then the other.[37]

2. UNCERTAINTY AVOIDANCE.   Uncertainty is a critical factor of the environment in which organizations live. Organiza-

tions seek to avoid uncertainty. The first rule is: solve pressing problems rather than developing long-run strategies. The requirement that events in the distant future be anticipated is avoided by using decision rules that emphasize short-run feedback. The second rule is: negotiate with the environment. The requirement that future reactions of other parts of the environment be anticipated is avoided by imposing plans, standard operating procedures, industry traditions, and uncertainty-absorbing contracts.[38]

3. PROBLEMISTIC SEARCH. Since Cyert and March argue that organizations use acceptable level goals and select the first alternative they meet that satisfies these goals, the theory of organizational search is critical. Organizational search is problemistic search. Search is stimulated by a specific problem and motivated to find a solution to that problem. Search follows simple-minded rules that direct the searcher first to the neighborhood of problem symptoms, then to the neighborhood of the current alternative. Search is biased by the special training and experience of the various parts of the organization, the interaction of hopes and expectations, and the communication distortions reflecting unresolved conflict.[39]

4. ORGANIZATIONAL LEARNING. Organizational behavior (characterized by the three concepts) is relatively stable. Organizations are, however, dynamic institutions. They change adaptively as the result of experience. Over time, organizational learning produces changes in goals, attention rules, and search procedures.[40]

This process-oriented model of the firm has been applied to actual business behavior with some measure of success. The four relational concepts lend themselves to the language of computer programming. Though Cyert and March produce a rather successful simulation model of a quite unexciting example (one department of a large retail department store), Geoffrey Clarkson's application of a similar model to simulate an individual trust officer in selecting a portfolio is more interesting.[41] Yair Aharoni employs a modified version of the theory with considerable success to the foreign investment decision process of businesses (though he finds the process too complicated for any simple computer simulation).[42]

Interesting points of tangency with the behavioral theory of the firm can be found in a number of studies of governmental

organizations. Patrick Crecine applies the basic model to simulate the behavior of government units in municipal budgeting.
Wildavsky's work on national budgeting exhibits a quite similar
model. Eckstein's *British National Health Service,* Sayer and
Kaufman's *Governing New York City,* and Thompson's *The Regulatory Process in OPA Rationing* reflect an analogous orientation.[43] Unfortunately, no one has yet studied the behavior of the
organizations concerned with foreign policy in terms of March
and Simon's model.[44]

Organizational Process Paradigm

This capsule account of organizational theory and economics
provides a context within which to outline an organization process paradigm relevant to foreign policy and international politics. While not employed in the present literature, this paradigm
should suggest perspectives that will be valuable in the future.
Without the necessary, but missing, behavioral studies of the
organizational components of governments, the present formulation must be more an expression of the prospects than of the
payoffs in this area of inquiry. Nevertheless, what is now known
about the behavior of organizations is enough to suggest some
limits on the use of Model I in explaining and predicting governmental behavior.[45]

I. *Basic Unit of Analysis: Governmental Action as Organizational Output.* The happenings of international politics
are, in three critical senses, outputs of organizational processes. First, actual occurrences are organizational outputs.
For example, Chinese entry into the Korean War — that is,
the fact that Chinese soldiers were firing at U.N. soldiers
south of the Yalu in 1950 — is an organizational action: the
action of soldiers in platoons, which form companies, which
in turn comprise armies, responding as privates to lieu-
tenants who are responsible to captains and so on to the
commander, moving into Korea, advancing against enemy
troops, and firing according to fixed routines of the Chinese
army. The decisions of government leaders trigger organizational routines. Government leaders can trim the edges of

this output and can exercise some choice in combining outputs. But most of the behavior is determined by previously established procedures.

Second, existing organizational routines for employing present physical capabilities constitute the range of effective choice open to government leaders confronted with any problem. Only the existence of men who were equipped and trained as armies and capable of being transported to North Korea made entry into the Korean War a live option for the Chinese leaders. The fact that the fixed programs (equipment, men, and routines that exist at the particular time) exhaust the range of buttons that leaders can push is not always perceived by these leaders. But in every case it is critical for an understanding of what is actually done.

Third, organizational outputs structure the situation within the narrow constraints of which leaders must make their "decisions" about an issue. Outputs raise the problem, provide the information, and take the initial steps that color the face of the issue that is turned to the leaders. As Theodore Sorensen has observed: "Presidents rarely, if ever, make decisions — particularly in foreign affairs — in the sense of writing their conclusions on a clean slate. . . . The basic decisions, which confine their choices, have all too often been previously made."[46] To one who understands the structure of the situation and the face of the issue — both determined by the organizational outputs — the formal choice of the leaders is frequently anti-climactic.

Analysis of formal governmental choice centers on the information provided and the options defined by organizations, the existing organizational capabilities that exhaust the effective choices open to the leaders, and the outputs of relevant organizations that fix the location of pieces on the chess board and shade the appearance of the issue. Analysis of actual government behavior focuses on executionary outputs of individual organizations as well as on organizational capabilities and organizational positioning of the pieces on the chess board.

II. *Organizing Concepts*
  A. *Organizational Actors.* The actor is not a monolithic "nation" or "government" but rather a constellation of

loosely allied organizations on top of which government leaders sit. This constellation acts only when component organizations perform routines. In the U.S. government, the departments or agencies — for example, the Navy, the Department of State, the CIA — are typically the principal agents.*

B. *Factored Problems and Fractionated Power.* Surveillance of the multiple facets of foreign affairs requires that problems be cut up and parceled out to various organizations. Within the U.S. government, the Department of State has primary responsibility for diplomacy, the Department of Defense for military security, the Treasury for economic affairs, and the CIA for intelligence.

To avoid paralysis, primary power must accompany primary responsibility. The Defense Department purchases weapons required for national security; the CIA gathers relevant intelligence. Where organizations are permitted to do anything, a large part of what they do will be determined within the organization. Thus each organization perceives problems, processes information, and performs a range of actions in quasi-independence (within broad guidelines of national policy).

The overriding fact about large organizations is that their size prevents any single central authority from making all important decisions or directing all important activities. Factored problems and fractionated power are two edges of the same sword. Factoring permits more specialized attention to particular facets of problems than would be possible if government leaders tried to cope with the problems by themselves. But that additional attention must be paid for in the coin of discretion for *what* an organization attends to, and *how* organizational responses are programmed.

---

*Organizations are not monolithic. The proper level of disaggregation depends upon the objectives of the analysis. This paradigm is formulated with reference to the major organizations that constitute the U.S. government. Reformulation for the principal organizational components of each of the departments and agencies — for example, disaggregating the Navy into the "brown shoe Navy" (aircraft carriers), "black shoe Navy" (traditional surface ships), the submariners, and the nuclear propulsion club (Polaris) would be relatively straightforward.

C. *Parochial Priorities and Perceptions.* Primary responsibility for a narrow set of problems encourages organizational parochialism, which is enhanced by factors such as: (1) selective information available to the organization, (2) recruitment of personnel into the organization, (3) tenure of individuals in the organization, (4) small group pressures within the organization, and (5) distribution of rewards by the organization. Clients (e.g., interest groups), government allies (e.g., congressional committees), and extra-national counterparts (e.g., the British Ministry of Defense for the Defense Department's Office of International Security Affairs or the British Foreign Office for the State Department's Office of European Affairs) galvanize this parochialism. Thus organizations develop relatively stable propensities concerning operational priorities, perceptions, and issues. For example, the military services are manned by careerists on a structured ladder. Promotion to higher rungs is dependent on years of demonstrated, distinguished devotion to a service's mission. Work routines, patterns of association, and information channels combine with external pressures from organized groups and friends in Congress to make quite predictable a service's continual search for new hardware consistent with currently assigned roles and missions — for instance, the Air Force's pursuit of a new manned bomber.

D. *Action as Organizational Output.* The preeminent feature of organizational activity is its programmed character: the extent to which behavior in any particular case is an enactment of preestablished routines.* In producing outputs, the activity of each organization is characterized by:

---

*This characterization of organizational activity (constraints defining acceptable performance, standard operating procedures, search rules, etc.) depends on more detailed features of an organization and its members. Rules for promotion and reward, budgeting procedures, information accounting-control procedures, and procedures for recruitment and socialization to the norms of the organization, as well as members' operating styles and attitudes and their extent of professionalization, affect the form and the stability of the characteristics outlined below. No doubt, the environment and the surrounding culture also affect these characteristics, though how and to what extent is less clear. For a suggestive examination of the last question, see Michel Crozier, *The Bureaucratic Phenomenon*, Chicago, 1964.

1. *Goals: Constraints Defining Acceptable Performance.*
   The operational goals of an organization are seldom
   revealed by formal mandates. Rather, each organization's operational goals emerge as a set of constraints
   defining acceptable performance. Central among these
   constraints is organizational health, defined usually
   in terms of bodies assigned and dollars appropriated.
   The set of constraints emerges from a mix of the
   expectations and demands of other organizations in
   the government, statutory authority, demands from
   citizens and special interest groups, and bargaining
   within the organization. These constraints represent
   a quasi-resolution of conflict — the constraints are
   relatively stable, so there is some degree of resolution;
   but the constraints are not compatible, hence it is only
   a quasi-resolution. Typically, the constraints are formulated as imperatives to avoid roughly specified dis-
   comforts and disasters. For example, the behavior of
   each of the U.S. military services (Army, Navy, and
   Air Force) seems to be characterized by effective imperatives to avoid: (1) a decrease in dollars budgeted,
   (2) a decrease in manpower, (3) a decrease in the
   number of key specialists (e.g., for the Air Force,
   pilots), (4) reduction in the percentage of the military budget allocated to that service, (5) encroach-
   ment of other services on that service's roles and
   missions, and (6) inferiority to an enemy weapon of
   any class. The fourth constraint is at the heart of
   what many civilians in the Office of the Secretary of
   Defense found puzzling in the outburst of the Air
   Force over the Kennedy administration's first budget
   — which increased total Air Force dollars by approximately 4 percent. That budget also reduced the Air
   Force's percentage of the defense pie.
2. *Sequential Attention to Goals.* The existence of conflict among operational constraints is resolved by the
   device of sequential attention. As a problem arises,
   the subunits of the organization most concerned with
   that problem deal with it in terms of the constraints
   they take to be most important. When the next problem arises, another cluster of subunits deals with it,
   focusing on a different set of constraints.

3. *Standard Operating Procedures.* Organizations perform their "higher" functions, such as attending to
problem areas, monitoring information, and preparing relevant responses for likely contingencies, by
doing "lower" tasks — for example, preparing budgets, producing reports, and developing hardware.
Reliable performance of these tasks requires standard
operating procedures (SOPs). Rules of thumb permit
concerted action by large numbers of individuals,
each responding to basic cues. The rules are usually
simple enough to facilitate easy learning and unambiguous application. Since procedures are "standard"
they do not change quickly or easily. Without such
standard procedures, it would not be possible to perform certain concerted tasks. But because of them,
organizational behavior in particular instances appears unduly formalized, sluggish, and often inappropriate. Some SOPs are simply conventions that make
possible regular or coordinated activity. But most
SOPs are grounded in the incentive structure of the
organization or even in the norms of the organization or the basic attitudes and operating style of its
members. The stronger the grounding, the more resistant SOPs are to change.

4. *Programs and Repertoires.* Organizations must be
capable of performing actions in which the behavior
of hundreds of individuals is precisely coordinated.
Assured performance requires sets of rehearsed SOPs
for producing specific actions, e.g., fighting enemy
units or answering an embassy's cable. Each cluster
comprises a "program" (in the language of drama
and computers) that the organization has available
for dealing with a situation. The list of programs relevant to a type of activity, e.g., fighting, constitutes
an organizational repertoire. The number of programs in a repertoire is always quite limited. When
properly triggered, organizations execute programs;
programs cannot be substantially changed in a particular situation. The more complex the action and the
greater the number of individuals involved, the more
important are programs and repertoires as determinants of organizational behavior.

5. *Uncertainty Avoidance.* Organizations do not attempt to estimate the probability distribution of future occurrences. Rather, organizations avoid uncertainty. By arranging a *negotiated environment,* organizations regularize the reactions of other actors with whom they have to deal. The primary environment (relations with other organizations comprising the government) is stabilized by such arrangements as agreed budgetary splits, accepted areas of responsibility, and established practices. The secondary environment (relations with the international world) is stabilized between allies by the establishment of contracts (alliances) and "club relations" (U.S. State Department and British Foreign Office or U.S. Treasury and British Treasury). Between enemies, contracts and conventional practices perform a similar function — for example, the rules of the "precarious status quo" that President Kennedy referred to in the missile crisis.

Where the international environment cannot be negotiated, organizations deal with remaining uncertainties by establishing a set of *standard scenarios* that constitute the contingencies for which they prepare. For example, the standard scenario for Tactical Air Command of the U.S. Air Force involves combat with enemy aircraft. Planes are designed and pilots trained for this contingency. Though this capability has proved of less relevance in more probable contingencies, e.g., close-in ground support in limited wars like Viet Nam, the scenario has been slow to change.

6. *Problem-directed Search.* Where situations cannot be construed as standard, organizations engage in search. The style of search and its stopping point are largely determined by existing routines. Organizational search for alternative courses of action is problem-oriented: it focuses on the atypical discomfort that must be avoided. It is simple-minded: the neighborhood of the symptom is searched first, then the neighborhood of the current alternative. Patterns of search reveal biases that reflect factors such as specialized training, experience of various parts of

the organization, and patterns of communication within the organization.

7. *Organizational Learning and Change.* The parameters of organizational behavior mostly persist. In response to nonstandard problems, organizations search and routines evolve, assimilating new situations. Such learning and change follow in large part from existing procedures, but marked changes in organizations do sometimes occur. Conditions in which dramatic changes are more probable include:

   a. *Budgetary Feast.* Typically, organizations devour budgetary feasts by proceeding down the existing shopping list. Nevertheless, government leaders who control the budget and are committed to change can use extra funds to effect changes.

   b. *Prolonged Budgetary Famine.* Though a single year's famine typically results in few fundamental changes in organizational structure and procedures, it often causes a loss of effectiveness in performing certain programs. Prolonged famine, however, forces major retrenchment.

   c. *Dramatic Performance Failures.* Dramatic change occurs usually in response to major disasters. Confronted with an undeniable failure of procedures and repertoires, authorities outside the organization demand change, existing personnel are less resistant to change, and key members of the organization are replaced by individuals committed to change.[47]

E. *Central Coordination and Control.* Governmental action requires decentralization of responsibility and power. But problems do not fit neatly into separable domains. Each organization's performance of its job has major consequences for other departments. Important problems lap over the jurisdictions of several organizations. Thus the necessity for decentralization runs headlong into the requirement for coordination. (Those who advocate one horn or other of this dilemma — responsive action entails decentralized power versus coordinated action requires central control — account for a considerable part of the demand for government reorganization.)

The necessity for coordination and the centrality of

foreign policy to the welfare of the nation guarantee the involvement of government leaders in the processes of the organizations that share power. Each organization's propensities and routines can be affected by the intervention of government leaders. Central direction and persistent control of organizational activity, however, is not possible. The relations among organizations and between organizations and government leaders depend critically on a number of structural variables, including the (1) nature of the job, (2) performance measures and information available to government leaders, (3) system of rewards and punishments for organizational members, and (4) procedures by which human and material resources get committed. For example, to the extent that rewards and punishments for the members of an organization are distributed by higher authorities, these authorities can exercise some control by specifying criteria for evaluating organizational output. These criteria become constraints within which organizational activity proceeds. Constraints, however, are crude instruments of control. Specification of relevant operational criteria for the activities of most government organizations is incredibly difficult. Moreover, in the U.S. government, the leader's control over critical rewards and punishments is severely limited.

Intervention by government leaders does sometimes change the activity of an organization in an intended direction, but instances are fewer than might be expected. As Franklin Roosevelt, the master manipulator of government organizations, remarked:

> The Treasury is so large and far-flung and ingrained in its practices that I find it is almost impossible to get the action and results I want. . . . But the Treasury is not to be compared with the State Department. You should go through the experience of trying to get any changes in the thinking, policy, and action of the career diplomats and then you'd know what a real problem was. But the Treasury and the State Department put together, are nothing as compared with the Na-a-vy. . . . To change anything in the Na-a-vy is like punching a feather bed. You punch it with your right and you punch it with your left until you are finally exhausted, and then you find the damn bed just as it was before you started punching.[48]

John Kennedy's experience seems to have been similar:

"The State Department," he asserted, "is a bowl of jelly."[49] And lest the McNamara revolution in the Defense Department seem too striking a counter-example, the Navy's rejection of McNamara's major intervention in naval weapons procurement, the F-111B, should be studied as an antidote.

F. *Decisions of Government Leaders.* Organizational persistence does not preclude shifts in governmental behavior. Government leaders sit atop the conglomerate of organizations. In spite of the limits of the leadership's ability to control changes in a particular organization's goals or SOPs, many important issues of governmental action require that these leaders decide what organizations will play out which programs where. Thus some kinds of important shifts in the behavior of governments can take place with little change in a particular organization's parochialism and SOPs. The degree of these shifts is limited by the range of existing organizational programs.

The leadership's options for shifting governmental behavior at any point include: (1) triggering program A rather than program B within a repertoire, (2) triggering existing organizational routines in a new context, (3) triggering several different organizations' programs simultaneously. Additional leeway can be won by feeding an issue to one component of an organization rather than another, for example, raising a strategic issue in budgetary guise or vice versa. Over the longer run, leaders can create new organizations. Occasionally, they may even effect deliberate change in organizations by manipulating the factors that support existing organizational tendencies. Even in making these various choices, leaders rely for the most part on information provided by, estimates generated by, and alternatives specified by organizational programs.

III. *Dominant Inference Pattern.* If a nation performs an action of a certain type today, its organizational components must yesterday have been performing (or have had established routines for performing) an action only marginally different from today's action. At any specific point in time, t, a government consists of an established conglomerate of organizations, each with existing goals, programs, and repertoires. The characteristics of a government's action in any instance follows from those established routines, and from the choice made by government leaders — on the basis of information and estimates provided by existing routines — among established programs. The best explanation of an organization's behavior at t is $t - 1$; the best prediction of what will happen at $t + 1$ is t. Model II's explanatory power is achieved by uncovering the organizational routines and repertoires that produced the outputs that comprise the puzzling occurrence.

This inference pattern is illustrated clearly (though in terms of a quite different orientation) by Roberta Wohl-stetter's excellent study, *Pearl Harbor*.[50] The question addressed by this book is why America slept. That is, how could the United States have failed to anticipate the Japanese attack on Pearl Harbor, given the extraordinary amount and quality of intelligence available? The Rational Actor Model would seem to supply the answer: confusion or conspiracy, incompetence or design. By December 7, Admiral Kimmel, the Pacific Fleet Commander, had received the following information: a warning from the Navy on November 27, about possible attack, report of a change in Japanese codes (evaluated as very unusual), reports of Japanese ships in Camranh Bay, orders to be alert for Japanese action in the Pacific, messages deciphered from Japan's most secure code ordering Japanese embassies to destroy secret papers, FBI notice that the local Japanese consul was burning papers, government authorization to destroy all American codes and secret papers in outlying islands, and personal warnings from Admiral Stark in Washington. Assuming honesty and competence, a Model I analyst would be led to predict: (1) the fleet would be out of the harbor, (2) the island would be air patrolled, (3) the emergency warning center would be staffed, and (4) the Army would have been notified under the Joint Coastal Frontier Defense Plan. But each of these predictions would have proved incorrect. Instead the Navy's activity on December 7 was identical with its behavior on December 6, which differed imperceptibly from its behavior on December 5, and so on. Each of these details represents standard outputs of an organization functioning according to very established routines.

IV. *General Propositions*

  A. *Organizational Implementation.* Activity according to standard operating procedures and programs does not constitute far-sighted, flexible adaptation to "the issue" (as it is conceived by the analyst). Detail and nuance of actions by organizations are determined chiefly by organizational routines, not government leaders' directions. Model I's attempt to use these details to distinguish among alternative hypotheses about leaders' subtle plans is misguided.

    1. *SOPs.* SOPs constitute routines for dealing with *standard* situations. Routines allow large numbers of ordinary individuals to deal with numerous instances, day after day, without much thought. But this regularized capacity for adequate performance is purchased at the price of standardization. If the SOPs are appropriate, average performance — i.e., performance averaged over the range of cases — is better than it would be if each instance were approached individually (given fixed talent, timing, and resource constraints).[51] But specific instances, particularly critical instances that typically do not have "standard" characteristics, are often handled sluggishly or inappropriately.

    2. *Programs.* A program, i.e., a complex cluster of SOPs, is rarely tailored to the specific situation in which it is executed. Rather, the program is (at best) the most appropriate of the programs in the existing repertoire.

    3. *Repertoires.* Since repertoires are developed by parochial organizations for standard scenarios that the organization has defined, programs available for dealing with a particular situation are often ill suited to it.

     On December 7, 1941, what was Army Intelligence in Hawaii prepared to do? A single scenario — the prevention of sabotage — dominated the planning, and the responses available were quite limited. As Wohlstetter records: "Washington advised General Short on November 27 to expect 'hostile activities' at any moment, by which it meant 'attack on American positions from without,' but General Short understood this phrase to mean 'sabotage.' "[52] Predictably, Army Intelligence implemented its counter-sabotage routines, rather than taking any precautions against air attack.[53]

B. *Organizational Options.* The menu of alternatives defined by organizations in sufficient detail to be live options is severely limited in both number and character. The short list of alternatives reflects not only the cost of alternative generation but, more important, each organization's interest in controlling, rather than presenting, choices — for example, by serving up one real alternative framed by two extremes. The character of the alternatives, i.e., the location of the set of alternatives in the universe of possible alternatives relevant to the leader's objectives, differs significantly from the character of alternatives that would be presented by, say, a team of five disinterested experts. The difference is a function of the configuration of established organizations and their existing goals and procedures.[54]

1. Alternatives built into existing organizational goals — e.g., both incremental improvements in each military service's primary weapon system and major new developments in that line — will be adequate (i.e., compare favorably with the expert's list, though with less sensitivity to costs). In contrast, alternatives contrary to existing organizational goals — e.g., proposals for reducing the number of officers in a service — will be poor (i.e., compare poorly with the expert's list).

2. Alternatives requiring coordination of several organizations — e.g., multi-service weapon systems, like McNamara's TFX — are likely to be poor.

3. Alternatives in areas between organizations — e.g., weapon systems not represented by a major service component — are likely to be poor. For example, the requirement for central coordination of intelligence seems obvious. But failure of the alert system on three occasions prior to Pearl Harbor was not sufficient to generate a proposal for central coordination of intelligence and communication.[55] Nor in organizational terms could it have been. Naval Intelligence "obviously and correctly regarded its own sources as

superior" and had no incentives for merging with an inferior. Army Intelligence, G-2, had little interest in combined intelligence operations. Its relations with Naval Intelligence were "not very close because we had practically nothing in common. There was no combat at that time."[56]

C. *Limited Flexibility and Incremental Change.* Major lines of organizational action are straight — i.e., behavior at one time, t, is marginally different from behavior at $t - 1$. Simple-minded predictions work best: behavior at $t + 1$ will be marginally different from behavior at the present time.

1. Organizational budgets change incrementally — both with respect to totals and with respect to intra-organizational splits. Organizations could divide the money available each year by carving up the pie anew (in the light of objectives or changes in the environment), but, in fact, organizations take last year's budget as a base and adjust incrementally. Predictions that require large budgetary shifts in a single year between organizations or between units within an organization should be hedged.

2. Organizational priorities, perceptions, and issues are relatively stable.

3. Organizational procedures and repertoires change incrementally.

4. New activities typically consist of marginal adaptations of existing programs and activities.

5. A program, once undertaken, is not dropped at the point where objective costs outweigh benefits. Organizational momentum carries it easily beyond the loss point.

Army Intelligence was primarily in the business of detecting subversive activity.[57] But as early as May 1940, General Marshall requested that an evaluation branch be established within G-2 (Army Intelligence) for the "maintenance of current estimates of predicted activity in . . . the Far East."[58] This request fueled an increase in the number of officers on the G-2 staff from twenty-two to nearly eighty men by December 7, 1941. But as the Chief of Military Intelligence later testified, at the end of 1941, "military intelligence was specifically concerned . . . with anti-subversive precautions and operations."[59]

D. *Long-range Planning.* The existence of long-range planning units in the foreign policy departments of the U.S. government — e.g., the Policy Planning Staff in the Department of State — would seem to support Model I's implication that governments deal with the uncertain future by devising long-run plans. Model II's proposition, however, concerns the effective contribution of such units to the policy output. Long-range planning tends to become institutionalized (in order to provide a proper gesture in that direction) and then disregarded. "As far back as 1936 war games and drills in the Hawaiian Islands had been planned on the basis of a surprise attack on Pearl Harbor . . . defined as a surprise air raid by Japan."[60] G-2 had a plan known as "Orange," to provide for defense against such an attack. The general and admiral in command of air units in Hawaii had approved the requirements for that defense. But the actual organizational routines proceeded without reference to that planning exercise. "There had never been any attempt to cover the full 360 degrees around the islands by long-distance reconnaissance"; moreover, despite two alerts in July and October 1941, "before December 7 Short [the Army Commander] held no drill or alert in which the boxes of ammunition were opened."[61]

E. *Goals and Tradeoffs.* Since organizational goals are formulated as constraints — i.e., imperatives to avoid falling beneath specified performance levels, behavior departs from Model I's expectations.

1. Tradeoffs — i.e., hard choices among goals — are neglected.

2. Incompatible constraints are attended to sequentially, the organization satisfying one while simply neglecting another.[62]

The aerial arm of the U.S. Navy stationed in Hawaii had two imperatives: (1) to train pilots for an attack on the Japanese mandated islands and (2) to carry out distant reconnaissance of enemy activities.[63] Given the available aircraft, it was not possible to satisfy both imperatives, so the Navy concentrated on the first. In order to conserve resources for the primary mission (attack on the Japanese mandates), aircraft were returned to base on weekends, including Friday, for maintenance. Had a limited number of aircraft been attending to the second imperative on Sunday, December 7, the base would have had an hour's warning. But attention to that imperative had been neglected for concentration on preparations for an offensive attack.

F. *Imperialism.* Most organizations define the central goal of "health" in terms of growth in budget, manpower, and territory. Thus issues that arise in areas where boundaries are ambiguous and changing, or issues that constitute new territories, are dominated by colonizing activity.

When a breakthrough cracked the Japanese codes, the question in the Navy was less "What do these messages mean?" than "Who would perform the task of serious evaluation of enemy intentions?"[64] This issue pitted the Office of Naval Intelligence against the War Plans Division. Though it lacked Japanese linguists and specialists, the War Plans Division ("traditionally the more powerful agency") fought and won the right to "interpret and evaluate all information concerning possible hostile nations from whatever source received."[65]

G. *Options and Organization.* Organizations or subunits of an organization are often created in order to pay special attention to a neglected aspect of a problem. Leaders see this as a way of increasing options by providing information and alternatives that would otherwise be unavailable. But the existence of options affects the probabilities of choice, for the organizations created to provide an option also generate information and estimates that are tailored to make the exercise of that option more likely.

H. *Administrative Feasibility.* Adequate explanation, analysis, and prediction must include administrative feasibility as a major dimension. A considerable gap separates what leaders choose (or might rationally have chosen) and what organizations implement.

1. Organizations are blunt instruments.
2. Projects that demand that existing organizational units depart from their established programs to per-

form unprogrammed tasks are rarely accomplished in their designed form.

3. Projects that require coordination of the programs of several organizations are rarely accomplished as designed.

4. Where an assigned piece of a problem is contrary to existing organizational goals, resistance will be encountered.

5. Government leaders can expect that each organization will "do its part" in terms of what the organization knows how to do.

6. Government leaders can expect incomplete and distorted information from each organization about its part of the problem.

Washington's insensitivity to administrative feasibilities is clearly demonstrated by Pearl Harbor. Having ordered full cooperation and communication between the Army and Navy, the leaders in Washington assumed that in the period of increased danger the Army and Navy operations at Pearl Harbor would function as a finely tuned sensor. Indeed, according to subsequent testimony, Washington seems to have assumed fully informed, intelligent coordination between these two "eyes" of the government. But in fact: (1) there was no exchange of information between Army and Navy units at Pearl Harbor; (2) on the basis of quite separate sources and types of information, each had a quite different estimate of likely contingencies for the end of the year 1941; and (3) though each had three different stages of alert, these plans meant quite different things — according to the Navy plan "1" signified a full alert, whereas for the Army "1" conveyed sabotage (lowest level of alert) and "3" a full alert. Indeed, "even in Washington the services were usually in disagreement about (1) what information to send to the theaters, (2) how to word that information, (3) what situation dictated an alert order, and (4) precisely what kind of alert was indicated."[66]

I. *Directed Change.* Existing organizational orientations and routines are not impervious to directed change. Careful targeting of major factors that support routines

— such as personnel, rewards, information, and budgets — can effect major changes over time. But the terms and conditions of most political leadership jobs — short tenure and responsiveness to hot issues — make effective, directed change uncommon.

V. *Specific Propositions*

   A. *Deterrence.* The probability of nuclear attack is less sensitive to balance and imbalance, or stability and instability (as these concepts are employed by Model I strategists) than it is to a number of organizational factors. Except for the special case in which the Soviet Union acquires a credible capability to destroy the United States with a disarming blow, American superiority or inferiority affects the probability of a nuclear attack less than do a number of organizational facts.[67]

   B. *Soviet Force Posture.* Soviet force posture (i.e., the fact that certain weapons, rather than others, are produced and deployed) is determined by organizational factors such as the goals and procedures of existing military services and of research and design labs. Government leaders' choices determine budgetary totals and influence some major procurement decisions, but the bulk of the force posture emerges from the routine functioning of organizational units. The weakness of the Soviet Air Force within the Soviet military establishment seems to have been a crucial element in the Soviet failure to acquire a large bomber force in the 1950s (thereby faulting American intelligence predictions of a "bomber gap").[68] The fact that missiles were controlled until 1960 in the Soviet Union by the Soviet Ground Forces, whose goals and procedures reflected no interest in an intercontinental mission, was not irrelevant to the slow Soviet build-up of ICBMs (thereby faulting U.S. intelligence predictions of a "missile gap").[69] The influence of organizational factors, like the Soviet Ground Forces' control of missiles and that service's fixation on European scenarios, helps to explain the Soviet deployment of so many MRBMs that European targets could be destroyed three times over.[70] Recent weapon development — e.g., the testing of a Fractional Orbital Bombardment System (FOBS) and multiple warheads for the SS-9 — very likely reflects the activity and interests of a cluster of Soviet research and development organizations, rather than a decision by Soviet leaders to acquire a first-strike weapon system.[71] Careful attention to the organizational components of the Soviet military establishment (Strategic Rocket Forces, Navy, Air Force, Ground Forces, and National Air Defense), the missions and weapons systems to which each component is wedded (an independent weapon system assists survival as an independent service), and existing budgetary splits (which probably are relatively stable in the Soviet Union as they tend to be everywhere) offer potential improvements in medium-range and longer-range predictions.

VI. *Evidence.* This paradigm's stark statement of organizational tendencies constitutes a marked shift of perspective. Examination of government action in terms of these roughly formulated concepts and propositions can be fruitful. For example, with a minimum of information about the organizations that constitute a government and their routines and SOPs, an analyst can significantly improve some expectations generated by the Rational Actor Model. But in order for the paradigm to get a strong grip on a specific case, the bare bones of this generalized statement must be fleshed out by information about the characteristics of the organizations involved.

Additional research should strengthen this paradigm. First, behavioral studies of various governmental organizations should permit greater differentiation within the broad class now lumped together simply as organizations. Second, study of the behavior of various classes of organizations should permit identification of the factors that support behavioral tendencies. This will also lead to a more precise formulation of the concepts and propositions of the paradigm. Third, studying instances of dramatic organizational change will make it possible to pinpoint conditions under which change is probable, and the levers a manager could manipulate to engineer improvements. Such studies should also shed light on the difficult question of why a given set of SOPs happens to exist in a particular organization.

The Organizational Process Paradigm Applied

To illustrate how Model II might be applied to problems typically treated by the classical model, let us reconsider the question of why the Soviet Union is simultaneously pursuing detente and deploying an antiballistic missile system. A Model II analyst demands no ingenious rationale for these two divergent patterns of activity; his organizational orientation leads him to expect that the left and right hands of a government often operate independently. Nor do the details of the ABM system or particular characteristics of detente provide clues to the true Soviet intentions, for these features are more a function of organizational procedures than of a coordinated choice. To find the key to this puzzle, the Model II analyst would examine the organizational interests, demands, and independent actions that yield these divergent patterns.[72]

What organization is purchasing the Soviet ABM capability? Understanding the actions of that organization requires answers to three more specific questions: (1) What slice of the defense budget does that organization have, and how stable has its slice been? (2) What perceptions and priorities are engrained in that organization? (3) What programs and standard operating procedures are built into that organization?

Public evidence suggests that the Soviet ABM system is being purchased by the Air Defense Command (PVO). This organization's slice of the Soviet defense budget has probably been large and relatively stable. This is the organization that reportedly spent extensively on anti-aircraft artillery from 1945 to the early 1960s. Perhaps by the late 1960s there seemed few additional locations within the Soviet Union for the deployment of conventional anti-aircraft capability. Thus the PVO may have both the budget and the need for a project like ABM.

The priorities and perspectives of the PVO are decidedly defense oriented. Any organization that could justify such extensive expenditures on anti-aircraft artillery would obviously be interested in defense against missiles. The fact that its anti-aircraft system was relatively ineffective did little to deter deployment. Similarly, the ineffectiveness of the present ABM system may not be particularly daunting. Nor is there reason to believe that this organization will consider or be impressed by arguments about possible U.S. reactions to Soviet defensive actions. Finally, if the PVO "keeps on doing what it's doing," an extensive ABM system will be acquired. The organization's established procedures and programs — e.g., reported development of ABMs since the mid-1950s and continuous deployment of at least one major defensive system since 1945 — would lead to deployment by continuation. To decide against deployment would require a major shift in established trends. Thus, organizational pressures seem sufficiently strong to account for ABM deployment to date. Given the secrecy that pervades the Soviet system — which restricts the flow of information, communication, and criticism that would encourage a more comprehensive view of various Soviet programs — and the characteristic lack of understanding and interest on the part of Soviet political leaders in the details of force posture, it is not at all surprising that this purchase should have proceeded (with tacit "approval" of the leaders) while the leadership group and, especially, the scientific community were pursuing detente.

Model II thus brings into question the traditional (Model I) conception of an "arms race" between the United States and the Soviet Union. Different organizations within a government — each with its own definition of its problem and its own effective constraints — seek certain weapon systems. Military organizations tend to keep doing what they are doing — e.g., to replace cavalry with cavalry — at least until a catastrophe in war occurs. Though governments are not entirely unresponsive to enemy purchases and other activities, changes in the overall budget and changes among missions and organizations are marginal. Soviet responses to American procurement typically involve not the choice of the rational countermove but rather a delayed option for something on the menu of one of the present organizations. As A. W. Marshall has argued, the history of Soviet purchases from 1946 to 1962 reveals an interaction between American and Soviet force postures that is muffled, lagged, and very complex.

Nuclear Strategy

In the standard intuitive typology, no class of decisions is more suited to analysis according to the Rational Actor Model than nuclear strategy. As noted in Chapter 1, the most developed area of this literature is the theory of deterrence, which has a single central concern: prevention of the explosion of enemy weapons on U.S. territory. The literature has focused almost exclusively on issues of "stability" and "balance," yielding propositions like Wohlstetter's and Schelling's that the probability of nuclear war is reduced not by the balance but rather by the stability of the balance.[73] What these propositions assert are syllogisms that turn on the pivot of what a rational leader could choose (or perhaps of what argument could prevail among rational leaders). But extensive and exclusive discussion of such issues is relevant only because "balance" and "stability" are believed to be the critical determinants of the occurrence that this literature discusses — namely the explosion of nuclear weapons on U.S. territory.

The organizational process paradigm suggests that the scenarios that dominate the existing strategic literature are considerably less interesting than a range of additional scenarios that arise irrespective of conditions of balance and imbalance, stability and instability. First, if the undesired event occurs, it will be as a consequence of organizational activity: the firing of rockets by a member of a missile group. This raises a central question: What is the enemy's *control* system? If the physical mechanisms and the SOPs permit multiple centers at which a choice can be made to launch nuclear weapons against the United States, the probability of the undesired event rises considerably higher than it would over most conceivable ranges of imbalance and instability. Examination of this issue might suggest that an enemy be given information about mechanical devices for maximizing central control over nuclear launches.

Second, what patterns of regularized behavior has the enemy developed for bringing his strategic capabilities to *alert status*? If these routines are loose, an accident may occur. If the procedures are so unregularized that the forces have never been brought to alert status, this is a critical piece of information about the dimension of risk and the difficulty of de-escalation. Prior to the outbreak of World War I, if the Russian tsar had understood the consequences — in terms of organizational processes — of his order for full mobilization, he would have known that he had chosen war.[74]

Third, organizational processes fix the range of effective choices open to enemy leaders. What plans and procedures will the leaders face when the showdown comes? Reportedly, the plans available to the U.S. President when Kennedy entered the White House provided that, in the case of a nuclear showdown, the President would pick up a special telephone and listen to a discussion between the relevant military and intelligence experts that would conclude with a recommendation, "O.K., Mr. President, go!" The menu of choice made available to the Russian tsar in 1914 included only full mobilization and no mobilization. Partial mobilization was not an option offered by the organization. Similarly, the German railroad timetables required that troops be loaded at specific times if they were to be at particular locations at specific other times.[75] The German General Staff's war plans did not require war. But once war was begun, established routines for fighting the war did require that it be fought on both the Eastern and the Western fronts.

Fourth, outputs of routine organizational procedures set the chessboard at which government leaders look when they confront the problem of choice. How are the enemy troops trained, and how are nuclear weapons deployed? In the quite conceivable case of the outbreak of hostilities in Berlin, organizational factors will be at least as important in the scenario as any "rational" considerations of stability. The deployment, training, tactical nuclear equipment, and SOPs of the Soviet troops in East Germany will determine the face of the issue for the Soviet leaders, as well as the way in which the leaders' choice is implemented.

Fifth, how likely are organizational processes to produce accidental firings? During the early 1950s the U.S. Air Force reportedly functioned according to a "fail-safe" system — in no case could the United States fail to destroy the Soviet Union. The notion of a "Doomsday Machine" was dreamed up to illustrate how much cheaper it would be to guarantee destruction of the Soviet Union in every case in which there was an attack on the United States — if that were the only goal. Reduction of American losses and protection against responding irrevocably to false alarms are also values for which the system must be designed. These values require some reduction in the deterrence of the rational enemy (with which standard deterrence theory is concerned) in order to encourage the organization controlling the strategic capability to develop safety systems.

Many aspects of these issues have arisen in the context of arms control. The most sophisticated deterrence theorists, especially Schelling and the Wohlstetters, have contributed significantly to thought about these issues. But the discussion of deterrence by students, the military, and many policy makers persists in terms of the framework in which stability and balance are the focus, without the integration of these further considerations.

4

Cuba II: A Second Cut

"The President believed he was President and that, his wishes having been made clear, they would be followed and the [Turkish] missiles removed."[1] So Robert Kennedy recalled President Kennedy's dismay in late October 1962 when he discovered that American missiles had *not* been removed from Turkey — in spite of the fact that he had twice ordered their withdrawal. If the United States attacked the Soviet missiles in Cuba, the Russians could reciprocate by attacking the American missiles in Turkey, and the President would face the decision of whether to reply with nuclear weapons against the Russian homeland. No one saw this issue more clearly than the President. On Saturday, October 27, when the ExCom was considering an attack on the Soviet missiles in Cuba, the President put his finger on the problem of the Turkish missiles. "It isn't the first step that concerns me, but both sides escalating to the fourth and fifth step — and we don't go to the sixth because there is no one around to do so."[2]

If events had followed this path — the United States attacks Soviet missiles in Cuba; the Soviets attack American missiles in Turkey; the United States reciprocates against the missile bases in the Soviet Union involved in the attack on Turkey; holocaust — historians would find the cause of the conflagration in the clash of national interests and large purposes. The persistence of the Turkish missiles might be noted as anecdote but would figure only as an aside in the explanation of the nuclear war. Facts like this one, which follow for the most part from the routine behavior of the large organizations that constitute governments, are typically underplayed in accounts of important events — nowhere more so than in the published accounts of the missile crisis. In contrast, this analysis attempts to focus seriously on the organizationally determined features of the missile crisis that set the drumbeat to which the actors marched.

From this perspective, what is most puzzling about the Cuban missile crisis arises from three central events: (1) the construction of Soviet offensive missiles in Cuba, (2) the imposition of a U.S. blockade of Cuba, and (3) the withdrawal of Soviet missiles from Cuba. Two of these events, the first and third, resulted from actions of Soviet organizations. We can see the behavior: missiles being constructed in Cuba; missiles being returned to the Soviet Union. But the actor is, in an important sense, a black box — albeit a box with several holes. Absence of information provides fertile soil for speculation, and there has been no lack of it about the missile crisis. Restrained hypothesizing, focusing primarily on Soviet organizations, can provide an interesting antidote to prevailing conjectures about Soviet objectives and calculations. The second event — the blockade — stemmed from activities of organizations that make up the U.S. government. A complete picture of this event would require a great deal more information about each organization's functions in this crisis than is readily available. But if the tentative hypotheses of organization theory are used to sift the available information, the results are suggestive.

The Deployment of Soviet Missiles in Cuba

The Soviet Build-up in Detail

Most explanations of the construction of Soviet missiles in Cuba focus on several of its salient characteristics. These features serve as criteria against which alternative hypotheses about the Soviet objectives can be tested. The question becomes: What objectives would have led the Soviets to choose an action with these specific characteristics? Analysts argue that a given hypothesis about the Soviet objective is preferable to alternative hypotheses on the grounds that only the motive specified by the preferred hypothesis accounts for the fact that the Soviets chose an action with the given characteristics. For example, the size of the Soviet deployment and the simultaneous emplacement of intermediate-range ballistic missiles (IRBMs) and medium-range ballistic missiles (MRBMs), some analysts argue, exclude an explanation of the action in terms of Cuban defense. But this behavior supports the hypothesis that the Soviet objective was a rapid build-up of missile power, since a nation with this objective would have reasonably chosen to install a large number of both MRBMs and IRBMs.

A full characterization of the Soviet construction of missiles in Cuba includes many details that do not seem amenable to any hypothesis of this type. Careful examination of these puzzling features raises serious doubts about the use of characteristics of the action as a principal guide to Soviet intentions.

In retrospect, American sources permit the construction of a reliable, detailed series of snapshots of the Soviet arms build-up that culminated in the conversion of Cuba into a major strategic missile base.[3] Soviet arms had been sent to Cuba since the summer of 1960, but in early 1962 there was a lull.[4] Soviet dry-cargo arrivals in Cuba averaged only fifteen per month for the first half of 1962, and the ships carried few weapons. In late July, Soviet shipments of arms resumed at a markedly increased pace. Thirty-seven Soviet dry-cargo ships arrived at Cuban ports during August, and some twenty of these carried arms shipments. By September 1, Soviet equipment in Cuba included: surface-to-air missiles (SAMs), cruise missiles, patrol boats, over 5,000 Soviet technicians and military personnel, and large quantities of transportation, electronic, and construction equipment.[5]

The first Soviet strategic offensive missiles reached Cuban soil that September. Measuring 59.6 feet in length (without the 13.7-foot nose cone), and 5.4 feet in diameter, these MRBMs were secretly transported to Cuba beneath the decks of Soviet ships that had been designed with extra large hatches for lumber trade.[6] The *Omsk*, which brought the first MRBMs, docked at the port of Mariel on September 8 and was followed by a second large-hatch ship, the *Poltava*, on the fifteenth.[7] Thereafter, additional MRBMs, missile trailers, fueling trucks, special radar vans, missile erectors, materials for building nuclear warhead storage bunkers, and other equipment related to the strategic missiles arrived and were rushed to construction sites (some of which had been prepared in advance). Similar equipment for IRBMs was also arriving. Nor were the September shipments restricted to strategic offensive missiles. Throughout that month the steady stream of Soviet ships brought another class

of offensive weapons, the IL-28 jet bombers, as well as the first
of the Soviets' most advanced jet fighters (MIG-21s), and additional SAMs, cruise missiles, and patrol boats.[8] On September
22, a joint communiqué issued in Moscow made the first official
announcement that the Soviet Union had agreed to help Cuba
meet the threat from "aggressive imperialist quarters" by delivering "armaments and sending technical specialists for
training Cuban servicemen."[9]

October shipments brought more of the same at an even
faster pace, until October 24 — the day on which the American
quarantine of Cuba began. Indeed, eighteen dry-cargo ships
were on the seas, en route to Cuba, when the quarantine was
announced.[10] Even without the arms which those ships carried,
the catalogue of military equipment on the island included:

1. MRBMS.   There were six field sites for the MRBMs, four
located in an area near San Cristobal, 50 miles southwest of
Havana, and two located near Sagua la Grande, 135 miles east
of Havana. Each of the sites included four launch positions,
mobile ground-support equipment, nuclear warhead storage facilities, and eight missile shelter tents, indicating that the Soviets intended to have a refire capability for each of their
launching positions. In total, six sites, each with four launchers,
each launcher with two missiles, meant forty-eight MRBMs.
These MRBMs had ranges up to 1,100 nautical miles.[11] Only
forty-two of these missiles ever reached Cuba.[12]

2. IRBMS.   Three fixed sites for IRBMs were under construction. Two of the sites were located at Guanajay near Havana and one at Remedios (which was in an earlier stage of
construction). At each of the sites, four launch positions, concrete control bunkers, nuclear weapon storage facilities, and
missile servicing facilities were under construction. In total,
three sites, each with four launching positions, meant twelve
IRBM launchers. A reload capability for each would have involved twenty-four IRBMs. The range of Soviet IRBMs was up
to 2,200 nautical miles. Though the related equipment for these
missiles was present, and the sites were under construction,
no IRBMs reached Cuban soil.[13] Presumably some of the Soviet
ships that returned to the Soviet Union rather than challenge
the American quarantine carried IRBMs.

3. IL-28s.   Forty-two unassembled IL-28s (Beagle Bombers) arrived at two Cuban airfields (San Julian and Holguin).
These jet bombers had a capability of delivering nuclear or non-

nuclear payloads of 6,000 pounds to a range of 600 nautical miles and returning to their home base. Only seven of these planes were finally assembled.[14]

4. SAMS. Twenty-four SA-2 sites ringed the isle of Cuba in a tight-knit perimeter air defense. Each site consisted of six launchers, each with a missile in place and three reload missiles available. These anti-aircraft missiles had a capability to strike targets at altitudes of up to 80,000 feet and a horizontal range of 30 nautical miles. In addition, large amounts of anti-aircraft artillery were installed for low-level air defense.[15]

5. CRUISE MISSILES. At least four coastal cruise missile sites were established. These sites, located near key beach and harbor areas, consisted of two thirty-four-foot launchers, guidance equipment, and a number of missiles. With a range of 40 nautical miles, cruise missiles posed a threat to ships and amphibious landings.[16]

6. KOMAR GUIDED MISSILE PATROL BOATS. Twelve high-speed KOMAR patrol boats were operating from Mariel and Banes. Weighing sixty-six tons and measuring eighty-three feet in length, each boat featured two twenty-foot cruise type missiles with a range of 10 to 15 nautical miles.[17]

7. MIG-21 AIRCRAFT. Forty-two of the latest Soviet high-performance MIG-21 aircraft were delivered to Cuban airfields. Equipped with air-to-air missiles, these interceptors were capable of speeds of up to 1,000 knots at 40,000 feet. More than forty of the earlier model MIG-15s and MIG-17s had been sent to Cuba prior to the July build-up.[18]

8. SOVIET PERSONNEL. There were some 22,000 Soviet soldiers and technicians in Cuba to assemble, operate, and defend these weapons. Soviet ground forces were deployed at four major installations (at Artemisa and Santiago de las Vegas in western Cuba, near Remedios in central Cuba, and near Holguin in eastern Cuba). Each of these installations included a regimental size armored group with modern Soviet ground force fighting equipment, including thirty-five to forty T-54 medium tanks, FROG tactical nuclear rockets (with a range of 20 to 25 nautical miles), and the Soviet army's most modern antitank missile, SNAPPER.[19]

Transportation of these armaments and related equipment required over 100 shiploads.[20] Construction and protection of them required over 22,000 Russians. There can be no doubt that the Soviets were engaged not only in a provocative, but also in a really massive, military build-up in Cuba. Presumably, coordination of their activities involved a plan calling for the introduction of less provocative defensive weapons first, followed by a second stage in which offensive weapons (the ballistic missiles and IL-28 bombers) would arrive.[21] Available evidence about the Soviet action might therefore be thought to be a source of clues to Soviet plans and thus to their intentions in embarking on this adventure.

Careful examination of the panoply of Soviet actions, however, raises many more questions than it answers. Perhaps the most striking question is why the Soviets were so insensitive to the possibility of U-2 observance of their operation. Having captured one of these high altitude planes in 1960, the Soviets could harbor no illusions about its capability. Thus, as the American photo reconnaissance expert Amron Katz has argued, the Soviet Union "could not have expected that their missile sites in Cuba would escape detection, given the likelihood of closely spaced surveillance."[22] They had to anticipate U-2 flights and to design the operation accordingly, if they were to avoid being found out. But consider what they actually did:

1. SAMS.   The SA-2s the Soviets shipped to Cuba were very sophisticated anti-aircraft missiles. SAMs of this variety had downed American U-2s over the Soviet Union in 1960 and over Communist China on September 9, 1962. (One of the SAMs based in Cuba was to shoot down a U-2 on October 27.) The perimeter defense that the Soviets were installing could therefore have effectively denied the U-2 free air space over Cuba. But the SAM network did not begin to operate until *after* the arrival and construction of the strategic offensive missiles. Indeed, it seems that the SAMs did not become operational until October 27 — after most of the MRBMs had achieved operational readiness.[23] This failure, in particular, puzzled President Kennedy. As Sorensen recalled, "Why the Soviets failed to coordinate the timing is still *inexplicable*."[24]

2. RADAR.   Construction of the Soviet radar is equally curious. Simply, the Soviets failed to complete the radar system prior to the introduction of the MRBMs and as a result denied themselves a monitor of U-2 activity. Observation of U-2 overflights would have provided a valuable clue about when the United States discovered the offensive missiles.[25]

3. CAMOUFLAGE.   Construction of Soviet MRBM and IRBM sites in Cuba proceeded without any attempt at camouflage. In the light of their awareness of U-2 overflights, this behavior

seems so puzzling that some analysts have been driven to the hypothesis that the Soviets must have wanted the United States to discover the missiles while they were being constructed. Such a hypothesis is inconsistent with earlier Soviet behavior, and it neglects the further fact that after the United States publicly disclosed what the Soviets were doing, they proceeded to camouflage the sites.[26] As Robert Kennedy recalled, "It was never clear why they waited until that late date to do so."[27]

4. CONSTRUCTION PACE. As the Wohlstetters state, "There has been almost universal agreement on the logistic efficiency of the Soviet operation [in constructing MRBMs]."[28] The speed at which the Soviets were able to install these missiles was indeed "remarkable."[29] Still, the Soviets did not bring in lights and begin round-the-clock construction until after the United States announced the blockade. If at the outset they had restricted construction activity to hours of darkness and camouflaged the sites during the day, they might have escaped detection.[30]

5. MISSILE SITES. The SAM, MRBM, and IRBM sites constructed in Cuba were built to look exactly like the SAM, MRBM, and IRBM sites in the Soviet Union. Soviet SAM sites were placed in the established Soviet pattern for defense of strategic missile installations.[31] (This clue led to American discovery of the missiles on October 14. Defense Intelligence Agency analysts noticed that the positioning of SAMs around San Cristobal was identical with the trapezoidal patterns with which photo analysts were familiar as a result of U-2 flights over the Soviet Union.) Moreover, the Soviets constructed MRBM and IRBM sites in a similar orderly fashion. MRBM sites consisted of four launch areas, each with one launcher and two missiles; a central propellent storage facility; and a fenced, 60-foot-by-75-foot nuclear warhead storage bunker (constructed from quarter-section, prestressed concrete arches, with drive-through entry-ways.)[32] IRBM sites were constructed as follows: four launch pads, grouped in two pairs, 750 feet apart, were served by a central control bunker. Each launch pad had a launch ring and flame deflector at the center. A fenced, 114-foot-by-60-foot nuclear warhead storage bunker was positioned at the side. (Again, it was the established Soviet four-slash "signature" of excavations for concrete revetment and associated equipment that alerted American intelligence analysts to the Soviet deployment of IRBMs.)[33] Interpreting the Soviet construction activity was not difficult, since American analysts had not only photos of similar missiles in the Soviet Union but also a manual of Soviet

missile construction, which Penkovskiy had delivered to United States intelligence.[34]

A second set of questions is raised by various "inconsistencies" in the Soviet operation. Juxtaposition of (1) the extraordinary secrecy shrouding the shipment of missiles to Cuba and transport of them from ports to construction sites, and (2) the complete lack of camouflage at the construction sites suggests one major inconsistency. A second discrepancy arises from Soviet behavior after announcement of the blockade. Then, and only then, did the Soviets begin camouflaging what had already been publicly identified. Similarly, after the United States had announced the blockade, Soviet troops at San Cristobal began constructing permanent barracks, while at San Julian the Soviets continued unpacking and assembling IL-28 trainers before assembling the combat aircraft. A related inconsistency stems from the contrast between the speed of certain operations (MRBM construction) and the sluggishness of others (SAM construction). But the most puzzling inconsistency of all is the simultaneous construction of MRBMs and IRBMs. Given the importance of finishing the MRBMs quickly, how can one explain the effort to install the more expensive, less salvageable, and more conspicuous IRBM sites at the same time they were building MRBM sites?

There is a third quandary that stems from the strategic character of the offensive missiles. For what contingencies were these missiles designed? While American strategic superiority would have made any Soviet first strike insane, could the missiles have been used in a retaliatory strike? All of the sites were "soft" and therefore extremely vulnerable to U.S. attack. The Soviets made no effort to harden them; nor were they constructed with an eye to future hardening. Moreover, the Soviets transported two strategic missiles for each launcher. Obviously, they intended a refire capability. But under what circumstances can an opportunity for refire be imagined? In any contingency, the Soviets would be fortunate to launch a single salvo from these missiles — avoiding American preemption. At that point the United States would undoubtedly destroy the sites before there was any possibility of reloading and refiring. So these reload missiles, which constituted half of the original deployment, were essentially useless. Indeed, there seems only one imaginable contingency in which the Soviets might have had an opportunity to fire a second missile from these soft sites. If, prior to

American discovery of the missiles, these missiles were launched against the United States in a first strike, the second missiles might have been loaded onto the launchers and fired in a second salvo. But the seventy-two missiles planned for these installations still left the Soviets with less than half of the strategic capability of the United States. And it is highly improbable that additional missile sites could have been constructed prior to American discovery of the Soviet activity.[35]

Fourth, the behavior of the Soviet military personnel in Cuba seems mildly schizophrenic. Though they made considerable effort to disguise their identity (for example, troops did not wear uniforms but rather appeared in slacks and sport shirts), a number of indelible signals revealed their presence. The "young, trim, physically fit, suntanned" technicians who arrived in civilian clothes at Cuban docks formed in ranks of fours and moved out in truck convoys.[36] An even more startling signal was noted by Representative Mahon in the House Appropriations Hearing. "It seems a little singular," he observed, "that these units would display large insignia descriptive of them in the area of the barracks and concentrations of men. Does this mean anything to you?" In fact, Soviet units did decorate the area in front of their barracks with standard Soviet ground force insignia representing both infantry and armor forces, elite guard badges, and even a Red Army Star.[37] The equipment the Soviet troops brought with them provides a further mystery. Why did they need so many tanks? Why did they bring their latest SNAPPER anti-tank missiles? The positioning of this equipment, especially the MIGs, is also difficult to understand. As Robert Kennedy mused, "The Russians and Cubans had inexplicably lined up their planes wing tip to wing tip on Cuban airfields, making them perfect targets."[38]

Finally, it is difficult to understand why the Soviets attempted so many complicated operations simultaneously. The string of puzzles generated by the Soviet performance is reminiscent of the Kennedy administration's first adventure in Cuba.

Organizational Implementation

Some of the anomalies in the Soviet build-up must be traced to errors and blunders of specific individuals in the Soviet Union. (The Soviet equivalent of the "Taylor Report" on the Bay of Pigs would make interesting reading.) But many pieces of this maze of seeming contradictions become considerably less puzzling if one assumes the perspective of an observer of the outputs of Soviet organizations. Information about these organizations and their specific functions is sparse in the public literature. But informed speculation is possible if one keeps in mind the typical behavior of American counterparts.

The final decision to put missiles in Cuba must have been made in the Presidium, but the details of the operation — that is, the path from the general decision to the actual appearance of operational missiles in Cuba — were probably delegated to appropriate Soviet organizations. Standard Soviet operations, particularly where nuclear weapons are involved, impose secrecy beyond anything approached in the American government. This operation was a strict Soviet secret. Thus each organization's tendency to "do what it knows how to do" was reinforced by a lack of information about the activity of other organizations and the impossibility of an overview of the whole operation.

The clandestine manner in which the missiles were shipped, unloaded, and transported to construction sites reveals the hand of Soviet intelligence agencies. Secrecy is their standard operating procedure. Clandestine Soviet arms shipments traditionally fall to the GRU (Soviet military intelligence).[39] Devices of deception characterize all their operations. (Similar secrecy had marked earlier arms shipments to Indonesia and Egypt, in spite of the fact that in those cases such precautions were unnecessary.) The exclusion of all Cubans from the ports and missile sites suggests that the KGB (the Communist Party intelligence and security organ) was responsible for this part of the operation.[40] But once the weapons and equipment were delivered to the construction sites, another organization became the central actor. SAMs belong to Air Defense Command.[41]

For the manager of a SAM site, location of the sites and construction of the missiles were technical problems. Protection of a strategic missile installation required a particular configuration of SAM battalions. Thus Cuban SAM sites were constructed in the typical trapezoidal pattern for no better — and no worse — reason than that this is the way Soviet SAM construction teams position SAMs. Nothing in the organization's repertoire reflected any awareness of the possible clues this pattern might present to foreign intelligence.

Strategic offensive missiles belonged to a quite separate Soviet military service, the Strategic Rocket Forces.[42] Never had an

MRBM or IRBM left Soviet soil. Few, if any, of the men assigned to install the missiles had traveled outside the Soviet Union. Soviet strategic rocket teams came with their equipment (including the trailer-erectors on which the MRBMs had been hauled through Red Square in the Moscow parades), their materials (including prefabricated concrete archways), and their know-how, to an unfamiliar island 8,000 miles away.[43] At the sites, each team did what it knew how to do — emplace missiles — literally according to the book. Each MRBM site consisted of four launchers, because an MRBM site has four launchers. At each IRBM site the two pairs of identical launchers were separated by 750 feet, because that is the established distance between IRBM launchers. Two missiles were transported for each launcher, because MRBM launchers have a refire capability (after all, something had to go under the second missile shelter tent). Missile sites had never been camouflaged in the Soviet Union. Why should a missile construction crew think of camouflage now? Indeed, that would have been a hindrance to that organization's objective: rapid completion of sites according to schedule. No attempt was made to harden the missile sites, not because of any intention to launch a first strike, but, rather, because no Soviet missile sites had ever been hardened. Soviet strategic rocket forces did not harden sites in the Soviet Union and had no equipment or procedures for such an operation.

Why the Air Defense Forces failed to achieve an operational SAM defense before the Strategic Rocket Forces began constructing MRBMs is not clear. Available evidence suggests that the Strategic Rocket Forces may have achieved a breakthrough in constructing MRBMs. If so, the operation would have proceeded much faster than the SAM plan anticipated. But the SAM network should have been finished before MRBM construction was begun. SAM construction teams seem to have found it necessary to relocate several sites because of unanticipated swamps.[44] Radar problems must have contributed to the confusion. The operation probably began with the understanding that the Cubans had an operational radar system. Indeed, they had. That system, however, was incapable of detecting a U-2 at an altitude of fourteen miles. After this discovery, a Soviet radar system was begun, but it was not completed until about October 27.

Other anomalies in Soviet missile construction flow from standard operating procedures. In spite of the American President's announcement of discovery of the missiles, Soviet forces began building permanent barracks in Cuba — right on schedule. Nuclear warhead storage bunkers were constructed with fixed dimensions and requisite material, according to established specifications — otherwise they might not have passed standard inspection tests for storage bunkers. Even the assembly of the IL-28 bombers continued in the established pattern (trainers before combat bombers), after the blockade had been announced, presumably because the tactical air force plan called for training Cubans while the other planes were being assembled. Similarly, tanks, antitank missiles, and other unusual equipment came with the regiments of the Soviet army, not because these particular weapons were appropriate for defense of the missiles against a possible attack by the Americans or Cubans, but simply because this equipment was standard gear for a battle-ready regiment.

Some of the puzzles about the military behavior may also reflect additional strains stemming from the Soviet leadership's attempt to make the military services implement decisions that ran contrary to these organizations' operational goals. That there was a deep split between the Party, especially Party boss Khrushchev, and the military, is no secret. The military seems to have been suspicious of Khrushchev's scheme and to have opposed the Presidium's adventurism in sending missiles to Cuba.[45] Suspicion of Khrushchev had recently been fueled, first by his attempt to reduce the standing forces by over one-third (from 3,623,000 to 2,140,000); second, by a Party-engineered attempt to introduce military *shefstvo* ("employment of military personnel from the conventional forces in civilian agricultural and industrial establishments");[46] and third, by Khrushchev's attempt to tighten his control over the military through a program spearheaded by General Epishev's appointment as head of the Main Political Administration (Party political control of the military with the function of indoctrination and supervision).[47]

Two pieces of evidence indicate conflict between the leadership and the military over missiles for Cuba. First, around the time of the final decision to install missiles in Cuba, Khrushchev replaced Moskalenko, a Deputy Minister of Defense and Commander-in-Chief of the Strategic Rocket Forces — the primary organization in this venture — with one of his own men, Biryuzov. Shortly after the venture failed, Moskalenko returned to his position as a Deputy Minister of Defense.[48] A second clue is suggested by the differences between the editorial position of the organ of the Ministry of Defense, *Red Star*, and that of the central Party organ, *Pravda*. Careful comparison of these editorials during the crisis highlights the military paper's "tougher and less conciliatory attitude toward U.S. demands."[49] After the crisis, both the extensive educational efforts by the Party against "some people" and numerous, strong statements by generals in *Red Star* support this hypothesis.

While reconstructions of this sort must be speculative, it seems not unlikely that the group within the Strategic Rocket Forces that favored this venture and engineered it under Biryuzov's authority was primarily concerned with the strategic missile balance. This group was especially alert to information about U.S. strategic capabilities and eager to provide a counterweight. Strategic missiles in Cuba were appealing on these terms to this organizational unit, but MRBMs were not enough. IRBMs were required to hit SAC bomber bases and American missiles. When the Presidium directed this component of the Strategic Rocket Forces to "place missiles in Cuba," they determined to do the job right — i.e., to install a large number of missiles, especially IRBMs. It seems quite possible that the leadership was unaware of these adjustments in "details," for Khrushchev later reported to the Supreme Soviet: "The government of Cuba asked the Soviet government this summer to provide additional help. Agreement was reached on a number of new measures, including the stationing of a few dozen Soviet *medium-range ballistic missiles* in Cuba."[50]

Organizational Chessboard and Options

Observers of organizational output are primarily attuned to persistence in established patterns, details of operations that follow from standard operating procedures, difficulties that arise from old programs played out in new contexts, slips between semi-independent organizations, and complications stemming from leaders' attempts to force organizations to act contrary to existing goals. While minor modifications in organizational routines occur constantly, major organizational changes typically follow, rather than precede, major crises. Nevertheless, the political leaders who sit atop government organizations do make major decisions about *which* organizations shall play out *what* programs *where*. Often this means the performance of existing organizational programs in different contexts, a new combination of routines from several organizations, and even, occasionally, rapid changes in existing organizational programs. Furthermore, each organization consists of components with somewhat different operational goals. Political leaders can affect the relative influence of these organizational components. Aspects of each of these increments of change must have contributed to the rather sharp shift in Soviet behavior that characterized the Cuban missile venture.

The presence of Soviet missiles in Cuba cannot be understood apart from the political leaders' decision to direct Soviet organizations to install them. But what were the terms of choice? No dramatic event, but rather the steady grinding of organizations fixed the pieces on the chessboard that the Soviet leaders faced when making this decision. In solving this problem, the leaders must have chosen among options defined by organizations on the basis of information provided by organizations. Specification of the behavior that resulted in the installation of missiles in Cuba is difficult: speculation must be done largely in the dark. But if the available data is teased, an admittedly speculative but instructive account can be put together.

The operation of established organizations according to existing procedures created a problem that had become severe by 1960 and that grew in gravity through 1961. By early 1962, the Presidium could not avoid a nasty strategic issue. While the United States was rapidly building up its nuclear capability to destroy Soviet cities, Soviet forces were growing very slowly, with most of the increase coming in MRBMs and IRBMs, capable of hitting Western Europe but not the United States.

This difference had its origins in the Soviets' failure to capitalize on their initial space spectacular in 1957 by building a large fleet of ICBMs. This failure has generated debate among sovietologists about the Kremlin's objectives. One important, neglected aspect of the puzzle is the behavior of the organizations involved. Until 1960, no branch of the Soviet military establishment had strategic rockets as its primary mission. Rather, military missiles belonged to the artillery section of the Soviet Ground Forces.[51] The mission of the artillery section as well as the experience and training of its officers encouraged activity related to the support of Soviet ground forces in Europe. As a result, the Soviets had produced some 750 MRBMs and IRBMs, three times European overkill.[52] The standard scenarios of this organization must have been two: (1) artillery rockets defending the Soviets from German or NATO invasions, and, perhaps, (2) Soviet rockets supporting the Soviet army's advance through Europe. A capability for direct attack against the United States was thus a secondary and perhaps even a peripheral goal of the Soviet army.

The Soviet space and military missile programs had been closely linked from their inception.[53] According to a Soviet academician, L. I. Sedov, a leading Soviet scientist and spokesman on aerospace matters, "There is one large team in Russia that handles all space projects. The same key men are in charge of guidance, tracking, and other segments for each of the projects. It is a very large team and it can well take care of several projects in parallel. . . . We have no distinction between military and civilian projects."[54] Some of the scientists, engineers, and technicians who managed the first Sputnik must have been interested in military applications of space technology. Some military and political leaders saw enormous potentials. Khrushchev, in particular, seems to have seen space rockets as a harbinger of Soviet preeminence and to have expected rapid assimilation of these missiles as a major feature of Soviet military might. But the goals and procedures of the established organization that would have had to adopt and integrate this weapon — namely, the Soviet Ground Forces — were not amenable. There is no evidence that the military establishment showed any interest in the space rockets that research labs had developed; they did not procure and deploy missiles until the design bureaus developed rockets that could support the Soviet army in European engagements.

Having discovered the limits of the power of the Presidium to effect major changes in the established orientation of the Soviet Ground Forces, the leadership took a new tack. On January 14, 1960, Khrushchev announced before the Supreme Soviet a strategic "new look." Wars of the future would be fought not by armies but rather by strategic nuclear rockets. Thus, nuclear rockets should become the dominant weapon in the Soviet arsenal. Frustrated by the Soviet Ground Forces' sluggishness in deploying rockets, Khrushchev announced the creation of a new service within the Soviet military — the Strategic Rocket Forces — which would assume this mission. Soviet Ground Forces would be cut by over one-third, and these resources would be applied to the Soviet Rocket Forces. As Khrushchev stated:

The military air force and navy have lost their previous importance. . . . Almost the entire military air force is being replaced with rocket equipment . . . while surface ships can no
longer play the part they once did. In our country, the Armed
Forces have been to a considerable extent converted to rockets
and nuclear arms. At the present time the defense capabilities
of a country are not determined by the number of soldiers
under arms. Under present conditions, wars would not be carried out as before and there would be little resemblance to
previous wars. . . . War would begin in the heart of the warring
countries [and] not a single capital [or] major industrial and
administrative center would escape the attack, not merely during the first days, but during the first minutes of the war.[55]

The success of this effort was again limited by organizational resistance. The new Strategic Rocket Forces did establish
some new organizational goals and routines. But since most of
its men, and especially its leadership, simply changed offices
and insignia, its orientation and procedures differed less markedly from those of the artillery section of the Ground Forces than
the Soviet leaders had hoped. Components of this new organization must have pushed for rapid development and deployment of
ICBMs. But these components were weaker than those committed to the traditional artillery mission. Thus, the build-up of
MRBMs and IRBMs capable of striking European targets continued. If the Strategic Rocket Forces had received the budget
increases announced by Khrushchev, resources would have been
available for secondary goals, that is, for ICBMs as well as for
the MRBMs. An announcement by the Chairman of the Communist Party to the Supreme Soviet, however, does not effect a
major reallocation of resources among Soviet services. Though
the Strategic Rocket Forces received an increase in funds (over
what they had received as part of the Soviet Army) and the
Soviet Ground Forces were cut slightly, the budget shifted much
less than had been promised. By August 1961, Khrushchev announced a halt to reductions in the Soviet Ground Forces. The
development and deployment of ICBMs proceeded at snail's pace.

In hailing Soviet space triumphs and boasting about Soviet
rocket capabilities, the leadership had begun to claim what
Americans were avowing: the Soviet Union had a much larger
ICBM force than the United States. But to the group in the
Soviet Strategic Rocket Forces that knew the facts, these claims
became a matter of concern. The younger, elite, college-educated
men of the Soviet military, who had been drawn to the rocket

forces and who seem to have comprised a large part of the ICBM-oriented component of this service, took seriously the issue of the strategic nuclear balance. This component of the organization listened for information about American strategic capabilities. Thus, the U.S. government's announcement in November 1961 that there had been no missile gap, and that American strategic capabilities were now significantly superior to those of the Soviet Union, sounded an alarm.[56] The proposal for the installation of missiles in Cuba may well have emerged from this group — after a breakthrough in routines substantially reduced MRBM installation time.[57]

The Presidium agreed that Soviet strategic capabilities should be built-up rapidly. But neither the behavior of the Strategic Rocket Forces nor the existing budgetary split among the Soviet military services offered much hope. Organizational demands in other sectors of the economy excluded the possibility of a massive increase in the Soviet strategic rocket budget. These pieces having been fixed on the chessboard by organizational moves, the options available to the leadership were severely limited. Indeed, the deployment of existing equipment and routines — the MRBMs and IRBMs — in a new place, Cuba, may have seemed the only live option.

Even that alternative had to be made "live," since it went against the grain of existing practice in the more conservative Soviet military establishment, especially the Ground Forces. It was probably opposed by the major component of the Strategic Rocket Forces. But it must have been favored by the component concerned with the strategic balance. To permit these young Turks to implement their option, Khrushchev replaced Moskalenko — the older, artillery-trained head of the Strategic Rocket Forces — with a Ukrainian political client, Biryuzov.[58] Thus, an organizational component of the Strategic Rocket Forces seems to have proposed the option, defined its details (for example, how fast MRBMs could be constructed), and implemented the choice.

The Imposition of a U.S. Blockade of Cuba

Organizational Intelligence

At 7 P.M. on October 22, 1962, President Kennedy delivered the major foreign policy address of his career. Disclosing American discovery of the presence of Soviet strategic missiles

in Cuba, the President declared a "strict quarantine on all offensive military equipment under shipment to Cuba" and demanded
that "Chairman Khrushchev halt and eliminate this clandestine,
reckless, and provocative threat to world peace."[59] This decision
was reached at the pinnacle of the U.S. government after a critical week of deliberation. What initiated that crucial week were
photographs of Soviet missile sites in Cuba taken on October 14
by a U-2 aircraft piloted by Air Force Major Rudolf Anderson.
But these pictures might not have been taken until a week later.
In that case, the President speculated, "I don't think probably we
would have chosen as prudently as we finally did."[60] On the other
hand, if a U-2 had flown over certain areas of Cuba in the last
week of September, U.S. leaders might have received the information three weeks earlier.[61] What determined the context in
which American leaders came to choose the blockade was the
discovery of the missiles on October 14.

There has been considerable debate over alleged American
"intelligence failures" in the Cuban missile crisis. Critics have
faulted the intelligence community for "philosophical convic-
tions" that led it to downgrade evidence,[62] for "concentrating on
intentions rather than capabilities,"[63] and for explaining away
evidence in an attempt to "save a theory."[64] But what both critics and defenders have neglected is the fact that information
about Soviet missiles in Cuba came to the attention of the President on October 14 rather than three weeks earlier, or a week
later, as a consequence of the routines and procedures of the
organizations that make up the U.S. intelligence community.
These "eyes and ears" of the government function less as integral parts of a unitary head that entertains preconceptions and
theories than as organs that perform their tasks in a habitual
fashion. The job of intelligence requires an incredibly complex
organization, coordinating large numbers of actors, processing
endless piles of information. That this organization must function according to established routines and standard procedures
is a simple fact. The organizational routines and standard operating procedures by which the American intelligence community
discovered Soviet missiles in Cuba were neither more nor less
successful than they had been the previous month or were to be
in the months to follow.[65]

The available record permits a fairly reliable reconstruction
of the major features of the organizational behavior that resulted
in discovery of the Soviet missiles. Intelligence on activities

within Cuba came from four primary sources: shipping intelligence, refugees, agents within Cuba, and U-2 overflights.[66] Intelligence on all ships going to Cuba provided a catalogue of information on the number of Soviet shipments to Cuba (eighty-five by October 3), the character of these ships (size, registry, and the fact that several of the large-hatch lumber ships were used), and the character of their cargoes (transport, electronic, and construction equipment, SAMs, MIGs, patrol boats and Soviet technicians).[67] Refugees from Cuba brought innumerable distorted reports of Soviet missiles, Chinese soldiers, etc. For 1959 — before the Soviet Union had begun sending any arms whatever to Cuba — the CIA file of reports devoted solely to missiles in Cuba was five inches thick.[68] The low reliability of these reports made their collection and processing of marginal value. Nevertheless, a staff of CIA professionals at Opa Locka, Florida, collected, collated, and compared the results of interrogations of refugees — though often with a lag, since refugees numbered in the thousands. Reports from agents in Cuba produced information about the evacuation of Cubans from the port of Mariel and the secrecy that surrounded unloading and transport of equipment (trucks were lowered into the holds, loaded, and hoisted out covered with tarpaulins), a sighting and sketch of the rear profile of a missile on a Cuban highway heading west, and a report of missile activity in the Pinar del Rio province.[69] But this information had to be transferred from sub-agent to master-agent and then to the United States, a procedure that usually meant a lag of ten days between a sighting and arrival of the information in Washington. The U-2 camera recorded the highest quality U.S. intelligence. Photographs taken from a height of fourteen miles allowed analysts to distinguish painted lines on a parking lot, or to recognize a new kind of cannon on the wing of an airplane.[70] U-2s flew over Cuba on August 29, September 5, 17, 26, 29, and October 5 and 7 before the October 14 flight that discovered the missiles.[71] These earlier flights gathered information on SAM sites, coastal defense missile sites, MIGs, missile patrol boats, and IL-28 light bombers.[72]

Intelligence experts in Washington processed information received from these four sources and produced estimates of certain contingencies. Hindsight highlights several bits of evidence in the intelligence system that might have suggested the presence of Soviet missiles in Cuba. Yet the notorious "September estimate" concluded that the Soviet Union would not intro-

duce offensive missiles into Cuba.[73] No U-2 flight was directed
over the western end of Cuba between September 5 and October
4.[74] No U-2 flew over the western end of Cuba until the flight
that discovered the Soviet missiles on October 14.[75] Can these
"failures" be accounted for in organizational terms?

On September 19, when the highest assembly of the American intelligence community, the United States Intelligence
Board (USIB), met to consider the question of Cuba, the "system"
contained the following information: (1) shipping intelligence
about the arrival in Cuba of two large-hatch Soviet lumber ships,
the *Omsk* and the *Poltava,* which the intelligence report also
noted were riding high in the water; (2) refugee reports of count-
less sightings of missiles, plus a report that Castro's private
pilot, after a night of drinking in Havana, had boasted: "We
will fight to the death and perhaps we can win because we have
everything, including atomic weapons"; (3) a sighting by a CIA
agent of the rear profile of a strategic missile; (4) U-2 photos
from flights on August 29 and September 5 and 17, showing
the construction of a number of SAM sites and other defensive
missiles.[76]

Not all this information, however, was on the desk of the
estimators. Information does not pass from the tentacle to the top
of the organization instantaneously. Facts can be "in the system" without being available to the head of the organization.
Information must be winnowed at every step up the organizational hierarchy, since the number of minutes in each day limits
the number of bits of information each individual can absorb.
It is impossible for men at the top to examine every report
from sources in 100 nations (25 of which had as high a priority
as Cuba). But those who decide which information their boss
shall see rarely see their bosses' problem. Finally, facts that
with hindsight are clear signals are frequently indistinguishable
from surrounding "noise" before the occurrence.

Intelligence about large-hatch ships riding high in the water
did not go unremarked. Shipping intelligence experts spelled out
the implication: the ships must be carrying "space consuming"
cargo.[77] These details were carefully included in the catalogue
of intelligence on shipping. For experts alert to the Soviet Union's
pressing requirement for ships, however, neither the facts nor
the implication carried a special signal. The refugee report of
Castro's pilot's remark had been received at Opa Locka along
with reams of inaccurate and even deliberately false reports

spread by the refugee community. That report and a thousand others had to be checked and compared before being sent to Washington. The two weeks required for initial processing could have been shortened by a large increase in resources devoted to this source of information.[78] But the yield of this source was already quite marginal, and there was little reason to expect that a change in procedures, reducing transmission time to one week, would be worth the cost. The CIA agent's sighting of the rear profile of a strategic missile had occurred on September 12; transmission time from agent sighting to arrival of the report in Washington typically took nine to twelve days. That report arrived at CIA headquarters on September 21, two days *after* the USIB meeting. Shortening the transmission time would have imposed severe cost in terms of danger to sub-agents, agents, and communication networks.

U-2 flights had produced no hard indication of the presence of offensive missiles. The flight over western Cuba on September 5 revealed SAM installations approaching completion. Then on September 9, a U-2 on "loan" to the Chinese Nationalists was shot down over mainland China.[79] Recalling the outcry that followed the downing of Francis Gary Powers' U-2 over the Soviet Union on May 1, 1960, the intelligence community feared lest this incident trigger an international stage show that could force the abandonment of U-2 flights, eliminating its most reliable source of information. The Committee on Overhead Reconnaissance (COMOR), which approved each U-2 flight pattern, was quickly convened.[80] The State Department pressed arguments about the political consequences if another U-2 should be shot down, for example, over Cuba. As a result, COMOR decided that rather than flying up one side of the island and down the other, future flights should "dip into" Cuban airspace and peer as much as possible from the periphery. COMOR also decided at this meeting that flights should concentrate on the eastern half of Cuba rather than on the western tip, where SAMs were known to be approaching operational readiness.[81]

Given the information available to them on September 19, then, the chiefs of intelligence made a reasonable judgment in predicting that the Soviets would not introduce offensive missiles into Cuba.[82] And the information available to them included everything that they could reasonably expect.

The fourteen days between the September 19 estimate and the October 4 decision by COMOR to direct a special flight over western Cuba added a number of pieces to the picture. First came a report "having to do with an area in Pinar del Rio Province . . . associated in generic terms with the possibility of missile activities."[83] Then on September 21 the agent's sighting of the rear profile of a missile (nine days before) reached the desk of the heads of the CIA and the Defense Intelligence Agency (DIA).[84] Shortly afterward, the refugee report of Castro's pilot's claim also arrived. On September 27 a "hard copy" report of the agent's sighting, which had been circulated as an "advance report" on September 21, arrived.[85] This presumably included a sketch of the missile. By that time, Colonel Wright of the DIA, who had been studying the pattern of SAM installations photographed by the U-2 flight over western Cuba on September 5, had noted that the trapezoidal pattern resembled photographs of SAM installations designed to protect strategic missiles in the Soviet Union.[86]

These pieces of information led some DIA analysts between September 27 and October 2 to the hypothesis that the Soviets were placing strategic missiles in the San Cristobal area.[87] The CIA marked the central and western parts of Cuba "suspicious" on September 29 and on October 3 certified them the highest priority for aerial reconnaissance. Thus when McCone assembled COMOR on October 4, in spite of State Department qualms about possible consequences of a loss of a U-2 over Cuba, the decision for an overflight of western Cuba was reached.[88] The gradual accumulation of pieces of evidence leading to the hypothesis that the Soviet Union was installing missiles and then to the decision to dispatch a U-2 over the western tip of Cuba is again routine and nonstartling from an organizational perspective.

The ten-day delay between decision and flight is another organizational story.[89] At the October 4 meeting, where the decision to dispatch the flight over western Cuba was made, the State Department spelled out the consequences of the loss of a U-2 over Cuba in the strongest terms. The Defense Department took this opportunity to raise an issue important to its concerns. Given the increased danger that a U-2 would be downed, the pilots should be officers in uniform rather than CIA agents, so the Air Force should assume responsibility for U-2 flights over Cuba. To the contrary, the CIA argued that this was an intelligence operation and thus within the CIA's jurisdiction. Besides, CIA U-2s had been modified in certain ways that gave them advantages over Air Force U-2s in avoiding Soviet SAMs. Five days passed while the State Department pressed for less risky alternatives, and the Air Force (in Department of Defense guise) and the CIA engaged in territorial disputes. On October 9, COMOR approved a flight plan over San Cristobal, but, to the CIA's dismay, the Air Force rather than the CIA would take charge of the mission. At this point details become sketchy, but several members of the intelligence community have speculated that an Air Force pilot in an Air Force U-2 attempted a high altitude overflight on October 9 that "flamed out," i.e., lost power, and thus had to descend in order to restart its engine.[90] A second round between Air Force and CIA followed, as a result of which Air Force pilots were trained to fly CIA U-2s. A successful overflight did not take place until October 14.

This ten-day delay constitutes some form of "failure." In the face of well-founded suspicions about offensive Soviet missiles in Cuba that posed a critical threat to the most vital U.S. interests, squabbling between organizations whose job it is to produce this information seems entirely inappropriate. But for each of these organizations, the question involved the issue: *Whose* job was it to be? Resolution of this issue would not only decide which organization controlled U-2 flights over Cuba; it would also prejudice the broader issue of control of all U-2 intelligence activities — the subject of a long-standing territorial dispute. Therefore, though the delay was in one sense a "failure," it was also a nearly inevitable consequence of two facts: many jobs do not fall neatly into precisely defined organizational jurisdictions; and vigorous organizations are imperialistic.

Organizational Options

Deliberations of leaders in ExCom meetings produced broad outlines of alternatives. Details of the alternatives, and blueprints for their implementation, had to be specified by the organization that would be responsible for execution. These organizational outputs effectively answered the question: What, specifically, *could* be done?

Discussion in the ExCom quickly narrowed the live options to two: an air strike and a blockade. The choice of the blockade instead of the air strike turned on two points: (1) the argument from both morality and tradition that the United States could not perpetrate a "Pearl Harbor in reverse"; (2) the belief that a "surgical" air strike was impossible.[91] Whether the United States would choose to strike first may have been a question of morality. Whether the United States was able to perform the surgical strike was a factual question about capabilities.

Initially, the members of the ExCom strongly favored the air strike. As Sorensen recalls, "The idea of American planes suddenly and swiftly eliminating the missile complex with conventional bombs in a matter of minutes — a so-called 'surgical' strike — had appeal to almost everyone first considering the matter, including President Kennedy on Tuesday and Wednesday."[92] According to Robert Kennedy's record, "The general feeling in the beginning was that some form of action was required. . . . Most felt, at that stage, that an air strike against the missile sites could be the *only course.*"[93] What effectively foreclosed that option was the Air Force's assertion that the air strike the leaders wanted could not be carried out with high confidence of success.[94] Indeed, after having tentatively chosen the course of prudence — given that the surgical air strike was not an option — Kennedy seemingly reconsidered. On Sunday morning, October 21, he called the Air Force experts to a special meeting in his living quarters, where he probed once more for the option of a *"surgical"* air strike.[95] General Walter C. Sweeney, Commander of Tactical Air Command, stated confidently again that the Air Force could guarantee no higher than 90 percent effectiveness in a surprise air strike.[96] That "fact" was false.

Organizations defined what the President believed U.S. military equipment and personnel were capable of performing in the Cuban missile crisis. Specification of the air strike alternative provides a classic case of *military estimates.* One of the alternatives outlined by the ExCom was named "air strike"; the technical job of preparing a detailed plan for this alternative was delegated to the Air Force. The military chiefs took this assignment with confidence that they were preparing not just an option (which the ExCom might consider) but an operational plan for the military course of action to which the leaders were committed. The process by which this plan unfolded was long and rather complex. The major features of it, however, can be summarized.

From the perspective of the military planners, the issue was straightforward: elimination of the Communist Cuban thorn. Their problem was to guarantee that the job would be done successfully. The Services had prepared and coordinated a contingency plan for military action against Castro — in case an opportunity should arise.[97] That plan deeply reflected the lesson that these organizations had learned from the Bay of Pigs: the Kennedy administration could not be trusted to do what was required in the heat of military action. When *these* leaders wanted military action, they would have to sign on to a plan that called for massive military force. The contingency plan for destruction of Castro was substantial. The assignment posed for the military planners on Tuesday, October 16, included a further, complicating factor. The leaders needed an immediate estimate of the earliest date on which the military machine would be ready to act. Caught in the middle of a crisis, under pressure for action at the earliest date, the Services acted according to procedures. In preparing the ExCom's "surgical air strike" option, the Air Force planning unit simply took the existing contingency plan out of the safe and made modifications aimed at the Soviet missiles. The contingency plan emphasized U.S. security requirements that might be affected by military action against Cuba. Thus the "air strike" option served up by the Air Force called for extensive bombardment of all storage depots, airports, and (in deference to the Navy) the artillery batteries opposite the naval base at Guantánamo, as well as all missile sites.[98] The Air Force could carry out this attack on Tuesday, October 23.

Political leaders do not normally examine the details of war plans. In that respect, this was a normal case. But the members of the ExCom repeatedly expressed bewilderment over Air Force assertions that the air strike would call for as many as 500 sorties, involve extensive collateral damage, and so forth. Both the leaders and the military spoke of an "air strike," but they were referring to quite different things. The surgical air strike the governmental leaders wanted, and which they thought was being discussed, was never examined in detail by Air Force planners during the first week of the crisis. By the end of the first week, the misunderstanding became apparent to several of the leaders. At that point, the Joint Chiefs declared firmly that all the targets called for by the existing plan were vital to U.S. security. To limit the attack any further would pose an "unacceptable risk." But by that time, the leaders had opted for a blockade.

In that choice they were influenced not only by the confusion between a "surgical" and a "massive" air strike but also by an even more curious misestimation. The ExCom asked the Air Force estimators whether the air strike could guarantee destruction of all operational missiles. The Commander of the Tactical Air Command replied that the air strike would certainly destroy 90 percent of the missiles but that it was not possible to guarantee 100 percent effectiveness.[99] According to Sorensen's record, "Even then, admitted the Air Force — and this in particular influenced the President — there could be no assurance that all the missiles would have been removed or that some of them would not fire first."[100] Few assertions could have made the air strike less attractive to the leaders of the U.S. government.

The Air Force planners' estimate that an air strike could not guarantee destruction of the missiles was not grounded in any careful study. Rather, the conclusion emerged according to the standard operating procedures of the Air Force. First, the estimaters consulted American manuals to determine the characteristics and capabilities of Soviet weapons in Cuba. According to the manuals, the MRBMs the Soviets were installing were classified "mobile, 'field-type' missiles" with a range of up to 1,100 nautical miles.[101] Second, they consulted U-2 photographs to establish the numbers, location, and readiness of the missiles: as many as twenty-four MRBMs would be operational when the United States attacked. The location of the sites was well established. Third, the planners consulted manuals on the capabilities of American aircraft to attack these sites simultaneously, as well as on the destructiveness and accuracy of various bombs that the planes could deliver. In this way they calculated the required number of sorties. The 10 percent uncertainty about destruction of all the missiles stemmed from the planners' belief that since the Soviet missiles were "mobile," they might be moved just before or during the attack and fired from a new position.

During the second week of the crisis, civilian experts examined the surgical air strike. Careful study revealed that these missiles were mobile in the sense that small houses are mobile: that is, they could be moved and reassembled in six days.[102] After the missiles were reclassified "movable," and detailed plans for surgical air strikes specified, this strike was added to the list of live options for the end of the second week.

Organizational Implementation

ExCom members distinguished several gradations of block-ade: offensive weapons only, all armaments, and all strategic goods including POL — petroleum, oil, and lubricants. The task of specifying the *details* of the option named "blockade" belonged to the Navy. Before the President announced the blockade on Monday evening, the first stage of the Navy's blueprint was in motion, and a problem loomed on the horizon.[103] The Navy had a detailed plan for the blockade. The President had several less precise but equally determined notions about what should be done and when and how. For the Navy, the issue was one of effective implementation of a military mission — without the meddling and interference of political leaders. For the President, the problem was to pace and manage events in such a way that the Soviet leaders would have time to see, think, and blink.

Observers of such conflicts naturally side with the responsible political leaders against the parochial organizations. But the tendency should be resisted in this case, for implementation of the proclaimed quarantine was no small order. First, the quarantine area included nearly one million square miles of water. The size of the Navy's job — and the measure of its success — contrasts sharply with another it was assigned in the first week of the Kennedy administration. Then, exiles hijacked a Portuguese passenger ship in the mid-Atlantic, and the United States volunteered to find it. After fourteen days of search, the Navy finally managed to locate the ship. As the Chief of Naval Operations explained at the time: "It's a big ocean."[104] Meanwhile, the ocean had not shrunk. But this time the Navy launched a larger effort — some 180 ships — and the task was more confined: naval reconnaissance planes had spotted all Soviet ships and plotted their position, speed, and direction, and ships from the mid-Atlantic had to approach Cuba by one of five navigable channels.

This operation was complicated, however, by a second factor — one unique in naval history and, indeed, unparalleled in modern relations between American political leaders and military organizations.[105] Advances in the technology of communications made it possible for political leaders in the basement of the White House to talk directly with commanders of destroyers stationed along the quarantine line. Advances in the technology of mass destruction created the possibility that acts by men on a single destroyer in that quarantine line could rapidly escalate to bring death to millions of Americans. Thus the governmental leaders had both the capability and the incentive to reach out beyond the traditional limits of their control. Maps in the "Situation Room" in the basement of the White House tracked the movement of all Soviet ships.[106] The members of the ExCom knew each of the ships by name and argued extensively about which should be stopped first, at what point, and how. Sorensen records "the President's personal direction of the quarantine's operation . . . his determination not to let needless incidents or reckless subordinates escalate so dangerous and delicate a crisis beyond control."[107] Thus, for the first time in U.S. military history, local commanders received repeated orders about the details of their military operations directly from political leaders — contrary to two sacred military doctrines. This circumvention of the *chain of command* and the accompanying countermand of the *autonomy of local commanders* created enormous pain and serious friction.

A surface chronology establishes a context within which questions arise. The President first heard a discussion of how the blockade would actually operate at the formal meeting of the National Security Council on Sunday, October 21, which ratified the ExCom's blockade decision.[108] Admiral George Anderson, Chief of Naval Operations, described the plans and procedures.[109] Each approaching ship would be signaled to stop for boarding and inspection. If the ship failed to respond, a shot would be fired across its bow. If there was still no satisfactory response, a shot would be fired into the rudder to cripple but not to sink. "You are certain that can be done?" the President inquired. "Yes, Sir!" responded the Admiral.[110] Monday evening as the President publicly announced the U.S. intention to impose "a strict quarantine on all offensive military equipment under shipment to Cuba," Naval Task Force 136 steamed toward the appointed line "flank speed 27 knots, in Cruise Condition 3 — no lights, limited radio communication, secondary batteries manned."[111] On Tuesday the ExCom hammered out the specific features of the quarantine: force should be used "only to the extent necessary"; ships that failed to comply with directions about identification and inspection would be disabled and taken into custody but not sunk; initially POL would be excluded; operation of the quarantine would not begin until the following day.[112] Tuesday evening, after OAS approval had been obtained, the President issued the Quarantine Proclamation, which stated that the quarantine would become effective on Wednesday, October 24, at 10 A.M. E.D.T.[113] According to the public record, the first Soviet ships approached the quarantine on Wednesday but halted just before challenging it. The first contact with a Soviet ship occurred Thursday morning when the tanker *Bucharest* crossed the line but on Presidential order was allowed to continue after merely identifying itself.[114] American warships shadowed the *Bucharest* as it proceeded toward Cuba while the ExCom discussed whether to intercept it.[115] The first boarding occurred Friday morning when the *Marcula,* a Lebanese freighter under charter to the Soviets, was stopped, boarded, and inspected before being allowed to pass.[116]

Any analyst sensitive to organizational perspectives will surmise that this schedule must have caused serious problems between the Navy and the government leaders. The ExCom's willingness to give the Soviet leaders more time to consider their choice, to delay the procedures of the blockade until there could be no question about the Soviet leaders' communicating repeatedly with the Soviet ship captains, to permit ships to pass through the blockade while waiting for a ship of just the right type, was in the words of one high-ranking naval officer, "a hell of a way to run a blockade."[117] A careful reading of available sources uncovers an instructive incident. On Tuesday evening, British Ambassador David Ormsby-Gore, who had attended a briefing on the details of the blockade, suggested to the President that the plan for intercepting Soviet ships far out of reach of Cuban jets did not facilitate Khrushchev's hard decisions.[118] Why not make the interception much closer to Cuba and thus give the Russian leader more time? According to the public account and the recollection of a number of the men involved, Kennedy, "agreeing immediately, called McNamara and, over emotional Navy protests, issued the appropriate instruction."[119] As Sorensen records, "In a sharp clash with the Navy, he made certain his will prevailed."[120] The Navy's blueprint for the blockade was thus changed by drawing the blockade much closer to Cuba. This incident would seem to suggest that organizational plans and procedures can be changed by political leaders successfully and at small cost.

Anyone with a serious organizational orientation, however, will be wary of this account. Though alternative versions must be somewhat speculative, more careful examination of the available evidence confirms other suspicions. According to the public chronology (1) on Tuesday evening the President ordered the quarantine drawn in closer to Cuba; (2) on Wednesday morning the quarantine became effective; (3) on Thursday morning the first Soviet ship (*Bucharest*) was hailed; and (4) on Friday morning the first ship (*Marcula*) was boarded. Thus Soviet ships were first hailed and boarded at the line established after the President's order that the quarantine line be moved. But according to the statement issued by the Department of Defense at the time of the first boarding, a party from the American destroyers *John R. Pierce* and *Joseph P. Kennedy, Jr.,* boarded the *Marcula* "at 7:50 A.M., E.D.T., 180 miles northeast of Nassau." [121] Other sources reveal that the *Marcula* had been trailed since 10:30 the previous evening.[122] Simple calculation allows one to locate the point at which the *Marcula* met the American quarantine line: approximately 500 miles out from Cuba's eastern tip, along the Navy's original line.[123] Existing accounts to the contrary, the blockade was *not* moved as the President ordered.

What did happen is not entirely clear. It is certain, however, that Soviet ships passed through the line along which American destroyers had posted themselves before the official "first contact" with the Soviet ship. On October 26, a Soviet tanker arrived in Havana and was welcomed by a dockside rally honoring the crew for "running the blockade." Photographs of this vessel show the name *Vinnitsa* in Cyrillic letters on the side of the vessel.[124] But according to the official U.S. position, the first tanker to pass through the blockade was the *Bucharest,* which was hailed by the Navy on the morning of October 25. Again simple mathematical calculation excludes the possibility that the *Bucharest* and the *Vinnitsa* were the same ship, since a tanker traveling at ten to twenty knots could not reach Havana from the blockade line in a single day.[125] It seems probable, then, that the Navy's resistance to the President's order that the blockade be drawn in closer to Cuba forced the President to allow one or several Soviet ships to pass through the blockade after it was officially operative.[126]

The attempt to leash the Navy's blockade operation had a price. On Wednesday morning, October 24, what the ExCom had been awaiting occurred: the eighteen dry cargo ships heading toward the quarantine stopped dead in the water. This was the occasion of Dean Rusk's remark, "We're eyeball to eyeball and I think the other fellow just blinked."[127] But the Navy had another interpretation: the ships had simply stopped to pick up more Soviet submarine escorts. Orders went out immediately that Soviet ships were to be given every opportunity to turn back.[128] Ships approaching the area should be hailed and trailed, but no ships should be stopped without further orders. Nevertheless, the President expressed concern that the Navy — already frustrated because of the leashing of its designed blockade — might blunder into an incident. Sensing the President's fears, McNamara decided to explore the organization's procedures and routines for making the first interception. Calling on the Chief of Naval Operations in the Navy's inner sanctum, the Navy Flag Plot, McNamara put his questions harshly.[129] Precisely what would the Navy do when the first interception occurred? Anderson replied that he had outlined the procedures in the National Security Council meeting and that there was no need to discuss it further. Angered but still calm, McNamara began to lecture the admiral. According to Elie Abel's reconstruction of that lecture, McNamara firmly explained that:

> The object of the operation was not to shoot Russians but to communicate a political message from President Kennedy to Chairman Khrushchev. The President wanted to avoid pushing Khrushchev to extremes. The blockade must be so conducted as to avoid humiliating the Russians; otherwise Khrushchev might react in a nuclear spasm. By the conventional rules, blockade was an act of war and the first Soviet ship that refused to submit to boarding and search risked being sent to the bottom. But this was a military action with a political objective. Khrushchev must somehow be persuaded to pull back, rather than be goaded into retaliation.[130]

Sensing that Anderson was not moved by this logic, McNamara returned to the line of detailed questioning. Who would make the first interception? Were Russian-speaking officers on board? How would submarines be dealt with? At one point McNamara asked Anderson what he would do if a Soviet ship's captain refused to answer questions about his cargo. At that point the Navy man picked up the *Manual of Naval Regulations* and, waving it in McNamara's face, shouted, "It's all in there." To which McNamara replied, "I don't give a damn what John Paul Jones would have done. I want to know what you are going to do, now."[131] The encounter ended on Anderson's remark: "Now, Mr. Secretary, if you and your Deputy will go back to your offices, the Navy will run the blockade."[132]

The Withdrawal of Soviet Missiles from Cuba

Chairman Khrushchev's announcement on Sunday, October 28, that "the arms which you describe as offensive [will be] crated and returned to the Soviet Union" marked the climax of the crisis.[133] A week of intense interaction between the United States and the Soviet Union preceded that announcement. That interaction was in large part a by-product of action within each nation — action that pitted government leaders against organizations whose outputs they sought to control. Indeed, the similarities between the phrases with which the groups who sat on top of each government characterized "the problem" are suggestive. As Soviet ships approached American warships stationed along the quarantine line, the American leaders sent a letter to the Soviets expressing concern "that we both show prudence and do nothing to allow events to *make the situation more difficult to control* than it is."[134] Later a Soviet reply emphasized the danger, "Contact of our ships . . . can spark off the fire of military conflict after which any talks would be superfluous because other forces and other laws would begin to operate — the *laws of war.*"[135] As the climax of the crisis drew near, developments were, in the American phrase, "approaching a point where *events could have become unmanageable.*"[136] The Russians chose another metaphor: the logic of war. "If indeed war should break out, then it would not be in our power to stop it, for such is the logic of war."[137]

Inside the Soviet Union

An understanding of the Soviet withdrawal must begin with an appreciation of the sense in which the missile crisis constituted for the Soviets a "Pearl Harbor in reverse." During the crisis, the leaders of the U.S. government vigorously debated whether the United States could perpetrate a "Pearl Harbor" — whether President Kennedy could be a "Tojo." There, "Pearl Harbor" referred to the Japanese decision to launch a surprise attack. But this symbol has another connotation as well. Especially for readers of Roberta Wohlstetter's artful account of

Pearl Harbor, this word refers to the American failure to read the handwriting on the wall.[138] It is in this sense that the Cuban missile crisis is essentially the Soviet Union's "Pearl Harbor."

Having initiated a course of action more provocative than Roosevelt's pressure on Japan, the Soviet leaders should have been alert for evidence of American preparations to seize the initiative. The clues available to them seem overwhelming. That the United States had good intelligence on the Soviet build-up was clear. A State Department briefing to reporters on August 24, Presidential statements on September 4, 7, and 13, and Undersecretary of State Ball's testimony on October 3 catalogued the Soviet build-up accurately. On September 4, in response to private assurances from Khrushchev relayed via Dobrynin to Robert Kennedy, the Presidential release itemized precisely the Soviet build-up and warned of American watchfulness for "offensive missiles."[139] On October 13, in a long conversation, Chester Bowles needled Ambassador Dobrynin on the question of whether the Soviet Union intended to insert "offensive weapons" in Cuba.[140] And on October 18, in reply to the solemn assurances from Soviet Foreign Minister Gromyko that the Soviet Union was not installing offensive missiles, the President sent for and read carefully to him the list of public statements that Kennedy had made in September warning the Soviet Union against putting missiles in Cuba.[141] Could the Soviet leaders have failed to recognize that the United States was alert to the possibility of Soviet emplacement of offensive missiles in Cuba?

In this setting, the behavior of the U.S. government during the week from October 15 to the American "first strike" on October 22 could have indicated only one thing: U.S. discovery of the Soviet move and preparation for action. At the first meeting of the ExCom (October 16) the President increased the U-2 surveillance of Cuba significantly.[142] Standard observance of U-2 flights would indicate that something was up. The American government attempted to impose secrecy and initiated a program of cover and deception.[143] The President kept up appearances of normalcy, receiving astronauts and foreign dignitaries and flying to Connecticut and Cleveland to keep commitments. But what John McCone called the "high-priced help" of the government met almost continuously for an entire week.[144] Not until Thursday did someone notice that their official limousines, bearing easily identified license plates, had been assembling outside the State Department and White House.[145] Lights burning late in the Pentagon and State Department, cots being moved into offices, and the sudden unavailability of top-level officials also conveyed strong signals that it was "crisis time." (A quick check of which lights were burning in what sections of which rings and floors of the Pentagon might have pinned down the location of the crisis.)

On Tuesday, October 16, President Kennedy learned that the Soviets had placed missiles in Cuba. Within thirty-six hours, British intelligence had pieced together the facts and alerted British Ambassador David Ormsby-Gore.[146] On Friday, Ormsby-Gore cabled his government that the United States had probably discovered Soviet offensive weapons in Cuba and was preparing the first move in an impending crisis.[147] (Little wonder, then, at his lack of surprise when Kennedy leaked the secret to him on Sunday.) By Saturday, Alfred Friendly of *The Washington Post* and James Reston of *The New York Times* had the story.[148] After Reston called George Ball and then McGeorge Bundy, it was clear that he lacked few of the details. The President telephoned the publishers of the *Times* and the *Post* requesting that they not "give the game away" in Monday's newspapers.[149] But where were the Russians?

During the crisis, Roger Hilsman, Director of Research and Intelligence for the State Department, argued that the Soviet Union knew that the United States had discovered the missiles.[150] *Post hoc*, he argues that they must have known.[151] The evidence available to them was overwhelming. This hypothesis, however, has difficulty accounting for the behavior of Soviet leaders in the first forty-eight hours after the United States announced its discovery. That behavior gives every indication of unanticipated surprise. Dobrynin, dumbfounded when Secretary Rusk informed him of the crisis, left the State Department visibly shaken. For several days he insisted that there were no Soviet missiles in Cuba, as did Soviet Ambassador Zorin at the United Nations. Khrushchev's refusal to accept the quarantine proclamation, public replies to U Thant and Bertrand Russell, his two secret letters to the President, and finally the harangue to which he subjected William Knox suggest the thrashing about of a surprised and uncertain man.[152] Knox, President of Westinghouse International, was visiting in Moscow when he received an urgent invitation to meet Chairman Khrushchev in the Kremlin.[153] For three hours, the Chairman treated Knox to a string of threats, complaints, and peasant jokes. Acknowledging the presence of Soviet missiles in Cuba, Krushchev asserted that Soviet ships would not yield to American piracy; Soviet submarines would sink U.S. destroyers if they attempted to stop Soviet ships. But within hours, Soviet ships were stopping and changing course rather than challenging the American blockade. Moreover, Hilsman's hypothesis cannot account for the fact that more than fifteen hours after the United States had informed the Soviets of discovery of the missiles, "There had been no general alert of the Soviet forces in Cuba or around the globe."[154] This evidence convinced most of the participants — and convinces most analysts — that the Soviet Union failed to uncover American plans for an initial move. Soviet intelligence proved to be less than the omniscient genie that Americans so often fear.

The Soviet decision to place missiles in Cuba must have been taken within a very narrow circle and implemented with utmost secrecy. That Dobrynin, the Soviet Ambassador to the United States, was ignorant of the move would not be unusual. The Japanese Ambassador was not informed of Pearl Harbor; the German Ambassador in Moscow was not informed of Barbarossa; Adlai Stevenson was not informed of the Bay of Pigs. Unaware of Soviet action, Dobrynin had no eye for the signs that were all over Washington. Similarly, many of the "americanologists" and most of Soviet intelligence that deals with raw data must not have known that the Soviet Union was placing missiles in Cuba. Thus information, which would have amounted to clues for one who knew, got lost in the hierarchical process of selection. Finally, the bits of information were gathered by several different large organizations, each of which transmitted and processed it according to routine procedures. After the fact, more information than would have been required to know what was happening could have been found "in the Soviet intelligence system."

In the wake of this reverse "Pearl Harbor," the Soviet leaders were confused. For several days many Soviet spokesmen were talking, but each with a different tongue. Dobrynin and Zorin denied the presence of missiles in Cuba. Khrushchev admitted that the missiles were there and threatened to sink American ships if they attempted to interfere with Soviet shipments. Presidium members absent from Moscow were not summoned, and some of those who were in the capital were not consulted.[155] A tanker "sneaked through" the blockade but several Soviet dry cargo ships stopped and the large-hatch ships returned to the Soviet Union. A conciliatory note was sounded in Khrushchev's personal Friday letter and reflected in an approach by Fomin, the head of Soviet Intelligence in Washington. Saturday, the Presidium's letter demanded that American missiles in Turkey be removed in exchange for Soviet withdrawal of missiles in Cuba, and a Soviet SAM downed an American U-2 over Cuba. Sunday, Khrushchev announced that the missiles would be withdrawn.

Some analysts have fitted these actions into a rational mold. It is just as easy to speculate about the organizational information and options that influenced these choices and actions. And various events could be interpreted as consequences of organizational procedures. For example, there is some evidence to support the speculation that Soviet government leaders did not make the decision to shoot down the American U-2 over Cuba on the final Saturday; before the crisis, orders had been issued for active defense of Cuba against U-2 overflights. On Saturday, October 27, the SAMs and radar networks finally reached operational readiness. That day the Soviet Air Defense units acted on the previous orders, which the leaders had neglected to withdraw, and shot down the first available U-2. Prudence, however, requires that the limits of confidence in the details of these explanations be acknowledged.

Inside the United States

American intra-national relations in the critical week of the crisis constitute a catalogue of friction and frustration as political leaders in the name of flexibility and options attempted to interfere with organizational routines and procedures. The struggle over where and how the quarantine would be implemented has been noted above. Political leaders insisted that the blockade be drawn close to Cuba. The Navy maintained its position — 500 miles out from Cuba. Political leaders forced the Navy to allow Soviet ships to pass through the blockade until Thursday and did not allow a boarding until Friday.

But the operation of the blockade produced an even more startling result, the full impact of which became clear only with the publication of Robert Kennedy's intensely personal memoir of the crisis. The most moving passage in his account provides a unique picture of the American government's leaders at the limits of their control and awaiting the crunch.

It was now a few minutes after 10:00 o'clock [Wednesday, October 24]. Secretary McNamara announced that two Russian ships, the *Gagarin* and the *Komiles,* were within a few miles of our quarantine barrier. The interception of both ships would probably be before noon Washington time. Indeed, the expectation was that at least one of the vessels would be stopped and boarded between 10:30 and 11:00 o'clock.

Then came the disturbing Navy report that a Russian submarine had moved into position between the two ships.

It had originally been planned to have a cruiser make the first interception, but, because of the increased danger, it was decided in the past few hours to send in an aircraft carrier supported by helicopters, carrying antisubmarine equipment, hovering overhead. The carrier *Essex* was to signal the submarine by sonar to surface and identify itself. If it refused, said Secretary McNamara, depth charges with a small explosive would be used until the submarine surfaced.

I think these few minutes were the time of gravest concern for the President. Was the world on the brink of a holocaust? Was it our error? A mistake? Was there something further that should have been done? Or not done? His hand went up to his face and covered his mouth. He opened and closed his fist. His face seemed drawn, his eyes pained, almost gray. We stared at each other across the table. For a few fleeting seconds, it was almost as though no one else was there and he was no longer the President.

Inexplicably, I thought of when he was ill and almost died; when he lost his child; when we learned that our oldest brother had been killed; of personal times of strain and hurt. The voices droned on, but I didn't seem to hear anything until I heard the President say: "Isn't there some way we can avoid having our first exchange with a Russian submarine — almost anything but that?" "No, there's too much danger to our ships. There is no alternative," said McNamara. "Our commanders have been instructed to avoid hostilities if at all possible, but this is what we must be prepared for, and this is what we must expect."

We had come to the time of final decision. . . . I felt we were on the edge of a precipice with no way off. This time, the moment was now — not next week — not tomorrow, "so we can have another meeting and decide"; not in eight hours, "so we can send another message to Khrushchev and perhaps he will finally understand." No, none of that was possible. One thousand miles away in the vast expanse of the Atlantic Ocean the final decisions were going to be made in the next few minutes. President Kennedy had initiated the course of events, but he no longer had control over them. He would have to wait — we would have to wait. The minutes in the Cabinet Room ticked slowly by. What could we say now — what could we do?[156]

This account captures the agony in the ExCom over the *initial* encounter of American and Soviet ships and stresses these men's concern about the fact that the initial encounter would involve a Soviet submarine. As the President said: "Anything but that." What neither the President nor his colleagues knew, however, was that *prior* to the experience through which they were living, American destroyers had encountered Soviet submarines — according to the Navy's standard operating procedures. McNamara discovered this during the course of his Wednesday evening visit to the Flag Plot.

On Monday, when U.S. forces went to alert, the Navy, according to established plans, set out to demonstrate the validity of its long-standing argument about the efficacy of Anti-Submarine Warfare (ASW). The Navy maintained that its "Hunter-Killer" ASW program was very effective. All it required was more resources. Many political appointees in the Department of Defense argued that ASW amounted to trying to "bail out the ocean with a bucket." What more opportune test than this crisis? As Admiral Anderson, the Chief of Naval Operations, boasted at a Navy League banquet after the crisis, "The presence of many Russian submarines in Caribbean and Atlantic waters provided perhaps the finest opportunity since World War II for U.S. Naval Anti-Submarine Warfare forces to exercise their trade, to perfect their skills and to manifest their capability to detect and follow submarines of another nation."[157] Testifying before the House Armed Services Committee in 1963, Admiral Anderson stated: "Our aircraft and ships were searching an area of some 3.5 million square miles for Russian ships and submarines. They were engaged in *the most extensive* and, I might add, *the most productive*, anti-submarine warfare operations since World War II."[158] In what sense was this operation "productive"? Naval destroyers had succeeded in locating and staying on top of Soviet submarines that came within 600 miles of the American mainland (that is, submarines close enough to launch missiles against the United States).[159] Moreover, according to standard "Hunter-Killer" procedures, the Navy had forced several Soviet submarines to surface.[160]

A third encounter pitted the Secretary of Defense's "no cities doctrine" (enunciated in his Ann Arbor speech of June 1962) against the alert procedures of the Strategic Air Command. According to the "no cities" doctrine, in the case of a nuclear war, the United States intended to launch weapons in a controlled fashion at Soviet military forces, rather than spasmodically destroying Soviet population and cities. Such an attack, it was hoped, would encourage the Soviet Union to attack only American military centers, since additional U.S. capability would deter Soviet counter-population attacks. Nevertheless, on Monday, October 22, Strategic Air Commander General Thomas S. Power dispersed his B-47 bombers, loaded with nuclear bombs, to forty civilian airports across the country.[161] The "no cities" doctrine was laid to rest. So "programmed" was SAC's dispersal of bombers that B-47s moved to civilian airports in the southeastern United States — within the range of the operational MRBMs in Cuba.

Informal sources provided the President with information concerning another frustration. On an earlier flight to Palm Beach, he had noted American fighters "lined up wing to wing," an easy target for an attacker.[162] After returning to Washington, he directed civil defense authorities to see that the aircraft were dispersed. Thus, at the ExCom meeting on Tuesday, October 23, when the Air Force reported that "the Russians and Cubans had inexplicably lined up their planes wing tip to wing tip, making them perfect targets," the President immediately raised a question. Had our airplanes been dispersed?[163] The Air Force representatives insisted that the planes had not been "wing to wing" and they were now well dispersed. Without informing the Florida bases, the President ordered independent aerial photographs of the area, and these revealed, to the embarrassment of some, that our aircraft were indeed still highly concentrated.[164]

Established, rather boring, organizational routines determined hundreds of additional, seemingly unimportant details — any one of which might have served as a fuse for disaster. Consequently, each provided a source of potential friction between leaders and organizations. Here, one instance must stand as a symbol for the rest. During the second week of the crisis, a member of the ExCom discovered, largely by accident, that a U.S. intelligence ship was carrying out its mission "very close to the coast of Cuba."[165] A Presidential order sufficed to have it moved considerably further out to sea. This incident took five minutes of the ExCom's time. For several years after the crisis, this fact seemed so trivial that it escaped note by accounts and analyses. But the procedures of that intelligence ship were not unlike those of the two now-famous U.S. intelligence ships: the *Liberty* (attacked by Israel during the 1967 Israeli-Arab war) and the *Pueblo* (captured by North Korea in 1967 when operating close to the shores of North Korea). In the aftermath of these incidents, it is less difficult to appreciate the potential significance of that detail.

Saturday, October 27, was the blackest and most frustrating day of the crisis. That morning the ExCom convened at 10 o'clock to draft a reply to Khrushchev's secret Friday letter. But at 10:17 A.M., "the news tickers cleared the first bulletin of a new note from Khrushchev then being broadcast by Radio Moscow."[166] The Soviets had reversed the position of the Friday letter. American missiles in Turkey would have to be withdrawn in exchange for Soviet withdrawal of Cuban missiles. The President winced: the assurances given to him the day before by State Department Soviet specialists about the strong Soviet signal had evaporated. Before the ticker stopped, a second bombshell landed. The ExCom was informed that at about 10:15 A.M. an American U-2 had been downed over Cuba by a Soviet SAM.[167] Soviet SAMs were now operational, and they had been used. On the previous Tuesday the ExCom had discussed what would be done if a U-2 were shot down and decided that the United States would retaliate with a strike against a single SAM site.[168] But now that the time had come to implement that decision, killing Russians in the process, and possibly leading to war, the President reconsidered. Perhaps, he suggested, he might "wait one more day — for more information on what happened to our planes and for Khrushchev's final negotiating position."[169] Robert Kennedy asked for absolute verification that the plane had been shot down by a Soviet SAM. Another member of the ExCom recalled that the Air Force might have taken the Tuesday decision as authorization to proceed with the retaliation. A series of rapid calls just managed to intercept Air Force implementation of what it had taken to be "orders" — but not without strenuous objections. Word was received that two low-level reconnaissance planes had drawn fire; the President ordered these flights halted and canceled the flare-drop flight scheduled for that night because of the danger that the flares might be taken for air-to-ground fire from planes.[170] At this point, some members of the Air Force began murmuring about an American "fold-in."

In this context, on Saturday afternoon, an incident stranger than "Strangelove" occurred.[171] A U-2 reported to be "on a routine air-sampling mission," picked the wrong star for its return and was over the Soviet Union.[172] The U-2 pilot had issued an open radio signal for help. Soviet fighters had scrambled. American fighters were attempting to rendezvous with the U-2 to escort it home. The President listened painfully as Roger Hilsman related these facts, but then broke the unbearable tension with an ironic laugh, "There is always some son-of-a-bitch who doesn't get the word." Perplexed as he awaited the outcome, the President considered the incredible implications of this unauthorized act. Why should the Soviet Union not regard this as last-minute reconnaissance in preparation for a nuclear attack? As Khrushchev himself asked in his letter announcing withdrawal of the missiles:

> One of your reconnaissance planes intruded over Soviet borders in the Chukotka Peninsula area.... The question is, Mr. President: How should we regard this? What is this, a provocation? One of your planes violates our frontier during this anxious time we are both experiencing, when everything has been put into combat readiness. Is it not a fact that an intruding American plane could be easily taken for a nuclear bomber, which might push us to a fateful step; and all the more so since the U.S. Government and Pentagon long ago declared that you are maintaining a continous nuclear bomber patrol?[173]

Were the organizations on top of which the President was trying to sit going to drag the country over the nuclear cliff in spite of all his efforts?

This query led to the final and most revealing frustration of the crisis. Saturday morning as the implications of the second Soviet letter were discussed, Kennedy boiled with anger. He distinctly recalled having ordered the removal of the Jupiters from Turkey. He had raised the question in a National Security Council meeting in early 1961.[174] The Joint Congressional Committee on Atomic Energy had recommended the removal of all Jupiters from both Italy and Turkey.[175] In early 1962 an administration study had concluded that the missiles were worthless and should be withdrawn.[176] Dean Rusk had been assigned to raise this issue with the Turkish and Italian foreign ministers during the NATO meetings at Oslo in May 1962,[177] but when Turkish Foreign Minister Selin Samper resisted, the matter was dropped. Frustrated at this inaction, Kennedy had

resorted to the most binding mechanism in the U.S. government
for registering decisions on matters of national security — a
National Security Council Action Memorandum (NASAM). In
the third week of August 1962, a NASAM ordered removal of
the missiles, and he personally directed George Ball (in Rusk's
absence) to pay the political price and remove the missiles.[178]
Ball discussed the matter with the Turkish Ambassador in
Washington and received a warning that the removal of the
missiles would have most harmful effects on Turkish public
opinion. So nothing happened. The Jupiters were still in Turkey,
now a principal target for the Soviets, if they should respond to
an American attack on Soviet missiles in Cuba. The Saturday
letter demanding a trade would legitimate, in the eyes of the
world, the Soviet Union's strike against Turkish missiles if the
United States struck Cuban missiles first. Was he, the President
of the United States, in charge of this incredible machine called
the U.S. government or not? At the Saturday afternoon meeting
as his frustration swelled, the President could control his anger
no longer. "Get those frigging missiles off the board!" he reportedly shouted.

The President thus decided to withdraw American missiles
from Turkey in order to remove the target that the Soviet Union
could legitimately strike when the United States performed the
hard actions that would have to be chosen on Sunday.[179] A
response to the letters of Friday and Saturday was drafted and
dispatched. That reply demanded Soviet withdrawal of Cuban
missiles and promised an American guarantee against invasion
of Cuba in return, without mentioning the Turkish missiles. But
the mood of the ExCom was dark. Some of the political leaders
understood Kennedy's frustration and accepted his order that
the Turkish missiles be removed as the only way of dealing with
the organizations constituting the U.S. government in this next
and hardest phase of the crisis. To a number of others, particularly the military who were present or who learned of the decision as the meeting was debriefed by staffs in the Pentagon and
elsewhere, the point was clear: the President had cracked and
folded.

The Turkish missiles had "stickability." This time, as in
the two previous cases, the President's order could not remove
the missiles instantly. Rather, it moved men in the Pentagon to
begin examining the technical requirements for defusing the
missiles, weighing the implications of this action for our NATO

allies, drafting cables, and so forth. Given sufficient time, the President would almost certainly have had his way (though initial development suggested that the missiles would not have been withdrawn either as quickly or as smoothly as he desired). But before the grinding of the machinery in Washington had led to actual defusing and withdrawal of missiles in Turkey, the operation was overtaken by events. On Sunday morning, October 28, the Soviet leaders announced that they were withdrawing their missiles in Cuba, without reference to the Turkish missiles.

5

Model III: Governmental Politics

Model II's grasp of government action as organizational output, partially coordinated by a unified group of leaders, balances the classical model's efforts to understand government behavior as choices of a unitary decisionmaker. But the fascination of Model II analysis should not be allowed to blur a further level of investigation. The "leaders" who sit on top of organizations are not a monolithic group. Rather, each individual in this group is, in his own right, a player in a central, competitive game. The name of the game is politics: bargaining along regularized circuits among players positioned hierarchically within the government. Government behavior can thus be understood according to a third conceptual model, not as organizational outputs but as results of these bargaining games. In contrast with Model I, the Governmental (or Bureaucratic) Politics Model sees no unitary actor but rather many actors as players — players who focus not on a single strategic issue but on many diverse intra-national problems as well; players who act in terms of no consistent set of strategic objectives but rather according to various conceptions of national, organizational, and personal goals; players who make government decisions not by a single, rational choice but by the pulling and hauling that is politics.

The apparatus of each national government constitutes a complex arena for the intra-national game. Political leaders at the top of the apparatus are joined by the men who occupy positions on top of major organizations to form a circle of central players. Those who join the circle come with some independent standing. Because the spectrum of foreign policy problems faced by a government is so broad, decisions have to be decentralized — giving each player considerable baronial discretion.

The nature of foreign policy problems permits fundamental disagreement among reasonable men about how to solve them. Analyses yield conflicting recommendations. Separate responsibilities laid on the shoulders of distinct individuals encourage differences in what each sees and judges to be important. But the nation's actions really matter. A wrong choice could mean irreparable damage. Thus responsible men are obliged to fight for what they are convinced is right.

Men share power. Men differ about what must be done. The differences matter. This milieu necessitates that government decisions and actions result from a political process. In this process, sometimes one group committed to a course of action triumphs over other groups fighting for other alternatives. Equally often, however, different groups pulling in different directions produce a result, or better a resultant — a mixture of conflicting preferences and unequal power of various individuals — distinct from what any person or group intended. In both cases, what moves the chess pieces is not simply the reasons that support a course of action, or the routines of organizations that enact an alternative, but the power and skill of proponents and opponents of the action in question.

This characterization captures the thrust of the bureaucratic politics orientation. If problems of foreign policy arose as discrete issues, and decisions were determined one game at a time, this account would suffice. But most "issues" — e.g., Viet Nam, or the proliferation of nuclear weapons — emerge piecemeal over time, one lump in one context, a second in another. Hundreds of issues compete for players' attention every day. Each player is forced to fix upon his issues for that day, deal with them on their own terms, and rush on to the next. Thus the character of emerging issues and the pace at which the game is played converge to yield government "decisions" and "actions" as collages. Choices by one player (e.g., to authorize action by his department, to make a speech, or to refrain from acquiring certain information), resultants of minor games (e.g., the wording of a cable or the decision on departmental action worked out among lower-level players), resultants of central games (e.g., decisions, actions, and speeches bargained out among central players), and "foul-ups" (e.g., choices that are not made because they are not recognized or are raised too late, misunderstandings, etc.) — these pieces, when stuck to the same canvas, constitute government behavior relevant to an issue. To explain why a particular formal governmental decision was made, or why one pattern of governmental behavior emerged, it is necessary to identify the games and players, to display the coalitions, bargains, and compromises, and to convey some feel for the confusion.

This conception of national security policy as political resultant contradicts both public imagery and academic orthodoxy. Issues vital to national security are considered too important to be settled by political games. They must be "above" politics: to accuse someone of "playing politics with national security" is a most serious charge. Thus, memoirs typically handle the details of such bargaining with a velvet glove. For example, both Sorensen and Schlesinger present the efforts of the ExCom in the Cuban missile crisis as essentially rational deliberation among a unified group of equals. What public expectation demands, the academic penchant for intellectual elegance reinforces. Internal politics is messy; moreover, according to prevailing doctrine, politicking lacks intellectual substance. It constitutes gossip for journalists rather than a subject for serious investigation. Occasional memoirs, anecdotes in historical accounts, and several detailed case studies to the contrary, most of the foreign policy literature avoids bureaucratic politics.

The gap between academic literature and the experience of participants in government is nowhere wider than at this point. For those who participate in government the terms of daily employment cannot be ignored: government leaders have competitive, not homogeneous interests; priorities and perceptions are shaped by positions; problems are much more varied than straightforward strategic issues; management of piecemeal streams of decisions is more important than steady-state choices; making sure that the government does what is decided is more difficult than selecting the preferred solution.* As the

---

*The tendency of participants in American government to understand these facts when thinking about an issue within the U.S. government, but to downgrade them and rely instead on Model I concepts and logic when thinking about other national governments, is well illustrated by an anecdote told by Henry S. Rowen. Shortly after taking a job in the U.S. government, Rowen attended a meeting of twelve representatives from different agencies on the

first Secretary of Defense, James Forrestal, once observed: "I have always been amused by those who say they are quite willing to go into government but they are not willing to go into politics. My answer . . . is that you can no more divorce government from politics than you can separate sex from creation."[1]

A small but increasing number of analysts have begun to examine the effect of these conditions on government actions. The first section of this chapter examines the work of several of these analysts, thus providing a foundation for a Governmental Politics Model. Unfortunately, the interests of these analysts have not led them to invest much labor in squeezing their insights into propositions. Consequently, the paradigm stated in the section beginning on page 162 can be no more than a tentative formalization. The application of the paradigm to several policy problems examined in preceding theoretical chapters is illustrated in the final section of this chapter.

The Governmental Politics Model Illustrated

Analyses of a Model III variety have attracted increasing attention since 1960. That year marked the publication of *Presidential Power* by Richard E. Neustadt and the legitimation of the political analysis of the Presidency that it embodied.[2] While attempts to analyze governmental action as the result of politics had been made earlier, Neustadt's work stands as the most forceful and subtle. President-elect Kennedy's enthusiastic recommendation of the book to inquiring columnists and his appointment of Neustadt as a principal transition adviser put the study on the required reading list among activists jockeying for a position in the new administration, journalists, and analysts interested in understanding the American Presidency. (Kennedy claimed afterward to be the best publicity agent a political scientist ever had.)

---

problem of desalination in the Middle East. After more than an hour of discussion of U.S. policy, no one was in doubt about the fact that each of the representatives favored a policy that conflicted sharply with the policies of the others. Moreover, several of the agencies were carrying out directly contradictory courses of action. But when the group turned to the next item on the agenda, everyone proceeded to talk about "the Israeli policy on desalination" as if a consistent course of action had been chosen by a single rational individual in the light of broad national goals.

The style of Neustadt's analysis reflects his experience in government, especially on Truman's White House staff. The conceptual model implicit in his thinking is thus most easily identified by characteristic phrases:

> The constitutional convention of 1787 is supposed to have created a government of "separated powers." It did nothing of the sort. Rather, it created a government of *separated institutions sharing powers.*[3]

Because participants in the government have independent bases, power (i.e., effective influence on outcomes) is shared. Constitutional prescription, political tradition, governmental practice, and democratic theory all converge to accentuate differences among needs and interests of individuals in the government, and to divide influence among them. Each participant sits in a seat that confers separate responsibilities. Each man is committed to fulfilling his responsibilities as he sees them. Thus those who share with the President the job of governance cannot be entirely responsive to his command. What the President wants will rarely seem a trifle to the men from whom he wants it. Besides, they are bound to judge his preferences in the light of their own responsibilities, not his.

> Presidential power is the *power to persuade.*[4]

> Underneath our images of Presidents-in-boots, astride decisions, are the half-observed realities of *Presidents-in-sneakers*, stirrups in hand, trying to induce particular department heads, or Congressmen or Senators, to climb aboard.[5]

In status and formal powers the President is chief. Every other participant's business somehow involves him. But his authority guarantees only an extensive clerkship. If the President is to rule, he must squeeze from these formal powers a full array of bargaining advantages. Bolstered by his "professional reputation" and "public prestige," the President can use these advantages to translate the needs and fears of other participants into an appreciation that what he wants of them is what they should do in their own best interest. His bargaining advantages are rarely sufficient to assure enactment of his will, but they are his only means of ensuring an impact on governmental action.

> They [the participants] bargain not at random but *according to the processes,* conforming to the prerequisites, responsive to the pressures of their own political system.[6]

The game of Presidential persuasion is not played at random. Rather, certain processes structure the play. Processes are regularized channels for bringing issues to the point of choice. Presidential attention becomes fixed, and bargaining earnest, only as issues are rendered actionable by moving along lines of process toward deadlines.

> Not action as an outcome but his [the President's] *impact on the outcome* is the measure of the man.[7]

> The things a President must think about if he would build his influence are not unlike those bearing on the *viability of public policy*. . . . A President who sees his power stakes sees something very much like the ingredients that make for viability in policy.[8]

The focus of Neustadt's attention is not action as the result of a bargaining game but rather Presidential *choice*. To understand policy, one must peek over the President's shoulder. What *can* be done is best understood by looking over the shoulder of the President-in-boots. What *is* done can best be understood by examining the skill of the President-in-sneakers as he probes the demands, the risks, and the threats to his own personal influence; as he persuades, cajoles, and spurs other members of the government to act accordingly.

> Each [government] is a more or less complex arena for internal bargaining among the bureaucratic elements and political personalities who collectively comprise its working apparatus. Its action is the product of their interaction. . . . *Relationships between allies are something like relationships between two great American departments.*[9]

Applied to relations between nations, this model directs attention to intra-national games, the overlap of which constitutes international relations.

The palace perspective that gives *Presidential Power* its sharp focus attempts to elucidate policy as the result of Presidential politics. Neustadt's later works move in the direction of an analysis of policy as the result of political bargaining in which other actors as well as the President are important players.[10] Nevertheless, he does not shed his commitment to a king's-eye view that leads him to picture policy as the crystallization of Presidential choice, action as the consequence of Presidential authorization, and activity by other players as a means of widening — or failing to widen — Presidential options.

Unfortunately, what is reputed to be the finest existing study of a crisis in international relations, Neustadt's "Skybolt Report," is not available in a public version.[11] His analytic style is clear, however, in his case study of President Truman's failure to stop American troops at the "narrow waist" in their advance up the Korean peninsula.[12] The United States entered the war with the explicit, limited intention of repelling the North Korean attack. The American-drafted U.N. Resolution of June 27, 1950, recommended only "such assistance to the Republic of Korea as may be necessary to repel the armed attack and restore international peace and security in the area."[13] By June 1951, the United States had repulsed the nearly disastrous Chinese attack and was pursuing the retreating army northward.* But in this second march up the Korean peninsula, American troops halted at the 38th parallel — dismissing the territory between that line and the waist as "real estate." Why then — in the face of the probability of Chinese entry into the war — had American troops advanced across the 38th parallel, across the waist, and toward the Chinese border in November 1950? Neustadt's answer to the question focuses on the President's failure to perceive the risks to his own personal power, risks that endangered his prestige with the public outside Washington.

Truman's behavior permits no doubt about his priorities. His *Memoirs* paraphrase the National Security Council minutes of June 29, 1950:

> I stated categorically that . . . I wanted to take every step necessary to push the North Koreans back behind the 38th Parallel. But I wanted to be sure that we did not become so deeply committed in Korea that we could not stop to take care of other situations as might develop. . . . I wanted it clearly understood that our operations were designed to restore peace there and to restore the border.[14]

There were many things he wanted more than unification of Korea. As Neustadt records:

> He wanted to affirm that the UN was not a League of Nations, that aggression would be met with counter-force, that "police

---

*A historical reminder: the United States entered the Korean War in June 1950, and marched northward, approaching the Chinese border by November 1950. In the last week of November, a Chinese Communist offensive began and drove MacArthur back down the peninsula. By late January 1951, U.S. troops were again on the offensive. In July 1951, truce talks began.

actions" were well worth the cost, that the "lesson of the 1930's" had been learned. He wanted to avoid "the wrong war, in the wrong place, at the wrong time," as General Bradley put it — and any "War," if possible. He wanted NATO strengthened fast, both militarily and psychologically. He wanted the United States rearmed without inflation, and prepared, thereafter, to sustain a level of expenditure for military forces and for foreign aid far higher than had seemed achievable before Korea. He also wanted to get on with the Fair Deal, keeping Democrats in office, strengthen his congressional support from North and West, and calm the waters stirred by men like Senator McCarthy.[15]

These priorities make all the more tragic his failure to halt American troops along a line at which the Chinese attack might have been avoided or repelled.

Neustadt traces the elements of the tragedy. In August 1950, when plans for the Inchon landing were approved, Truman might have publicly nailed down the aims stated in June — namely, restoration of South Korean borders. Crossing into North Korea in September 1950 might have been justified on grounds other than unification. In October 1950 the target of a "better line of defense" at the waist might have been proclaimed. But the crux of the puzzle arises in the days between November 9 and the Chinese attack on November 28.

By late October, as U.S. troops marched up North Korea toward the Chinese border, the Chinese presence in Korea was confirmed. In the first week of November, MacArthur insisted upon bombing Yalu bridges because troops "pouring" South threatened "ultimate destruction of U.N. forces."[16] Before November 10 the following facts were accepted: military action with existing forces could not achieve the military target — namely destruction of enemy forces; no more troops could be spared for MacArthur; negotiation with the Chinese would be necessary. "As Truman's *Memoirs* show, the policy dilemma was implicitly *accepted* by all parties to a National Security Council discussion on November 9."[17] The occupation of North Korea could not follow from military action alone. Either it would have to be given up entirely or it would follow from negotiation with the Chinese Communists. Yet the November 9 meeting ended with a decision that MacArthur's directives should be "kept under review" pending State Department efforts at clarification of Peking intentions and the possibilities of negotiation.[18] In accepting this decision, Truman was simply postponing a change of MacArthur's orders, "yet this postponement of decision proved to be one of the most decisive actions Truman ever took."[19] For this delay made MacArthur — the general whose personal views so differed from those of his commander-in-chief that Truman had considered firing him in August, who had the prestige of a general gathering victories, the pressures of a military man rushing to achieve his objectives before the politicians took over, who was pursuing his objectives with the discretion of earlier orders — "the judge and arbiter of White House risks."[20]

Why did no one try to alter MacArthur's orders in the two weeks that followed? Pentagon analysts were convinced by mid-November that Chinese soldiers were massing South of the Yalu. Bradley, the Chairman of the Joint Chiefs of Staff; Marshall, the Secretary of Defense; and Acheson, the Secretary of State — each expressed intense concern about MacArthur's failure to concentrate his forces. The British kept urging a pullback to the waist. The Chiefs of Staff implored caution on MacArthur's part. He demurred; they did not override him. Why did no one go to the President and recommend that the postponement of a change of orders now be rescinded? Neustadt's answer is simple enough: "Everyone thought someone else should go."[21] The details of his answer are best captured in his own words.

> Before November 25 the men who had concluded two weeks earlier that Truman should not change MacArthur's orders were agreed, it seems, in wishing that he would. The diplomatic emphasis of earlier discussion ceased to obscure military risks; when those grew sharp enough, it reinforced them. The logic of November 9 led to an opposite conclusion some days later, in the light of what these men had come to fear. On November 9 the Chairman of the Joint Chiefs, Bradley, had waived military risks in deference to foreign policy . . . but policy had not envisaged tactical disaster; policy suggested its avoidance at all costs. When worry grew, the military chiefs deferred to State; let Acheson, as guardian of "policy," ask Truman to reverse MacArthur. But Acheson, already under fire from the Capitol, was treading warily between the Pentagon and that inveterate idealist about generals, Harry Truman. In immediate terms the risk was "military"; if it justified reversing the commander in the field, then the Joint Chiefs must make the judgment and tell Truman. So Acheson is said to have insisted, understandably enough, and there the matter rested. On a "military" issue the Chiefs of Staff were loath to balk the victor of Inchon, whose tactics might be better than they seemed 8000

miles away. As for the Secretary of Defense, he had preceded Acheson in State and had been Army Chief of Staff when Bradley was a subordinate commander. Since his return to government Marshall had leaned over backwards not to meddle with the work of his successors in *their* jobs. He had also leaned over backwards not to revive the old Army feud between him and MacArthur. What Acheson and Bradley were not ready to initiate, Marshall evidently felt he could not take upon himself.[22]

What is the moral of the story? Agreement on what must be done about "the issue" does not suffice to guarantee action. Differences in roles, responsibilities, perceptions, and priorities among players focusing on slightly different faces of a complex issue permitted each player to expect that someone else would do what was required. Natural reticence, i.e., hesitant silence and only partially intended soft-spokenness, among players and between each player and the President combined with a moderate portion of misperception and confusion to allow inaction in a case where the substantive recommendation was not in dispute. Characteristically, Neustadt's understatement leaves the lesson to the reader: if here, then elsewhere how much more?

A second, more explicitly theoretical source of the bureaucratic politics analyses of the 1960s flows from the works of Gabriel A. Almond and Charles E. Lindblom. Almond's *American People and Foreign Policy,* published in 1950, formulates a set of concepts and terms for analyzing American foreign policy as the result of pluralist politics.[23] An outer circle of participants is composed of the "general public," a group normally ignorant of and indifferent to foreign policy matters, unless aroused about some highly visible issue. The "attentive public" sits one ring closer to the center, is informed and interested in foreign policy problems, and provides the audience for discussion among the elites. Center stage is surrounded by the "policy and opinion elites" who give structure to the public discussion and open avenues of access to the various groupings. Finally, the "official policy leadership" are the actors. The elite structure is characterized by a large number of autonomous and competing groups: autonomous, since power is widely dispersed among participants and drawn from a variety of independent sources; competing, since participants differ about both ends and means; and groups, since only by coordination can individuals assemble sufficient power to achieve their proposals. Almond's terminology thus represents the application of a pluralist model to foreign policy decisions.[24]

The mechanism of decentralized coordination has provided the focus of Charles Lindblom's work. From his "Bargaining: The Hidden Hand in Government," through his most famous article, "The Science of Muddling Through," to his books *The Intelligence of Democracy* and *The Policy-Making Process,* Lindblom has explored the character of bargaining and expounded the virtues of incremental muddling as opposed to comprehensive choice as the mode of policy making.[25] Attacking a variant of what we have termed Model I, Lindblom develops an alternative. His alternative, which he labels "successive limited comparisons," is spelled out in terms of a series of contrasts with the characteristics of the rational model:[26]

1. The selection of values and goals is not distinct from empirical analysis of alternative actions for achieving the goals; rather the two processes are intermingled.

2. Since ends and means are not distinct, means-ends analysis is often inappropriate or limited.

3. The test of a "good" policy is typically that various analysts find themselves directly agreeing on a policy (without agreeing that it is the most appropriate means to an end).

4. Analysis is drastically limited. Important policy outcomes are neglected. Important alternative policies are neglected. Important affected values are neglected.

5. By proceeding incrementally and comparing the results of each new policy with the old, actors reduce or eliminate reliance on theory.

The more recent literature of bureaucratic politics includes both attempts at explicit characterization of this framework and case studies from this perspective. The convergence of government experience (Neustadt) and theoretical formulation (Almond and Lindblom) is clearest in Warner Schilling's study, "The Politics of National Defense: Fiscal 1950."[27] Schilling opts for a bureaucratic politics framework explicitly at the outset when outlining his concept of budgeting as a political process. The process is characterized by (1) problems that have no right answer: "There is no determinant answer to the question of how much to spend for defense"; (2) participants whose policy differences stem from both intellectual and institutional differences; (3) processes that distribute power and advantages differentially among participants; (4) a "strain towards agreement" that encourages compromise and consensus; and (5) outcomes that result from conflict, coalition, and bargaining.[28] Schilling claims that, as a result of this process, American foreign policy often exhibits a variety of symptoms that constitute a policy syndrome: (1) "no policy at all"; (2) "compromised policy"; (3) "paper policy"; (4) "blind policy"; (5) "slow policy"; (6) "leaderless policy"; and (7) "gyroscopic policy."[29]

Using this framework, Schilling analyzes the fiscal 1950 budget, first describing the political process through which that budget was determined and then examining the relationship between that process and the content of the budget. The budgetary process involved round-robin bargaining with Secretary of Defense Forrestal as the pivot. Truman and James Webb (Director of the Bureau of the Budget) fixed a $14.4 billion ceiling for defense spending. What the Pentagon judged as necessary for the national defense could not be bought for this amount. Forrestal's initial ploy was to approach the Joint Chiefs of Staff with a proposition: they would meet the $14.4 billion ceiling with an unbalanced force posture, i.e., one that satisfied strategic bombing requirements but left the Navy and Army bare. Truman and Webb would then see the holes in the military forces, particularly the limited war capabilities, and raise the ceiling. The Army and Navy chiefs were unwilling to risk their hides on such a gamble. So Forrestal approached Secretary of State Marshall. But Marshall's first concern was Europe, and prudence required that he "save the leverage he possessed on the President's budget for protection and advancement of his own claims on Federal revenue."[30] Alone, Forrestal went to the President, but Truman's mind was elsewhere. He seems to have believed his economic experts' assurances that a defense budget of more than $15 billion would mean "national bankruptcy." Silencing the Joint Chiefs was the only military problem that captured his attention. Forrestal thus returned empty-handed to the Chiefs, reporting, "In the person of Harry Truman, I have seen the most rocklike example of civilian control that the world has ever witnessed."[31] Forrestal presented the budget to Congress — in terms that appeared "general and vacuous." JCS pleadings sounded to economy-minded Congressmen like evidence of "separatism" and the need for "reorganization." Not surprisingly, then, fiscal 1950 displays the features of Schilling's "syndrome."[32]

The Common Defense by Samuel P. Huntington analyzes U.S. defense policies and force postures from the end of the Second World War to 1960 in terms of another variant of a governmental politics model.[33] Huntington focuses specifically on one segment of military policy — namely, "decisions on the overall size of the military effort, force levels, and weapons."[34] These decisions are explained not as the product of expert planning but rather as the "result of controversy, negotiations, and bargaining among officials and groups with different interests and perspectives."[35] His distinction between *"executive"* and *"legislative"* processes symbolizes this contrast. A policymaking process is executive to the extent that: "(1) the participating units differ in power (i.e., are hierarchically arranged); (2) fundamental goals and values are not at issue; and (3) the range of possible choice is limited."[36] In contrast, a policymaking process is legislative to the extent that: "(1) the units participating in the process are relatively equal in power (and consequently must bargain with each other); (2) important disagreements exist concerning the goals of policy; and (3) there are many possible alternatives."[37]

According to Huntington during the period he examined, decisions about force levels and weapons were determined by a structured "legislative" process. The Joint Chiefs of Staff and the National Security Council — "the two most important committees in the executive branch of the national government" — served as the forum for balancing interests.[38] These committees produced three regular pieces of executive legislation on programs. First, National Security Council (NSC) papers, especially the annual NSC paper, contained "a broad outline of the aims of U.S. national strategy and a more detailed discussion of the military, political, economic, and domestic elements to support the overall national strategy."[39] Second, the Joint Chiefs of Staff counterpart to the NSC annual policy paper, the Joint Strategic Objectives Plan (JSOP), "estimates the military requirements for cold, limited, or general war, and includes a determination of the military forces together with their disposition and employment necessary to implement the military strategy derived from the 'Basic National Security Policy.' "[40] The third document, the annual formulation of force requirements, was then drawn up by the military Chiefs on the basis of the NSC and JCS papers. When approved by the administration, this document served as the guidelines for the appropriations and expenditures required by military services in the executive budget. This legislative process exemplified the traditional tactics of congressional legislation: (1) "avoiding controversial issues, delaying decisions on them, referring them to other bodies for resolution";[41] (2) "compromise and logrolling, that is, trading off subordinate interests for major interests";[42] (3) "expressing policies in vague generalities, representing the 'lowest common denominator' of agreement in which all can acquiesce";[43] (4) "basing policies upon assumptions which may or may not be realistic."[44]

Another example of recent analysis from this perspective is Roger Hilsman's *To Move a Nation* (published in 1967).[45] Before entering the government with the Kennedy administration, Hilsman had formulated a version of the Governmental Politics Model — one heavily influenced by the theoretical works of Almond, Lindblom, and Dahl.[46] The framework used in the analysis of the major foreign policy decisions of the Kennedy administration and formulated explicitly at the end of *To Move a Nation* has been refined both by his experience in the government and by the works of Schilling, Huntington, Neustadt, and Schelling.[47]

Following Almond, Hilsman conceives of the policymaking process as a series of concentric circles. The innermost circle contains the President and the men in the departments and agencies who must carry out foreign policy decisions. Beyond this core lie other departments of the executive branch, and other layers in the basic departments and agencies. Finally, there is the open arena of "attentive publics," which includes Congress, press, and interest groups. Policy is made primarily in the innermost circle. But whether in the inner sanctum or when involving second-ring and third-ring participants, policymaking is politics.[48] Decisionmaking as a political process exhibits three characteristics: (1) "a diversity of goals and values that must be reconciled before a decision can be reached";[49] (2) "the presence of competing clusters of people within the main group who are identified with each of the alternative goals and policies";[50] (3) "the relative power of these different groups of people included is as relevant to the final decision as the appeal of the goals they seek or the cogency and wisdom of their arguments."[51] Policymaking is therefore a process of "conflict and consensus building." The advocate of a particular policy must build a consensus to support his policy. Where there are rival advocates or rival policies, there is competition for support, and all the techniques of alliance appear — persuasion, accommodation, and bargaining.[52]

Hilsman's account of Kennedy's foreign policy is "a story of *battles*, battles over national policy."[53] "Given the difficulty of the problems, it was inevitable and even desirable that participants in these battles disagreed in their judgments. Given the importance of the stakes involved, it was entirely appropriate that they fought hard and passionately."[54] Thus leaks of secret material to the Congress or press, attempts to force the President to adopt the only right path, and outright falsification or deception, as well as the more conventional techniques of bargaining, are typically observed. On one occasion in 1963, several important decisions about Viet Nam were made at a National Security Council meeting.[55] After the meeting, Secretary of Defense Robert McNamara, the Chairman of the Joint Chiefs of Staff Maxwell Taylor, the President's Special Assistant McGeorge Bundy, Presidential Assistant Michael Forrestal, and Assistant Secretary of State Hilsman went to the Situation Room to draft a cable reflecting the decisions. The cable was finished before the group could see the President, so only Bundy, Forrestal, and Hilsman waited. When the three finally entered the President's office, Kennedy said: "And now we have the 'inner club.'" Bundy later explained to Hilsman what this meant:

> He meant that we had together the people who had known all along what we would do about the problem, and who had been pulling and hauling, debating and discussing for no other purpose than to keep the government together, to get all the others to come around.[56]

While Bundy's elaboration may exaggerate the extent to which the inner circle had known what the government would decide, it does define clearly the character of the activity both in the National Security Council and in the cable drafting. In this case, the President and his men played well and presumably achieved a decision resembling their preference.

Sometimes Neustadt's "President-in-sneakers" is the central political gamesman. Sometimes the President merely observes the pulling and hauling among various groups within the government. Sometimes the President is the target of the tactics of a bureaucratic group. Hilsman relates an instructive example from the Eisenhower administration.[57] In 1957, President Eisenhower appointed the Gaither Committee to study the major strategic issue of the day, American nuclear capability. When it became clear that the committee was going to be critical of the administration's posture, publication of the report was suppressed. Having lost this battle, the advocates of the committee's proposals regrouped for a second: whether there would be two or two hundred top secret copies of the report. This battle they won. In the same week that the President failed to accept the proposals recommended by the report, Chalmers Roberts of *The Washington Post* published an account covering two newspaper pages, containing an accurate and complete version both of the top secret report and of its recommendations.[58]

Finally, a growing number of case studies of decisions in foreign policy trace the bureaucratic politics of particular decisions, actions, and policies.[59] Paul Hammond has produced three of the most interesting studies. The first, "Directives for the Occupation of Germany," centers on the problem of drafting concrete orders for U.S. troops occupying Germany.[60] The chief economic issue for American occupying forces was whether to "de-industrialize" Germany. When Germany surrendered on May 7, 1945, this issue became urgent. On May 11, President Truman signed the major directive on German economic policy, JCS-1067, ordering the U.S. Supreme Commander, General Eisenhower, both to "prevent Germany from 'ever again' becoming a threat to the peace of the world" and to prevent "such civil unrest as would endanger the occupying forces."[61] The former clause was a slightly veiled reference to the Morgenthau Plan; the latter referred to the consequences that State and War Department planners predicted would follow if the Morgenthau Plan were implemented. The balance of politics within the administration prevented any clear guidelines and thus permitted American military commanders to settle the issue.

Hammond traces the sources of this stalemate: the competition and confusion of a small group of players including President Roosevelt, Secretary of the Treasury Morgenthau, Secretary of War Stimson, and Secretary of State Hull. The stage for this battle was set by Roosevelt's operating style — his tendency to guard his options until the end and his willingness to encourage the principal members of his government to get involved in an issue on the assumption that he agreed with their substantive recommendation. In a brilliant ploy at Montreal on September 15, 1944, Morgenthau won both Roosevelt's and Churchill's signatures to a document ordering the dismemberment of Germany, the destruction of all industry, and the creation of a pastoral dairyland. Over the eight months that followed, however, Morgenthau badly misperceived Roosevelt's retreat. Stimson used his influence with the President to weaken Roosevelt's commitment to Morgenthau's plan, which Stimson regarded as absurd, while taking advantage of his position as Secretary of War to hedge against it. Though the State Department had little influence, Hull and his deputies functioned centrally in the various drafting committees and there had some impact. In the end, Truman signed the compromised, somewhat contradictory directive, and the American military commands proceeded with a relatively free hand.

Hammond's second study, "Super Carriers and B-36 Bombers," contrasts the major strategic purchases of the late 1940s.[62] These decisions settled the issue of military capabilities for U.S. defense and foreign policy in the early 1950s. But for the participants, these decisions appeared in quite a different guise. The decision against supercarriers emerged from the battle among Denfeld and Radford for the Navy; Symington and Vandenberg for the Air Force; Johnson, the new Secretary of Defense; Webb, the Director of the Bureau of the Budget; and President Truman. For Denfeld and Radford, supercarriers represented the Navy's guarantee of survival, their ticket to the future. For Symington and Vandenberg, supercarriers posed a clear threat to the Air Force monopoly on atomic delivery capabilities. Secretary of Defense Johnson had been appointed on a platform of one billion dollars of economy in defense spending. Thus he took the issue of supercarriers to the Chiefs, where it was rejected two to one, whereupon he scrapped the program on the grounds of "professional military" advice. Webb and Truman accepted this instance of applied economizing with few regrets.

The decision to procure B-36 bombers reassembled the same cast with the addition of the House Armed Services Committee. Cancellation of the supercarriers caused Radford to fear for the life of the Navy. In retaliation, he mounted a fierce attack both on the B-36 itself and on the concept of strategic bombing. Suspicious of Johnson, Radford shifted the battleground to the House Armed Services Committee. This provided the forum for the "revolt of the admirals." Emphasizing superior preparation and exploiting dissent within naval ranks, Symington and Vandenberg turned the hearings to the advantage of the Air Force. Congressional appreciation of the merits of strategic bombing was simply reenforced, and the Air Force got its bombers.

Hammond's third case study, "NSC-68," traces the tangled pattern that produced the first comprehensive review of U.S. national security policy.[63] In 1949 Paul Nitze, head of the Policy Planning Staff in the State Department, became convinced the budgetary ceilings were severely limiting U.S. foreign policy. He decided to do something about it. The Policy Planning Staff circulated several studies of the relative economic capacities of the United States and the Soviet Union, as well as of problems of European defense, in an attempt to generate interest in a major reconsideration of national strategy. Sydney Souers, Executive Secretary of the National Security Council, bought the idea and prompted the National Security Council to order a general study. The reconsideration in which Nitze was interested, however, required a stronger mandate. The H-bomb decision provided the occasion to get that mandate. With the aid of Secretary of State Acheson and Chairman Lilienthal of the Atomic Energy Commission, Nitze managed to couple to the H-bomb decision a directive authorizing a joint State-Defense overall reassessment of strategic issues. Both were approved on January 30, 1950.

Nitze and the Policy Planning Staff guided the study by their willingness to "do the work." The benevolent presence and occasional intervention of Secretary Acheson on Nitze's behalf also enhanced his position. Secretary of Defense Johnson, leader of the economy drive, stood aloof from the study and hampered Department of Defense and Joint Chiefs of Staff participation. Nevertheless, before the study was completed in mid-March, General Landon (who had been assigned to the study by the JCS because of his commitment to existing budget levels) supported the recommendations. Landon guided the paper through the Pentagon, acquiring the signatures of all three service Secretaries and the Joint Chiefs. Outmaneuvered, Johnson was forced to join Acheson in recommending the paper to President Truman. On April 12, the President gave his tentative approval to the paper and referred it to the NSC for cost estimates. These estimates were being formulated when the eruption of the

Korean War made NSC-68 a blueprint for tripling the defense budget.

A Governmental (Bureaucratic) Politics Paradigm

Within the ballpark outlined by this rapid tour through the literature, a tentative governmental or bureaucratic politics paradigm can be formulated. The primary source of the paradigm is the model implicit in Neustadt's work, though his concentration on Presidential action has been generalized to a concern with action as a resultant of political bargaining among a number of independent players, the President being only a "superpower" among many lesser but considerable powers.⁶⁴ The paradigm takes seriously Schilling's contention that the substantive problems are so inordinately difficult that differences about goals, alternatives, and consequences are inevitable. Thus the process of conflict and consensus building described by Hilsman becomes crucial. Characterization of the techniques employed starts from Huntington's insight that the activity resembles bargaining in legislative assemblies, though his contention that the process is "legislative" overemphasizes participant equality as opposed to the hierarchy that structures the game.⁶⁵

I. *Basic Unit of Analysis: Governmental Action as Political Resultant.* The decisions and actions of governments are intranational political resultants: *resultants* in the sense that what happens is not chosen as a solution to a problem but rather results from compromise, conflict, and confusion of officials with diverse interests and unequal influence; *political* in the sense that the activity from which decisions and actions emerge is best characterized as bargaining along regularized channels among individual members of the government. Following Wittgenstein's employment of the concept of a "game," national behavior in international affairs can be conceived of as something that emerges from intricate and subtle, simultaneous, overlapping games among players located in positions in a government. The hierarchical arrangement of these players constitutes the government.* Games proceed neither at random nor at leisure.

---

*The theatrical metaphor of stage, roles, and actors is more common than this metaphor of games, positions, and players. Nevertheless, the rigidity connoted by the concept of "role" both in the theatrical

Regular channels structure the game; deadlines force issues to the attention of incredibly busy players. The moves, sequences of moves, and games of chess are thus to be explained in terms of the bargaining among players with separate and unequal power over particular pieces, and with separable objectives in distinguishable subgames.

In analyzing governmental actions — for example, U.S. government efforts to retard the spread of nuclear weapons — one must examine all official actions of the U.S. government that affect this outcome. U.S. government actions affecting the spread of nuclear weapons include the State Department's efforts to gain adherence to the Nonproliferation Treaty, Presidential offers of guarantees to non-nuclear nations against nuclear blackmail; Atomic Energy Commission (AEC) tests of nuclear explosives for peaceful purposes (that consequently provide a convenient shield for non-nuclear powers' development of nuclear devices); withdrawal of U.S. forces from the Far East (which may increase the concern of some Japanese and Indians about their national security); statements by the AEC about the great prospects for peaceful nuclear weapons (designed to influence AEC budgets); an AEC commissioner's argument, in the absence of any higher level decision, to a Brazilian scientist about the great virtues of peaceful nuclear explosives; and U.S. government refusal to confirm or deny the reported presence of nuclear weapons aboard ships calling in foreign ports. As this list suggests, it is important to recognize that governmental actions relevant to some issues are really an agglomeration or collage composed of relatively independent decisions and actions by individuals and groups of players

---

sense of actors reciting fixed lines and in the sociological sense of fixed responses to specified social situations makes the concept of games, positions, and players more useful for this analysis of active participants in the determination of national foreign policy. Objections to the terminology on the grounds that "game" connotes nonserious play overlook the concept's application of most serious problems both in Wittgenstein's philosophy and in contemporary game theory. Game theory typically treats more precisely structured games, but Wittgenstein's examination of the "language game" wherein men use words to communicate is quite analogous to this analysis of the less specified game of bureaucratic politics. Wittgenstein's employment of this concept forms a central strand in his *Philosophical Investigations*. See also Thomas C. Schelling, "What Is Game Theory?" in James Charlesworth, *Contemporary Political Analysis*, New York, 1967.

in a broader game, as well as formal governmental decisions and actions that represent a combination of the preferences and relative influence of central players or subsets of players in more narrowly defined games. For purposes of analysis, it will often be useful to distinguish among: (1) governmental actions that are really agglomerations of relatively independent decisions and actions by individuals and groups of players, (2) *formal* governmental decisions or actions that represent a combination of the preferences and relative influence of *central* players in the game, (3) formal governmental decisions and actions that represent a combination of the preferences and relative influence of a special *subset* of players in the game.

II. *Organizing Concepts.* The organizing concepts of this paradigm can be arranged as strands in the answers to four interrelated questions: Who plays? What determines each player's stand? What determines each player's relative influence? How does the game combine players' stands, influence, and moves to yield governmental decisions and actions?

A. Who plays? That is, whose interests and actions have an important effect on the government's decisions and actions?

1. *Players in Positions.* The governmental actor is neither a unitary agent nor a conglomerate of organizations, but rather is a number of individual players. Groups of these players constitute the agent for particular government decisions and actions. Players are men in jobs.

Individuals become players in the national security policy game by occupying a position that is hooked on to the major channels for producing action on national security issues. For example, in the U.S. government the players include *Chiefs:* the President, the Secretaries of State, Defense, and Treasury, the Director of the CIA, the Joint Chiefs of Staff, and, since 1961, the Special Assistant for National Security Affairs;[66] *Staffers:* the immediate staff of each Chief; *Indians:* the political appointees and permanent government officials within each of the departments and agencies; and *Ad Hoc Players:*

actors in the wider government game (especially "Congressional Influentials"), members of the press, spokesmen for important interest groups (especially the "bipartisan foreign policy establishment" in and out of Congress), and surrogates for each of these groups. Other members of the Congress, press, interest groups, and public form concentric circles around the central arena — circles that demarcate limits within which the game is played.*

Positions define what players both may and must do. The advantages and handicaps with which each player can enter and play in various games stem from his position. So does a cluster of obligations for the performance of certain tasks. The two sides of this coin are illustrated by the position of the modern Secretary of State. First, in form and usually in fact, he is a senior personal adviser to the President on the political-military issues that are the stuff of contemporary foreign policy. Second, he is the colleague of the President's other senior advisers on problems of foreign policy, the Secretaries of Defense and Treasury, and the Special Assistant for National Security Affairs. Third, he is the ranking U.S. diplomat in negotiations with foreign powers. Fourth, he serves as the primary representative of the administration's foreign policy in Congress. Fifth, he is an educator of the American public about critical issues of foreign affairs and a defender of the actions of the administration. Sixth, he serves as an administration voice to the outside world. Finally, he is Mr. State Department or Mr. Foreign Office, "leader of officials, spokesman for their causes, guardian of their interests, judge of their disputes, superintendent of their work, master of their careers."[67] But he is not first

---

*For some purposes, organizations and groups can be treated as players. In treating an organization or group as a player, it is important to note the differences among (1) summarizing the official papers that emerge from an organization as coherent calculated moves of a unitary actor; (2) treating the actions of the head of an organization, whose goals are determined largely by that organization, as actions of the organization; and (3) summarizing the various actions of different individual members of an organization as coherent strategies and tactics in a single plan.

one and then the other: all these obligations are his simultaneously. His performance in one affects his credit and power in the others. The perspective he gets from the daily work he must oversee — the cable traffic by which his department maintains relations with other foreign offices — conflicts with the President's requirement that he serve as a generalist and coordinator of contrasting perspectives. The necessity that he be close to the President restricts his ability to represent the interests of his department. When he defers to the Secretary of Defense rather than fighting for his department's position — as he often must — he strains the loyalty of his officialdom. In the words of one of his Indians: "Loyalty is hilly, and it has to go down if it is going to go up."[68] Thus he labors under the weight of conflicting responsibilities.

A Secretary of State's resolution of these conflicts depends not only upon the position, but also upon the player who occupies it. For players are also people; men's metabolisms differ. The hard core of the bureaucratic politics mix is personality. How each man manages to stand the heat in *his* kitchen, each player's basic operating style, and the complementarity or contradiction among personalities and styles in the inner circles are irreducible pieces of the policy blend. Then, too, each person comes to his position with baggage in tow. His bags include sensitivities to certain issues, commitments to various projects, and personal standing with and debts to groups in the society.

B. What determines each player's stand? What determines his perceptions and interests that lead to a stand?

    1. *Parochial Priorities and Perceptions.* Answers to the question "What is the issue?" are colored by the position from which the question is considered. Propensities inherent in positions do not facilitate unanimity in answering the question "What must be done?" The factors that encourage organizational parochialism also exert pressure upon the players who occupy positions on top of (or within) these organizations. To motivate members of his organization, a

player must be sensitive to the organization's orientation. The games into which the player can enter and the advantages with which he plays enhance these pressures. Thus propensities and priorities stemming from position are sufficient to allow analysts to make reliable predictions about a player's stand in many cases. But these propensities are filtered through the baggage that players bring to positions. Some knowledge of both the pressures and the baggage is thus required for sound predictions.

2. *Goals and Interests.* The goals and interests that affect players' desired outcomes include national security interests, organizational interests, domestic interests, and personal interests. Some national security objectives are widely accepted — for example, the interest in U.S. avoidance of foreign domination and the belief that if the United States were to unilaterally disarm other nations would use military force against it and its allies with serious adverse consequences. But, in most cases, reasonable men can disagree about how American national security interests will be affected by a specific issue. Thus other interests as well affect an individual's stand on an issue of national security or foreign policy. Members of an organization, particularly career officials, come to believe that the health of their organization is vital to the national interest. The health of the organization, in turn, is seen to depend on maintaining influence, fulfilling the mission of the organization, and securing the necessary capabilities. While many bureaucrats are unconcerned with domestic affairs and politics and do not ask themselves how a proposed change in policy or behavior would affect domestic political issues, the President and senior players will almost always be concerned about domestic implications. Finally, a player's stand depends on his personal interests and his conception of his role.

3. *Stakes and Stands.* Games are played to determine decisions and actions. But decisions and actions advance and impede each player's conception of the national interest, his organization's interests, specific programs to which he is commited, the welfare

of his friends, and his personal interests. These overlapping interests constitute the *stakes* for which
games are played. *Stakes* are an individual's interests
defined by the issue at hand. In the light of these
stakes, a player decides on his *stand* on the issue.

4. *Deadlines and Faces of Issues.*   "Solutions" to strategic problems are not found by detached analysts
focusing coolly on *the* problem. Instead, deadlines
and events raise issues and force busy players to take
stands. A number of established processes fix deadlines that demand action at appointed times. First,
in the national security arena, the budget, embassies'
demands for action-cables, requests for instructions
from military groups, and scheduled intelligence reports fix recurring deadlines for decision and action.
Second, major political speeches, especially Presidential speeches, force decisions. Third, crises necessitate decisions and actions. Because deadlines raise
issues in one context rather than in another, they
importantly affect the resolution of the issue.

When an issue arises, players typically come to
see quite different *faces of the issue.* For example,
a proposal to withdraw American troops from Europe
is to the Army a threat to its budget and size, to the
Budget Bureau a way to save money, to the Treasury
a balance-of-payments gain, to the State Department
Office of European Affairs a threat to good relations
with NATO, to the President's congressional adviser
an opportunity to remove a major irritant in the
President's relations with the Hill. (Chiefs, especially, tend to see several faces of the issue simultaneously.) But the face of the issue that each
player sees is not determined by his goals and interests alone. By raising an issue in one channel rather
than in another, deadlines affect the face an issue
wears.

C. What determines each player's impact on results?
1. *Power.*   Power (i.e., effective influence on government decisions and actions) is an elusive blend of at
least three elements: bargaining advantages, skill and
will in using bargaining advantages, and other players' perceptions of the first two ingredients. The

sources of bargaining advantages include formal authority and responsibility (stemming from positions); actual control over resources necessary to carry out action; expertise and control over information that enables one to define the problem, identify options, and estimate feasibilities; control over information that enables chiefs to determine whether and in what form decisions are being implemented; the ability to affect other players' objectives in other games, including domestic political games; personal persuasiveness with other players (drawn from personal relations, charisma); and access to and persuasiveness with players who have bargaining advantages drawn from the above (based on interpersonal relations, etc.). Power wisely invested yields an enhanced reputation for effectiveness. Unsuccessful investments deplete both the stock of capital and the reputation. Thus each player must pick the issues on which he can play with high probability of success.

D. What is the game? How are players' stands, influence, and moves combined to yield governmental decisions and actions?

1. *Action-channels.* Bargaining games are neither random nor haphazard. The individuals whose stands and moves count are the players whose positions hook them on to the action-channels. An action-channel is a regularized means of taking governmental action on a specific kind of issue. For example, one action-channel for producing U.S. military intervention in another country includes a recommendation by the ambassador to that country, an accessment by the regional military commander, a recommendation by the Joint Chiefs of Staff, an evaluation by the intelligence community of the consequences of intervention, a recommendation by the Secretaries of State and Defense, a Presidential decision to intervene, the transmittal of an order through the President to the Secretary of Defense and the JCS to the regional military commander, his determination of what troops to employ, the order from him to the commander of those troops, and orders from that commander to the individuals who actually move in-

to the country. Similarly, the budgetary action-channel includes the series of steps between the Budget Bureau's annual "call for estimates," through departmental, Presidential, and congressional review, to congressional appropriation, Presidential signature, Bureau of Budget apportionment, agency obligation, and ultimately expenditure.

Action-channels structure the game by preselecting the major players, determining their usual points of entrance into the game, and distributing particular advantages and disadvantages for each game. Most critically, channels determine "who's got the action" — that is, which department's Indians actually do whatever is decided upon.

Typically, issues are recognized and determined within an established channel for producing action. In the national security area, weapons procurement decisions are made within the annual budgeting process; embassies' demands for action-cables are answered according to routines of consultation and clearance from State to Defense and White House; requests for instructions from military groups (concerning assistance all the time, concerning operations during war) are composed by the military in consultation with the Office of the Secretary of Defense, the Secretary of State, and the White House; crises responses are debated among White House, State, Defense, CIA, Treasury, and ad hoc players.

2. *Rules of the Game.* The rules of the game stem from the Constitution, statutes, court interpretations, executive orders, conventions, and even culture. Some rules are explicit, others implicit. Some rules are quite clear, others fuzzy. Some are very stable; others are ever changing. But the collection of rules, in effect, defines the game. First, rules establish the positions, the paths by which men gain access to positions, the power of each position, the action-channels. Second, rules constrict the range of governmental decisions and actions that are acceptable. The Constitution declares certain forms of action out of bounds. In attempting to encourage a domestic industry — for example, the computer industry — to

take advantage of certain international opportunities, American players are restricted by antitrust laws to a much narrower set of actions than, for example, are players in Japan. Third, rules sanction moves of some kinds — bargaining, coalitions, persuasion, deceit, bluff, and threat — while making other moves illegal, immoral, ungentlemanly, or inappropriate.

3. *Action as Political Resultant.* Government decisions are made, and government actions are taken, neither as the simple choice of a unified group, nor as a formal summary of leaders' preferences. Rather, the context of shared power but separate judgments about important choices means that politics is the mechanism of choice. Each player pulls and hauls with the power at his discretion for outcomes that will advance his conception of national, organizational, group, and personal interests.*

Note the *environment* in which the game is played: inordinate uncertainty about what must be done, the necessity that something be done, and the crucial consequences of whatever is done. These features force responsible men to become active players. The *pace of the game* — hundreds of issues, numerous games, and multiple circuits — compels players to fight to "get others' attention," to make them "see the facts," to assure that they "take the time to think seriously about the broader issue." The *structure of the game* — power shared by individuals with separate responsibilities — validates each player's feeling that "others don't see my problem," and "others must be persuaded to look at the issue from a less parochial perspective." The *law of the game* — he who hesitates loses his chance to play at that point and he who is uncertain about his recommendation is overpowered by others who are sure —

*How each player ranks his interests as they are manifest as stakes at particular points in the game is a subtle, complex problem. In one sense, players seem to have gone through a Model I analysis. American culture tends to legitimize national interests and to render "political considerations" beyond the pale. This makes it difficult for many players to articulate, even to themselves, the priorities that their behavior suggests.

pressure players to come down on one side of a 51 to 49 issue and play. The *reward of the game* —effectiveness, i.e., impact on outcomes, as the immediate measure of performance — encourages hard play. Thus, most players come to fight to "make the government do what is right." The strategies and tactics employed are quite similar to those formalized by theorists of international relations.

Advocates fight for outcomes. But the game of politics does not consist simply of players pulling and hauling, each for his own chosen action, because the terms and conditions of players' employment are not identical. Chiefs and Indians are often advocates of particular actions. But staffers fight to find issues, state alternatives, and produce arguments for their Chiefs. Presidential staffers — ideally — struggle to catch issues and structure games so as to maximize both the President's appreciation of advocates' arguments and the impact of Presidential decision. Chiefs sometimes function as semi-staffers for the President. The President's costs and benefits often require that he decide as little as possible, keeping his options open (rather than coming down on one side of an uncertain issue and playing hard).

When a governmental or Presidential decision is reached, the larger game is not over. Decisions can be reversed or ignored. As Jonathan Daniels, an aide to Franklin Roosevelt, noted:

> Half of a President's suggestions, which theoretically carry the weight of orders, can be safely forgotten by a Cabinet member. And if the President asks about a suggestion a second time, he can be told that it is being investigated. If he asks a third time, a wise Cabinet officer will give him at least part of what he suggests. But only occasionally, except about the most important matters, do Presidents ever get around to asking three times.[69]

And even if not reversed or ignored, decisions still have to be implemented. Thus formal governmental decisions are usually only way-stations along the path to action. And the opportunity for slippage between decision and action is much larger than most analysts have recognized. For after a decision, the game expands, bringing in more players with more diverse preferences and more independent power.

Formal decisions may be very general or quite specific. In some cases, the players who reach a formal decision about some action that the government should take will have no choice about who will carry it out. But in other cases, there will be several subchannels leading from decision to action. For example, negotiations with foreign governments are usually the concern of the State Department but can be assigned to a special envoy or to the intelligence services. Where there are several subchannels, players will maneuver to get the action into the channel that they believe offers the best prospect for getting their desired results.

Most decisions leave considerable leeway in implementation. Players who supported the decision will maneuver to see it implemented and may go beyond the spirit if not the letter of the decision. Those who opposed the decision, or opposed the action, will maneuver to delay implementation, to limit implementation to the letter but not the spirit, and even to have the decision disobeyed.

III. *Dominant Inference Pattern.* If a nation performed an action, that action was the *resultant* of bargaining among individuals and groups within the government. Model III's explanatory power is achieved by displaying the game —the action-channel, the positions, the players, their preferences, and the pulling and hauling — that yielded, as a resultant, the action in question. Where an outcome was for the most part the triumph of an individual (e.g., the President) or group (e.g., the President's men or a cabal) this model attempts to specify the details of the game that made the victory possible. But with these as with "orphan" actions, Model III tries not to neglect the sharp differences, misunderstandings, and foul-ups that contributed to what was actually done.

IV. *General Propositions.* The difficulty of formulating Model III propositions about outcomes can be illustrated by con-

sidering the much simpler problems of a theorist attempting
to specify propositions about outcomes of a card game he
has never seen before but which we recognize as poker. As
a basis for formulating propositions, the analyst would want
information about (1) the rules of the game: are all positions
equal in payoffs, information, etc., and if not, what are the
differences? (2) the importance of skill, reputation, and
other characteristics that players bring to positions: if important, what characteristics does each player have? (3) the
distribution of cards, i.e., the advantages and disadvantages
for the particular hand; (4) individual players' valuation of
alternative payoffs, e.g., whether each simply wants to maximize his winnings or whether some enjoy winning by
bluffing more than winning by having the strongest cards.
This partial list suggests how difficult the problem is, even
in this relatively simple, structured case.* The extraordinary
complexity of cases of bureaucratic politics accounts in part
for the paucity of general propositions. Nevertheless, as the
paradigm has illustrated, it is possible to identify a number
of relevant factors, and, in many cases, analysts can acquire
enough information about these factors to offer explanations
and predictions.

A. *Political Resultants.* A large number of factors that
   constitute a governmental game intervene between "issues" and resultants.

   1. The peculiar preferences and stands of individual
      players can have a significant effect on governmental
      action. Had someone other than Paul Nitze been head
      of the Policy Planning Staff in 1949, there is no rea-
      son to believe that there would have been an NSC-68.
      Had MacArthur not possessed certain preferences,
      power, and skills, U.S. troops might never have
      crossed the narrow neck.

   2. The advantages and disadvantages of each player
      differ substantially from one action-channel to an-
      other. For example, the question of economic direc-
      tives for Germany was considered by the U.S.
      government in a military context. If the issue had
      arisen through international monetary channels,

---

*An analogous difficulty is faced by economists trying to formulate
propositions in oligopoly theory.

players in the Treasury would have had more leverage in pressing their preferences.

3. The mix of players and each player's advantages shift not only *between* action-channels but also *along* action-channels. Chiefs dominate the major formal decisions on important foreign policy issues, but Indians, especially those in the organization charged with carrying out a decision, may play a major role thereafter.

B. *Action and Intention.* Governmental action does not presuppose government intention. The sum of behavior of representatives of a government relevant to an issue is rarely intended by any individual or group. Rather, in the typical case, separate individuals with different intentions contribute pieces to a resultant. The details of the action are therefore not chosen by any individual (and are rarely identical with what any of the players would have chosen if he had confronted the issue as a matter of simple, detached choice). Nevertheless, resultants can be roughly consistent with some group's preference in the context of the political game.

1. Most resultants emerge from games among players who perceive quite different faces of an issue and who differ markedly in the actions they prefer.

2. Actions rarely follow from an agreed doctrine in which all players concur.

3. Actions consisting of a number of pieces that have emerged from a number of games (plus foul-ups) rarely reflect a coordinated government strategy and thus are difficult to read as conscious "signals."

C. *Problems and Solutions*

1. "Solutions" to strategic problems are not discovered by detached analysts focusing coolly on *the* problem. The problems for players are both narrower and broader than *the* strategic problem. Each player focuses not on the total strategic problem but rather on the decision that must be made today or tomorrow. Each decision has important consequences not only for the strategic problem but for each player's stakes. Thus the gap between what the player is focusing on (the problems he is solving) and what a strategic analyst focuses on is often very wide.

2. Decisions that call for substantial changes in governmental action typically reflect a coincidence of Chiefs in search of a solution and Indians in search of a problem. Confronting a deadline, Chiefs focus on an issue and look for a solution. Having become committed to a solution developed for an earlier, somewhat different and now outmoded issue, Indians seek a problem.[70]

D. *Where you stand depends on where you sit.*[71] Horizontally, the diverse demands upon each player shape his priorities, perceptions, and issues. For large classes of issues — e.g., budgets and procurement decisions — the stance of a particular player can be predicted with high reliability from information about his seat. For example, though the participants in the notorious B-36 controversy were, as Eisenhower put it, "distinguished Americans who have their country's good at heart," no one was surprised when Admiral Radford (rather than Air Force Secretary Symington) testified that "the B-36, under any theory of war, is a bad gamble with national security," or when Air Force Secretary Symington (rather than Admiral Radford) claimed that "a B-36 with an A-bomb can take off from this continent and destroy distant objectives which might require ground armies years to take and then only at the expense of heavy casualties."[72]

E. *Chiefs and Indians.* The aphorism "Where you stand depends on where you sit" has vertical as well as horizontal application. Vertically, the demands upon the President, Chiefs, Staffers, and Indians are quite distinct, first in the case of policymaking, and second in the case of implementation.

The foreign policy issues with which the President can deal are limited primarily by his crowded schedule. Of necessity, he must deal first with what comes next. His problem is to probe the special face worn by issues that come to his attention, to preserve his leeway until time has clarified the uncertainties, and to assess the relevant risks.

Foreign policy Chiefs deal most often with the hottest issue *du jour*, though they can catch the attention of the President and other members of the government for most issues they take to be very important. What they cannot guarantee is that "the President will pay the price" or that "the others will get on board." They must build a coalition of the relevant powers that be. They must "give the President confidence" in the choice of the right course of action.

Most problems are framed, alternatives specified, and proposals pushed, however, by Indians. Indians' fights with Indians of other departments — for example, struggles between International Security Affairs of the Department of Defense and Political-Military of the State Department — are a microcosm of the action at higher levels. But the Indians' major problem is how to get the *attention* of Chiefs, how to get an issue on an action-channel, how to get the government "to do what is right." The incentives push the Indian to become an active advocate.

In policymaking, then, the issue looking *down* is options: how to preserve my leeway until time clarifies uncertainties. The issue looking *sideways* is commitment: how to get others committed to my coalition. The issue looking *upward* is confidence: how to give the boss confidence to do what must be done. To paraphrase one of Neustadt's assertions, the essence of *any* responsible official's task is to persuade other players that his version of what needs to be done is what their own appraisal of their own responsibilities requires them to do in their own interests.[73]

For implementation of foreign policy decisions, vertical demands differ. The Chief's requirements are two, but these two conflict. The necessity to build a consensus behind his preferred policy frequently requires fuzziness: different people must agree with slightly different things for quite different reasons; when a government decision is made, both the character of the choice and the reasons for it must often remain vague. But this requirement is at loggerheads with another: the necessity that the choice be enacted requires that footdragging by the unenthusiastic, and subversion by the opposed, be kept to a minimum. Nudging the footdraggers and corraling the subversives constitute difficult tasks even when the decision is clear and the watchman is the President. And most oversight, policing, and spurring is done not by the President but by the President's men or the men who agree with the government decision. Men who would move the machine to act on what has been decided demand clarity.

F. *The 51–49 Principle.* The terms and conditions of the game affect the time that players spend thinking about hard policy choices and the force and assurance with which they argue for their preferred alternative. Because he faces an agenda fixed by hundreds of important deadlines, the reasonable player must make difficult policy choices in much less time and with much less agonizing than an analyst or observer would. Because he must compete with others, the reasonable player is forced to argue much more confidently than he would if he were a detached judge.

G. *Inter- and Intra-national Relations.* The actions of one nation affect those of another to the degree that they result in advantages and disadvantages for players in the second nation. Thus players in one nation who aim to achieve some international objective must attempt to achieve outcomes in their intra-national game that add to the advantages of players in the second country who advocate an analogous objective.

H. *The face of the issue differs from seat to seat.* Where you sit influences what you see as well as where you stand (on any issue). Rarely do two sets of eyes see the same issue. President Truman never saw the issue of defense in the military budget of 1950. Arguments about security and the forces required to support our foreign policy appeared purely as military strategies for expanding the budgets of the services concerned.

I. *Misperception.* The games are not played under conditions of perfect information. Considerable misperception is a standard part of the functioning of each government. Any proposal that is widely accepted is perceived by different men to do quite different things and to meet quite different needs. Misperception is in a sense the grease that allows cooperation among people whose differences otherwise would hardly allow them to coexist.

J. *Misexpectation.* The pace at which the multiple games are played allows only limited attention to each game and demands concentration on priority games. Thus players frequently lack information about the details of other players' games and problems. In the lower priority games, the tendency to expect that someone else will act in such a way that "he helps me with my problem" is unavoidable. In November 1950, each man expected that someone else would go to the President to get MacArthur's orders changed.

K. *Miscommunication.* Both the pace and the noise level merge with propensities of perception to make accurate communication difficult. Because communication must be quick, it tends to be elliptic. In a noisy environment, each player thinks he has spoken with a stronger and clearer voice than the others have actually heard. At the Key West meeting of March 1947, the Chiefs understood Forrestal to say that the President had decided to purchase a flush deck carrier. Forrestal heard the Chiefs' acceptance of the President's decision as their approval of the merits of a flush deck carrier. These differences came to light only when the issue was reopened.[74]

L. *Reticence.* Because each player is engaged in multiple games, the advantages of reticence — i.e., hesitant silence and only partially intended soft-spokenness — seem overwhelming. Reticence in one game reduces leaks that would be harmful in higher priority games. Reticence permits other players to interpret an outcome in the way in which the shoe pinches least. It gives them an ill-focused target of attack. Reticence between Chiefs and Staffers or Indians permits each Indian to offer a charitable interpretation of the outcome — the proposal that simply never moves, for example, or the memo that dies at an interagency meeting of Chiefs. And at least it reduces explicit friction between a Chief and his men. Neustadt's example of the reticence of various Chiefs in speaking to Truman about leashing MacArthur is classic.

M. *Styles of Play.* There are important differences in the behavior of (1) bureaucratic careerists, whether civilian or military, (2) lateral-entry types, and (3) political appointees. These differences are a function of longer-range expectations. The bureaucrat must adopt a code of conformity if he is to survive the inevitable changes of administration and personnel, whereas the lateral-entry type and the political appointee are more frequently temporary employees, interested in policy. The political appointees have a very limited tenure in office and thus impose a high discount rate, that is, a short-time horizon on any issue. Careerists know that presidents come and presidents go, but the Navy . . .

Style of play is also importantly affected by the terms of reference in which a player conceives of his action. Some players are not able to articulate the bureaucratic politics game because their conception of their job does not legitimate such activity. On the other hand, Acheson maintained that the Secretary of State works "in an environment where some of the methods would have aroused the envy of the Borgias." The quality he distinguished from all others as the most necessary for an effective American Secretary of State was "the killer instinct."[75]

V. *Specific Propositions*
A. *Nuclear Crises*

1. A decision to use nuclear weapons is less likely to emerge from a game in which a political leader (whose position forces upon him the heat of being a Final Arbiter) has most of the chips than from a game in which the military have most of the chips.

2. The probability of the U.S. government making a decision to use more military force (rather than less) in a crisis increases as the number of individuals who have an initial, general, personal preference for more forceful military action increases in the following positions: President, Special Assistant for National Security Affairs, Secretaries of Defense and State, Chairman of the JCS, and Director of the CIA.

3. In a nuclear crisis, the central decisions will be hammered out *not* in the formal forums, e.g., the National Security Council, but rather by an *ad hoc* group that includes the President, the heads of the major organizations involved, plus individuals in whom the President has special confidence.

4. These individuals' perception of the issue will differ

radically. These differences will be partially predictable from the pressure of their position plus their personality.

B. *Military Action*

1. For any military action short of nuclear war, decision and implementation will be delayed while proponents try to persuade opponents to get on board.

2. Major decisions about the use of military tend not simply to be Presidential decisions, or majority decisions, but decisions by a large plurality.

3. No military action is chosen without extensive consultation of the military players. No decision for a substantial use of force, short of nuclear war, will be made against their advice, without a delay during which an extensive record of consultation is prepared.

VI. *Evidence.* Information about the details of differences in perceptions and priorities within a government on a particular issue is rarely available. Accurate accounts of the bargaining that yielded a resolution of the issue are rarer still. Documents do not capture this kind of information. What the documents do preserve tends to obscure, as much as to enlighten. Thus the source of such information must be the participants themselves. But, *ex hypothesis*, each participant knows one small piece of the story. Memories quickly become colored. Diaries are often misleading. What is required is access, by an analyst attuned to the players and interested in governmental politics, to a large number of the participants in a decision before their memories fade or become too badly discolored. Such access is uncommon. But without this information, how can the analyst proceed? As a master of this style of analysis has stated, "If I were forced to choose between the documents on the one hand, and late, limited, partial interviews with some of the principal participants on the other, I would be forced to discard the documents."[76] The use of public documents, newspapers, interviews of participants, and discussion with close observers of participants to piece together the bits of information available is an art. Transfer of these skills from the fingertips of artists to a form that can guide other students of foreign policy is this model's most pressing need.

The Governmental Politics Model Applied

A Model III approach to problems considered in earlier chapters accents new dimensions. The Soviet Union's simultaneous purchase of ABMs and pursuit of detente emerge as separate resultants of different bargaining games. A full understanding would require specific information about the players, their advantages, and the overlapping games from which relevant decisions and actions resulted. In the absence of this information, however, one can consider more general characteristics of the Soviet national security game.

The dominant feature of bureaucratic politics in the Soviet Union is the continuous "struggle for power." An occupant's position in the central game is always uncertain and risky. Members of the Politburo and Central Committee are aware of the historical tendency for one man to become preeminent. Thus while a central problem of life for the leader is managing to stay on top, a large part of the problem for Politburo members is how to keep the leadership collective. This fact yields a relevant proposition: policy issues are inextricably intertwined with power plays. Reorganizations, or shifts in resources, constitute redistributions of advantages and disadvantages in the central game.

Presidium and Central Committee Secretariat members have typically risen through, and assumed special responsibility for, various departments and subdepartments. These organizational associations color players' perspectives and priorities. Individuals in these organizations constitute each player's power base. Because of personal histories and constituent pressures, a number of central players must have taken visible stands for ABM deployment, and for detente. In the absence of a deadline forcing a decision in the central Soviet game between ABM and detente, it seems likely that advocates of each have been allowed to tend their own gardens. (Indeed, if one assumes that the Soviet government is analogous to the U.S. government, advocates of the two tracks argue that there is really no conflict between the two.) Thus the two courses of action probably emerged, and are likely to be sustained.

A necessity for budgetary cuts or a requirement to respond to a strong American initiative for an agreement limiting ABM deployment might present an opportunity for advocates of detente to interfere with the established programs and procedures of the PVO. Indeed, stopping deployment of ABMs would constitute a major defeat for several central players and a redistribution of the power base of certain ministers and Presidium members. It is important to recognize, however, that this conflict would arise from unavoidable choices on concrete issues rather than by internal disagreement about the consistency of strategic policies.

Nuclear Strategy

In thinking about the problem of deterrence, a Model III analyst begins from the proposition that if a nuclear attack occurs, it will have emerged as a resultant of bargaining in the attacking government. Rather than Model I's focus on balance and stability, or Model II's focus on organizational routines, a Model III analyst is concerned with the features of the internal politics of a government that might produce this decision.

First, which players can decide to launch an attack? Whether the effective power over this action is controlled by an individual, a minor game, or the central game is critical.

Second, though Model I's confidence in deterrence relies on the assumption that, in the end, nations will not commit suicide, Model III recalls historical precedents. Admiral Yamamoto, who designed the Japanese attack on Pearl Harbor, told the members of the Japanese government accurately: "In the first six months to a year of war against the U.S. and England I will run wild, and I will show you an uninterrupted succession of victories; I must also tell you that, should the war be prolonged for two or three years, I have no confidence in our ultimate victory."[77] But Japan attacked. Such a precedent suggests three key questions. One: Could any member of the government solve *his* problem by attack? What patterns of bargaining could yield attack as a resultant? The major difference between a stable balance of terror and a questionable one may simply be that most members of the government appreciate fully the consequences of attack in the case of the former and are thus on guard against this decision. Two: What stream of decisions might lead to an attack? At what point in that stream do the potential attacker's politics lie? If members of the U.S. government had known more about the succession of decisions from which the Japanese attack on Pearl Harbor emerged, they would have been aware of a considerable probability of that attack. Three: How might miscalculation and confusion generate foul-ups that yield attack as a resultant? For example, in a crisis or after the beginning of conventional war, what happens to the information available to, and the effective power of, members of the central game?

A final element of importance in thinking about nuclear attacks is the probable differences in perceptions and priorities of central leaders. Pressures encourage both the Soviet Chairman and the U.S. President to feel the distance between their own responsibilities and those of other members of their central games. Each lives with the daily responsibility for nuclear holocaust. Neither will be overly impressed by differences between the death of one million and one hundred million of his own citizens when choosing to take, or to refrain from taking, a risk. Each will be more sensitive to the other's problem than is any other member of the central game. Both may well appreciate the extent to which the "kings" are partners in the game against nuclear disaster. Both will be interested in private communication with each other. If channels can be arranged, such communication offers the most promising prospect of resolution of a crisis.

6

Cuba II: A Third Cut

"The fourteen people involved [in the ExCom] were very significant — bright, able, dedicated people, all of whom had the greatest affection for the U.S. . . . If six of them had been President of the U.S., I think that the world might have been blown up."[1] This remark of Robert Kennedy's overstates the risks inherent in the course of action advocated by his opponents — the air strike — as compared with those of the blockade, which he favored. But his memoir of the Cuban missile crisis does no disservice to those fourteen men* in recognizing that they differed sharply about what should be done.[2] Given the difficulty of the problem, the differences in their jobs, and the individuality of each man, who would expect otherwise? That each of these men fought hard for the course of action he judged to be right should not be surprising. With the life of the nation in the balance, should anyone expect less?

---

*The members of the ExCom Kennedy listed in his *Thirteen Days* were: Secretary of State Dean Rusk, Secretary of Defense Robert McNamara, Director of the CIA John McCone, Special Assistant for National Security Affairs McGeorge Bundy, Secretary of the Treasury Douglas Dillon, Special Counsel Theodore Sorensen, Chairman of the Joint Chiefs of Staff Maxwell Taylor, Undersecretary of State George Ball, Deputy Undersecretary of State Alexis Johnson, Assistant Secretary of State (Latin American Affairs) Edwin Martin, State Department Soviet expert Llewellyn Thompson, Deputy Secretary of Defense Roswell Gilpatric, Assistant Secretary of Defense (International Security Affairs) Paul Nitze, former Secretary of State Dean Acheson, and former Secretary of Defense Robert Lovett. Actually, this list includes fifteen, in addition to the President and the Attorney General himself.

Historians and analysts of great events tend to obscure differences among governmental leaders and to neglect the distance between these leaders' reasonable but competing recommendations and a chosen, implemented course of action. Information about such factors is difficult to acquire. To some, these features seem overly petty or personal. For others, hindsight so clarifies the uncertainties that failures become errors and successes become the only reasonable choice. To most historians and analysts, the idea that events of such consequence should turn on ephemeral details like the pulling and hauling of individuals within a government appears radically malproportioned. But — as Robert Kennedy's remark reminds us — in the Cuban missile crisis the preferences of the leaders of the U.S. government covered a spectrum from "doing nothing" to "launching a surprise military invasion of Cuba." An understanding of why, on October 24, 1962, the United States was blockading (rather than invading or ignoring) Cuba thus requires careful attention not only to the arguments for that course of action but also to the essentially political process by which the blockade emerged as the American government's choice.

Because of the centrality of this crisis to the Presidency of John Fitzgerald Kennedy and the numerous accounts of his administration that followed his assassination, public documentation of what the members of the U.S. government were seeing, thinking, and doing is considerably richer than for most events, even after the classified documents are opened. Moreover, the critical nature of this event etched its details sharply in the memories of the participants. The availability of this information so soon after the crisis presents an unusual opportunity for recollections to be compared. As a result, the "story" of the blockade — the details of the perceptions, the analyses, and the politics of individual players out of which the blockade emerged — can be told with confidence.

Unfortunately, this cannot be said about the other major puzzles of the Cuban missile crisis: Soviet deployment of offensive missiles in Cuba and Soviet withdrawal of missiles from Cuba. These events resulted in large part from activity internal to the Soviet government. Lack of information about the perceptions, thoughts, and actions of individuals within the Soviet government should limit the confidence with which its actions are explained — and here, it does. Accordingly, this chapter departs from the chronological order of events, treating the three puzzles in descending order of availability of information and confidence. An explanation of the blockade will provide a basis for explaining the withdrawal of the missiles that will offer some clues about why the Soviets shipped missiles to Cuba.

The Imposition of a Blockade by the United States

The Politics of Discovery

The ExCom's choice of the blockade cannot be understood apart from the context in which the necessity for choice arose. Though a government post-mortem on the crisis concluded that "there was no action that the U.S. could have taken before we actually did act," this judgment is incorrect.[3] Had a U-2 flown over the western end of Cuba three weeks earlier, it could have discovered the missiles, giving the administration more time to consider alternatives and to act before the danger of operational missiles in Cuba became a major factor in the equation.[4] Had the missiles not been discovered until two weeks later, the blockade would have been irrelevant, since the Soviet missile shipments would have been completed. The state of mind of various American governmental officials on the Cuban issue formed a second crucial feature of the context. What the presence of Soviet missiles in Cuba meant to these individuals could not be separated from their statements and stances on this question, both within the administration and before the country. A series of overlapping bargaining games determined both the *date* of the discovery of the Soviet missiles and the *impact* of the discovery on the administration. An explanation of the politics of the discovery is consequently a considerable piece of the explanation of the U.S. blockade.

Cuba was the Kennedy administration's "political Achilles' heel."[5] This vulnerability had three related causes. First, the Bay of Pigs operation in April 1961 (Cuba I) raised the most serious internal doubts about the President's judgment, the wisdom of his advisers, and the quality of their advice. No subsequent major issue of national security was decided without bringing Theodore Sorensen and Robert Kennedy into the process. When the President referred to Cuba as his "heaviest political cross," he referred to the inside of his administration as well as to the outside.[6] Second, Cuba I had taught the public unfortunate lessons: that Cuba constituted a serious threat to U.S. security, that calls for the overthrow of Castro's Communism had some legitimacy, that U.S. policy could cater to hawkish appetites. Third, the failure of the invasion had made Kennedy appear indecisive. By attempting to overthrow Castro with a clandestine force but bungling the job (in part because of dovish squeamishness), the President and his advisers were left standing in a position not unlike Chamberlain's after Czechoslovakia. Having been tried and found wanting, they were liable to be overwhelmed by the pressures to overreact in the next case.

The Republican Party did not miss the administration's vulnerability. The months preceding the Cuban missile crisis were also months before the off-year congressional elections, and the Republican Senatorial and Congressional Campaign Committee had announced that Cuba would be "the dominant issue of the 1962 campaign."[7] What the administration billed as a "more positive and indirect approach of isolating Castro from the developing, democratic Latin America," Senators Keating, Goldwater, Capehart, Thurmond, and others attacked as a "do-nothing" policy.[8] In statements on the floor of the House and Senate, in campaign speeches across the country, and in interviews and articles carried by national news media, Cuba — particularly the Soviet program of increased arms aid — served as a stick for stirring the domestic political pot.[9] In contrast to the administration's inaction, which was allowing additional Soviet arms shipments to Cuba, critics called for a blockade, an invasion, or simply "action."

These attacks drew blood. Prudence demanded a vigorous administration reaction, and the President decided to meet the issue head-on. His best hope was to overwhelm the critics with a barrage of official statements disclaiming any Soviet provocation in Cuba, thus deflating the opposition's case. So the administration mounted a forceful campaign of denial designed to discredit critics' claims. The President himself manned the front line of this offensive, though most administration officials participated. In his news conference on August 29, President Kennedy attacked as "irresponsible" calls for an invasion of Cuba, stressing rather "the totality of our obligations" and promising to "watch what happens in Cuba with the closest attention."[10] On September 4, he issued a strong statement denying any provocative Soviet action in Cuba.[11] On September 13 he lashed out at "loose talk" calling for an invasion of Cuba.[12] The day before the flight of the U-2 that discovered the missiles, he campaigned in Capehart's Indiana against those "self-appointed generals and admirals who want to send someone else's sons to war."[13]

Undersecretary of State George Ball testified before a congressional committee on October 3:

> Our intelligence is very good and very hard. All the indications are that this is equipment which is basically of a defensive capability and it does not offer any offensive capability to Cuba as against the United States or the other nations of the Hemisphere.[14]

On Sunday, October 14, on ABC's *Issues and Answers,* Presidential Assistant McGeorge Bundy was denying the presence of Soviet offensive missiles in Cuba just as a U-2 was taking its first pictures of them. In response to Edward P. Morgan's probing about the "interpretation of the military installations in Cuba which the administration emphasizes are defensive in nature and not offensive" Bundy asserted: "I *know* that there is no present evidence, and I think that there is no present likelihood that the Cubans and the Cuban government and the Soviet government would, in combination, attempt to install a major offensive capability."[15]

On Monday, October 15, a phone call reached Assistant Secretary of State Edwin Martin just as he finished delivering a speech to the National Press Club. His speech addressed the question of Soviet activity in Cuba and argued that the build-up was "basically defensive in character."[16] The phone call informed Martin of the U.S. discovery of offensive missiles.

In the campaign to puncture the critics' charges, the administration found that the public needed positive slogans. Thus, Kennedy fell into a tenuous semantic distinction between "offensive" and "defensive" weapons. This distinction originated in Kennedy's September 4 statement, which announced that there was no evidence of "offensive ground-to-ground missiles" and warned that "were it to be otherwise, the gravest issues would arise."[17] His September 13 statement pivoted on the distinction between "defensive" and "offensive" weapons and made a firm commitment to action if the Soviet Union attempted to introduce the latter into Cuba.[18] Congressional committees elicited testimony from administration officials that read both this distinction and the President's commitment into the *Congressional Record.*[19]

This is a classic illustration of the effect of the "backdrop"

— in this instance, the opposition and congressional committees — on policymaking in crises. A number of Republicans tried to make electoral capital of this foreign policy issue, but provoked a response that had significant consequences for U.S. policy. For most of the congressional participants, the character of this response was unanticipated and irrelevant to their purposes. For several skilled congressional players, however, the venture succeeded: the administration was pinned down on a response to Soviet offensive missiles in Cuba, and the President's options were narrowed. But an equally important, more subtle, and less noted effect of this "action in the wings" occurred in games within the administration.

What the President least wanted to hear, the CIA found it difficult to say plainly. On August 22, before the administration's campaign against the critics had begun, John McCone met privately with the President, McNamara, and Rusk to voice suspicions that the Soviets were preparing to introduce offensive missiles in Cuba.[20] Kennedy heard this as what it was: the suspicion of a professional anti-Communist. McNamara seems to have feared that McCone's aggressiveness might push the administration into unwarranted action. Both McNamara and Rusk disagreed with McCone, arguing that available evidence indicated only a defensive build-up. Both Secretaries reiterated the prevailing view that the Kremlin would never take the risk of installing offensive weapons in Cuba.[21]

To what extent McCone may have been relying on evidence provided by Phillippe Thyraud De Vosjoli can only be a matter of speculation.[22] De Vosjoli — whose activities have been publicized and exaggerated in Leon Uris' novel *Topaz* — served as the head of French intelligence in the United States, and in this period the French intelligence services (Service de Documentation Exterieure et de Contre-Espionage) and the CIA cooperated closely. Because the CIA apparatus in Cuba had been decimated in the aftermath of the Bay of Pigs, French intelligence activity in Cuba was a major source of U.S. information. According to De Vosjoli's published account, his role in these events began in July 1962. In late July reliable intelligence reported a dramatic increase in shipments to the Port of Mariel. After a conversation with McCone, De Vosjoli made a trip to Cuba in August. According to his account:

> When I left Washington for Havana in August, I had a very good idea of what to look for, and the operation I organized

produced an enormous amount of information — as many as 50 or 100 separate reports a day. Naturally enough, not all of the intelligence was of the same quality, but most of the evidence pointed in the same direction . . . Russian rockets. . . . What I learned I passed on to Paris and shared with the American intelligence authorities. . . . I have had the thanks, in private, of John McCone.[23]

Having had his say with the President, McCone left Washington for a month's honeymoon on the Riviera. Fretting at Cap Ferrat, he bombarded his deputy, General Marshall Carter, with telegrams on September 7, 10, 13, and 16.[24] But Carter, knowing that McCone had informed the President of his suspicions and had been given a cold reception, was reluctant to distribute these telegrams outside the CIA.[25] Early in September an American U-2 strayed over Siberia for nine minutes.[26] On September 9 a U-2 flown by Chinese Nationalists was downed over mainland China.[27] When the Committee on Overhead Reconnaissance (COMOR) convened on September 10, there was a sense of urgency.[28] Loss of another U-2 might so inflame world opinion that cancellation of U-2 flights would be necessary. The intelligence community feared for the life of its "eyes." The President's campaign against critics' charges of Soviet provocation in Cuba had begun. To risk a U-2 shootdown over Cuba was to risk chopping off the limb on which the President was sitting. At that meeting, COMOR decided to shy away from the western end of Cuba (where SAMs were becoming operational) and modify the flight pattern of the U-2s in order to reduce the probability that a U-2 would be lost.[29]

The United States Intelligence Board (USIB) met on September 19 to *approve* the now notorious estimate concerning Soviet offensive missiles in Cuba.[30] The draft they approved conveyed hints both of the bargaining from which the draft had emerged and of the sensitivity of the players to the spectrum of issues. On September 13 the President had affirmed that there were no Soviet offensive missiles in Cuba and had committed his administration to action if such missiles were discovered. Administration officials being called to testify before congressional committees were denying that there was any evidence whatever of offensive missiles in Cuba. The implications of a National Intelligence Estimate concluding that the Soviets were introducing offensive missiles into Cuba could not be lost on the men who constituted America's highest intelligence assembly.

Though McCone thought that the Soviets were introducing missiles into Cuba, he was on the Riviera. The President had heard
the hypothesis, so Deputy Director Carter waited for harder evidence. Given this climate of opinion and cluster of considerations, the USIB, on the basis of the information available,
unanimously accepted the proposed National Intelligence Estimate.

The necessity of official adherence to administration guidelines led some members of the military and intelligence com-
munities who disagreed with the administration position to
resort to unofficial channels, particularly Congress and the
press.[31] Senator Kenneth Keating, Representative Paul Kitchin,
and others were receiving information from within the administration. To insure against leaks if intelligence on offensive weapons did become available, President Kennedy ordered special
security arrangements, including a special code, PSALM, which
restricted information about offensive weapons to a limited
number who had special need to know.[32]

The October 4 COMOR decision to direct a flight over the
western end of Cuba in effect overturned the September estimate,
without, however, officially raising that issue. This decision represented the victory for which McCone had lobbied with the
President before the September 10 decision, in telegrams before
the September 19 estimate, and in person after his return to
Washington. Though the politics of the intelligence community
is closely guarded, several pieces of the story can be told.[33] By
September 27, Colonel John Wright and others in the Defense
Intelligence Agency (DIA) believed that the Soviet Union was
placing offensive missiles in the San Cristobal area.[34] That area
was marked suspicious by the CIA on September 29 and certified top priority on October 3. By October 4, McCone had the
evidence required to raise the issue officially. The members of
COMOR heard McCone's argument but were reluctant to make
the hard decision he wanted. American overflight of the western
end of Cuba was a matter of *real* concern. There was a significant probability that a U-2 would be downed. This hesitancy
accounts for the ten-day delay between decision and flight, but
the details of that bargaining must be held in abeyance. After
the missiles were discovered, the President reportedly remarked
to McCone, "You were right all along." "But for the wrong reasons," McNamara was quick to add.[35]

The Politics of Issues

The U-2 photographs presented incontrovertible evidence of Soviet offensive missiles in Cuba. This revelation fell upon politicized players in a complex situation. As one high official recalls, Khrushchev had caught us "with our pants down." What each of the central participants perceived, and what each did to cover both his own nakedness and the administration's embarrassment, provides a spectrum of issues.

On the morning of Tuesday, October 16, McGeorge Bundy went to the President's living quarters with the message: "Mr. President, there is now hard photographic evidence . . . that the Russians have offensive missiles in Cuba."[36] Much has been made of Kennedy's "expression of surprise."[37] But "surprise" fails to capture the character of his initial reaction. Rather, it was one of startled anger, most adequately conveyed by the exclamation: "He can't do that to *me!*"[38] That exclamation in this context was triple-barrelled. First, in terms of the President's attention and priorities at that moment, Khrushchev had chosen the most unhelpful act of all. In a highly sensitive domestic political context where his opponents demanded action against Soviet interests in Cuba, Kennedy was following a policy of reason and responsibility. In support of that policy, he had drawn a distinction between "defensive" and "offensive" weapons, staked his full Presidential authority on the flat statement that the Soviets were not placing offensive weapons in Cuba, and warned unambiguously that offensive missiles would not be tolerated.[39] Second, the major thrust of his administration's policy toward the Soviet Union had been aimed at relaxing tension and building trust through trust. At considerable political cost, he was attempting to leash the anti-Communist Cold Warriors and to educate officials as well as the public out of prevailing devil theories of Soviet Communism. He and his closest advisers had made considerable effort to guarantee that all communication between the President and the Chairman would be straightforward and accurate. Contact had been made; Khrushchev was reciprocating; mutual confidence was growing. As part of this exchange, Khrushchev had assured the President through the most direct and personal channels that he understood Kennedy's domestic problem and would do nothing to complicate it. Specifically, Khrushchev had given the President solemn assurances that the Soviet Union would not put offensive missiles in Cuba.[40] But then *this* — the Chairman had *lied* to the President. Third, Khrushchev's action challenged the President personally. Did he, John F. Kennedy, have the courage in the crunch to start down a path that had a real chance of leading to nuclear war? If not, Khrushchev would win this round. More important, he would gain confidence that he could win the next as well — simply by forcing Kennedy to choose between a nuclear path and acquiescence. Kennedy had worried, both after the Bay of Pigs and after the Vienna meeting with Khrushchev, that the Chairman might have misjudged his mettle. This time Kennedy determined to stand fast.

For this President of the United States, nothing short of a forceful response would suffice: the missiles must be removed. To fail to act forcibly would (1) undermine the confidence of the members of his administration, especially those who had so firmly defended his policy toward Cuba; (2) convince his permanent government that this administration had no leader and cultivate their willingness to challenge all of his policies; (3) cut the ground out from under his fellow Democrats (most of whom were standing on his Cuban policy) with the congressional elections less than three weeks away; (4) destroy his reputation with all but a few members of Congress; (5) create public distrust of his word and his will; (6) encourage friends and foes of the United States abroad to doubt his courage and commitments; (7) invite a "second Bay of Pigs," thereby sealing the fate of his administration: a short chapter in the history books entitled "Crucified over Cuba"; (8) feed doubts in his own mind about himself. As Roger Hilsman, one of the "President's men" in this crisis, has written: "The United States might not be in mortal danger but the administration most certainly was."[41] Douglas Dillon, a Republican member of the Cabinet, passed a blunt note across the table at one ExCom meeting:

> Have you considered the very real possibility that if we allow Cuba to complete installation and operational readiness of missile bases, the next House of Representatives is likely to have a Republican majority? This would completely paralyze our ability to react sensibly and coherently to further Soviet advances.[42]

The reaction of these varied constituents appeared most plainly in the response of congressional leaders when, two hours before the President's announcement to the world, he informed them of the decision to respond to the Soviet action with a quarantine. Reacting harshly to a McNamara-Rusk-McCone briefing, Senator Richard Russell stated that "he could not live with himself if he did not say in the strongest possible terms how important it was that we act with greater strength."[43] Second to speak was Senator William Fulbright. He firmly opposed Kennedy's quarantine, urging "military action rather than such a weak step as a blockade."[44] Almost unanimously the leaders of Congress recommended an air strike or invasion.[45]

It is impossible to determine what weight each of these various considerations may have had in the President's mind. No doubt the calculations rehearsed above do not capture all his thoughts.[46] But it is clear that the entire circle of pressures to which he as President had to be responsive pushed him in a single direction: strong action. Indeed, the record leaves no doubt that from the outset he was determined to act forcefully.[47] Halfway down that road of firm action, feeling the heat of the risks involved, John Kennedy raised the question of why he had ever begun. There was more than humor in Robert Kennedy's reply. "I just don't think there was any choice," he said, "and not only that, if you hadn't acted you would have been impeached." "That's what I think," the President replied, "I would have been impeached."[48] The nonforcible paths — avoiding military measures, resorting instead to diplomacy — could not have been more irrelevant to *his* problem.

These two tracks — "doing nothing" and "taking a diplomatic approach," as the alternatives were labeled in the ExCom — were the solutions initally advocated by two of his principal advisers to the issues they saw. For Secretary of Defense McNamara, the missiles raised the specter of nuclear war. In an effort to combat this specter, he framed the issue as a straightforward strategic problem. To understand the issue, one had to grasp two obvious but difficult points. First, the missiles represented an inevitable occurrence: narrowing of the missile gap. It simply happened sooner rather than later. Second, the United States could accept this occurrence since its consequences were minor: seven-to-one missile superiority, one-to-one missile equality, one-to-seven missile inferiority — the three postures are nearly identical. McNamara's statement of this argument at the first meeting of the ExCom was summed up in the phrase "a missile is a missile."[49] "It makes no great difference," he

maintained, "whether you are killed by a missile from the Soviet Union or Cuba."[50] The Soviet missiles in Cuba constituted
no important change in the balance of power.

The perceptions of McGeorge Bundy, the President's Special
Assistant for National Security Affairs, are difficult to reconstruct. He too seems to have been impressed primarily by the
potential in the proposed military actions for escalation to nuclear war, since initially he was the advocate of a diplomatic
approach. Several forms of diplomatic approach were outlined,
but Bundy argued most persuasively for either confronting
Soviet Foreign Minister Gromyko (who happened to be in the
United States) with the evidence and demanding withdrawal,
or directly approaching Khrushchev in a similar manner.[51] As
he pointed out, this approach would give Khrushchev an opportunity to withdraw the missiles quietly, without humiliation. It
might avoid any confrontation whatever. It reduced the length
of time this secret would have to stay bottled up inside the U.S.
government. Moreover, Bundy argued, consider the alternatives:
each called for springing the discovery on Khrushchev when
announcing to the American people and the world the chosen
course of action. This amounted to a suspension of the rules of
diplomacy.[52] To make this a public issue engaging Khrushchev's
and the Soviets' prestige in the eyes of the world, before trying
traditional diplomatic channels, would be at best shortsighted.
Finally, in terms of the argument that became the touchstone
of these deliberations, a diplomatic approach *closed no other
options*. If Khrushchev refused or delayed, an alternative could
then be publicly announced, and the administration would be
shielded from criticisms that it had provoked a public confrontation without first attempting diplomatic negotiations.

Bundy's argument was powerful. His arguments were always powerful. But the tone of the argument and the fact that
later in the week he became an advocate of the air strike leave
some doubt about his "real" reaction. Was he laboring under
his acknowledged burden of responsibility in Cuba I? Was he
playing the role of devil's advocate in order to make the President probe his own initial reaction? As one of Bundy's colleagues
is reported to have commented: "You don't know what he thinks.
I don't know what he thinks. The President doesn't know what
he thinks. And I sometimes wonder whether he knows what he
thinks."[53] As Bundy recalls his own reaction, "I almost deliberately stayed in the minority. I felt that it was very important to
keep the President's choices open."[54]

Attorney General Robert Kennedy saw clearly the political wall against which Khrushchev had backed his brother. But he found himself hemmed in by two additional barriers as well. First, like McNamara, he was haunted by the prospect of nuclear doom. Was Khrushchev going to force the President into an insane action? Second, more than any other member of the group, he saw a vital issue posed by the traditions and moral position of the United States. Was his brother going to blacken the name of the United States in the pages of history? At the first meeting of the ExCom, he scribbled a note, "I now know how Tojo felt when he was planning Pearl Harbor."[55] In opposing former Secretary of State Acheson, RFK developed this analogy:

> Whatever validity the military and political arguments for an attack [had] . . . America's traditions and history would not permit such a course of action. Whatever military reasons he [Acheson] and others could marshal, they were nevertheless, in the last analysis, advocating a surprise attack by a very large nation against a very small one. This . . . could not be taken by the U.S. . . . Our struggle against Communism throughout the world was far more than physical survival — it had as its essence our heritage and our ideals, and these we must not destroy.[56]

In a phrase, a sudden attack would be "a Pearl Harbor in reverse."[57] From the outset Robert Kennedy probed for an alternative to the air strike.

The initial reaction of Theodore Sorensen, the President's Special Counsel and "alter ego," fell somewhere between the President and his brother. Like the President, Sorensen felt the poignancy of betrayal. If the President had been the architect of the policy the missiles punctured, Sorensen was the draftsman. Khrushchev's deceitful move demanded a strong counter-move. But, like Robert Kennedy, Sorensen feared lest shock and disgrace lead to disaster. Chosen by the President to be his primary reporter on the discussions in the ExCom, Sorensen guarded against becoming an advocate. Instead, in the ExCom he conceived his role to be one of assisting in "prodding, questioning, eliciting arguments and alternatives and keeping the discussions concrete and moving ahead."[58] But because his memos posed for the President the issues, arguments, and questions, his personal reactions mattered.

To the Joint Chiefs of Staff the issue was clear. *Now* was the time to do the job for which they had been preparing contingency plans. Cuba I had been badly done; Cuba II would not be.

The missiles provided the *occasion* to deal with the issue they were prepared for: ridding the Western Hemisphere of Castro's Communism. The security of the United States required a massive air strike, leading to an invasion and the overthrow of Castro.[59] Convinced that this time the President had no real alternative, the Joint Chiefs advocated their option with an abandon that amazed other members of the ExCom.[60] For example, after Air Force Chief of Staff Curtis LeMay had argued strongly that a military attack was essential, the President asked what the response of the Russians might be. General LeMay replied: "There would be no reaction."[61] The President was not convinced. As he recalled on the day the crisis ended, "An invasion would have been a mistake — a wrong use of our power. But the military are mad. They wanted to do this. It's lucky for us that we have McNamara over there."[62]

There were other, more persuasive advocates of military action. Acheson, Nitze, Dillon, and McCone formed a natural alliance. To them the overriding issues were two: the security of the United States together with its position of leadership in the Western Hemisphere and Western Europe. The situation permitted little time for deliberation. The Soviet missiles in Cuba "were fast becoming an acute danger and should be removed by military action before they became operational."[63] As Acheson recalls his own argument:

> As I saw it at the time, and still believe, the decision to resort to the blockade was a decision to postpone the issue at the expense of time within which the nuclear weapons might be made operable. The Soviet Union did not need to bring any more weapons into Cuba. . . . The nuclear weapons already there . . . were capable of killing eighty million Americans. That was enough.[64]

As Nitze maintained, when starting down a path that might lead to war, any man with a responsible regard for the lives of American citizens had to distinguish sharply between the consequences of war before and after those missiles became operational.

Furthermore, Acheson argued that the blockade simply delayed the hard choice that would at some point have to be faced. After a week of blockading, a number of Soviet missiles would be operational and what would the options be? To enforce the demand that Khrushchev withdraw the missiles, the President would have had to threaten or perform a larger air strike. In that context, however, the chances that the Soviet missiles would fire were much higher. Thus the dilemma.[65]

Acheson considered the objection that an air strike might provoke a spasmodic response. He has recorded his argument:

> This would be possible, of course; but analysis seemed to show it unlikely. (Incidentally, General de Gaulle did not believe that the Kremlin would have responded with either action). One must recall that the Russian Ambassador and the Foreign Minister were asserting to the President that no offensive nuclear weapons had been installed in Cuba by the Soviet Union. Their representatives at the United Nations continued to repeat this even after Mr. Stevenson had asserted the contrary in the Security Council. So far, then, as the public record was concerned, a sudden air attack by us on non-populated areas of Cuba would have been an attack not on the Soviet Union but on something — not people — in Cuba. This would hardly have called for a reflex attack on the United States at the expense of reciprocal destruction of the Soviet Union.
>
> The Russians would have been better advised to stick to their story that no nuclear weapons were in Cuba and charge that we had nervously fired at shadows created by our own fears.[66]

Secretary of State Rusk's reaction was both dramatic and enigmatic. On the one hand, he represented the counsel of doom, predicting that "if we take a strong action the allies and Latin Americans will turn against us and if we take a weak action they will turn away from us," and coining phrases like "nuclear incineration."[67] On the evening before the President's public announcement of the crisis, Rusk told his staff, "By this time tomorrow, Gentlemen, we will be in a flaming crisis."[68] On the morning after the speech, he pronounced: "We have won a considerable victory. You and I are still alive."[69] On the other hand, his substantive reactions are inscrutable. Initially, he was reluctant to participate in the ExCom, missing meetings and carefully withholding his own personal views. Undersecretary Ball represented the State Department and, in fact, most of the ExCom meetings took place in Ball's conference room on the seventh floor of the State Department. But on Thursday, October 18, Rusk spoke out vigorously: first as a dove, then as a hawk, and finally as an uncertain man. In an unusual, strong statement at the Thursday morning meeting, he argued against an air strike. But at the early evening session he read a paper he had prepared on his own position: "On the following Wednes-

day, after informing Macmillan, De Gaulle, Adenauer, and possibly Turkey and a few Latin Americans, a limited air strike
wiping out the missiles should be accompanied by a simultaneous Presidential announcement to the world and formal
reference to the UN and OAS."[70] After other participants pointed
out that this proposal simply neglected the issue of advance
warning, which was the problem over which the air strike advocates were stalled, Rusk "began to back away from his plan."[71]

In spite of such fluctuations, he seems never to have
wavered in his conviction that we must see it through. Indeed,
in concluding his written recommendation of the air strike, he
predicted, "If we don't do this we go down with a whimper. Maybe it's better to go down with a bang."[72]

Thus, the missiles posed no single issue. The players who
gathered at the pinnacle of the U.S. government perceived many
faces of quite different issues. And, in spite of efforts to classify
these men as "hawks" and "doves" — a metaphor coined during
this crisis — their initial reactions were much more diverse than
the metaphors suggest.[73]

The Politics of Choice

At the outset of the crisis, the individuals who convened at
the President's discretion as the ExCom whistled many different
tunes. Before the final decision was made and the vote taken,
the majority whistled a single tune: the blockade. The process
by which this consensus emerged is a story of the most subtle
and intricate probing, pulling, and hauling, leading, guiding, and
spurring. Reconstruction of the process must, of course, be
tentative.

The nonmilitary paths — doing nothing or taking a diplomatic approach — had powerful advocates. They minimized the
risk that U.S. action in response to the missiles in Cuba would
lead to nuclear war. In contrast, as the President later acknowledged, the path of forcible action "raised the prospect that it
might escalate . . . into a nuclear war."[74] Yet, by the afternoon of
the second day, serious discussion in the ExCom focused on two
military alternatives, the air strike and the blockade.[75]

Obviously, there were counter-arguments to either doing
nothing or going a diplomatic route. Acheson and Nitze attacked
McNamara's assertion that the Soviet missiles in Cuba constituted no change in the strategic balance: U.S. warning of an

attack would be cut from fifteen to three minutes; much of the American bomber force would become vulnerable; and the Soviet first-strike capability would be doubled. But did this amount to a significant change in the strategic balance, or rather, as McNamara suggested, simply a rapid narrowing of the missile gap? That was a matter of judgment. Similarly, the weight of Dillon's argument — that because "the fat was in the fire" military action was necessary before the missiles became operational — depended on one's interpretation of the meaning of "superiority," "equality," and "inferiority" in the nuclear age. As McNamara came to concede, the Soviet action did have some effect on the political balance. But did those consequences counsel an American choice of a course of action involving a high probability of nuclear war?

In opposing the diplomatic approach, Rusk, with the support of Llewellyn Thompson, argued that to inform Gromyko on Thursday, before the United States had decided on a course of action, would "let the initiative pass to the Soviets."[76] Deciding what to do when the United States held the tactical advantage was difficult enough. To forfeit that advantage and permit the Russians to respond before the United States had made a decision would unduly complicate the issue. To this line of argument, someone might have objected that the Soviets could be told on Saturday, after the U.S. decision. But that alternative, like the direct approach to Khrushchev, ran into a second line of counter-arguments. On the one hand, if the U.S. message simply demanded withdrawal of the missiles, Khrushchev could equivocate while the missiles became operational. On the other hand, if the message threatened military action on a specific date unless the missiles were withdrawn, Khrushchev could hide the missiles. He might commit the Soviet Union to retaliate against any American attack on the missiles. As Sorensen argued, this message would constitute "the kind of ultimatum which no great power could accept."[77] Finally, the President had stated one further argument at the first meeting of the group: there was great advantage in announcing our discovery and our response simultaneously.[78] This time the Soviets should react to our initiative.

Unquestionably, the diplomatic channel might have vastly complicated the issue. Khrushchev could try to conceal the missiles — but he could do that after the United States announced a blockade. Khrushchev might commit himself to retaliate against an attack — but he could do that after a blockade was announced. A message that demanded withdrawal of the missiles by a specific date would be an ultimatum of sorts — but an ultimatum of that sort would be required at the end of a week of the blockade. Using diplomatic channels might allow Khrushchev to seize the tactical advantage. But what real option would that close? As Bundy observed, this approach just might dissolve the crisis without any public conflict. Again, the issue came down to matters of judgment.[79]

Arguments in the Excom for and against the nonmilitary tracks involved difficult estimates, interpretations, and matters of judgment. Indeed, in retrospect, an analyst weighing all available arguments could decide either way. But, as Sorensen's record of these events reveals, the rapid abandonment of the nonmilitary path resulted less from the balance of argument than from the intra-governmental balance of power. "The President had rejected this course from the outset."[80]

Initially, the President wanted a clean, surgical air strike. On Tuesday, when he informed U.N. Ambassador Adlai Stevenson about the missiles, he mentioned only two alternatives: "I suppose the alternatives are to go in by air and wipe them out, or to take other steps to render the weapons inoperable."[81] Stevenson was so stunned by what seemed to be a settled decision that he delivered a distressed, hand-written note to the President early Wednesday morning. The note warned that: "To risk starting a nuclear war is bound to be divisive at best, and the judgments of history seldom coincide with the tempers of the moment. . . . I confess I have many misgivings about the proposed course of action."[82] But neither Stevenson nor his argument carried much weight. What prevented the air strike was a fortuitous coincidence of a number of factors — the absence of any one of which might have permitted that option to prevail.

First, McNamara's vision of the nuclear specter set him firmly against the air strike. His initial attempt to frame the issue in strategic terms struck Kennedy as particularly inappropriate, given the President's problem. Once McNamara realized that the President required a strong response, he and his deputy Gilpatric seized the blockade as a fallback. McNamara formulated the dominant argument for this alternative: it would "maintain the options" and "leave us in control of events."[83] When this Secretary of Defense — whose department had the action, whose reputation in the Cabinet was unequaled, in whom the President had demonstrated full confidence — marshaled the arguments for the blockade and refused to be moved, the blockade became a formidable alternative.

Second, Robert Kennedy — the President's closest confidant — pressed the "Tojo" analogy. Acheson challenged RFK's "thoroughly false and pejorative analogy."[84] As Acheson recalls, he pointed out

> that at Pearl Harbor the Japanese without provocation or warning attacked our fleet thousands of miles from their shores. In the present situation the Soviet Union had installed missiles ninety miles from our coast — while denying they were doing so — offensive weapons that were capable of lethal injury to the United States. This they were doing a hundred and forty years after the warning given in President Monroe's time that the United States government would regard an attempt by any European power to extend its "system to any portion of this hemisphere as dangerous to our peace and safety" and as manifesting "an unfriendly disposition toward the United States." . . . How much warning was necessary to avoid the stigma of "Pearl Harbor in reverse"?[85]

This dispute over analogies Acheson dismissed as "dialectical" rather than serious.[86] What worried Acheson was that Robert Kennedy "seemed at the time — a view strengthened by his account — to have been moved by emotional or intuitive responses more than by the trained lawyer's analysis of the dangers threatened and of the relevance of these to the various actions proposed."[87] But Acheson's lecture did not move Robert Kennedy. Moreover, both RFK's analogy and his moral argument against the air strike struck a responsive chord in the President. (After these arguments had been stated so strongly, the President scarcely could have followed his initial preference without seeming to become what RFK had condemned.)

The President learned of the missiles on Tuesday morning. On Wednesday morning, in order to mask the discovery from the Russians, Kennedy flew to Connecticut to keep a campaign commitment, leaving RFK as the unofficial chairman of the group. By the time the President returned on Wednesday evening, a critical third piece had been added to the picture. McNamara had presented his argument for the blockade; Robert Kennedy had supported McNamara; Sorensen had joined the coalition. A "triple alliance," consisting of the advisers in whom the President had the greatest confidence and with whom he was personally most compatible, had emerged. This association deeply affected the lives of these men, as well as the course of events. As McNamara warmly recalls: "Common exposure to danger forges bonds and understanding between men stronger than those formed by decades of close association. So it was that I came to know, admire, and love Robert F. Kennedy by his behavior during the Cuban missile crisis."[88]

Fourth, the coalition that had formed behind the President's initial preference gave him reason to pause. *Who* supported the air strike — the Chiefs, McCone, Rusk, Nitze, and Acheson — counted as much as *how* they supported it. This *entente cordiale* was not composed of the President's natural allies. This point struck the President squarely as he listened to one of these "allies" answer a question about the Soviet response to an air strike. "I know the Soviets pretty well," this extra-governmental member of the ExCom replied. "I think they'll knock out our missile bases in Turkey." "What will we do then?" "Under our NATO Treaty, we'd be obligated to knock out a base inside the Soviet Union." "What will they do then?" "Why, then we hope everyone will cool down and want to talk."[89]

Fifth, a piece of inaccurate information, which no one probed, permitted the blockade advocates to fuel potential uncertainties in the President's mind. As Robert Kennedy's memoir reports, McNamara

> reinforced his position [against the air strike] by reporting that a surprise air strike against the missile bases alone — a surgical air strike, as it came to be called — was militarily impractical in the view of the Joint Chiefs of Staff, that any such military action would have to include all military installations in Cuba, eventually leading to an invasion.[90]

RFK and Sorensen met the President at the airport Wednesday evening with this information. In Sorensen's four-page memorandum outlining the areas of agreement and disagreement, the strongest argument was simply that the air strike could not be surgical. After a day of probing, it seemed clear that what the Air Force was preparing under the rubric "air strike" was something quite different: a massive attack. The Joint Chiefs had declared that the security of the United States required no less than the proposed attack. Even then, the Air Force admitted, "there could be no assurance that all the missiles would have been removed."[91] As Sorensen records, "this in particular influenced the President."[92] Perhaps he was troubled by shades of Cuba I. In any case, once the surgical air strike that he wanted had been declared a null option, he decided not to attend that evening's session of the ExCom, but rather to ponder the coalition's argument for the blockade.

On Thursday, discussion at the ExCom continued, without the President (though some of his staff met with him that morning and afternoon). When the President convened the ExCom at the White House on Thursday evening, he "had already moved from the air-strike to the blockade camp."[93] After the arguments, he declared his tentative choice of the blockade and directed that preparation be made to put it into effect by Monday morning.[94] Though he returned to the question of a surgical air strike subsequently, he seems to have accepted the experts' opinion that this was no live option.[95] (The President's acceptance of this estimate suggests that he may have learned the lesson of the Bay of Pigs, "Never rely on experts," less well than he supposed.)[96] This information was incorrect. During the second week of the crisis, civilian experts examined the surgical air-strike option, discovered that it could be chosen with high confidence, and thus added it to the list of options for the end of the second week. Why no one probed the initial estimate earlier is an interesting question for further investigation.

Though he seems to have missed this issue during that week of deliberations, in his recollection of these events Acheson complains that

> the narrow and specific proposal, pressed by some of us, constantly became obscured and complicated by trimmings added by the military. To the proposal of immediate and simultaneous low-level bombing attacks on the nuclear installations, some wished to add bombing of airfields, SAM sites, and fighter aircraft; and others, the landing of ground troops to assure that the missiles were destroyed or removed. . . . *While a drill book might call for preliminary attack on Cuban defenses,* this was not necessary for the action we recommended.[97]

Pure foul-up and confusion are sufficient to account for the fact that most of the civilian members of the ExCom failed to see this point. Some it helped; some it hurt. Most of these men had never seen the details of any military plan. Even if someone had been suspicious of the counsel of the military, was there anyone who had the information, or the time, or the authority to challenge the Chiefs' assertions about these military plans — preeminent matters of military expertise — on the basis of a suspicion? Even if someone had commanded all these resources, he might have hesitated, for if the challenge were made unsuccessfully, at least a day of precious time that could have been spent on other high-priority issues would be gone; the Chiefs would be enraged; and his own influence in subsequent events would be sharply diminished. And if the challenge were successful, the U.S. government might attempt a course of military action to which the Chiefs — the men who would be managing the machinery of action — were opposed, over which they had been embarrassed, and for which they had predicted failure.

Why the Chiefs of Staff themselves failed to see the consequences of their "trimmings," and of the Air Force assertion that it could guarantee only 90 percent confidence of destroying all the missiles in the full-dress strike, is more puzzling. But questions of just this sort surround their behavior throughout the crisis. Indeed, their oversights seem to reflect the same insensitivity that the President referred to when, after the crisis, he expressed dismay "that the representatives with whom he met, with the notable exception of General Taylor, seemed to give *so little consideration to the implications of steps they suggested.*"[98] What the President had in mind were such contributions as the Chiefs' attempts to assure him that the Russians would make no response to an air strike and the argument of one of the Chiefs that we should use nuclear weapons in the strike since "our adversaries would use theirs against us in an attack."[99] The inflated air strike and the crucial (inaccurate) estimate stemmed from the same failure to understand the reasoning and the rhetoric of the administration. General Taylor, who had chaired the administration's study of what went wrong in the Bay of Pigs episode, may have been fortified by reluctance to be in charge of any half-hearted military action initiated by this administration. But the insensitivity of Air Force Chief of Staff Curtis LeMay, whose Indians prepared the air-strike plan and the estimate, is really not surprising. On Sunday, October 28, *after* the Russians agreed to withdraw their missiles, he suggested that "we attack Monday in any case."[100]

The decision to blockade thus emerged as a collage. Its pieces included the President's initial decision that something forceful had to be done; the resistance of McNamara, Robert Kennedy, and Sorensen to the air strike; the relative distance between the President and the air-strike advocates; and an inaccurate piece of information. To get from here to a government decision and then action, the members of the club had to get the air-strike advocates on board.

RFK and Sorensen were the engineers of consensus. According to RFK's published recollection of the ExCom deliberations, "There was no rank, and, in fact, we did not even have a chairman."[101] But the others recall that Robert Kennedy "soon emerged as the discussion leader."[102] RFK recalled that "the conversations were completely uninhibited and unrestricted."[103] Sorensen remarks on the "sense of complete equality."[104] Nevertheless, he allows that in "shaping our deliberations when the President was absent, the best performer . . . was the Attorney General."[105] McNamara has affirmed that it was Robert Kennedy "acting with his brother's consent, who did so much to organize the effort, monitor the results and assure the completion of work on which recommendations to the President were based."[106] Stevenson compared the Attorney General to "a bull in a china shop."[107] In another participant's words, "Bobby made Christians of us. We all knew little brother was watching; and keeping a little list of where everyone stood."[108] In any case, the group moved toward consensus.

Acheson, the leader of the air-strike advocates, attacked the Attorney General sharply on Wednesday. He received an invitation to visit the White House on Thursday. The President listened to his argument, but Acheson left with no question in his mind about where the buck stopped. That evening, Kennedy informed the entire group of his decision in favor of the blockade. Friday was to have been the day of consensus, culminating in a formal decision that would be announced to the nation on Sunday evening.[109]

But on Friday, as the President prepared to leave for a scheduled campaign trip to the Midwest, the Joint Chiefs of Staff delayed his flight in order to press their argument.[110] Disgusted, the President called in his brother and Sorensen and charged them to "pull the group together quickly."[111] Otherwise, "more delays and dissension would plague whatever decision he took."[112] Still, Friday morning's ExCom meeting reopened the matter. Over protests that a decision had been reached the night before, the air-strike advocates continued to press their arguments.[113] Tempers became so heated that Sorensen resorted to an uncharacteristic invocation of his special relationship with the President: "We [are] not serving the President well."[114] Finally, Robert Kennedy flatly stated that the President could not possibly order an air strike.[115] Sorensen agreed to write the first draft of a blockade speech.[116] The air-strike advocates had lost. Dean Acheson did not return to the meeting the next day but instead retired to his farm in Maryland.[117]

Saturday was the day of "decision." That morning the group approved — or at least acquiesced in — Sorensen's draft of a blockade speech.[118] Robert Kennedy, who had spoken with his brother several times by telephone on Friday, called the President at the Blackstone Hotel in Chicago and informed him that the group was "ready to meet with him." A formal meeting of the National Security Council — the first of this crisis week — was set for Saturday afternoon.[120] RFK's memoir of the crisis strains to build to a point to climax: "It was now up to one single man. No committee was going to make this decision."[121]

The National Security Council meeting resembled a Greek drama in which the players maneuvered according to the plot, which moved inexorably toward the predetermined outcome. McCone began with the latest photographic intelligence, a daily ritual of such solemnity that it was referred to by some as "saying grace."[122] Then the two basic tracks were presented in considerable detail. McNamara in a "brilliant architectonic presentation" argued for the blockade: it would "maintain the options"; it would be a first step, leaving open the alternatives of destroying the missiles or even of invading Cuba. If the blockade did not cause Khrushchev to back down, then the missiles would be destroyed before they became operational. A cost would be incurred whatever action we took, but the blockade appeared most likely to secure our limited objective, the removal of the missiles — at the lowest cost.[123] Bundy outlined the case for the air strike: it was the most direct and efficient means of eliminating the problem.[124] According to Sorensen's record, "At the conclusion of the presentations, there was a brief, awkward silence. It was the most difficult and dangerous decision any President could make, and only he could make it."[125] But Deputy Secretary of Defense Gilpatric broke the silence with the remark: "Essentially, Mr. President, this is a choice between limited action and unlimited action; and most of us think that it's better to start with limited action."[126] The President "nodded his agreement" to limited action.[127] But before making the decision final, he wanted to talk directly with the Air Force Tactical Bombing Command to make certain that a truly "surgical" air strike was not feasible.[128]

At this point, the discussion turned to diplomatic moves that might accompany announcement of a blockade. Adlai Stevenson, who had returned from New York specifically for this decisive meeting, proposed first "the demilitarization, neutralization and guaranteed territorial integrity of Cuba, thus giving up of Guantánamo which . . . was of little use to us, in exchange for the removal of all Soviet missiles on Cuba."[129] As an alternate or subsequent move, he suggested that the United States offer "to withdraw our Turkish and Italian Jupiter missile bases if the Russians would withdraw their Cuban missile bases, and send U.N. inspection teams to all the foreign bases maintained by both sides to prevent their use in a surprise attack."[130] In a follow-up memo, he argued that this political program would avoid comparisons with the Suez invasion, "The offer would not sound 'soft' if properly worded," he declared. "It would sound 'wise,' particularly when combined with U.S. military action."[131]

President Kennedy addressed himself to Stevenson's proposals and rejected both. First, the United States simply could not give up Guantánamo at this point. Second, though he had previously ordered withdrawal of the Jupiter missiles, he dismissed any possibility of making such a concession under pressure. Instead of becoming defensive, the President insisted that we press our indictment of the Soviet Union for its duplicity and its threat to world peace. Lovett, McCone, and others joined in a much sharper attack on Stevenson's diplomatic proposals.[132]

Interpretation of this exchange must be speculative. As noted earlier, the President himself warned historians about "this mine field of charges and counter-charges."[133] Here, we will simply record the speculation that Kennedy— who had requested that Stevenson return from New York for the Saturday meeting — had in fact sacrificed the Ambassador to the hawks in order to allow himself to choose the moderate, golden mean. "The bitter aftertaste of that Saturday afternoon in the Oval Room stayed with him [Stevenson] until his death."[134]

On Sunday morning Kennedy met once more with the Air Force bombing experts. To them, this meeting was their last chance. Again, they asserted that the air strike would have to be massive and that they could not guarantee that all the missiles would be destroyed. But, they argued, the President had to authorize the air strike. Kennedy listened carefully but held his course. According to RFK's account, Sweeney's assurances "ended the small, lingering doubt that might still have remained in his mind. It had worried him that a blockade would not remove the missiles — now it was clear that an attack could not accomplish that task completely, either."[135] But his statement at the Saturday meeting and this last-minute reconsideration also "prepared the record" in case his chosen course ran aground.[136] At least he would not be vulnerable to the charge that he had not heard the Air Force case.

Thus, the decision that Kennedy announced to the world on Monday evening, October 22, emerged — part choice and part result, a melange of misperception, miscommunication, misinformation, bargaining, pulling, hauling, and spurring, as well as a mixture of national security interests, objectives, and governmental calculations recounted in more conventional accounts.

Soviet Withdrawal of the Missiles from Cuba

The full story of the withdrawal of Soviet missiles cannot be told: the information is simply not available. Nevertheless, our account of the politics of the American blockade provides a suggestive base from which to consider the subtle overlap of intranational games that brought about withdrawal without war. A tentative, somewhat speculative outline should indicate the importance of probing the available evidence and of examining hypotheses of this sort in trying to understand the withdrawal.

A sign posted outside the ExCom's briefing room in the State Department read, "In a Nuclear Age, nations must make war like porcupines make love — carefully."[137] On Tuesday, October 23, the mating dance of the porcupines began: U.S. ships started forming a blockade that would intercept Soviet ships speeding toward Cuba. Each successive, hesitant, occasionally stumbling, but more often deliberate step in this dance reflects the complex internal politics that moved each nation.

The President and the Chairman

> Bullfight critics row on row,
> Crowd the enormous plaza de toros
> But only one is there who knows,
> And he is the one who fights the bull.[138]

There was more than irony in President Kennedy's recital of this poem in closing an off-the-record press conference on Tuesday, October 16.[139] For that day he learned that the Soviets were installing offensive missiles in Cuba. In the preceding 635 days as President, he lived with the knowledge that at any moment he might make a personal judgment that would put half the world in jeopardy. Every day this responsibility weighed on his thought and his sleep. The experience of this burden separated him, and his needs, from those around him — even his closest advisers.[140] They could know his burden intellectually; he actually experienced it emotionally. As he put it in his year-end interview for 1962: "The President bears the burden of responsibility. The advisers may move on to new advice."[141]

Until October 1962, this weight hung around his neck as a prospective responsibility. Now events forced the nuclear toreador into the ring. What he experienced in those days we cannot know. The burden of responsibility for actually *making* judgments that might cause the quick death of millions of human beings and the destruction of entire societies must have been overwhelming. While he could involve others in the choice, his was the responsibility for the outcome. This qualitative difference in responsibility must have exaggerated the differences between his perspective and that of the men around him.

The language Kennedy chose to characterize the crisis gives us a glimpse into his perspective. At one particularly difficult point during the thirteen days, the President emphasized, with characteristic understatement, the differences between himself and his associates: "I guess I'd better earn my salary this week."[142] Robert Kennedy recorded the President's brooding about

> the specter of the death of the children of this country and all the world — the young people who had no role, who had no say, who knew nothing, even of the confrontation, but whose lives would be snuffed out like everyone else's. They would never have a chance to make a decision. . . . Our generation had. But the great tragedy was that, if we erred, we erred not only for ourselves, our futures, our hopes, and our country, but for the lives, futures, hopes, and countries of those who had never been given an opportunity to play a role . . . to make themselves felt.[143]

"It was this," RFK recorded, "that troubled him most, that gave him such pain."[144] Could anyone else have presumed to formulate these troubles? In the ExCom meetings, again and again Kennedy pressed upon his advisers the *consequences* of their proposals. RFK captured one instance:

He stressed again our responsibility to consider the effect our action would have on others. NATO was supporting the United States, but were these countries truly and completely aware of the dangers for them? These hourly decisions, necessarily made with such rapidity, could be made only by the President of the United States, but any one of them might close and lock doors for peoples and governments in many other lands. We had to be aware of this responsibility at all times . . . aware that the President was deciding, for the U.S., the Soviet Union, Turkey, NATO, and really for all mankind.[145]

This global conception of responsibilities and consequences would hardly have been appropriate for anyone else.

Perhaps only President Kennedy's Soviet counterpart also knew what it was to be, in Richard Neustadt's apt phrase, a "Final Arbiter."[146] Khrushchev's statements about the crisis were, characteristically, more dramatic than Kennedy's. He recalled the "smell of scorching [that] hung in the air."[147] He warned Kennedy that if we "do not show wisdom . . . [we] will come to a clash, like *blind moles,* and then reciprocal extermination would begin."[148] His secret Friday letter concluded with the most penetrating metaphor of the crisis:

If you have not lost your self-control and sensibly conceive what this might lead to, then, Mr. President, you and I ought not now to pull on the ends of the rope in which you have tied the *knot of war,* because the more the two of us pull, the tighter the knot will be tied. And a moment may come when that knot will be tied so tight that even he who tied it will not have the strength to untie it, and then it will be necessary to cut that knot, and what that would mean is not for me to explain to you, because you yourself understand perfectly of what terrible forces our countries dispose.[149]

This nuclear crisis seems to have magnified both rulers' conceptions of the consequences of nuclear war, and each man's awareness of his responsibility for these consequences. This consciousness not only set each man apart from his associates; it set them apart in a way that left the two alone — together. For they were equally yoked with responsibility for irreparable consequences: either man could cause both to fail; each would have to cooperate if they were to succeed. Indeed, it is a central feature of the crisis that these two men were partners in a game against nuclear disaster.

This tenous "alliance" is reflected in their private communications where each insisted on persuading himself that they both understood their common interest. In a private letter to Khrushchev, accompanying the public statement on October 22, Kennedy stated: "I have not assumed that you or any other sane man would, in the nuclear age, deliberately plunge the world into war which it is crystal clear no country could win and which could only result in catastrophic consequences to the whole world, including the aggressor."[150] In a later reply, Khrushchev assured Kennedy: "We are of sound mind and understand perfectly well that if we attack you, you will respond the same way. But you too will receive the same that you hurl against us. And I think you also understand this. . . . This indicates that we are normal people, that we correctly understand and correctly evaluate the situation."[151]

This partnership is reflected further in each leader's willingness to distinguish explicitly between the other leader and members of the other leader's government. A private letter from Kennedy to Khrushchev on October 25 might have caused Khrushchev some difficulty if it had been available to all members of his government. Kennedy charged that "your military people set out recently to establish a set of missile bases in Cuba."[152] Moreover, he included the following sentence: "I repeat my regret that these events should cause a deterioration in *our* relations."[153] A later Khrushchev letter drew a similar distinction: "Although I trust your statement, Mr. President, there are irresponsible people who would like to invade Cuba now and thus touch off a war."[154] Khrushchev went on to remind Kennedy that

> In 1960 we shot down your U-2 plane, whose reconnaissance flight over the U.S.S.R. wrecked the summit meeting in Paris. At that time, you took a correct posture and denounced that criminal act of the former U.S. administration. But during your term of office as President another violation of our border has occurred, by an American U-2 plane. . . . A still more dangerous case occurred on 28 October, when one of your reconnaissance planes intruded over Soviet borders. . . . Imagine the responsibility you are assuming; especially now, when we are living through such anxious times.[155]

What were the implications of this unique perspective, this sense that their mutual survival was indivisible? First were the strong pressures for each ruler to become the guardian, within his own government, of his "partner's" perspective and problem.

One can only wonder whether Kennedy's advocate in the Kremlin was as diligent as he. Certainly Kennedy understood and played this role. As he put it: "Mr. Khrushchev and I are in the same boat in the sense of both having this nuclear capacity and both wanting to protect our societies."[156] Over and over, the President would develop an argument, beginning "If I were Khrushchev."[157] Many members of the ExCom heard the President reject one of their proposals with the assertion, "Khrushchev would never stand for it!"[158] Robert Kennedy recalls that "During the crisis, President Kennedy spent more time trying to determine the effect of a particular course of action on Khrushchev . . . than on any other phase of what he was doing. What guided all his deliberations was an effort not to disgrace Khrushchev."[159]

Several months after the crisis, in August 1963, some advisers pressed him to issue a public demand that Khrushchev withdraw all Soviet forces from Cuba within sixty days. Kennedy rejected the proposal out of hand: "There is one thing I have learned in this business," he said, "and that is not to issue ultimatums. You just can't put the other fellow in a position where he has no alternative except humiliation."[160] It seems clear that this was what Kennedy had in mind in drawing the moral of the crisis in his celebrated American University speech: "Above all, while defending our own vital interests, nuclear powers must avert those confrontations which bring an adversary to the choice of either a humiliating defeat or a nuclear war."[161]

A second implication was that each "king" seems to have felt obliged to take control of, and manage, the game within his own government. Kennedy reached out beyond the normal span of Presidential awareness and influence to watch as many details as possible, to recheck potential slip-ups, to force to the fore arguments and alternatives that might have been slighted, to guarantee that the mix of players produced a first-rate map of the issues and options. He guarded against actions that would engage Khrushchev's pride or face and thus "require a response . . . which, in turn, for the same reasons of security, pride, or face would bring about a counterresponse and eventually an escalation into armed conflict."[162] "If they suffer a defeat . . ." he mused, "it increases possibly the chance of war."[163] He insisted that communications with the Soviets be clear and, knowing that a large portion of noise was inevitable, stated his crucial points over and over through a variety of channels. He demanded that Khrushchev be given time, again and again delaying the ExCom's preference for quick, forceful U.S. action. Perhaps recalling his own initial inclination, he bought time within his circle — time for Khrushchev to choose sensibly, time for him to get his government together and to act wisely. As RFK's memoir concludes:

> The President believed from the start that the Soviet Chairman was a rational, intelligent man who, if given sufficient time and shown our determination, would alter his position. But there was always the chance of error, of mistake, miscalculation or misunderstanding, and President Kennedy was committed to doing everything possible to lessen that chance on our side.[164]

From Blockade to Withdrawal

The attempt of both President and Chairman to dominate their internal games is illustrated by several incidents along the path from blockade to withdrawal. First, faced with these fateful decisions, both the President and the Chairman bypassed the formally established machinery, the National Security Council and the Presidium, in favor of *ad hoc* groups. The group assembled by the President and later authorized by the National Security Council as the Executive Committee of the NSC included (1) the major Cabinet and agency officers with principal responsibility for political and military decisions, (2) Presidentially selected surrogates for major segments of the public — for example, Acheson, Lovett, and McCloy as representatives of the bi-partisan foreign policy establishment; and (3) a number of advisers who were present only because of Presidential choice — for example, Robert Kennedy and Sorensen. This group functioned with minimal reliance on the standard channels down into the second or third levels of the government, causing no little pain to the players left out of the action.[165] But the pressures to cut the group off from the bureaucracy were enormous, especially in light of the President's needs.

Khrushchev seems to have assembled an ExCom of his own, including Mikoyan, Kosygin, Suslov, Brezhnev, and Kozlov.[166] Presidium candidates were not summoned to Moscow, and Podgorny — the only full member not resident in the capital — apparently remained in Kiev. Some of the Presidium members who lived in Moscow seem to have been left out of the deliberations.[167] Of necessity, both the President and the Chairman shared the making of these decisions with those who shared power over political-military actions. But both also exercised discretion in the composition of their groups.

Second, the operation of the blockade and the testing of the blockade reveal elements of caution suggestive of an acute sense of the risks involved. Obviously, many features of the blockade were not controlled by the President. But in a number of incidents, Kennedy did manage to turn the balance in favor of more time for Khrushchev. On Wednesday, October 25, the day on which the blockade went into effect, the Russian tanker *Bucharest* reached the barricade. The tanker probably carried no contraband and could therefore be allowed to pass after simply identifying itself. On the other hand, some members of the Ex-Com argued that the *Bucharest* should be stopped and boarded "so that Khrushchev would make no mistake of our will or intent."[168] Kennedy postponed the decision, ordering American warships to trail the *Bucharest*. Later that evening he decided to let the ship go through to Cuba. "We don't want to push him [Khrushchev] to a precipitous action," Kennedy said. "Give him time to consider. I don't want to put him in a corner from which he cannot escape."[169] Kennedy also permitted an East German passenger ship to slip through the blockade before the Navy was finally allowed to stop and board the *Marcula*, a Soviet-chartered but Lebanese-owned ship personally selected by the President.[170]

What role Khrushchev played in the Soviet testing of the blockade is uncertain. He obviously had strong allies in the chiefs of the intelligence agencies, who were mindful of the possibility that if Soviet ships tried to challenge the blockade, the United States might capture their missiles and warheads. The manner in which the dry-cargo ships and submarine escorts drew up short of the blockade, missile-carrying ships returned to the Soviet Union, and ships likely not to offend the announced quarantine tested the blockade, indicates strong, central, cautious management.

Third, though many voices spoke through the multiple channels of communication between the United States and Soviet Union, the President and the Chairman were relatively successful in establishing a private "hot line" by which to reiterate what had to be understood.[171] Among the channels of communication flowing between Moscow and Washington in this period were: (1) public letters between the two heads of government;

(2) private letters between the two heads of government; (3) public and private statements by U.S. officials in Washington; the Party, government, and military press in Moscow; and public and private statements by officials of both governments at the United Nations; (4) news conferences; (5) messages through intelligence channels; (6) public and private letters to third parties; (7) leaks; and (8) private communications from JFK to RFK to Dobrynin to Khrushchev.

A myriad of "signals" — some compatible and others contradictory — were sent through these channels. The "messages" tended to be garbled for two reasons. First, single communications were aimed at many audiences — for example, a public Presidential letter being directed to the Soviet government, the American permanent government, the Congress, the American public, world opinion. Second, many different individuals within each government spoke, each with his own perspective and priorities. For example, on Friday, October 26, the State Department Press Officer, Lincoln White, went beyond the White House position, emphasizing to reporters a passage in the President's Monday night speech warning that if work on the missiles continued, "further action will be justified." This piece of communication brought the President's rage down on White's head.[172]

In order to reduce the contextual noise, Kennedy and Khrushchev sought out, and used, a private, secure "hot line." Several messages were relayed from the President to the Chairman, and vice versa, through RFK and Dobrynin.[173] This channel of communication became critical in the final days.

Fourth, what much of the U.S. government regarded as the "flap in the White House" underlined differences in perspective between the President and his officials. As the second week dragged on and considerations turned to further steps, the White House did begin to flap. The President in particular, but also others who assumed a Presidential perspective, actually thought their way down paths that led in only five steps to a major nuclear war. For example: (1) the United States attacks Soviet missiles in Cuba; (2) the Soviet Union attacks U.S. missiles in Turkey and Italy; (3) NATO attacks bases from which the attack on Turkey and Italy was launched; (4) the Soviets, fearing an American attack, launch ICBMs and bombers against the United States; (5) the United States decimates the Soviet Union. What they saw should have caused a little trembling. Moreover, Kennedy, in particular, saw how miscalculation, misunderstandings, and momentum could turn this path into a slippery slope. Having recently read Barbara Tuchman's book *The Guns of August,* he mused about the miscalculations of the Germans, the Russians, the Austrians, the French, and the British, the confusion within each government that allowed the lot to tumble into war.[174]

From the perspective of some members of the ExCom, and most members of the government outside the White House, the White House fear seemed alarmist. Viewed from the departments, "this exaggerated concern prompted consideration of improvident actions . . . and counseled hesitations where none were necessary."[175] As a major departmental report on the crisis concluded: "Since the United States could get its way without invoking nuclear weapons, the burden of choice rested entirely on the Soviets."[176] In its most extreme form, officialdom's view of the crisis was symbolized by a Defense Department civilian official's reactions to the Soviet ships halting before testing the U.S. blockade: "My God," he said, "someone should fire their game manager!"

While it is difficult to believe that the President actually felt that the chance of war was one-in-three, it should be easy to see why he had good reasons for substantial fears. He understood the frailty of his own government. Working to reduce his own government's foul-ups, he was nevertheless aware of the inevitability of misunderstandings, miscommunications, and misjudgments. Even if he managed to control his own machine, what about his "partner"? Reflecting on how the poor so-and-sos in the Kremlin were getting on, the President sensed the near impossibility, but unavoidable necessity, of two such complex machines interacting in a deliberate and controlled fashion.

The "Deal"

The blockade serves as the centerpiece in most analysts' explanations of the Soviet withdrawal of missiles from Cuba. It signaled the engagement of vital U.S. interests and a firm American commitment to elimination of the missiles. In that context, the Soviets had but one choice. This explanation is rejected by other analysts, who point out that the blockade failed to force withdrawal. Only when the United States took the further step of issuing an ultimatum that gave the Kremlin the choice between removing the missiles and having the United States remove them did Khrushchev announce the withdrawal. At least one analyst has argued that the matter is still more complicated. The Soviets withdrew after the U.S. ultimatum, but at a point when the President had begun to wobble (evidenced by his order to defuse U.S. missiles in Turkey). From the perspective of the present account, these available data can be combined in a further, more revealing interpretation.

Announced in the President's Monday speech, the quarantine became operational on Wednesday at 10 A.M. By Thursday evening, most members of the ExCom saw that the blockade was not working: while it prevented Soviet missile shipments to Cuba, construction of missiles already on the island rushed toward operational readiness. Thus they faced the issue of the next step. The consensus behind the blockade, such as it was, had been built on an agreement that if the blockade failed, then the United States would move to more forceful action, in particular the air strike. As the "slow agony" — Bundy's phrase for the blockade — became unbearable, the advocates of military action pressed their arguments.[177] Other possible steps were suggested — for example, adding petroleum, oil, and lubricants (POL) to the quarantine. The original blockade team, and especially the President, searched for an option that would stave off the air strike. But as RFK recalled,

> the feeling grew that this cup was not going to pass and that a direct military confrontation between the two great nuclear powers was inevitable. Both "hawks" and "doves" sensed that our combination of limited force and diplomatic efforts had been unsuccessful. If the Russians continued to be adamant and continued to build up their missile strength, military force would be the only alternative.[178]

Largely because of the mounting pressures within the administration, it was generally agreed that the next step could not be postponed for more than one or two days.

At Friday morning's meeting, the President ordered the State Department to ready plans for a civil government in Cuba, which would be established after the invasion and occupation. Don Wilson of USIA was authorized to print five million leaflets in Spanish explaining why the United States had been forced to attack Cuba. The names of all Cuban doctors in the Miami area were collected, should they be required. Discussion in the ExCom centered on casualties that the United States would incur in an invasion. The President said: "We are going to have to face the fact that, if we do invade, by the time we get to these sites, after a very bloody fight, they will be pointed at us. And we must further accept the possibility that when military hostilities first begin, those missiles will be fired."[179]

But Friday afternoon brought relief. First, at 1:30 that afternoon, John Scali, the State Department correspondent for ABC, "a man known to be trusted as a reliable and accurate reporter by the highest levels of the U.S. Government," received an urgent phone call from Alexander Fomin, a Soviet embassy official who was known to be the head of the KGB in Washington.[180] At a quickly arranged meeting, Fomin put to Scali a concrete proposal for resolving the crisis: "(1) The Soviet Union would agree to dismantle and remove the offensive missiles in Cuba. (2) It would allow United Nations inspection to supervise and verify the removal. (3) The Soviet government would pledge not to reintroduce missiles, ever, to Cuba. And (4) in return, the United States would pledge publicly not to invade Cuba."[181] He asked Scali to find out immediately from his "high-level friends in the State Department" how the U.S. government would react to this proposal. Scali went directly to Roger Hilsman, Director of the State Department's Bureau for Intelligence and Research, who took him to Rusk.

Though the channels were unorthodox, Rusk received the Fomin proposal seriously. The head of the KGB, who had his own direct channels of communication to the Kremlin, would not make such an approach lightly.[182] Rusk drafted two sentences, cleared them with the White House, and gave the handwritten note to Scali. It said: "I have reason to believe that the U.S.G. sees real possibilities and supposes that the representatives of the two governments in New York could work this matter out with U Thant and with each other. My impression is, however, that time is very urgent."[183] And he further emphasized to Scali, beating out his slow cadence with his fist, that time was short, very short — not more than two days.[184] Scali immediately took the message to Fomin, who assured him that it would be rushed to the very highest levels of the Kremlin.

At 6 P.M. the notorious "secret Friday letter" from Khrushchev arrived. Though several accounts of this letter have portrayed it as the "outcry of a frightened man," it was nothing of the sort.[185] It was a very personal letter, bearing the unmistakable marks of Khrushchev himself, long, sometimes rambling, and emotional. But, as RFK recorded, "it was not incoherent, and the emotion was directed at the death, destruction, and anarchy that nuclear war would bring to his people and all mankind. That, he said again and again and in many different ways, must be avoided."[186] Though the letter is still classified, it is of such importance that the pieces available in the public record should be compiled. The following reproduces both quotations and paraphrases from public sources.[187]

> The moment had come, Khrushchev wrote, to rise above "petty passion" and to stop the drift toward war before it was too late. Elections might seem important in some countries, but they were transient things. "If indeed war should break out, then it would not be in our power to stop it, for such is the logic of war. I have participated in two wars and know that war ends when it has rolled through cities and villages, everywhere sowing death and destruction."
>
> It was obvious that he and Kennedy could not agree on the significance of the missiles in Cuba. Kennedy was mistaken to think of them as offensive missiles. There was, however, no need to quarrel over definitions. It was apparent that he would never be able to persuade Kennedy that the missiles in Cuba were defensive weapons. As a "military man," the President ought to understand that missiles alone, even a vast number of missiles of varying ranges and explosive power, could not be a means of attack. Missiles were nothing but a means of extermination. To attack, you needed troops. Unless it was backed up by troops, no missile — not even a missile carrying a hundred-megaton nuclear warhead — could be offensive.
>
> The United States, he went on to say, should not be concerned about the missiles in Cuba; they would never be used to attack the United States and were there for defensive purposes only.
>
> You can be calm in this regard, that we are of sound mind and understand perfectly well that if we attack you, you will respond the same way. But you too will receive the same that you hurl against us. And I think that you also understand this. . . . This indicates that we are normal people, that we correctly understand and correctly evaluate the situation. Consequently, how can we permit the incorrect actions which you ascribe to us? Only lunatics or suicides, who themselves want to perish and to destroy the whole world before they die, could do this.
>
> "We want something quite different . . . not to destroy your country . . . but despite our ideological differences, to compete peacefully, not by military means."
>
> There was no purpose, he said, for us to interfere with any of his ships now bound for Cuba, for they contained no weapons.

The weapons required to defend the island were already there. He would not pretend that the Soviet Union shipped no weapons to Cuba. Not at all. Soviet weapons were indeed shipped to Cuba, but they had long since arrived.

Why had the Russians sent missiles into Cuba? Khrushchev said he would be quite frank. It was because there had been a landing at the Bay of Pigs. Cuba had been attacked and many Cubans had lost their lives. He had mentioned this to Kennedy at their Vienna meeting in June of 1961. The President had then assured him that the Bay of Pigs landing was a mistake. Khrushchev accepted the explanation. The President had repeated it, making the point that not all Chiefs of State were prepared to acknowledge their mistakes. Khrushchev honored such frankness. The Soviet leaders were no less courageous. They, too, had acknowledged the mistakes of the past — Stalin's mistakes — acknowledged and sharply condemned them.

The President had every right to be concerned with the peace and welfare of the American people. The Chairman of the Soviet Council of Ministers was no less concerned for his people. Both ought to be jointly concerned with saving the peace, because war in modern conditions would be a world war, a catastrophe for mankind.

"If assurances were given that the President of the United States would not participate in an attack on Cuba and the blockade lifted, then the question of the removal or the destruction of the missile sites in Cuba would then be an entirely different question. Armaments bring only disasters. When one accumulates them, this damages the economy, and if one puts them to use, then they destroy people on both sides. Consequently, only a madman can believe that armaments are the principal means in the life of society. No, they are an enforced loss of human energy, and what is more are for the destruction of man himself. If people do not show wisdom, then in the final analysis they will come to a clash, like blind moles, and then reciprocal extermination will begin."

This is my proposal, he said. No more weapons to Cuba and those within Cuba withdrawn or destroyed, and you reciprocate by withdrawing your blockade and also agree not to invade Cuba. Don't interfere, he said, in a piratical way with Russian ships. "If you have not lost your self-control and sensibly conceive what this might lead to, then, Mr. President, we and you ought not to pull on the ends of the rope in which you have tied the knot of war, because the more the two of us pull, the tighter the knot will be tied. And a moment may come when the knot will be tied so tight that not even he who tied it will not have the strength to untie it, and then it will be necessary to cut that knot, and what that would mean is not for me to explain to you, because you yourself understand perfectly of what terrible forces our countries dispose. Consequently, if there is no intention to tighten that knot, and thereby to doom the world to the catastrophe of thermonuclear war, then let us not only relax the forces pulling on the ends of the rope, let us take measures to untie that knot. We are ready for this."

Considered in tandem, Fomin's inquiry and Khrushchev's letter had the makings of a deal: (1) the Soviet Union would remove the missiles from Cuba, under U.N. observation; (2) the United States would remove the quarantine and pledge not to invade Cuba. Although Acheson predicted that the Soviets would never go through with such a deal, if these indeed were the terms, no one in the U.S. government could really oppose it.[188] A group in the State Department's Bureau of Intelligence and Research were assigned to spend the night preparing an analysis of Khrushchev's letter and Fomin's proposal — particularly to look for "any hookers" — to be ready for the ExCom meeting on Saturday morning. RFK reported

a slight feeling of optimism as I drove home from the State Department that night. The letter, with all its rhetoric, had the beginnings perhaps of some accommodation, some agreement. . . . I was also slightly more optimistic because when I left the President that night, he too was for the first time hopeful that our efforts might possibly be successful.[189]

Saturday was different. Indeed most participants remember it as "the blackest day" of the crisis, though individuals differ, to some extent, about why it was black. The ExCom assembled at 10 A.M. At 10:17 Robert Kennedy's glimmer of hope began to fade. The news ticker reported a new letter from Khrushchev, being broadcast by Radio Moscow. In contrast to the letter received on Friday, this one read more formally, bearing the signs of a document that had been approved by a large number of governmental officials before being dispatched by the Foreign Office. The contrast in substance overshadowed the difference in style. This letter *switched* the terms of the deal: American missiles in Turkey were demanded as the price for the removal of Russian missiles in Cuba.

You are worried over Cuba. You say that it worries you because it lies at a distance of ninety miles across the sea from the shores of the United States. However, Turkey lies next to us.

Our sentinels are pacing up and down and watching each other. Do you believe that you have the right to demand security for your country and the removal of such weapons that you qualify as offensive, while not recognizing this right for us?

You have stationed devastating rocket weapons, which you call offensive, in Turkey literally right next to us. How then does recognition of our equal military possibilities tally with such unequal relations between our great states? This does not tally at all. . . .

This is why I make this proposal: We agree to remove those weapons from Cuba which you regard as offensive weapons. We agree to do this and to state this commitment in the United Nations. Your representatives will make a statement to the effect that the United States, on its part, bearing in mind the anxiety and concern of the Soviet state, will evacuate its analogous weapons from Turkey.[190]

What did this shift mean? Had Khrushchev been overruled by members of the Presidium? Maybe other members of the Presidium, encouraged by the talk of a swap in Washington and London newspapers, had forced Khrushchev to up the ante.[191] "The change in the language and tenor of the letters from Khrushchev indicated confusion within the Soviet Union," Robert Kennedy recorded, "but there was confusion among us as well."[192] Doubts fed doubts as confusion spread around the conference table. Even the ExCom's Soviet expert, Llewellyn Thompson — whose reading of the Soviets up to this point had struck other members of the group as remarkably confident and remarkably accurate — was uncertain.[193] While there could be no doubt that members of the Presidium differed substantially among themselves, no one could be sure about the shape of these differences.[194]

Confusion fueled tension — and new sources of confusion further clouded the picture. First, McCone reported that "A single Soviet ship had detached itself from the others outside the quarantine line and was headed for Cuba."[195] Maybe the Soviets wanted to test the permeability of the quarantine. Or perhaps they planned to provoke an incident. Second, intelligence reported that work on the missile sites was now proceeding full speed, both day and night.[196] Furthermore, work was proceeding rapidly on "permanent and expensive installations of nuclear warhead storage bunkers and troop barracks."[197] The two letters could be a device for stalling while the missiles became operational. Third, and most distressing, Soviet SAMs had shot down a U-2 reconnaissance plane over Cuba. The Soviet SAM network was operational and the Soviets meant to use it.

The Soviets had fired the first shot, causing the first fatality of the crisis. The ExCom could no longer postpone the issue of military force. The conclusion seemed foregone. Earlier in the week, the ExCom had decided that if a U-2 were shot down, the United States would retaliate against a single SAM site. If a second U-2 were attacked, the United States would destroy all the SAM sites.[198] The Air Force had prepared an attack plan and was ready to go. In the ExCom, "There was almost unanimous agreement that we had to attack early the next morning."[199]

Then, at the point of actual implementation, the President's doubts emerged. "It isn't the first step that concerns me," he said, "but both sides escalating to the fourth and fifth step — and we don't go to the sixth because there is no one around to do so. We must remind ourselves we are embarking on a very hazardous course."[200] Over sharp disagreement, and to the dismay of many members of the group, Kennedy reversed the earlier decision, postponing the choice yet another day.[201] Maybe the plane had crashed accidentally. We should have a more careful review of the implications of various courses of action. Furthermore, he called off "the flare drop flights scheduled for that night . . . because of the danger that the flares might be taken for air-to-ground fire from the planes."[202] In the Pentagon, especially in the office of the Air Force Chief of Staff, the order to stop the Air Force reprisal was received with disbelief.

The Soviets had raised the ante. Had Kennedy folded, or simply checked? Around the government, and around the table, suspicion and tension mounted. And still there was the issue of a response to the two Soviet proposals. "Our little group, seated around the cabinet table in continuous session that Saturday," Sorensen writes, "felt nuclear war to be closer on that day than at any time in the nuclear age. If the Soviet ship continued coming, if the SAMs continued firing, if the missile crews continued working and if Khrushchev continued insisting on concessions with a gun at our head, then — we all believed — the Soviets must want a war and war would be unavoidable."[203]

As discussion returned to the question of a U.S. reply, Robert Kennedy recorded his judgment that the second Soviet proposal — missiles in Cuba for missiles in Turkey — "was not unreasonable and did not amount to a loss to the U.S. or to our NATO allies."[204] Indeed, because the Jupiter missiles in Turkey had been judged obsolete, the President had twice ordered their removal. In the spring of 1962, at Presidential insistence, Rusk had raised the issue with the Turkish Foreign Minister, heard loud objections, and allowed the matter to drop. For the Secretary of State, removal of obsolete missiles from Turkey did not justify a row with the Turkish government. The President had raised the matter a second time with Undersecretary of State Ball and made it plain that he wanted the missiles removed, even at some political cost. But again, State Department representatives found the Turks intransigent and decided against allowing the question to become a source of discontent in relations with Turkey and in the NATO alliance. Now Kennedy was forced to confront the Turkish missiles once more, and this time they were hostages of the Soviet Union. As RFK recorded, "He was angry."[205]

Could the United States withdraw the Turkish missiles under Soviet threat? No. Rusk and Ball argued that such a trade would "undermine the faith of the whole alliance in America's pledged word."[206] Thompson warned that "the Russians would certainly interpret the President's acceptance as proof of weakness."[207] Sorensen records that "the President had no intention of destroying the alliance by backing down."[208] As Kennedy had argued just one week earlier in rejecting Stevenson's suggestion of this trade, he could not make "concessions that could break up the Alliance by confirming European suspicions that we would sacrifice their security to protect our interests in an area of no concern to them."[209] Harold Macmillan recalled his support for the President's "most difficult decision . . . the refusal, against the advice of weaker brethren in America and elsewhere, to bargain the security of the Western world by yielding to the specious Russian offers of a face-saving accommodation at the expense of America's allies."[210] A formal White House statement was released, dismissing the Soviets' Saturday letter with reference to "inconsistent and conflicting proposals . . . [involving] the security of nations outside the Western hemisphere."[211]

Still the quandary persisted: How could the United States respond? In trying to devise a reply, "Fatigue and disagreement over the right course caused more wrangling and irritability than usual."[212] The Joint Chiefs of Staff joined the meeting to propose a solution: an air strike on Monday, followed shortly by an invasion. Robert Kennedy noted their argument: they had always felt the blockade "to be far too weak a course and that military steps were the only ones the Soviet Union would understand. They were not at all surprised that nothing had been achieved by limited force, for this is exactly what they had predicted."[213] The President restrained himself.

At some point in the deliberations, the President paused over the first-round implications of the option that was coming to seem more and more likely: an air strike or invasion of Cuba. What would happen, he asked, in Berlin or Turkey? "If we attacked Cuba, and the Russians reciprocated with an attack on Turkey, would or should the Turkish missiles be fired?"[214] At this point, he ordered that the missiles in Turkey be de-fused.[215] For some members of the group, this was the darkest moment of the day.

By early afternoon, Rusk and Ball, with the aid of Thompson, had drafted a note from Kennedy to Khrushchev rejecting the Turkish trade and demanding a halt to work on the missiles in Cuba. Robert Kennedy disagreed sharply with both the content and the tenor of the draft.[216] In desperation, he conceived an extraordinary diplomatic move, one later labeled a "Trollope Ploy," after a recurring scene in the writings of Victorian novelist Anthony Trollope in which a marriage-hungry maiden takes some imprudent gesture — for example, a squeeze on her hand — as an opportunity to accept a proposal of marriage. The United States should ignore the second letter, respond to the terms of the first letter as refined by Fomin's inquiry, and propose the following: an American pledge not to invade Cuba in return for the Soviet withdrawal of missiles in Cuba. As Robert Kennedy recalled

> There were arguments back and forth. There were sharp disagreements. Everyone was tense; some were already near exhaustion; all were weighted down with concern and worry.... When we almost seemed unable to communicate with one another, he [the President] suggested with a note of some exasperation that — inasmuch as I felt so strongly that the State Department's various efforts to respond were not satisfactory — Ted Sorensen and I should leave the meeting and go into his office and compose an alternative response.[217]

Robert Kennedy and Sorensen left, wrote a response accepting Khrushchev's first "offer," and presented it to the group. After minor refinement, the group followed the President's lead and accepted it. The essential points of this public letter read as follows:

The first thing that needs to be done . . . is for work to cease on
offensive missile bases in Cuba and for all weapons systems
in Cuba capable of offensive use to be rendered inoperable,
under effective United Nations arrangements. . . .

As I read your letter, the key elements of your proposals —
which seem generally acceptable as I understand them — are
as follows:

1. You would agree to remove these weapons systems from
Cuba under appropriate United Nations observation and supervision; and undertake, with suitable safeguards, to halt the
further introduction of such weapons systems into Cuba.

2. We, on our part, would agree — upon the establishment
of adequate arrangements through the United Nations to ensure
the carrying out and continuation of these commitments — (a)
to remove promptly the quarantine measures now in effect and
(b) to give assurances against an invasion of Cuba.[218]

To make sure Khrushchev could not misunderstand the
message, the President privately instructed Robert Kennedy to
deliver a copy of the letter to Dobrynin with a strong warning.
According to Sorensen's account, Robert Kennedy warned
Dobrynin: "The point of escalation was at hand; the United
States could proceed toward peace and disarmament, or we could
take 'strong and overwhelming retaliatory action . . . unless [the
President] received immediate notice that the missiles would be
withdrawn.' "[219] The President thus posed for Khrushchev a
choice between accepting the terms of the original deal and seeing his missiles in Cuba destroyed by a U.S. attack. The time
available for him to make up his mind and get his government
together was very short.

Given the President's unique perspective and his particular
problem (removal of the Russian missiles from Cuba without
war), this ultimatum seems puzzling, especially in the light of
his earlier preference for postponing forceful action. One can
understand how representatives of the State Department, who
had failed to negotiate removal of the Turkish missiles, might
be persuaded by the argument that a deal would split the NATO
allies. But the President had already been willing to pay part of
that price, since many Europeans would interpret the de-fusing
of the Turkish missiles as the first step in a deal, whatever the
United States said. Why should his concern for the problem that
withdrawal would mean for the NATO allies now dominate his
interest in giving Khrushchev an acceptable path away from
war? One can understand why, if it were simply a matter of
competitive bargaining between two nations in which one na-

tion's loss were the other's gain, the United States could not respond to the Friday letter, refuse the terms of the Saturday letter, and then offer a private deal on the side. This show of weakness might tempt the Soviets to demand more. But the earlier behavior of both leaders suggests recognition of their precarious partnership. Kennedy had demonstrated considerable attentiveness to Khrushchev's problem. Now Khrushchev seemed to be asking for a path by which to retreat, without humiliation within his own government.

In Presidential terms the case for a *private* carrot to balance the public stick seems compelling. The President should not be *seen* accepting Saturday's deal. Indeed, the arrangements would have to be made without the knowledge of most members of his own ExCom, let alone the rest of the government or the wider public. So (one might be led to speculate) he sent RFK to see Dobrynin.

This speculation was no more than that when it was first formulated. Had RFK not written his memoirs, and indeed, quite probably, had he had the opportunity to edit his first draft, these speculations would remain in the realm of the fanciful. A careful reading of *Thirteen Days,* however, discloses important, confirming evidence. Robert Kennedy recounted his visit with Dobrynin in considerable detail — including their discussion of missiles in Turkey.*

---

*Memoirs attributed to Khrushchev, *Khrushchev Remembers* (Boston, 1970), contain an interesting, rather fanciful account of the meeting between RFK and Dobrynin. "The climax came after five or six days when our ambassador to Washington, Anatoly Dobrynin, reported that the President's brother, Robert Kennedy, had come to see him. Dobrynin's report went something like this: 'Robert Kennedy looked exhausted. One could see from his eyes that he had not slept for days. He himself said that they had not been home for six days and nights. The President is in a grave situation, Robert Kennedy said, and he does not know how to get out of it. We are under very severe stress. In fact we are under pressure from our military to use force against Cuba. . . . We want to ask you, Mr. Dobrynin, to pass President Kennedy's message to Chairman Khrushchev through unofficial channels. President Kennedy implores Chairman Khrushchev to accept his offer and to take into consideration the peculiarities of the American system. Even though the President himself is very much against starting a war over Cuba, an irreversible chain of events could occur against his will. That is why the President is appealing directly to Chairman Khrushchev for help in liquidating this conflict. If the situation continues much longer, the President is not sure that the military will not overthrow him and seize power' " (pp. 497–98).

Can this private exchange be properly labeled a "deal"? What was above as well as what was below the line could not have been plainer. At the initial level, there could be no "deal." Let the issue be clear: the Russian missiles must be removed — with no strings attached. But at a second level, let there be no misunderstanding. The President had intended that the Turkish missiles be removed more than a year ago. Nothing had changed. And Khrushchev could be assured that they would be removed within a short time after the crisis. In RFK's words,

> I said that there could be no quid pro quo or any arrangement made under this kind of threat or pressure, and that in the last analysis this was a decision that would have to be made by NATO. However, I said, President Kennedy had been anxious to remove those missiles from Turkey and Italy for a long period of time. He had ordered their removal some time ago, and it was our judgment that, within a short time after the crisis was over, those missiles would be gone.[220]

Soviet Installation of the Missiles

To construct a plausible account of why the Soviets placed missiles in Cuba is not difficult. Indeed, it is embarrassingly easy to construct a large number of plausible accounts of this occurrence and extraordinarily difficult to distinguish among them. Given the limits of the available public information about the developments within the Soviet Union at that time, it is not possible to have high confidence in any single explanation.[221] Unfortunately, few published accounts of this event manage to communicate the extent to which they are, of necessity, tenuous, tentative, and uncertain. This account acknowledges these limits. Nevertheless, the perspective developed in the analysis of the blockade and the withdrawal will allow us to formulate several more confident, limited points and to produce an outline that, while uncertain and speculative, may be nonetheless of some heuristic value.

American Warning and Soviet Decision

The Kennedy administration reacted to the discovery of Soviet offensive missiles in Cuba with "shocked incredulity."[222]

We have analyzed the President's personal reaction above: "If Khrushchev could pull this after all his protestations and denials, how could he ever be trusted on anything?"[223] Sorensen recalls the group's reasoning: "The fact that Khrushchev had already made one major miscalculation — in thinking he could get away with missiles in Cuba — increased the danger that he would make more."[224] This feeling of shock over the proportions of Khrushchev's miscalculation shaped the ExCom's reading of the situation. The issue was posed: What objective could Khrushchev possibly have that would lead him to violate the President's confidence and fly in the face of solemn American warnings? No slim ambition would account for such a major error. The only hypothesis consistent with the facts was one of grand Cold War politics: Khrushchev intended the "supreme probe" of the United States' (or the President's) courage.[225]

This interpretation — by the administration and by a large number of subsequent analysts who have followed the administration's understanding of this point — fails to consider carefully the likely perceptions of people in Moscow at the time of the decision to place offensive missiles in Cuba.

Consider the evidence that could have been available. First, in the spring of 1961, the United States had invaded Cuba — in a half-hearted, hesitant fashion. Khrushchev seems to have been deeply puzzled by Kennedy's behavior in the Bay of Pigs episode. Perhaps Kennedy could stumble, or be forced by other members of his government, into military action against Cuba; but when the crunch came, he did not regard Cuba as sufficiently important to U.S. vital interests to justify decisive military action. Second, in the summer of 1961 the chairman of the Senate Foreign Relations Committee, Senator J. William Fulbright — whom, it was known, Kennedy had seriously considered appointing as his Secretary of State — made a speech on the floor of the Senate that seemed to invite the Soviets to consider moving missiles to Cuba.

> The possibility of Soviet missile bases and jet aircraft bases in Cuba is frequently noted. I suppose we would all be less comfortable if the Soviets did install missile bases in Cuba, but I am not sure that our national existence would be in substantially greater danger than is the case today. Nor do I think that such bases would substantially alter the balance of power in the world.

What would substantially alter the balance of power in the world would be precipite action by the United States resulting in the alienation of most of Latin America, Asia and Africa.[226]

Third, in the fall of 1961, the administration discovered that there was no "missile gap" and announced publicly that the United States had marked·missile superiority. The administration's program for a substantial American second-strike capability proceeded on track, and several officials, as well as a number of government consultants, began talking about the necessity for the Soviets to build up a second-strike capability of their own. Some Americans seemed to feel that both the United States and the Soviet Union would be safer if both had substantial missile capabilities.[227] Fourth, Soviet shipments of military equipment to Cuba had, after all, begun in the middle of 1960 and continued intermittently up to the time when the decision was made — without any serious suggestion that this might provoke U.S. action. Finally, up to the spring of 1962 — the latest point when the decision could have been made — the administration statements on Soviet arms to Cuba were quite restrained.

On the basis of this evidence, it would not have been difficult to argue in the spring of 1962 that the Kennedy administration's reaction to Soviet missiles in Cuba would be minimal. If the missiles were installed discreetly, so as to avoid making waves in American domestic politics, the administration would react with protests but inaction. Certainly, the available evidence does not exclude the possibility that the advocates of the Soviet decision argued solely in terms of objectives like Cuban defense or the build-up of Soviet strategic capabilities and that no one in the Soviet government had any intention whatever of probing American commitments or of posing a personal challenge to the President. In the spring of 1962, who could have predicted that Cuba would become a major campaign issue, forcing the President to draw a line between offensive and defensive weapons and commit himself to action against offensive weapons?

The administration reaction to the Soviet move erred in not recognizing the difference between the climate in which the Soviet leaders decided to install missiles in Cuba and the climate in which U.S. leaders discovered the Soviet missiles. But, it could be argued, this error was of little consequence, since *after* the administration became exercised about the Soviet build-up and *after* strong Presidential warnings, Khrushchev persisted in his chosen course. Indeed, at that point, Khrushchev spent the bank account of trust that he had built up with Kennedy, deliberately misleading the administration about Soviet plans.

A judgment on this issue requires careful examination of specific dates. On August 24, Roger Hilsman presented a background briefing on the summer build-up of Soviet arms in Cuba. At a press conference on August 29, the President took note of the Soviet build-up, but argued that available evidence suggested no threat that would justify U.S. action "at this time." On September 4, Ambassador Dobrynin met with Robert Kennedy and relayed instructions from Khrushchev "to assure President Kennedy that there would be no ground-to-ground missiles or offensive weapons placed in Cuba."[228] RFK warned him that "we were watching the build-up carefully and that it would be of the gravest consequence if the Soviet Union placed missiles in Cuba."[229] On the afternoon of September 4, the White House issued a special Presidential statement on Cuba warning that if the Soviets tried to bring offensive ground-to-ground missiles or other significant Soviet offensive capabilities to Cuba, "the gravest issues would arise." On September 6, Dobrynin met with Sorensen and assured him that the Soviets were doing nothing new or extraordinary in Cuba, that offensive weapons would not be brought to Cuba, and that the Soviet Union would try not to complicate the international situation before the American congressional elections. On September 11, the Soviet government authorized Tass to issue a statement on Soviet policy in Cuba denying that the Soviet Union would ever "set up in any other country — Cuba for instance — the weapons it has for repelling aggression." At his press conference on September 13, the President went beyond previous statements, warning that "if Cuba should possess a capability to carry out offensive actions against the U.S.," the United States would "do whatever must be done."

The first Soviet ship carrying MRBMs and missile base equipment docked in Cuba on September 8, followed by a second on September 15.[230] Construction of Soviet missile sites and deployment of the missiles and equipment began between September 15 and 20.[231] Thus, two serious private conversations and the President's first public warning on offensive missiles occurred before any Soviet missiles reached Cuba. Before missile construction began, the President made a second and even stronger commitment to action. At both points, Khrushchev and other members of the Soviet government had opportunities to reconsider in the light of the President's commitment and stop this dangerous venture.[232] Yet they persisted. And it is this that justifies the President's — and subsequent analysts' — reading of the action primarily as a probe of American commitments.

This argument makes a point, but, again, it misses an important distinction. For a government to make a decision, even a decision as important as sending missiles to Cuba, is one thing. Once made, to reverse such a decision is quite a different matter. The making of the decision must have required Khrushchev and others to take a stand on likely American reactions. At that time, opponents of the move must have argued that the United States would respond forcibly. The available evidence suggests that the military leaders, in particular, resisted what they regarded as a risky and unnecessary exposure of Soviet weapons and troops.[233] Could Khrushchev reopen the issue on the basis of arguments identical with those made by the original opponents of the action? Two months into a complex sequence of steps involving preparation of ports, surveys of missile sites, and deployment of SAMs, and two days before the arrival of missiles in Cuba, to stop those involved in the activity, who had now become committed to the action, on the basis of recent, uncertain warnings, would have been no easy matter. The argument is not that it would have been impossible to reopen the issue, reverse the Presidium decision, and recall the missiles. It is, rather, that for any other member of the Presidium to try to force a halt in the middle of the stream would have been extraordinarily difficult, and that for Khrushchev to switch horses and retreat on the basis of the available information would have been to open himself to charges from all sides, including the military who, now involved in the action, would have argued that Khrushchev had backed out of a sure success. The difference between (1) Khrushchev and the Presidium's deciding to move missiles to Cuba before any American warnings had been issued or commitments made and (2) Khrushchev and the Presidium's failing to reverse this decision — when, during implementation, the Kennedy administration did issue warnings and make commitments — is enormous. No one who lived through Cuba I should have misunderstood or underestimated the importance of that distinction. The distinction is not without implications for the extent to which one can justifiably interpret the Soviet action as a probe or challenge.

How Clear Was the American Warning?

It has been argued that because of the difficulty in reversing a Presidium decision and stopping a machine in motion, the U.S. government's unambiguous warnings that missiles would not be tolerated did not suffice. Certainly the warnings *seemed* unambiguous. Immediately upon learning of the missiles, Kennedy reviewed his public statements on what our reaction would be to offensive missiles in Cuba and concluded, as Sorensen records, that "his pledge to act was unavoidable," that he was "compelled to act."[234] But it may be worthwhile to consider further just how these commitments may have appeared, at the time, to a man in Moscow.

A careful reader of the President's personal statements up to the point at which the missiles were discovered (October 14) should have noted a strong personal commitment that Kennedy would not likely be inclined, or able, to escape. Nevertheless, even up to the day of discovery, a man in Moscow, listening to the array of messages emanating from Washington, could have had grounds for reasonable doubt about the U.S. government's reactions. His argument could have been that the Kennedy administration was reacting to the provocations of domestic critics, that these statements were aimed at Republican opponents rather than at the Soviet Union, that American campaigns included numerous promises and statements that had no substance, and thus that after the election, the administration would find some way to accommodate a Soviet *fait accompli*.

In considering how this hypothetical man in Moscow might have constructed the argument, one must consider the following. First, the administration had tried to play the Cuban issue in a low key. Only when attacked by Republican opponents had the President reacted to the Soviets' summer weapon build-up. And even then, his reaction had been one of denial that the Soviet behavior constituted a sufficient threat to justify U.S. action. These denials could not stand alone; the President had to say something to American voters about when the administration *would* act. In the light of this requirement, the remarks seemed restrained. Second, a great deal has been made of the President's sharp line between offensive and defensive weapons. But this distinction was made in several lines of a statement that consisted of many paragraphs. After the event, it stands out in bold relief, but at the time it was embedded in a great deal of noise. And again, it could have been a way of quieting domestic critics with a distinction that could, in the end, be fuzzed by talking about intentions, rather than capabilities.

Third, the administration had taken great pains to deny the presence of Soviet military troops in Cuba. After mid-July, the Soviet troops had begun arriving, but they did not wear uniforms. Given the amount of information that the United States had about Soviet military shipments to Cuba (as reported in the August 24 background briefing), one might have assumed that intelligence sources had picked up information about the Soviet troops as well. But up to the date of discovery, no American official had publicly acknowledged the presence of Soviet troops in Cuba.[235]

Finally, during the last week before discovery of the missiles, it seemed that the administration was indeed willing to tolerate the presence of Soviet *offensive* weapons in Cuba. Consider the facts. In drawing the line between offensive and defensive weapons, the President referred to weapons of "significant offensive capability," specifically mentioning "offensive ground-to-ground missiles."[236] In his address to the nation on October 22, the President pointed to three types of Soviet offensive weapons in Cuba: medium-range ballistic missiles, intermediate-range ballistic missiles, and "jet bombers, capable of carrying nuclear weapons." When Khrushchev agreed to withdraw offensive weapons from Cuba, Kennedy insisted on complete withdrawal of all three types of weapons. In congressional hearings after the crisis, Secretary McNamara testified that "three major offensive weapon systems were deployed in Cuba by the Soviet Union . . . medium-range ballistic missiles . . . intermediate-range ballistic missiles . . . and IL-28 bombers."[237] Thus, at least in retrospect, there was no ambiguity about what the U.S. government regarded as "offensive weapons," the presence of which would raise "the gravest issues."[238]

Yet, on October 14 — the day on which a U-2 would discover Soviet missiles in Cuba — McGeorge Bundy stated on ABC's *Issues and Answers* that the U.S. government was willing to accept the presence of at least one of these offensive weapon systems, namely the IL-28 bombers. Bundy asserted: "I *know* there is no present evidence, and I think there is no present likelihood that the Cubans and the Cuban Government and the Soviet Government would, in combination, attempt to install a major offensive capability."[239] But then he went on, "So far, everything that has been delivered in Cuba falls within the categories of aid which the Soviet Union has provided, for example, to neutral states like Egypt or Indonesia, and I should not be surprised to see additional military assistance of that sort."[240] The Soviet Union had, in fact, provided IL-28 bombers to Egypt and Indonesia. The United States had taken pictures on September 28 of crates on the deck of Soviet ships en route to Cuba, "crates of a peculiar size and shape that were similar to those the Soviets had used to ship IL-28 light bombers to Egypt and Indonesia."[241] Several days before the television broadcast, Bundy had received an intelligence brief showing "pictures of peculiarly shaped crates . . . and recalling the shipment of IL-28s to Egypt and Indonesia."[242] The conclusion that the administration had discovered a way to tolerate one type of offensive weapon in Cuba is unavoidable. Our "man in Moscow" was right about at least one out of the three weapon systems. Was it so certain that the administration might not have found other ways to tolerate the other weapon systems?

Many Problems: One Solution

As we have noted, any account of the details of the internal politics out of which the decision to send Soviet missiles emerged must be speculative. There should be some value, however, in taking advantage of the limited evidence that is available to construct one illustrative account of the actual decision. While it is not possible to identify with any confidence the players and games and their specific perceptions and priorities, it seems certain that explanations that assume complete coincidence of views about the problem, or even accounts exclusively in terms of Khrushchev's solution to his range of problems, are inaccurate. From the perspective of the present account, it seems likely that the decision emerged not from grand global planning — the Soviet government (or Khrushchev) standing back and considering, for example, where to probe the United States — but rather from a process in which a number of different individuals' quite distinct perceptions of separable problems snowballed into a single solution.

Unfortunately, not a great deal is known about the internal politics of high-level policy decisions in the Soviet Union.[243] The Presidium, which consists of the Chief Party politicians, functions as the supreme policymaking body. During 1962, Khrushchev's position of preeminence within the Presidium was not seriously challenged. Nevertheless, even if his power within the Soviet government exceeded that of Kennedy within the U.S. government — a proposition that many scholars would dispute — the evidence is overwhelming that Khrushchev was mortal; that he had no more than twenty-four hours a day; that he could attend to only a limited number of the major issues facing the Soviet government; that effective influence over policy was therefore dispersed to various other individuals, both within the Presidium and in the lower levels of the Party and the departments; that these individuals initiated many policies and resisted many choices initiated by each other and Khrushchev; and, finally, that these individuals eventually dismissed Khrushchev.

It appears that for the formulation and management of policy in various spheres, the Presidium members divided into a number of "teams." The team for military and intelligence issues consisted of five Presidium members — Khrushchev, Kozlov, Mikoyan, Kosygin, Brezhnev — plus Gromyko (the Minister of Foreign Affairs), Malinovsky (the Minister of Defense), Semichastny (the Chairman of the KGB), and Ustinov (the Chairman of the Supreme Economic Council.)[244] This group thus linked the chief politicians with the heads of operating departments, namely the Ministries of Foreign Affairs, Defense, Intelligence, and Economics. In addition, a question about Cuba would have involved the team that managed Soviet party relations with other parties in the international Communist movement. This group consisted of Khrushchev, Kuusinen and Suslov (both Presidium members), and two Secretaries from the Central Committee Secretariat — Ponomarev, who had responsibility for relations with nonbloc parties, and Andropov, who had responsibility for bloc parties.[245] These two "teams" must have constituted the circle in which the initial decision about missiles for Cuba was made.[246] And it seems fair to consider the problems that could have led to a position on this issue.

1. THE CUBAN PROBLEM. Since 1960, Castro had been requesting, and Moscow resisting, specific military security guarantees. For example, in July 1960 Khrushchev stated: "Figuratively speaking, in case of need Soviet artillerymen *can* support the Cuban people with their rocket fire."[247] Castro tried to translate this figurative warning as a guarantee of his regime, but

Khrushchev resisted.[248] During his visit to the United States in September 1960, Khrushchev was asked by a journalist: "Is it true that you stated that in case of a United States intervention against Cuba, the USSR would strike at the United States?" He evaded a reply by saying: "More or less true . . . you need not worry . . . since America is not going to attack Cuba."[249] In January 1961 Che Guevara asserted that it was "well known that the Soviet Union and all the socialist states are ready to go to war to defend our sovereignty and that a tacit agreement has been reached between our peoples."[250] But the Soviet Union said nothing. Even after the Bay of Pigs, the Soviet Union was not forthcoming with the desired guarantees.

Early in 1962, according to one of Castro's versions of these events, Castro pressed the Soviet Union once more, arguing on the basis of a phrase in President Kennedy's interview with Khrushchev's son-in-law Adzhubei that the United States was preparing a second Bay of Pigs. Castro's demands, juxtaposed with the Soviet reluctance, account for the strain that marked Cuban-Soviet relations through the spring of 1962. This strain peaked at the end of March with Castro's purge of the Soviet's man in Havana, Annibal Escalenté. Escalenté was one of the old-line Communists in Cuba who had been organizing Party cadres around Castro. Castro's indictment of him charged that he had been seeking to win over the rank and file of the new revolutionary party, thereby threatening the Castroite leadership.[251]

The purge posed a dilemma for the individuals directly responsible for relations between the Party in the Soviet Union and the Party in Cuba. Their hopes for surrounding Castro with more reasonable and committed Communists sank with Escalenté. Unless the Cuban government's policy of excluding old-line Communists could be reversed, the prospect of a Moscow-oriented Communist Party in Cuba would evaporate. Suslov and Ponomarev, the men specially charged with Party relations, would be responsible. Further deterioration could mean a serious rupture in relations between the Soviet Union and the only established Communist government in the Western Hemisphere.[252] Moreover, what if Castro's reports of an imminent U.S. invasion were correct? In spite of the earlier reluctance of military leaders and the Ministry of Foreign Affairs to give security guarantees for Cuba, something had to be done. Suslov and Ponomarev obviously had a problem and a deadline suffi-

cient to lead them to support strongly someone else's proposal
of missiles for Cuba, or even to generate the proposal.

2. THE STRATEGIC PROBLEM. Any member of the Soviet
government seriously concerned with the Soviet strategic capability against the United States, and informed of the facts, had
to be frightened by the end of 1961. When the Kennedy administration took office (January 1961), both Soviet and American
leaders were talking about a "missile gap," with the United
States on the short side. An informed Soviet strategist obviously
knew that the Soviet Union did not have, and was not procuring,
the missiles the Americans referred to. But as long as the Americans knew no better, the problem was manageable.

In November 1961, this solution exploded. American leaders announced the facts to the Soviets and the world: the United
States was not on the short side of the missile gap; rather,
United States strategic superiority was considerable.[253] Moreover,
the United States did not simply state the facts. By elaborate
procedures, including briefings for allies, some of whom were
known to be "leaky," the United States signaled to the Soviet
Union both that these were the facts and that these facts were
important.[254]

The implications of this announcement for the Soviet
strategists must have been staggering. First, American leaders
were broadcasting their strategic superiority: they would soon
be using it in more provocative ventures. On the eve of the crisis, October 16, 1962, an article published in *Red Star* reflected
this concern. Its author argued that overestimation of their nuclear superiority had led American leaders to embark on an
extremely aggressive policy and urged his comrades "to raise
vigilance . . . to be able, when it becomes necessary, to put a
strait jacket on the madmen."[255] Second, and even more
alarming, must have been the recognition of the possibility of a
major American intelligence breakthrough. If American information about the number of Soviet missiles was so accurate,
the United States might also have information about the location of the missiles. Soviet counter-intelligence seized Penkovskiy
in September 1962, after having watched him for a number of
months. Perhaps he and a ring of spies had delivered to the
United States the precise location of the small Soviet strategic
capability. Or perhaps the United States had achieved another
major new capability for observing Soviet territory (the Soviets
had earlier been amazed by the American U-2). In either case,
the "soft" Soviet missile fleet would be vulnerable to a preemp-

tive American strike, and indeed, if the United States deployed ICBMs at the announced rate through 1962, it might well have had, by the end of 1962, a very credible first-strike capability.

While these facts should have sufficed to persuade a reasonable man in the Soviet Union that there was a strategic problem, *who* in the Soviet Union combined a serious concern about strategic nuclear issues with access to and a recognition of the importance of these facts? Certainly the head of the KGB, for one, had both responsibility and information that would make him conscious of this problem. For another, any member of the Presidium with a special interest in strategic matters would have seen the issue — though there is little evidence of any serious thought about strategic matters by Presidium members at this time. The head of the Strategic Rocket Forces must have noticed these developments, though again, the scant evidence available suggests that Moskalenko's views agreed with those of older-line military opinion, being more concerned with building up the Soviet Army and its "artillery" support, namely MRBMs against Europe, than with ICBMs.[256] Some individuals within the Strategic Rocket Forces obviously did recognize the crisis for the Soviet strategic capability. Perhaps they formulated the argument about the necessity for immediate measures, lest the United States acquire a capability for a "timely blow" against the Soviet Union. An article in *Pravda* on May 3, 1962, cited a comment by President Kennedy on flexible response, interpreting the statement as a threat of a first strike in the event of a massive Soviet attack on Europe.[257] Khrushchev himself drew attention to this threat while on a trip to Bulgaria in May.[258]

The group within the Strategic Rocket Forces might also have devised a proposal to move MRBMs to Cuba, as a stop-gap measure — the only emergency step available that would deny the United States the first-strike capability. They would have had great difficulty in selling this line of argument within the Ministry of Defense. But the proposal, once formulated, could have been made through Party channels to Presidium members or staffers. The arguments for this proposal should have impressed some Presidium members. In any case, in April 1962, around the date when the decision must have been made, Moskalenko, the head of Strategic Rocket Forces, was replaced by Biryuzov, one of Khrushchev's Ukrainians.[259]

3. THE BERLIN PROBLEM. Khrushchev had tied his personal prestige to a solution to the Berlin problem.[260] Who persuaded him of the original venture remains obscure, but

beginning in November 1958 he initiated a series of zigs and zags aimed at a settlement, on Soviet terms, in Berlin.[261] On November 27, 1958, he issued an ultimatum demanding that West Berlin be transformed into a "de-militarized free city" within six months, or the Soviet Union would seek an independent solution.[262] This step failed. In the fall of 1959, he took a more friendly tack in his discussions of the issue with President Eisenhower at Camp David and got an agreement to reopen negotiations the following year. Those negotiations, planned for the summit meeting in Paris in May 1960, were canceled because of the U-2 incident. In June 1961, Khrushchev made new proposals on Germany and Berlin to Kennedy at Vienna. On June 15, he issued a second ultimatum: a peace settlement must be attained before the end of the year or the Soviets would sign a separate treaty with East Germany. A crisis heated up, as both sides explicitly increased defense expenditures, called up troops, and reinforced garrisons in Berlin. The Berlin Wall, begun on August 13, represented the high point of the crisis, though harassments and even a day-long confrontation between Soviet and American tanks followed. In October, Khrushchev recognized Western intransigence and withdrew his deadline for a second time.

It seemed certain that Khrushchev did not undertake these ventures alone. Various members of the Presidium and officials in lower levels of the government obviously saw Khrushchev's personal involvement in this matter and followed his lead in order to gain favor with him. By the spring of 1962, most of the individuals in the Party Secretariat and the Ministry of Foreign Affairs who worked on the Berlin problems had come to their jobs after Khrushchev's Berlin offensive had begun. They were therefore likely to be right-thinking types, conscious of the Chairman's strong inclinations, and concerned to find a solution to a problem that exercised him so. The visit of East Germany's Chancellor Ulbrecht at the end of February 1962 reminded these men, and Khrushchev as well, that something had to be done.[263] Ulbrecht left with some assurance that the Soviet government had not forgotten his problem and that a new offensive was being prepared.

Saddled with a demand to devise some new initiative, the men in the Secretariat confronted the problem. Two major offensives against Berlin had failed — to the discredit not only of Khrushchev but also of the men in their positions. Whatever the truth about the relative strategic power of the United States and the Soviet Union — and a member of the Secretariat with responsibility for Berlin would not be likely to have a good account of either Soviet or American nuclear capabilities — recent American statements indicated that the United States believed that it had superior forces. Certainly, another round of bluff and bluster was bound to fail. Thus, the Soviet Union had no means by which to achieve its objectives in Berlin — unless a way could be found to get more chips.

This recognition coincided not only with the facts but perhaps even more importantly with the objections of opponents of Khrushchev's Berlin adventures. According to Penkovskiy, the high councils of the military were very concerned about the "big risk" Khrushchev took in building the Berlin Wall and thereby risking a major war for which the Soviet forces were not ready.[264] Similarly, Penkovskiy reports that three Presidium members, Mikoyan, Suslov, and Kozlov, had reservations about Khrushchev's tough bluff in Berlin.[265] Both groups would resist a new round of Khrushchev's antics, predicting accurately its failure. But the objections of both groups could be outflanked if a way could be devised to change the strategic position and momentum. Whether this group in the Secretariat devised the Cuban military solution, or simply supported someone else's proposal, they had good reasons to lobby for the move.[266]

4. THE ECONOMIC PROBLEM. Because the Soviet economy was growing more slowly than the economic planners had predicted, competition for slices of the budget grew more severe. Early in 1961, the economic planners had pushed through a decision to cut back the Soviet military forces by one million men, but this decision came apart during the Berlin crisis. Military advocates won an increase in the military budget as a ploy in the Berlin crisis of 1961. In the planning stages of the budget for the following year, the military leaders made increased demands not only for the army but also for the Strategic Rocket Forces. These demands squeezed the funds available for the industrial sector, threatened the industrial sector's prospects for meeting assigned targets, and forced revision of the agreed economic plan. Certainly, Kosygin and other economic planners saw this problem. That they could have been attracted to a cheaper way of meeting Soviet strategic needs is easy to believe. But it seems probable that they would have supported a solution to someone else's problem, rather than deriving this as a solution to their own concern.

5. DOMESTIC CAMPAIGNS. An issue like missiles for Cuba

could not be unrelated to various current domestic campaigns being pursued by Khrushchev and others: a new round in the battle between anti-Stalinists and Stalinists, a doctrinal dispute about the predominance of economics over politics, and a struggle between party *apparatchiki* and industrial and agricultural managers that led to a proposal for dramatic organizational restructing.[267] No Presidium member, and few high-level members of the government, could keep foreign and domestic problems entirely separated. Of necessity, each was involved in many issues, both foreign and domestic, and each man's influence on any particular issue derived not only from his advantages in that game, but from his performance in the spectrum of issues with which he was involved. Indeed, each official's tenure in office depended on this performance. But because of the lack of information, we are forced simply to note these additional dimensions of the game, without speculating about their consequences for the decision to send missiles to Cuba.

How the separate players' various perceptions of quite different problems such as these finally converged in a single solution to these assorted problems is unknown. A number of plausible paths can be imagined by which an initial proposal, made as a solution to one problem, appealed to other individuals and groups for different reasons as solutions to their problems. For example, some Presidium members who were not impressed with the Soviets' obligations to Cuba, and who were suspicious of Khrushchev's ambitions in Berlin, nonetheless may have seen in the proposal a way of increasing strategic capabilities without significantly increasing the military budget. Given Khrushchev's known penchant for gambling, it seems likely that at some point he picked up the proposal and made it his own. There were many reasons why someone could support the proposal. There seems, nonetheless, to have been significant opposition to the move by some Presidium members who feared U.S. reaction as well as by the military and intelligence circles over the danger of exposing Soviet nuclear capabilities and troops less than ninety miles from the American mainland.[268] By some such succession of complex and probably confused steps, the Soviet government reached the decision to send missiles to Cuba.

7

Conclusion

In the preceding chapters, we have taken a "walk around" the Cuban missile crisis, with pauses at three vantage points. This allowed us to explore the central puzzles of the crisis. While the chapters do not settle the matter of what happened and why, they do uncover many previously underemphasized features, and they afford a rich source of hypotheses about the causes of various outcomes. At the same time, these three case studies offer evidence about the nature of explanations produced by different analysts. None of the three analysts simply described events. In attempting to explain what happened, each distinguished certain features as the relevant determinants. Each combed out the numerous details and factors in a limited number of causal strands that were woven into the "reasons" for a particular occurrence. Moreover, the three accounts emphasized quite different factors in explaining the central puzzles of the crisis. The sources of the difference are the conceptual models each analyst employed.

These conceptual models are much more than *simple* angles of vision or approaches. Each conceptual framework consists of a *cluster* of assumptions and categories that influence what the analyst finds puzzling, how he formulates his question, where he looks for evidence, and what he produces as an answer. The three cuts at the missile crisis demonstrate both the complexity of the models and the differences in analysis that they make.

Summing Up: Differences in Interpretation

In generating hypotheses about the missile crisis from alternative conceptual angles, these chapters present a number of
differences in emphasis and interpretation. Such incongruities
could be the starting point for a full-length historical study of
the crisis. Friends have persuaded me that so many participants
in the event have given so graciously of their time and information that I have incurred an obligation to try my hand at this
task as a further work. Here, however, a few preliminary obser-
vations seem in order.

There is an apparent incompatibility between the level of
discourse in the Model I account and that of the Model II and
Model III accounts. The Model I analyst approached the Soviet
installation of missiles in Cuba, the American naval blockade,
and the Soviet withdrawal of missiles as strategic choices. By
analyzing the strategic problem that the Soviet Union faced, and
the characteristics of the Soviet missile deployment, he produced
an argument for one goal (rectifying the nuclear balance) that
made the Soviet emplacement plausible. The American blockade
was explained simply as the U.S. value-maximizing choice.
Withdrawal of the missiles was understood as the only option
left for the Soviets after the United States signaled the firmness
of its intentions. While these explanations were offered without
detailed attention to the internal mechanisms of the governments,
the Model I analyst's appropriation of statements by officials
of the government as "the government view" and his use of
fine detail about the Soviet missile deployment as a criterion
for distinguishing among Soviet objectives would seem to imply
coincidence of perceptions, control of choice, and coordination
of movement within the government-as-unitary-actor.

As the Model II and Model III accounts of bureaucratic
machinations demonstrate, this was not in fact the case. Many
crucial details of implementation followed from organizational
routines rather than from central choice. The principal government leaders differed markedly in their perceptions of the problem, their estimates of the consequences of various courses of
action, and their preferred solutions. These facts force one to
wonder about the Model I account. The explanation proceeds
as if it were simply describing the process of governmental
reasoning, choice, and implementation. But since, as we have

seen, this account does not accurately describe the process, what does it describe? To whose objectives and reasons does the Model I analysis refer? In contrast with the Model II and Model III accounts, the Model I version seems somewhat disembodied.*

The Model I analyst fastened on particular characteristics of the Soviet installation of missiles, and of the blockade, as signals of central calculations and choices. The Soviet installation of more expensive and more visible IRBMs as well as MRBMs was taken by the Model I analyst as a major piece of evidence against which to test the competing hypotheses about Soviet intentions. He used this fact to disqualify the "Cuban defense" hypothesis on the grounds that MRBMs alone would have sufficed to guarantee the defense of Cuba. But the Model II analyst challenged the presumption that evidence of this sort can be used to identify governmental intentions. He explained the simultaneous installation of IRBMs and MRBMs as a consequence of organizational goals and routines. Similarly, the construction of MRBMs before completion of the SAM network, the positioning of Soviet missiles in the standard four-slice pattern, and the failure to camouflage the sites were explained by the Model II analyst as normal, organizational performance — rather than as occasions for extraordinary puzzlement.

The most glaring conflict between Model I's strategic summary of the event and Model II and Model III's examination of details of the process — organizational or political — reflects the incentives that each model produces for probing the facts. The Model I analyst's explanatory power derives primarily from his construction of a calculation that makes plausible the character of the action chosen, given the problem the nation faced. This construction requires a factual base. But the available, conventional facts usually suffice, since the essential element in the analyst's work is his reasoning, his thinking through the nation's problem.[1]

For example, most previous Model I analyses have accepted the blockade as a satisfactory base for building an explanation of the Soviet withdrawal. As our Model I account argued, this interpretation is incorrect. Ours is the first published account to emphasize the U.S. ultimatum to the Soviet Union as the central factor in the Soviet withdrawal. This interpretation

---

*This issue is considered further, beginning on page 252.

emerged from hard Model I reasoning plus a serious respect for the facts. Similarly, as the footnotes to Chapter 3 demonstrate, our account avoids a large number of specific errors that have been accepted in various previous accounts. Nevertheless, our Model I account accepts certain points that the Model II and Model III accounts find to be inaccurate, and it overlooks certain pieces of information that the Model II and Model III accounts notice.

The argument for permitting this is threefold. First, the present chapters mirror the author's experience with the models. The inaccuracies discovered in the Model I version and the new insights recorded in the Model II and Model III versions were found when probing data with the concepts of these models. Second, since the purpose of the Model I account is to present a strong, typical explanation, it seems fair to let the account reflect only conventional evidence plus additional facts that the model itself would naturally uncover. Third, most of the additional facts are not simple facts. Rather, they are points that emerge when one mixes traces of evidence with judgments; one is inclined to accept or reject the judgments depending on the logic of the model within which he is working.[2]

The alternative interpretations of the Soviet missile withdrawal provide the most suggestive instance of these differences among the models over evidence and interpretation. Our Model I analyst explained the withdrawal as a consequence of the American ultimatum. Most analysts will find this interpretation preferable to explanations that focus on the blockade. This explanation is certainly satisfactory in Model I terms. But the Model II and Model III analysts carry the argument a step further. They are naturally inclined to dig deeper into the evidence about organizations and internal politics. Though the information is incomplete, the Model II analyst uncovered and emphasized the importance of U.S. missiles in Turkey and a Presidential order that they be de-fused. This led him to hypothesize with respect to the final Saturday that either (1) an American ultimatum forced Soviet capitulation, or (2) while Kennedy was beginning to wobble, Khrushchev folded. From a Model III perspective, a further hypothesis emerged. The argument against a "deal" (i.e., withdrawal of Soviet missiles in Cuba for withdrawal of American missiles in Turkey) has — in Model I terms — been heretofore entirely compelling. In spite of the fact that the Soviets proposed precisely this arrangement in their Saturday letter, the United States simply could not accept such terms: it would shake the alliance; it would signal weakness; it would confuse the issue. No published analysis of the missile crisis has been able to escape this reasoning. But from a Model III perspective, it is hard to believe that John F. Kennedy should have been so insensitive to Khrushchev's problem as to refuse, in private, what he in fact planned — and had previously meant — to do. Robert Kennedy's last account of the crisis, published after our Model III analyst generated this hypothesis, suggests strongly that the Model III analysis is correct.

Between the Model II and Model III versions there are a number of additional differences in emphasis and interpretation. For example, the Model II explanation credited Kennedy's consultation of General Sweeney, the head of Tactical Air Command, on Sunday, October 20, as a *bona fide* last minute reconsideration. But the Model III understanding of this occurrence as "preparation of the record" seems closer to the mark.

More revealing is the divergence between Model II and Model III interpretations of the Air Force estimate of U.S. capabilities for a surgical air strike. From a Model II perspective, that inaccurate estimate — which in its error eliminated the Air Force's preferred course of action — emerged according to the established routines of the Air Force. In contrast, the Model III interpretation of this event highlighted both the overconfidence of the Air Force Chief of Staff, which reduced his suspicion of the estimate, and the willingness of other government leaders not to probe an estimate that served their purposes. The available evidence is insufficient to permit confident judgment between these hypotheses.

A large number of puzzles about this most important event are yet unresolved — leaving a real need for a thorough historical study of this crisis.

Summing Up: Different Answers or Different Questions?

Such variance among interpretations demonstrates each model's tendency to produce different answers to the same question. But as we observe the models at work, what is equally striking are the differences in the ways the analysts conceive of the problem, shape the puzzle, unpack the summary questions, and pick up pieces of the world in search of an answer. Why did the

United States blockade Cuba? For Model I analysts, this "why" asks for reasons that account for the American choice of the blockade as a solution to the strategic problem posed by the presence of Soviet missiles in Cuba. For a Model II analyst, the puzzle is rather: What outputs of which organizations led to this blockade? A Model III analyst understands the basic "why" as a question about the various problems perceived by relevant players and their pulling and hauling from which the blockade emerged.

Typically, the thing to be explained is designated by a rather vague, summary clause, accompanied by an implicit appendix that specifies the relevant aspects of the occurrence.[3] For a Model I analyst, "blockade" is an aggregate act. The perceived context, formal decision, and implementation are all aspects of one coordinated, rational choice. The Model II and Model III analysts insist on splitting up the blockade into a number of pieces. The Model II analyst focuses on slices like *when* the missiles were discovered, *how* the options were defined, and the *details* of the blockade's execution. The Model III analyst focuses both on the emergence of the blockade decision in the ExCom and on various aspects of implementation.

To explain the blockade, the Model I analyst examines the U.S. strategic calculus: the problem posed by the Soviet missiles, relevant American values, and U.S. capabilities. Explanation *means* placing the blockade in a pattern of purposive response to the strategic problem. For a Model II man, this "solution" emerges as the by-product of basic organizational processes. The analyst emphasizes organizational constraint in choice and organizational routines in implementation. Organizational processes produced awareness of the problem on October 14 (rather than two weeks earlier or later); organizational routines defined the alternatives; organizational procedures implemented the blockade. These features overshadow the "decisions" of the unified group of leaders within these constraints. Explanation starts with existing organizations and their routines at $t - 1$ and attempts to account for what is going on at time t. The Model III analyst accents the action of players in the relevant games that produced pieces of the collage that is the blockade. Bargaining among players who shared power but saw separate problems yielded discovery of the missiles on a certain date in a special context, a definition of the problem which demanded strong action, a coalition of Presidential intimates set on averting holo-

caust, failure to probe the the military estimate, and consequently a blockade. In the absence of a number of particular
characteristics of players and games, the action would not have
been the same.

The information required by Model II and Model III analysts
dwarfs that needed by a Model I analyst. An armchair strategist
(in Washington or even Cambridge) can produce accounts of
U.S. (or Soviet) national costs and benefits. Understanding the
value-maximizing choices of nations demands chiefly an analytic ability at vicarious problem solving. But analyses that concentrate on processes and procedures of organizations, or on
pulling and hauling among individuals, demand much more information. Some observers (particularly players in the game) rely
on a version of Model III for their own government's behavior,
while retreating to a Model I analysis of other nations. Thus *information costs* account for some differences among explanations. The difficulty of acquiring information, however, is no
more important than the differential capacity of different models
to recognize the relevance and importance of additional pieces of
information. For a Model I analyst, information about a split
between McNamara and the Joint Chiefs over the proper response to Soviet missiles constitutes gossip or anecdote but
not evidence about an important factor. Only Model II analysts
are willing to gather information about existing organizational
routines. Model III's delineation of positions, and its attention
to the advantages and disadvantages of various players, strikes
other analysts as an undue concern with subtlety.

Thus while at one level three models produce different
explanations of the same happening, at a second level the models
produce different explanations of quite different occurrences.
And indeed, this is my argument. Spectacles magnify one set of
factors rather than another and thus not only lead analysts to
produce different explanations of problems that appear, in their
summary questions, to be the same, but also influence the character of the analyst's puzzle, the evidence he assumes to be relevant, the concepts he uses in examining the evidence, and what
he takes to be an explanation. None of our three analysts would
deny that during the Cuban missile crisis several million people
were performing actions relevant to the event. But in offering his
explanation, each analyst attempts to emphasize what is relevant
and important, and different conceptual lenses lead analysts to
different judgments about what is relevant and important.

Where Do We Go from Here?

In the last several years it has been remarked with increasing frequency that American academic and professional thought about foreign affairs seems to have reached a hiatus. Strategic thought has made little progress since Schelling's *Strategy of Conflict*. Sovietology is just "more of the same." The arms control literature has been coasting on ideas generated by the time of the summer study of 1960. The new wave of revisionist studies of American foreign policy turns traditional interpretations on their head without really increasing our understanding. Diplomatic history shows little life.

Why should this be the case? My colleagues in Harvard's Research Seminar on Bureaucracy, Politics, and Policy have convinced me that my argument really backs into consideration of these larger issues: namely, where does our thinking about foreign affairs now stand? Where should we go from here? The answer provided by this study is half-baked and rather haphazard, since these are not questions with which it began. Still, the tentative answer it implies should be made explicit.

That most thinking about foreign affairs is dominated by one basic set of categories is hardly accidental. Confronted by a puzzling occurrence in international affairs, we naturally ask why, and try to understand how the nation involved could have chosen the action in question. Without thinking, we immediately begin talking about "Hanoi" or "Peking." We try to "see the problem from the North Vietnamese point of view" — that is, from the point of view of a reasonable leader sitting in Hanoi — and to reason why "he" chose the action in question. The analogy between nations in international politics and a coordinated, intelligent human being is so powerful that we rarely remember we are reasoning by analogy.

The contribution of the classical model (Model I) to our explanations, predictions, and analyses of foreign affairs is considerable. This lens reduces the organizational and political complications of a government to the simplification of a single actor. The array of details about a happening can be seen to cluster around the major features of an action. Through this lens the confused and even contradictory factors that influence an occurrence become a single dynamic: *choice* of the alternative that achieved a certain goal. Thus the Rational Actor Model permits us to translate the basic question, "Why did X happen?" into the question "Why did this nation do X?" The question then becomes: "What problem was the nation solving (or what goal was the nation achieving) in choosing X?" The classical model allows us to deal with the last question in the same way that we would answer a question about an individual's action.

Recall once more the Model I analyst's explanation of Soviet installation of missiles in Cuba. Confronted with the fact, he formulated the puzzle as a question about why the government chose this aggregate action. Explanation then consisted in constructing a calculation according to which the Soviet government reasonably chose to make the move. In producing the explanation, the Model I analyst proceeded as if his assignment had been: make a powerful argument for one objective that permits the reader to see how, given the strategic problem, if he had been playing the Soviet hand, he would have chosen that action. In more technical terms, the game is one of maximization under some set of constraints.[4]

The model employed in this explanation is not only the basic framework used by ordinary men and professional analysts in explaining occurrences in foreign affairs. It is even more essential. Perhaps the most fundamental method employed by human beings in their attempt to come to grips with the puzzling occurrences around them is to conceive of these occurrences not as simple phenomena or events (i.e., things that just happen) but rather as *action* (i.e., behavior expressing some intention or choice).[5] This is the way we explain our behavior to ourselves and to others: "I wanted X." "I chose Y." This is the way we understand the behavior of our fellow men.

For explaining and predicting the behavior of individual men, this general orientation toward purpose and rational choice seems to be the best available. The rationality of man's choices is, of course, "bounded" by things such as the availability of information and the difficulty of calculation. But as a baseline, if one knows how an individual has defined his problem and what resources he has available, his objectives provide a good clue to his behavior.

Difficulties arise when the thing to be explained is not the behavior of an individual but rather the behavior of a large organization or even a government. Nations can be reified, but at considerable cost in understanding. By personifying nations, one glides over critical characteristics of behavior where an organization is the main mover— for example, the fact that organizational action requires the coordination of large numbers of individuals, thus necessitating programs and SOPs. Thinking about a nation as if it were a person neglects considerable differences among individual leaders of a government whose positions and power lead them to quite different perceptions and preferences. Thus where the actor is a national government, a conception of action for objectives must be modified. (Perhaps the organizational and political factors could be formulated as "constraints" within which the government actually chooses, though this would require an analysis quite distinct from Simon's concern with "bounded rationality.")[6]

As we have noted earlier, the Model II and Model III accounts of questions treated ordinarily in standard Model I fashion highlight this difficulty. No longer is it possible to maintain that the Model I explanation is simply *describing* the processes within the national government. We are forced to recognize that in treating happenings as actions, and national governments as unitary purposive actors, we are "modeling." The fact that the assumptions and categories of this model neglect important factors such as organizational processes and bureaucratic politics suggests that the model is inadequate. Careful examination of the model's performance confirms this suspicion. For example, the U.S. intelligence estimate of September 19, 1962, contained a plausible strategic analysis showing that the Soviets would not place missiles in Cuba. If no missiles had been placed in Cuba, a Model I analyst would have explained this fact by reference to these reasons. Given that the Soviets did emplace missiles, the Model I analyst attempts to explain this event by constructing the strategic analysis that makes plausible their choice to do so. But the occurrence or nonoccurrence of the Soviet missile deployment in Cuba must have been determined by something more than these strategic reasons.

The present hiatus in thinking about problems of foreign affairs derives in large part from attempts to pursue Model I reasoning, without much self-consciousness, as the single form of analysis. Model I analysis can be valuable. It does permit a quick, imaginative sorting out of a problem of explanation or analysis. It serves as a productive shorthand, requiring a minimum of information. It can yield an informative summary of tendencies, for example, by identifying the weight of strategic

costs and benefits. But it is not itself a full analysis or explanation of an event, and it cannot stand alone. We must understand
much more clearly what a Model I analysis refers to, what part
of the problem it captures, how we should modify its rules for
the use of evidence, etc. Part of "where we should go from here"
is to develop Model I as one of several conscious and explicit
styles of analysis.

The burden of this study's argument, however, is that
larger payoffs in the future will come from an intellectual shift
of gears. We should ask not what goals account for a nation's
choice of an action, but rather what factors determine an outcome. The shift from Model I to the Model II and Model III forms
of analysis really involves a fundamental change in intellectual
style. From the basic conception of happenings as choices to be
explained by reference to objectives (on analogy with the actions
of individual human beings), we must move to a conception of
happenings as events whose determinants are to be investigated
according to the canons that have been developed by modern
science.

Model II and Model III summarize two bundles of categories and assumptions, and two distinctive logical patterns that
provide useful, emphatic shorthands in which governmental action can be explained and predicted. The separation of these
two models as alternative pairs of spectacles facilitates the generation of hypotheses and highlights features that might otherwise be overlooked. The focus on separable clusters of factors
with distinguishable logical thrusts makes persuasive the importance of certain factors that might not otherwise be so. But
this argument should not be misinterpreted as an assertion that
Model II and Model III are the *only* alternative conceptual models.
One of my colleagues in the Bureaucracy Research Seminar, John
Steinbruner, has stated a fourth conceptual model.[7] A number of
others are clearly possible. Nor should the fact that several are
stated, and additional models contemplated, be misunderstood
as a denial of the possibility of a grand model that would incorporate the features of all. The basic orientation toward outcomes
and their determinants invokes an image of an ideal model in
which all determinants and their relations could be specified (at
least probabilistically). The only issue here is one of the relative
merits of alternative paradigms versus a grand model at the
present stage of understanding.

Summary Outline of Models and Concepts

The Paradigm	Model I	Model II	Model III
	National government — **Black box** → Goals (objective function), Options, Consequences, Choice	National government — **Leaders** (A B C D E F G) → Organizations (A–G), Goals, SOPs and programs	National government (Players in positions A–F) → Players in positions (A–F); Goals, interests, stakes, and stands (r–z); Power; Action-channels
Basic unit of analysis	Governmental action as choice	Governmental action as organizational output	Governmental action as political resultant

Organizing concepts	National actor
	The problem
	Static selection
	  Action as rational choice
	  Goals and objectives
	  Options
	  Consequences
	  Choice
		Organizational actors (constellation of which is the government)
		Factored problems and fractionated power
		Parochial priorities and perceptions
		Action as organizational output
		Goals: constraints defining acceptable performance
		Sequential attention to goals
		Standard operating procedures
		Programs and repertoires
		Uncertainty avoidance (negotiated environment, standard scenario)
		Problem-directed search
		Organizational learning and change
		Central coordination and control
		Decisons of government leaders
			Players in positions
			Parochial priorities and perceptions
			Goals and interests
			Stakes and stands
			Deadlines and faces of issues
			Power
			Action-channels
			Rules of the game
			Action as political resultant

Dominant inference pattern	Governmental action = choice with regard to objectives	Governmental action (in short run) = output largely determined by present SOPs and programs Governmental action (in longer run) = output importantly affected by organizational goals, SOPs, etc.	Governmental action = resultant of bargaining
General propositions	Substitution effect	Organizational implementation Organizational options Limited flexibility and incremental change Long-range planning Goals and tradeoffs Imperialism Options and organization Administrative feasibility Directed change	Political resultants Action and intention Problems and solutions Where you stand depends on where you sit Chiefs and Indians The 51–49 principle Inter- and intra-national relations Misperception, misexpectation, miscommunication, and reticence Styles of play

The outline of a tentative, *ad hoc* working synthesis of the models begins to emerge if one considers the general questions that each model leads one to ask of a problem of explanation, analysis, or prediction.

Among the questions posed by Model I are:[8]

1. What is the problem?
2. What are the alternatives?
3. What are the strategic costs and benefits associated with each alternative?
4. What is the observed pattern of national (governmental) values and shared axioms?
5. What are the pressures in the "international strategic marketplace"?

Model II leads one to ask:

1. Of what organizations (and organizational components) does the government consist?
2. Which organizations traditionally act on a problem of this sort and with what relative influence?
3. What repertoires, programs, and SOPs do these organizations have for making *information* about the problem available at various decision points in the government?
4. What repertoires, programs, and SOPs do these organizations have for generating *alternatives* about a problem of this sort?
5. What repertoires, programs, and SOPs do these organizations have for *implementing* alternative courses of action?

The central questions posed by Model III include:

1. What are the existing action channels for producing actions on this kind of problem?
2. Which players in what positions are centrally involved?
3. How do pressures of job, past stances, and personality affect the central players on this issue?
4. What deadlines will force the issue to resolution?
5. Where are foul-ups likely?

Thus we can see how Model I emphasizes, on the one hand, the problem and context that create incentives and pressures for a government to choose a particular course of action, and, on the other, the national (or governmental) values and axioms that create propensities to respond in certain ways. Overarching problems and axioms summarize important differences between behavioral tendencies of nations. Were one ignorant, for example, of the differences between American national attitudes in the mid-1960s and those in the mid-1930s, he would miss fundamental factors in the foreign policy of the United States. The shared objectives of national leaders, and the pressures created by strategic problems influence the trend line of any nation's action. Indeed, it is not difficult to see how the factors summarized by Model I affect assumptions of players in the Model III game, the kinds of arguments that these men can make, and even the range of outputs that organizations examined by Model II are prepared to produce. For some purposes, then, Model I may provide a satisfactory summary of the longer-run patterns of a nation's foreign policy.[9]

Model II and Model III analysts, however, assume the influence of Model I factors, focusing within this environment — this set of market pressures — on the mechanism that produced a particular outcome. The problem, according to these analysts, is not to explain, for example, why the United States had 500,000 men in Viet Nam in the mid-1960s, rather than in the mid-1930s. The problem is, given the national values and leaders' objectives in the United States in the 1960s, why did the United States have 500,000 men in Viet Nam? Overarching ideas or the climate of opinion constitute a large part of the explanation of the differences between the 1930s (when the probability that any U.S. leader or governmental organization could have inserted 500,000 men in Viet Nam approached zero) and the 1960s (when the possibility of this outcome was closer to 0.2). But the Organizational Process and Governmental Politics Models assume the context, and focus on the problem of explaining the occurrence of an event that values and objectives made 20 percent probable.

Thus the models can be seen to complement each other. Model I fixes the broader context, the larger national patterns, and the shared images. Within this context, Model II illuminates the organizational routines that produce the information, alternatives, and action. Within the Model II context, Model III focuses in greater detail on the individual leaders of a government and the politics among them that determine major governmental choices. The best analysts of foreign policy manage to weave strands of each of the three conceptual models into their explanations. A number of scholars whom our analytic chapters have squeezed into a single box display considerable intuitive powers in blending insights from all three models. By drawing complementary pieces from each of these styles of analysis, explanations can be significantly strengthened. But we must pay more careful attention to the points at which the explanations are complementary and the junctures at which implications may be incompatible.[10]

As a final reminder of the importance of the differences in emphasis among the three models, consider the *lessons* that each model draws from the crisis. The most widely believed and frequently cited lessons of the crisis have emerged from Model I analysis. These include: (1) since nuclear war between the United States and Soviet Union would be mutual national suicide, neither nation would choose nuclear war, and nuclear war is therefore not a serious possibility; (2) in a world of rough nuclear parity, the United States can choose low-level military actions with no fear that they will escalate to nuclear war; (3) nuclear crises are manageable — that is, in situations involving the vital interests of the superpowers, the leaders of both nations will have little difficulty in thinking through the problem and its alternatives, finding limited actions (the blockade) that communicate resolve, and thus settling the issue (withdrawal of the missiles). According to these analyses, the missile crisis was one of the Kennedy administration's "finest hours," though the "flap in the White House" — the White House tendency to view the problem in apocalyptic terms — was not only unnecessary but positively dangerous. As we noted earlier, the major departmental postmortem on the crisis concluded that "this exaggerated concern [about the possibility of nuclear war] prompted consideration of improvident actions and counseled hesitation where none was due."[11]

Model II and Model III analysts caution against confidence in the impossibility of nations stumbling — "irrationally" — into a nuclear exchange, in the manageability of nuclear crises, or in our understanding of the ingredients of successful crisis management. According to Model II's account of the crisis, our success included crucial organizational rigidities and even mistakes. Except for the routines and procedures that produced an inaccurate estimate of our capability for a surgical air strike, the probability of war would have been much higher. Only barely did government leaders manage to control organizational programs that might have dragged us over the cliff. In several instances, we were just plain lucky. The lesson: nuclear crises between machines as large as the United States and Soviet governments are inherently chancy. The information and estimates available to leaders about the situation will reflect organizational goals and routines as well as the facts. The alternatives presented to the leaders will be much narrower than the menu of options that would be desirable. The execution of choices will exhibit unavoidable rigidities of programs and SOPs. Coordination among organizations will be much less finely tuned than leaders demand or expect. The prescription: considerable thought must be given to the routines established in the principal organizations before a crisis so that during the crisis organizations will be capable of performing adequately the needed functions. In the crisis, the overwhelming problem will be that of control and coordination of large organizations.

The lessons that emerge from Model III give one even less reason to be sanguine about our understanding of nuclear crises or about the impossibility of nuclear war. The actions advocated by leaders of the U.S. government covered a spectrum from doing nothing to an air strike. The process by which the blockade emerged included many uncertain factors. Had Cuba II been President Kennedy's first crisis, Robert Kennedy and Sorensen would not have been members of the group, and the air strike would probably have emerged. Had Kennedy proved his mettle domestically in a previous confrontation, the diplomatic track could have prevailed. The lessons in Model III terms, then, are that: (1) the process of crisis management is obscure and terribly risky; (2) the leaders of the U.S. government can choose actions that entail (in their judgment) real possibilities of escalation to nuclear war; (3) the interaction of internal games, each as ill-understood as those in the White House and the Kremlin, could indeed yield nuclear war as an outcome. From this perspective, the "flap in the White House" was quite justified — especially for men aware that the internal politics of the government whose behavior they were trying to influence must have been no less confusing and complex than their own. If a President and his associates have to try to manage a nuclear crisis, the informal machinery, free-wheeling discussions, and devil's advocacy exemplified by the ExCom have many advantages. But the mix of personality, expertise, influence, and temperament that allows such a group to clarify alternatives even while it pulls and hauls for separate preferences should be better understood before we start down the path to nuclear confrontation again. On the evidence of the Cuban missile crisis, clarification is scarcely assured.

Both these differences in emphasis among the models and a partial, working synthesis of the three can be illustrated by using the models to generate predictions. Strategic surrender is an important problem of international relations and diplomatic history. War termination is a new, developing area of the strategic literature. Both of these interests lead scholars to address a central question: *Why* do nations surrender *when*? Whether implicit in explanations or more explicit in analysis, diplomatic historians and strategists rely upon propositions that can be turned forward to produce predictions. Thus surrender offers an interesting issue for illustrative predictions. In spite of the risks of seeming dated, and being in error, a number of readers have persuaded me to reproduce some predictions presented in an earlier essay. The question addressed there was: Why will North Viet Nam surrender when? What follows is quoted *verbatim* from a paper delivered in September 1968 to the American Political Science Association.[12]

In a nutshell, analysis according to Model I asserts: nations quit when costs outweigh the benefits. North Viet Nam will surrender when it realizes "that continued fighting can only generate additional costs without hope of compensating gains, this expectation being largely the consequence of the previous application of force by the dominant side."[13] U.S. actions can increase or decrease Hanoi's strategic costs. Bombing North Viet Nam increases the pain and thus increases the probability of surrender. This proposition and prediction are not without meaning. That — "other things being equal" — nations are more likely to surrender when the strategic cost-benefit balance is negative is true. But nations rarely surrender when they are winning. The proposition specifies a range within which nations surrender. But over this broad range, the relevant question is: Why do nations surrender?

Model II and Model III analysts focus upon the government machine through which this fact about the international strategic marketplace must be filtered to produce a surrender. These analysts are considerably less sanguine about the possibility of surrender *at the point* that the cost-benefit calculus turns negative. Never in history (i.e., in none of the five cases I have examined) have nations surrendered at that point. Surrender occurs sometime thereafter. *When* depends on the processes of organizations and the politics of players within these governments — as they are affected by the opposing government. Moreover, the effects of the victorious power's action upon the surrendering nation cannot be adequately summarized as increasing or decreasing strategic costs. Imposing additional costs by bombing a nation may increase the probability of surrender. But it also may reduce it. An appreciation of the impact of the acts of one nation upon another thus requires some understanding of the machine that is being influenced. For more precise prediction, Model II and Model III require considerably more information about the organizations and politics of North Viet Nam than is publicly available. On the basis of the limited public information, however, these models can be suggestive.

Model II examines two subproblems. First, to have lost is not sufficient. The government must know that the strategic cost-benefit calculus is negative. But neither the categories nor the indicators of strategic costs and benefits are clear. And the sources of information about both are organizations whose parochial priorities and perceptions do not facilitate accurate information or estimation. Military evaluation of military performance, military estimates of factors like "enemy morale," and military predictions about when "the tide will turn" or "the corner will have been turned" are typically distorted. In cases of highly decentralized guerrilla operations, like Viet Nam, these problems are exacerbated. Thus strategic costs will be underestimated. Only highly *visible* costs can have direct impact on leaders without being filtered through organizational channels. Second, since organizations define the details of options and execute actions, surrender (and negotiation) is likely to entail considerable bungling in the early stages. No organization can define options or prepare programs for this treasonous act. Thus, early overtures will be uncoordinated with the acts of other organizations — e.g., the fighting forces — creating contradictory "signals" to the victor.

Model III suggests that surrender will not come at the point that strategic costs outweigh benefits, but that it will not wait until the leadership group concludes that the war is lost. Rather the problem is better understood in terms of four additional propositions. First, strong advocates of the war effort, whose careers are closely identified with the war, rarely come to the conclusion that costs outweigh benefits. Second, quite often from the outset of a war, a number of members of the government (particularly those whose responsibilities sensitize them to problems other than war, e.g., economic planners or intelligence experts) are convinced that the war effort is futile. Third, surrender is likely to come as the result of a political shift that enhances the effective power of the latter group (and adds swing members to it). Fourth, the course of the war, particularly actions of the victor, can influence the advantages and disadvantages of players in the loser's government. Thus, North Viet Nam will surrender not when its leaders have a change of heart, but when Hanoi has a change of leaders (or a change of effective power within the central circle). How U.S. bombing (or pause), threats, promises, or action in South Viet Nam affect the game in Hanoi is subtle but nonetheless crucial.

That these three models could be applied to the surrender of governments other than North Viet Nam should be obvious. But that exercise is left for the reader.

AFTERWORD

Implications and Issues
for Further Research, 1971

This study has obviously bitten off more than it has chewed. The arguments started and lines of inquiry begun must extend beyond the covers of this book. It may be useful, however, to spell out several implications of the argument and to identify a number of unsettled issues that require further research. What follows are a dozen implications and issues, the first six of general and practical character, the last six of narrower, more theoretical interest.

1. MODEL II AND MODEL III CUTS AT OTHER PROBLEMS OF FOREIGN POLICY AND INTERNATIONAL RELATIONS. Though preliminary and partial, the paradigms presented here do provide a basis for serious reexamination of many problems of foreign policy and international relations. Model II and Model III cuts at problems typically treated in Model I terms should permit significant improvements. Various areas of literature, for example, Sinology or diplomatic history, should be treated systematically from the perspectives of organizational processes and bureaucratic politics. In areas where Model I thinking is so entrenched that it discourages serious consideration of alternative hypotheses, it might be appropriate to ask analysts, after they have produced a Model I study, to then write further Model II and Model III cuts at the same issues. At a minimum, analysts should be encouraged to put on Model II and Model III spectacles in searching for hypotheses about any issue.

Full Model II and Model III analyses require large amounts

of information. But even in cases where information is severely limited, improvements are possible. Consider the problem of predicting Soviet strategic forces. In the mid-1950's Model I-style calculations led to predictions that the Soviets would rapidly deploy large numbers of long-range bombers. From a Model II perspective, both the frailty of the Air Force within the Soviet military establishment and the budgetary implications of such a build-up would have led analysts to hedge this prediction. Moreover, Model III would have pointed to a sure, visible indicator of such a build-up: noisy struggles among the service chiefs and Politburo members over major budgetary shifts. In the late 1950s and early 1960s, Model I calculations led to the prediction of an immediate, massive, Soviet deployment of ICBMs. Again, a Model II cut would have reduced this number because in the earlier period strategic rockets were controlled by the Soviet ground forces rather than an independent service, and in the latter period this would have necessitated major shifts in budgetary splits.

2. THE "BUREAUCRACY" PROBLEM. The factors highlighted by our Organizational Process and Governmental Politics Models provide a base from which to begin to formulate the bureaucracy problem.

Few issues about the American government are more critical today than the matter of whether the federal government is capable of governing. Specifically, the issue is whether the U.S. government is capable of translating intentions into outcomes. Any careful review of the outcomes produced by the American government over the past decade will make the point of this question painfully obvious. Some radical critics focus on the seeming inability of the government to deliver even available, well-understood solutions to problems that most Americans recognize and want solved — for example, hunger in the United States — and conclude that the "system" should be destroyed. This radical despair is not unlike the frustration of many governmental analysts and operators as they reflect on the fate of their best-laid plans and solutions.

But what is the problem? The classical frame of reference finds it difficult to formulate, since the assumptions and categories of Model I seem to require an analyst to choose between pinning bad outcomes on bad intentions (villains or conspirators) and explaining the outcomes as aberrations from the normal processes of government. Even when Model I analysts reach

beyond the assumptions of the classical model to identify "bureaucracy" as the source of the problem, their orientation con-
strains their grasp of the issue.

The argument developed in this book suggests that bureaucracy is indeed the least understood source of unhappy outcomes
produced by the U.S. government. Calls for the elimination of
bureaucracy are, however, nonsolutions. Large organizations
that function according to routines, and politics among individuals who share power, are inevitable features of the exercise of
public authority in modern society. Perhaps much of the "Permanent Government" created in the 1930s to implement various
New Deal programs has outlived its usefulness. But if these organizations are to be destroyed, they will have to be replaced by
other large organizations. Otherwise, various public functions
that American citizens now expect from the federal government
will not be performed. These new organizations will develop
goals that are in part their own, and they will establish programs
and SOPs for doing business. Where these organizations are
forced to deal with problems that are not well understood — for
example, poverty — their performance is likely to appear sluggish and inappropriate to external critics, and their patterns of
behavior are likely to seem encrusted and incapable of change
to outsiders who try to make a revolution during their season
inside.

Similarly, the major features of the current bureaucratic
political game may make creative, or even reasonable, solutions
unlikely. But if these features are changed, for example, by
electing Congressmen or Presidents of a new caste or appointing
Cabinet officers or deputy assistant secretaries from a new breed,
a new game with a new distribution of influence will form. And
in that game, governmental officials who differ substantially
over issues and solutions will advance their preferred proposals
by the processes of internal politics. Again, especially in the case
of problems that are not well understood, critics who feel confident about their definition of the problem and their preferred
solution will find the actions of the government that emerge
from current games disappointing, and occasional insiders are
likely to find embarrassingly slow the process of consensus-
building and maneuvering required to achieve a desired action.

Thus there is no escaping the need for a better understanding of bureaucracy: of the Model II and the Model III factors that

make for many unhappy outcomes in the present system and that will have to be changed, with meticulous care, on the basis of considerable understanding, if changes in this system are to increase the probability of happy results.

3. ANALYSIS, GOVERNMENTAL ACTIONS, AND OUTCOMES. Improvement in the capabilities of analysts and operators to achieve desired actions and outcomes will require (1) narrowing the "analysis gap," (2) upgrading current policy analysis, and (3) finding new ways of thinking about the "system" for selecting and implementing actions.

As presently practiced, most analysis of public policy issues consists in solving analytic problems, that is, identifying preferred proposals for attacking a defined policy problem. For example, analyses of the problems of NATO defense attempt to distinguish the preferred package of troops and weapons for meeting the range of plausible contingencies. Good analysis clarifies objectives, explores alternatives, ranks alternatives in terms of relevant objectives, and selects the preferred option. The development of techniques like systems analysis and cost-benefit analysis permit highly refined Model I-style analysis.

According to prevailing practice, analysis stops when a preferred analytic solution to the problem has been identified. Analysts seem to assume either that the preferred solution will command agreement and thus be adopted and implemented or that in any case their job ends and someone else's (perhaps the politician's) begins at that point.

If one is primarily interested in what the government actually does, the unavoidable question is: What percentage of the work of achieving a desired governmental action is done when the preferred analytic alternative has been identified? My estimate is about 10 percent in the normal case, ranging as high as 50 percent for some problems. What remains — namely, the gap between preferred solutions and the actual behavior of the government — we label the "analysis gap" or "missing chapter" in conventional analysis.

If analysts and operators are to increase their ability to achieve desired policy outcomes, they will have to develop ways of thinking analytically about a larger chunk of the problem. It is not that we have too many good analytic solutions to problems. It is, rather, that we have more good solutions than we have appropriate actions. Thus we shall have to find ways of thinking harder about the problem of "implementation," that is, the path between preferred solution and actual performance of the government.

This perspective suggests that the central questions of policy analysis are quite different from the kinds of questions analysts have traditionally asked. Indeed, the crucial questions seem to be matters of planning for management: How does an analyst or operator think about moving from the preferred solution to the actual governmental action? Among the questions that an analyst concerned with this gap must consider are: Is the desired action on the agenda of issues that will arise in the current climate? If not, can it be forced onto the agenda? What are the various bundles of action-channels and sequences of action-channels for producing the desired action? Can new action-channels be devised? How will the key players along those action-channels regard this proposal? Which players will have to agree and which to acquiesce? What means are available to whom for persuading these players? Is the desired action consistent with existing programs and SOPs of the organizations that will deliver the behavior? If not, how can these organizational procedures be changed?

More systematic and rigorous ways of asking and answering these questions should increase analysts' and operators' effectiveness not only in achieving actions but also in judging the *administrative feasibility* of preferred solutions. For the argument is not simply that analysis needs to be extended beyond the identification of preferred solutions to implementation. It is also that ways must be found of *inserting* organizational and political factors into the initial analysis, into the selection of the preferred alternative.

For solving problems, a Model I-style analysis provides the best first cut. Indeed, for analyzing alternatives and distinguishing the preferred proposal, there is no clear alternative to this basic framework. In order to make a Model I-style analysis manageable, analysts simplify the problem by abstracting from the real-world situation. For example, analyses of the purchase of a major piece of hardware, e.g., a fighter for the military services or computer facilities for the health services, attempt to distinguish the most cost-effective alternative. By examining the benefits derived from the marginal dollars in each of the alternative investments, the analyst is able to distinguish one of the alternatives as the most beneficial. But such analyses omit factors like the existing configuration of organizations that will employ the hardware, the norms and procedures of these organizations, the extent of support for these norms and programs, the political configuration on top of and outside of the relevant organizations, etc. In order to distinguish the alternative that will produce the most cost-effective action, these factors would have to be built into the problem being solved. Formally, many of these factors can be posed as additional "constraints." How such factors can be built into analysis in practice is a most difficult issue for further research.

Moreover, a serious concern with using analysis to improve policy outcomes must not be limited to improving analysis of particular problems. Rather, we must find new ways of thinking about improving the capabilities of the "system" to select and implement actions. The central questions concern the impact of the structure of political games, and the character of organizations, on policy outcomes. For example, what information do existing organizational procedures make available at what points and how can this information be improved? How can organizations be encouraged to produce a longer list of alternatives? Can means be devised for checking the programs that organizations are prepared to implement and making the repertoire of programs more relevant? What structure of a bureaucratic political game facilitates the identification of issues and production of a good map of alternatives and arguments? How does structure affect the representation of interests and provision of a forum for relevant participants? The arguments developed in this study should facilitate formulation of a long list of questions of this sort about the impact of structural arrangements on policy analysis and policy outcomes. These questions present a promising area for further research.

4. NORMATIVE CONSIDERATIONS.   This study has suggested that when analysts focus on an outcome in international affairs, the name of the game is *explanation*. But this is not entirely fair. The haphazard state of the literature of foreign affairs derives in part from the fact that analysts are engaged in a number of other activities as well. Sometimes in asking "why" of an outcome, they seek an *evaluation* or *justification* rather than an explanation. For example, in examining the U.S. blockade, an analyst may be interested not only in an explanation of that ac-

tion but also in the question of whether the President and his associates were justified in choosing a course of action that entailed such a high probability of nuclear war.

An analogue of the conceptual model that we have specified as Model I serves as the basis for most evaluation of actions in international politics. A rational analysis of the problem, alternatives, and consequences provides the benchmark against which the behavior of the governments is tested.

But if one accepts a Model II or Model III explanation of a governmental action, does this not require him to modify the norms he uses in evaluating that behavior? For example, the Organizational Process Model leads an analyst to expect routine behavior in implementation, rather than complete flexibility in tailoring action to the specific situation. A Model II analyst might ask whether established routines were appropriate. But should he not tend to accept — and justify — behavior that would appear, from a Model I perspective, in error? Model III leads the analyst to expect much pulling and hauling, and consequently large errors as a result of innumerable, small slips. Perhaps his touchstone for failure could be labeled "for want of a nail a shoe is lost . . ." Since he recognizes many reasons for losing nails, should this not limit his willingness to allocate large slices of blame — especially for "failures" to make grand departures?

5. PREDICTIONS AND WARNING SIGNS. The utility of the models in activities other than explanation derives in large part from their effect on analysts' expectations about future outcomes. While most analysts' predictions tend to be generated in terms of some variant of Model I, the attempt to make predictions based on Model II and Model III should permit improvements. But the issue of prediction raises a number of questions that have not been addressed in this study and that provide a fascinating agenda for further work.

Predictions are important, inevitable elements in the structure of our opinions about policy issues, and in any policy analysis or recommendation. These predictions are most often implicit. Most analysts formulate predictions in an intuitive fashion, without much explicit thought. But in making predictions, analysts are forced to relate and weight hundreds of factors known to be relevant to the outcome. Would making explicit predictions about outcomes, and assessing other analysts' implicit predictions, be a useful way of clarifying thought about policy problems and improving analysis and advice? Specifically, should we accept the precept: *a good, simple-minded test of someone's expertise in a particular area is whether he can win money (on average) in a series of bets with other reasonable men about outcomes in that area?*

For what classes of outcomes do propositions that emerge from Model II and Model III have the most power, that is, permit the greatest improvement in prediction?

Should the objective of studies of internal mechanisms of governments be an explicit statement of factors and relations — a series of simultaneous equations — or rather simply a map of factors to which an analyst should be sensitive, but which he must weigh and relate in his own gut?

What are the major drawbacks to the simple-minded demand for predictions about outcomes, and what does the literature on the logic of prediction and forecasting suggest about ways of overcoming them?

This cluster of issues forms a major problem for further steps in the analysis of foreign policy, and indeed of all public policy.

Model II and Model III cuts should not only improve analysts' specific predictions; they should also sensitize analysts to certain warning signs about the behavior of nations that they might otherwise overlook. A Model II perspective should encourage analysts to worry about the mechanisms by which partial commitments become overcommitments. For example, any organizational process analyst would have bet that in allowing MacArthur to provide air cover for the South Koreans on June 26, 1950, Truman had virtually decided for American intervention with a significant force. No Model II analyst could have expected that President Johnson's decision to bomb North Viet Nam in February 1965 (and thus of necessity to provide bases for bombers, storage sites for bombs, and security for both) would be separate from the introduction of American troops. Only by neglecting the questions posed by Model II could an analyst assume that organizational options, e.g., significant capabilities for fighting limited war, can be created without also raising the probability that these options will be exercised. In the words of Senator Richard Russell, a seasoned observer of military organizations, "If Americans have the capability to go anywhere and do anything, we will always be going somewhere and doing something."

Model III should lead an analyst to post cautions about the necessity for complementarity among personalities and operating styles in the highest circles. Some ingredients and certain combinations tend to spoil the soup — or at least to make it less savory. For example, each new American administration goes through a transition period in which large errors are likely to occur: Truman's cancellation of Lend-Lease, Kennedy's Bay of Pigs, and Johnson's Viet Nam. These "transition phenomena" resulted in large part from the newness of players both to one another and to the machines on top of which they were placed.

6. APPLICATIONS OF THE MODELS TO OTHER AREAS OF PUBLIC POLICY.   That analogues of the three models can be used to analyze outcomes in areas of public policy outside foreign and military affairs should be obvious. Several such analyses have been published, for example, Theodore Marmor's excellent study, *The Politics of Medicare*. Others are in progress. Further specification of the analogues, and application of them to various additional areas, constitutes a significant "target of opportunity."

7. THEORIES OF FOREIGN POLICY AND INTERNATIONAL RELATIONS.   The argument of this book implies a position on the problem of "the state of the art" of theorizing about foreign policy and international relations.

That the best explanations of foreign affairs are insightful, personalistic, and noncumulative has often been noted. The field is so unstructured that each scholar is encouraged to make a personal contribution by expressing his understanding in a vocabulary that captures what is unique about his insight. Such insights, however, are not easily applied by less brilliant students of foreign policy to new cases. Consequently, perceptive analyses of particular happenings tend simply to illuminate those occurrences rather than to contribute to an accumulating body of systematic knowledge.

Some analysts justify this condition as a consequence of the character of the enterprise. The complexities of the reality with which the analyst of foreign affairs is concerned create a conflict between insight and cumulation. Juxtaposition of the necessity for insight and the requirement of communication poses a paradox: well-defined concepts shackle the analyst's ability to grasp insights that require well-defined concepts to communicate. In explaining occurrences, then, the foreign policy analyst is a historian, and Clio is a muse. As one major proponent of this position has declared, "Understanding is the enemy of prediction."

While accepting the characterization of the present condition of foreign policy analysis, most international relations theorists draw quite different conclusions. These symptoms constitute evidence of the lack of theory in international relations and the bankruptcy of analysis without theory. Under the banner "There is no theory in international relations" international relations theorists march off to explore new frontiers.

The fact that almost as much time has been spent lamenting the lack of theory, and theorizing about theory in international relations, as has been invested in producing substantive work suggests that the "discipline" is retarded. But this study adopts a third posture toward the problem — one quite distinct from the first two. A concern for systematic foreign policy analysis does not entail a demand for *a priori* theorizing on new frontiers or *ad hoc* appropriation of "new techniques." The present condition of foreign policy explanations can be taken as an indicator that the "state of the art" is stunted rather than bankrupt. What is required, at least as the first step, is noncasual examination of the present product: inspection of existing explanations, articulation of the conceptual models employed in producing them, formulation of the propositions relied upon, analysis of the logic of the various intellectual enterprises, and reflection on the questions being asked. These preliminary matters — formulating questions with clarity and self-consciousness about categories and assumptions so that fruitful acquisition of large quantities of data is possible — are still a major hurdle in considering most important problems. As a second step, foreign policy and international relations theorists must begin systematic acquisition and processing of data. Most theorists have little respect for "case studies" — in large part because of the a-theoretical character of case studies of the past. But the only substitute for detailed examination of particular events and problems is construction of theory in the absence of specific information. What we need is a new kind of "case study" done with theoretical alertness to the range of factors identified by Models I, II, and III (and others) on the basis of which to begin refining and testing propositions and models.

8. CLARIFICATION AND REFINEMENT OF MODELS I, II, AND III. The present formulation of Models I, II, and III is a first step. These models must be refined, their applicability clarified, and variants identified. Given any action, an imaginative analyst should always be able to construct some rationale for the government's choice. (Indeed, in a democratic system, it is necessary

that reasons be produced for whatever is done.) By imposing, and relaxing, constraints on the parameters of rational choice (as in variants of Model I), analysts can construct a large number of accounts of any act as the rational choice. But what does such an account imply? What are the rules of evidence and inference by which one distinguishes among various accounts of a particular action as a rational choice? What evidence counts for or against an assertion about, for example, Soviet intentions? Analysts who rely on Model I in explaining occurrences by reference to national goals and intentions summarize a large number of specific factors. But if we are to be clearer about specific determinants of occurrences, it will be necessary to decompose these summary statements.

As suggested in Chapter 1, I have begun a further study of the Rational Actor Model in which I attempt to distinguish between Model I statements about (1) pressures created by the international environment, that is, pressures that would be felt by any national government; (2) the logic of a situation or problem; (3) shared national values and assumptions; and (4) values or assumptions shared by a group of national leaders. But considerably more refinement is necessary before Model I analysis can make more systematic contributions to the question of determinants of governmental actions.

Model II's explanation of action at t in terms of activity at $t - 1$ is explanation. The world is contiguous. But governments sometimes make sharp departures. Can an Organizational Process model be modified to suggest where change is likely? Attention to organizational change should afford greater understanding of why particular programs and SOPs are maintained by identifiable types of organizations and also how a manager can improve organizational performance. Model II concentrates on the aggregate behavior of organizations rather than on individuals within organizations. What kinds of individuals, personnel systems, and norms are consistent with the kind of organizational behavior identified by Model II? In the present formulation of Model II, a unified group of leaders makes decisions within organizational constraints. Other accounts of these central decisions could be meshed with the organizing concepts of Model II.

Model III tells a fascinating story, but it is enormously complex. The information requirements are often overwhelming, and many of the details of the bargaining may be superfluous.

How can such a model be made parsimonious? The use of this model requires more satisfactory accounts of each player's position, more careful specification of various action-channels, etc. The current statement of the model concentrates on the governmental machine, but external groups could be included by broadening the model. Model III permits a number of low-level propositions about the behavior of players or their likely stand on various issues. How these propositions can be combined to yield propositions about more aggregate governmental actions is a central difficulty.

9. RELATIONS AMONG THE MODELS: PARTIAL V. GENERAL ANALYSIS. The three models are obviously not exclusive alternatives. Indeed, the paradigms highlight the partial emphasis of each framework — what each magnifies and what it leaves out. Each concentrates on one class of variables, in effect, relegating other important factors to a *ceteris paribus* clause. The models can therefore be understood as building blocks in a larger model of the determinants of outcomes.

The developed sciences have little hesitation about partial models. The fact that additional factors are known to be relevant to a class of outcomes does not necessarily mean that it is always helpful to try to incorporate these factors into an analytic model. In contrast, the aspiring sciences tend to demand general theory. In satisfying this demand, they often force generalization at the expense of understanding. Refining partial paradigms, and specifying the classes of actions for which they are relevant, may be a more fruitful path to limited theory and propositions than the route of instant generalization.

It is not difficult to sketch the outline of a general model. The concepts of each conceptual model could be represented as factors relevant to governmental action in foreign affairs. And the collection of factors in each of the models could then be combined into a full function — or a set of simultaneous equations — that represent the determinants of these actions. Given our present understanding of the factors involved, and our lack of understanding of the relations among them, however, this "grand model" is really a metaphor.

10. THE TYPOLOGY PROBLEM. The three models are not equally applicable to any governmental action or outcome. A typology of actions and outcomes, some of which are more amenable to treatment in terms of one model and some to another, should be developed.

The highest of high-level crises, the events of October 1962, do not constitute a typical occurrence. *Prima facie*, the missile crisis would seem to be an ideal Model I case. The strategic competition, the obvious threat to shared values, the awareness of central leaders about the details of governmental actions, and the overwhelming importance of the President and the Chairman do make Model I analysis powerful. Even in this case, Model II and Model III add a lot. But the shape of this study is biased by focusing on this high-level crisis rather than on the more routine behavior of governments.

For explaining actions where national security interests dominate, shared values lead to a consensus on what national security requires, and actions flow rather directly from decisions, Model I is useful. Thus to predict that if the Soviet Union doubles its defense expenditures, the U.S. defense budget will rise, Model I is sufficient. For explaining the specific characteristics of a governmental action performed by a large organization, Model II is most powerful. Decisions that emerge from intra-governmental debate at the highest levels are the stuff of Model III. But these three clues are no typology. For a refined typology, we do not even have a satisfactory list of the relevant dimensions. Among the dimensions that should be considered are: crisis to noncrisis contexts, decisions to actions, short-term to long-term, more Presidential involvement to Presidential unawareness, potential political saliency to no political saliency; as well as the substance of the issue: military force, budget, diplomacy, etc. But can the typology neglect specific characteristics of the structure of the government and the individuals in it? A typology of decisions and actions that would serve as a guide to the analyst about predominant reliance for a first cut constitutes an important next step in research.

11. ADDITIONAL PARADIGMS. These three models of the determinants of governmental action do not exhaust the dimensions on which they are arranged. Along one dimension, they represent different levels of aggregation: nations (or national governments), organizations, and individuals. Along a second dimension, they represent different patterns of activity: purposive action toward strategic objectives, routine behavior toward different organizational goals, and political activity toward competing goals. It is not accidental that explanations offered in the literature of foreign policy cluster around these three patterns. But models that mix characteristics of the three are clearly

possible. One of the more interesting and promising is a cross between Model I and Model III, focusing in the case of the United States, on the President as the rational actor whose purposes nevertheless include more than mere strategic values and whose activities require sneakers as well as boots. Similarly, by treating organizations as political players, Model II and Model III can be blended.

But these three paradigms neglect or underplay a number of further aspects of governmental behavior. Additional paradigms focusing, for example, on individual cognitive processes, or the psychology of central players, or the role of external groups, must be considered.

12. FACTORS BEYOND GOVERNMENTAL ACTION. Governmental action forms but one cluster of factors relevant to outcomes in foreign affairs. Most students of foreign policy adopt this focus. Most explanations of occurrences center on government action. Nevertheless, the dimensions of the chessboard, the character of the pieces, and the rules of the game — factors considered by international systems theorists — constitute the context in which the chess pieces are moved. This context includes diverse factors such as gross topography, frontiers, climate, religion, national character–institutions–style, natural resources, demography, capital resources, skill and training, technology, GNP, and morale. How these factors affect the models of governmental behavior is yet another important issue for further research.

Notes

Preface

1. John F. Kennedy, "Preface" to Theodore Sorensen, *Decision-Making in the White House: The Olive Branch and the Arrows,* New York, 1963.
2. The Rand Corporation has a continuing "Organizational Behavior" project. The Brookings Institution has begun a project on Bureaucracy and Foreign Policy. The Institute of Politics in the John F. Kennedy School of Government at Harvard University has a Faculty Seminar on Bureaucracy, Politics, and Policy. The Social Science Division at California Institute of Technology is starting a study of organizational behavior in government.

Introduction

1. Deaths of this order of magnitude would have occurred only in the worst case.
2. Theodore Sorensen, *Kennedy,* New York, 1965, p. 705.
3. Harold Macmillan, "Introduction" to Robert F. Kennedy, *Thirteen Days: A Memoir of the Cuban Missile Crisis,* New York, 1969, p. 17.
4. In attempting to understand problems of foreign affairs, analysts engage in a number of related but logically separable enterprises: (1) description, (2) explanation, (3) prediction, (4) evaluation, and (5) recommendation. This study focuses primarily on explanation and, by implication, prediction.
5. For the purpose of this argument we shall accept Carl G. Hempel's characterization of the logic of explanation: an explanation "answers the question 'Why did the explanadum-phenomenon occur?' by showing that the phenomenon resulted from certain particular circumstances, specified in $C_1, C_2 \ldots C_k$, in accordance with the laws $L_1, L_2 \ldots L_r$. By pointing this out, the argument shows that, given the particular circumstances

and the laws in question, the occurrence of the phenomenon *was to be expected;* and it is in this sense that the explanation enables us to *understand why* the phenomenon occurred" (*Aspects of Scientific Explanation,* New York, 1965, p. 337). While various patterns of explanation can be distinguished (*viz.,* Ernest Nagel, *The Structure of Science: Problems in the Logic of Scientific Explanation,* New York, 1961), satisfactory scientific explanations exhibit this basic logic. Consequently prediction is essentially the converse of explanation.

6. Model I has been variously labeled the rational-policy model, the unitary-purposive model, and the purposive-actor model.

7. Model III might have been labeled administrative, internal, governmental, machine, or even palace politics. "Politics" signifies the subtle pulling and hauling in intricate games that characterize the action. "Bureaucratic" signifies that the action is located in the bureaucratized machine that is the executive, or administration, or (in the United Kingdom) government.

8. In strict terms, the "outcomes" these three models attempt to explain are essentially the behavior of national governments, i.e., the sum of official behavior of all individuals employed in a government, relevant to an issue. These models focus not on a state of affairs, i.e., a full description of the world, but upon national decisions and implementation. This distinction is stated clearly by Harold and Margaret Sprout, "Environmental Factors in the Study of International Politics," in James Rosenau (ed.), *International Politics and Foreign Policy,* Glencoe, Ill., 1961, p. 116. This restriction excludes explanations offered principally in terms of international systems theories. Nevertheless, it is not severe, since few interesting explanations of occurrences in foreign policy have been produced at that level of analysis. According to David Singer, "The nation state — our primary actor in international relations . . . is clearly the traditional focus among Western students and is the one which dominates all of the texts employed in English-speaking colleges and universities" ("The Level-of-Analysis Problem in International Relations," in Klaus Knorr and Sidney Verba (eds.), *The International System,* Princeton, N.J., 1961). Similarly, Richard Brody's review of contemporary trends in the study of international relations finds that "scholars have come increasingly to focus on acts of nations. That is, they all focus on the behavior of nations in some respect. Having an interest in accounting for the behavior of nations in common, the prospects for a common frame of reference are enhanced."

Chapter 1   Model I: The Rational Actor

1. Arnold Horelick and Myron Rush, *Strategic Power and Soviet Foreign Policy,* Chicago, 1965, chs. 11–12. Based on A. Horelick, "The Cuban Missile Crisis: An Analysis of Soviet Calculations and Behavior," *World Politics,* April 1964.

2. Ibid., p. 154.

3. *The New York Times*, February 18, 1967.

4. Ibid.

5. Hans Morgenthau, *Politics Among Nations*, 4th edition, New York, 1970, p. 185.

6. Ibid., p. 186.

7. Ibid., p. 5.

8. Ibid., p. 6.

9. Stanley Hoffmann, *Daedalus*, Fall 1962; reprinted in *The State of War*, New York, 1965.

10. Ibid., p. 171.

11. Ibid., p. 189.

12. Following Robert MacIver; see Stanley Hoffmann, *Contemporary Theory in International Relations*, Englewood Cliffs, N.J., 1960, pp. 178–79.

13. Thomas Schelling, *The Strategy of Conflict*, New York, 1960, p. 232. This proposition was formulated earlier by Albert Wohlstetter in "The Delicate Balance of Terror," *Foreign Affairs*, January 1959. Consider Schelling's discussion of deterrence. How does he characterize the essentials of the situations and behavior in question? Deterrence is concerned with influencing the choices that another party will make and doing it by influencing his expectations of how we will behave. It involves confronting him with evidence for believing that our behavior will be determined by his behavior. Thus, according to the analysis, the aspects of the concept that demand clarification are as follows. First, what combination of value systems for the two participants — ōf the "payoffs" in that languagè of game theory — makes a deterrent threat credible? Second, how do we measure the mixture of conflict and common interest required to generate a deterrence situation? Third, what communications are required and what means of authenticating the evidence communicated? Fourth, what kind of rationality is required — knowledge of his own value system, an ability to perceive alternatives and to calculate with probabilities, an inability to disguise his own rationality? Fifth, what is the need for trust or enforcement of promises? Sixth, what are the devices by which one commits himself to acts that otherwise he would be known to shrink from, considering that if a commitment makes the threat credible enough to be effective it need not be carried out? (See Schelling, op. cit., pp. 13 ff.)

14. Schelling, op. cit., p. 4.

15. Morgenthau, op. cit., p. 5; Stanley Hoffmann, "Roulette in the Cellar," in *The State of War*, and *Contemporary Theories of International Relations*, pp. 178–79; K. Archibald (ed.), *Strategic Interaction and Conflict*, Berkeley, 1966; and Schelling, op. cit.

16. This chapter examines several exceptions to this generalization. Sidney Verba's excellent essay "Assumptions of Rational-

ity and Non-Rationality in Models of the International System"
is less an exception than it is an approach to a somewhat
different problem. Verba focuses upon models of rationality
and irrationality of *individual* statesmen, in Knorr and Verba
(eds.), *The International System*, Princeton, 1961.

Although this conceptual model has received scant notice in
the literature on foreign policy, a considerable discussion of
closely related notions is taking place in economic, decision,
and game theory. Thus, in attempting to explicate the implicit
model, this chapter refers to, draws from, and hopefully makes
some contribution to those efforts — without, however, assuming any familiarity with that literature.

17. Bernadotte Schmitt, "1914 and 1939," *Journal of Modern History*, Vol. 31, June 1959.

18. Sidney Fay, *The Origins of the World War*, Vol. 2, New York,
1928, p. 55.

19. Bernadotte Schmitt, "Fifty Years of Exploring History," *The
Fashion and Future of History*, Cleveland, 1960, pp. 4–5.

20. Arthur Schlesinger, Jr., "The Historian and History," *Foreign
Affairs*, April 1963, p. 494.

21. For an elaboration of this proposition see John Passmore, "Explanation in Everyday Life, in Science, and in History," *History
and Theory*, Vol. 2, No. 2, 1962.

22. Schelling, op. cit., p. 13.

23. Ibid., p. 253. This is perhaps the central proposition about
limited war that emerges from a cluster of analyses published
around 1960. See Morton Halperin, *Limited War in the Nuclear
Age*, p. 13: "If and when the strategic balance becomes more
stable, that is, when both sides have strategic forces so well
protected that there is no perceived advantage in striking first,
the effect of the strategic balance will change. . . . Both sides
are more likely to run risks in a local war when they are com-
placent about the stability of the strategic balance."

24. Schelling, op. cit., pp. 75, 262–63. Halperin (ch. 3, op. cit.)
makes a persuasive argument that in the Korean War the two
sides observed quite different, asymmetrical limits that emerged
less from battlefield bargaining than from the kinds of factors
emphasized by Model II and Model III.

25. Glen Snyder, in *Deterrence and Defense* (Princeton, 1961), exhibits a precise formulation of this basic model. In addressing
the problem of deterrence, he asserts: "The probability of any
particular attack by the aggressor is the resultant of essentially
four factors which exist in his 'mind.' All four taken together
might be termed the aggressor's 'risk calculus.' They are (1)
his valuation of his war objectives; (2) the cost which he expects to suffer as a result of various responses by the deterrer;
(3) the probability of various responses, including 'no response'; and (4) the probability of winning the objectives with
each possible response" (p. 12). According to this principle,
Snyder explains U.S. success in deterring an attack on NATO

as a consequence of the negative expected value of this alternative in the Soviet risk calculus. "If the expected value [of any
particular attack] were negative, or positive but less than the
positive expected value of non-military alternatives, the Soviets
would be deterred" (p. 12). This framework also leads him to
single out the degree of stability in the balance of terror as the
crucial factor determining the likelihood that an accidental firing of a single missile would escalate to a full-blown nuclear
war. "The danger that the accidental firing of one or a few missiles will touch off the ultimate holocaust depends crucially on
the degree of stability in the balance of terror, i.e., the degree to
which each side's forces approach a sufficient first-strike capability" (p. 111).

26. Herman Kahn, *On Escalation,* New York, 1965, pp. 12–13.

27. Ibid., p. 16.

28. Ibid., p. 25.

29. Ibid., p. 211.

30. Ibid., pp. 211–12 n.

31. Ibid., p. 212.

32. Ibid. Emphasis in original.

33. Albert Wohlstetter, "Analysis and Design of Conflict Systems,"
    in E. S. Quade (ed.), *Analysis for Military Decision,* Rand
    Corporation, 1964, p. 131.

34. Ibid. Emphasis added. Wohlstetter uses this as an explicit
    "minimax" or "worst case" analysis. In correspondence he has
    suggested that the model he employs would be better labeled a
    "model of bounded irrationality."

35. Paul Nitze, Remarks to the Institute for Strategic Studies, Lon-
    don, December 11, 1961; quoted in William Kaufmann, *The
    Nuclear Strategy,* New York, 1964, p. 110.

36. Schelling in Archibald (ed.), op. cit., p. 150.

37. Kaufmann, op. cit., p. 114.

38. Robert McNamara, Address at the Commencement Exercises,
    University of Michigan, Ann Arbor, June 16, 1962. Emphasis
    added. Quoted in Kaufmann, op. cit., p. 115. In fairness to
    McNamara, it should be noted that after this assertion he goes
    on to examine other possible causes of a nuclear war: "The
    mere fact that no nation could rationally take steps leading to
    a nuclear war does not guarantee that a nuclear war cannot
    take place."

39. Horelick and Rush, op. cit., p. 9.

40. Horelick and Rush argue: "From the initiation of the Berlin
    crisis in 1958 until the 1962 encounter in Cuba, the attempt to
    deceive the West regarding Soviet missile capabilities had a
    central place in Soviet policy. The deception directly affected
    Soviet cold war objectives and the methods used in pursuing
    them. To understand Soviet foreign policy in those years, there-

fore, it is necessary to inquire ... why the Soviet leaders permitted the United States to widen substantially its margin of strategic superiority, even after the USSR had acquired the technical means of reducing it" (op. cit., p. 105).

41. Ibid.

42. Ibid.

43. Ibid.

44. Ibid., p. 106.

45. Another sovietologist, H. S. Dinerstein, offers an analysis in similar terms of the earlier development of Soviet forces and strategy, with greater emphasis on the interaction of military doctrine and Soviet forces. See his book *War and the Soviet Union,* New York, 1959. With care characteristic of biblical hermeneutics, he scrutinizes available Soviet press and professional journals (which at the time he wrote were quite limited) and compares various statements about Soviet intentions, strategy, and military doctrine with evidence about the Soviet force posture in order to discover basic Soviet intentions. Intentions require certain strategic plans, which in turn determine the structure of Soviet forces. Thus, Dinerstein explains particular Soviet force postures or weapons by reference to the military doctrine and objectives from which the force structure can be deduced. Conversely, what the Soviet objective must have been is discovered by projecting from force posture and military doctrine to the objective which it rationally served (p. 13). Dinerstein's central argument proceeds as follows: "Once it had been decided that the major mission of the Soviet armed forces was to fight a full-scale war if the need arose, the choice of strategies open to the planners was automatically narrowed.... The Soviet strategy, therefore, is to destroy the enemy's military forces before those forces can destroy Soviet population and cities. This strategy has the greatest promise of success if the Soviet Union is able to initiate the use of nuclear weapons.... Soviet strategic plans, then, demand the ability to destroy a large part of the presumptive enemy's war-making force at its bases.... Such requirements necessitate a striking force able to hit with considerable precision" (pp. 24–25). It would require considerable ingenuity to reconcile this analysis with facts which became incontrovertible only after this study was published: namely, the small Soviet bomber fleet, the Soviet failure to purchase a substantial ICBM force, and the lack of precision of the Soviet missiles.

46. Allen Whiting, *China Crosses the Yalu,* New York, 1960, p. 159.

47. Ibid., p. 151. Emphasis added.

48. Ibid.

49. Ibid., pp. 151–52. What permits Whiting to sort through Peking's commissions and omissions and on this basis to offer such a confident explanation of Chinese decisions? "The logic behind final decision has been deduced," Whiting states, "upon the

assumption that the Chinese leaders calculated the expected costs, risks, and gains associated with alternate courses of action. In brief, it has been assumed that Chinese Communist behavior is rationally motivated" (p. ix).

50. Morton Halperin and Dwight Perkins, *Communist China and Arms Control*, New York, 1965.

51. Ibid., p. 1.

52. Ibid., p. 10.

53. Ibid., pp. 1–2.

54. Dinerstein, op. cit., p. 25.

55. Merton Peck and Frederic Scherer, *The Weapons Acquisition Process*, Boston, 1962.

56. Ibid., pp. 285–86.

57. Ibid., p. 286.

58. Ibid., pp. 226 ff.

59. Henry Kissinger, *Nuclear Weapons and Foreign Policy*, New York, 1957, p. 8.

60. Ibid.

61. Ibid., p. 5.

62. Ibid., p. 6.

63. Ibid., p. 34.

64. Henry Kissinger, *The Necessity for Choice*, New York, 1961, pp. 1–4.

65. Kissinger, *Nuclear Weapons and Foreign Policy*, p. 4.

66. Kissinger, *The Necessity for Choice*, p. 7. Though relying primarily on this style of explanation, Kissinger is also a perceptive observer of the haphazard process by which many American doctrines and actions emerge. See, for example, the final chapter of *Nuclear Weapons and Foreign Policy;* the final chapter of *The Necessity for Choice;* "Domestic Structure and Foreign Policy," *Daedalus,* Spring 1966, and "Bureaucracy and Policymaking," in *Bureaucracy, Policy and Strategy*, Security Studies Paper Number 17, University of California, Los Angeles, 1968. This last piece suggests a substantially different approach, even for explanations, that is more consistent with Model III.

67. Morgenthau, op. cit., pp 5–6. Emphasis added.

68. Ibid., p. 5. Emphasis added.

69. Arnold Wolfers, "The Actors in International Politics," in William Fox (ed.), *Theoretical Aspects of International Relations*, Notre Dame, 1959, p. 83.

70. Ibid., p. 98.

71. Ibid.

72. James Rosenau (ed.), *International Politics and Foreign Policy*, Glencoe, Ill., 1961.

73. Ibid., pp. 1–3.

74. Ibid., p. 78.
75. Ibid.
76. Ibid.
77. Raymond Aron, *Peace and War: A Theory of International Relations,* New York, 1966, p. 16. Emphasis in the original.
78. Ibid.
79. Ibid., p. 17.
80. Ibid., p. 177; see also pp. 177–83.
81. This basic conception of meaning is taken from Hilary Putnam, "The Analytic and the Synthetic," *Minnesota Studies in the Philosophy of Science,* Vol. 2, 1963.
82. This term is Herbert Simon's, from his *Models of Man,* New York, 1957, p. 196. R. S. Peters has argued the general point with care in *The Concept of Motivation,* London, 1958.
83. As Seymour Martin Lipset has stated, "The major assumption in the social sciences generally . . . is that people seek ego gratification — that this is their goal or end" (in Archibald (ed.), op. cit., p. 150).
84. J. Von Neumann and O. Morgenstern, *Theory of Games and Economic Behavior,* Princeton, 1947.
85. Hobbes' concept has been discussed with care by Carl Friedrich, *Man and His Government,* New York, 1963, pp. 159 ff. See also Carl Friedrich (ed.), *Rational Decision,* Nomos VII, Englewood Cliffs, N.J., 1964. It has also been restated by Max Weber, *The Theory of Social and Economic Organizations,* A. M. Henderson (trans.), Talcott Parsons (ed.), Glencoe, Ill., 1947, pp. 115–18; and *The Methodology of the Social Sciences,* New York, 1949, pp. 52–53; Talcott Parsons, *The Structure of Social Action,* 2nd edition, New York, 1949, p. 58; and Herbert Simon, *Administrative Behavior,* New York, 1943, p. 67.
86. Anatol Rapport, in *Two-Person Game Theory: The Essential Ideas* (Ann Arbor, Mich., 1966), requires an integral ratio; but see Simon, *Models of Man,* p. 244.
87. For a mathematical formalization of this classical rational model, see Herbert Simon, "A Behavioral Model of Rational Choice," *Quarterly Journal of Economics,* February 1955. The Rational Actor Paradigm formulated in this chapter could be formalized along the lines of Simon's model. Statistical decision theory and game theory have modified this model for probabilistic situations. See D. Luce and H. Raiffa, *Games and Decisions,* New York, 1957, esp. ch. 13; W. Baumol, *Economic Theory and Operations Analysis,* Englewood Cliffs, N.J., 1961, esp. ch. 19; H. Raiffa, *Decision Analysis,* Boston, 1970.
88. Anthony Downs, *An Economic Theory of Democracy,* New York, 1957, p. 4.
89. Ibid.
90. John Harsanyi, "Some Social Science Implications of a New Approach to Game Theory," in Archibald (ed.), op. cit., p. 1.

91. Ibid., p. 139. Emphasis added.

92. Strictly speaking, it is possible to guarantee only optimal probability, i.e., the highest expected value. Sometimes the actual outcome must fall on the small tail of the curve. A frequent error in interpretations of events in foreign policy is the conclusion from a single outcome — e.g., discovery of Soviet missiles in Cuba — that someone must have mis-estimated a probability. It may be the case that an event which is improbable nevertheless occurs.

93. Both defenses — comprehensive rationality and rationality limited to a stylized definition of the situation — have become fashionable targets of attack. Objections raised by a considerable, but uneven, body of literature can be grouped in three clusters. The first cluster of critics objects to the requirement that the entire decision tree be generated. This demands more than man's limited intellectual capacities. For example, in our chess player's problem of rational choice, although there are only thirty possible moves in an average chess situation, consideration of all possible countermoves and counters to countermoves and so on leads to a number on the order of 10^{120} paths from the state of the board to the end of the game. A machine examining one of these paths every millionth of a second would require 10^{95} years to decide on its first move.

    A second cluster of critics — see R. J. Hall and C. J. Hitch, "Price Theory and Economic Behavior," *Oxford Economic Papers*, May 1939 — combine practical objections of the first type with a methodological "principle of realism," condemning the rational model as "unrealistic." Since decisionmakers do not consciously rank all goals and consider all alternatives in choosing, it is argued that this model cannot be used to explain or predict decisionmakers' choices. This objection stems from a basic misconception of the function of theoretical models in explanation and prediction. The regularity with which this error is resurrected in the social sciences is disheartening. The natural sciences and the philosophy of science have relegated it to an appropriate methodological dump.

    That the model of rational action is not as "realistic" as some alternative models of action is agreed. But "realism" is no simple sieve for separating acceptable and unacceptable models. To the extent that the model is offered as a description — and I am unaware of anyone who has recommended it on these grounds alone — sharp divergence between the model and observed conditions in the world must be censored. But for explanation and prediction, this lack of realism need be no drawback — as long as the rules of correspondence, relating concepts of the model to observed phenomena, are reasonably clear.

    To reject criticisms of the rational model based on the principle of realism is not necessarily to accept Milton Friedman's argument that "unrealism" is the mark of all powerful theory.

See M. Friedman, "The Methodology of Positive Economics," in his *Essays in Positive Economics*, Chicago, 1953. In arguing that the single criterion for judging models is their predictive power and, moreover, that predictive power requires unrealism, Friedman is extreme — almost to the point of being deliberately perverse.

Students of the genealogy of arguments will recognize that this essay's approach to the problem of conceptual models and their criticism represents a third-generation position. The essay might simply have attacked the Rational Actor Model and its employment in the literature as "unrealistic." The decisions and actions of national units are chosen not by monolithic actors, it would be pointed out, but rather by a conglomerate of distinct individuals who constitute a government. Moreover, these individuals choose not in terms of a consistent ranking of strategic goals, but rather on the basis of various individuals' rankings of a much wider range of values. This first-generation argument would resemble most attacks on Hans Morgenthau's theory of international politics. At a second-generation level, this essay might have assumed Friedman's position — a flair that is becoming increasingly popular in political science. As such, it would present first-generation attacks on the model and then remove their sting by pressing Friedman's principle of unrealism. The function of models is prediction, it would be argued; thus predictive power is the sole criterion for judging the adequacy of models. Predictive power requires an unrealistic model. First-generation critiques therefore support rather than detract from the model's adequacy. Fortunately, the reader has been spared both of these possible essays. But the rejection of these alternatives conveys important insight into the character of this study's argument. For we have assumed, in effect, a third-generation posture.

A final group of critics of the rationality model seize the most serious objection: *conceptually*, the model's requirement that *all* alternatives be considered and *all* consequences evaluated is not as precise as it might seem. The typical assumption that payoff functions, alternatives, and consequences are properties of an *objective situation* in which real alternatives, consequences, and utilities exist may be understandable in the case in which the choosing subject is a rat and the observer a man (especially if the man designed the experimental situation). The alternative paths in the maze and the consequences of each path (whether or not the rat gets the cheese) are precise and determinant. In a constructed game, sense can be made of the notion of all alternatives and all consequences. But in most situations in which action is required, the notion of all alternatives, or even of a rule for generating all possible alternatives (given unlimited time), is simply unclear. What objective situation makes sense of the concept of all possible consequences and their values in an ordinary situation from the everyday world, for example, foreign aid?

These objections cut. What they imply for a workable concept of rational action, however, is less straightforward than some critics have supposed. That the comprehensive rationality model is limited to artificial situations does not entail that only a *behavioral* rational model is applicable to situations in the natural world (contra Simon). Indeed, a slightly modified sibling of the comprehensive rationality model can be made sufficiently clear to be acceptable and can do much of the work of its stronger brother. The modified rationality model simply relaxes the comprehensive rationality model's requirement that "all" alternatives and "all" consequences be generated and emphasizes the heart of the model: value-maximizing choice within the large set of alternatives and consequences that are considered. For purposes of mathematical calculation, this introduces an unacceptable degree of indeterminacy. But for the explanation of typical behavior, the requirement that the *purposive* character of the action be revealed may suffice.

94. Robert Merton, *Social Theory and Social Structure,* enlarged edition, New York, 1968, pp. 69–72.

95. Analogies between Model I and the concept of explanation developed by R. G. Collingwood, William Dray, and other "revisionists" among philosophers concerned with the critical philosophy of history are not accidental. For a summary of the "revisionist" position see Maurice Mandelbaum, "Historical Explanation: The Problem of 'Covering Laws,'" *History and Theory,* Vol. 1, No. 3, 1960.

96. Though a variant of this model could easily be stochastic, this paradigm is stated in nonprobabilistic terms. In contemporary strategy, a stochastic version of this model is sometimes used for predictions; but it is almost impossible to find an explanation of an occurrence in foreign affairs that is consistently probabilistic. Obviously, the stochastic model could be modified for a game theory version. And indeed, the modification required for a number of other variants, for example, a cybernetic model, should follow, in a straightforward manner, modifications of the classical theory of the firm. For a discussion of these variations, see Joseph McGuire, *Theories of Business Behavior,* Englewood Cliffs, N.J., 1964, pp. 18 ff.

97. This model is an analogue of the theory of the rational entrepreneur developed extensively in economic theories of the firm and the consumer. These two propositions specify the "substitution effect." Refinement of this model and specifications of additional general propositions by translating from the economic theory are straightforward.

98. *The New York Times,* March 22, 1969.

99. The author's study of the classical model and its variants should be available shortly.

100. By including internal governmental values in the preference function of the leader, e.g., the President or Chairman, this variant can become a cross between Model I and Model III.

101. Whiting, op. cit. p. ix. Emphasis added.
102. Nathan Leites, *A Study of Bolshevism,* Glencoe, Ill., 1953.
103. Other conspiracy theorists who ascribe whatever occurs to the choice of some actor, e.g., the establishment, or the military-industrial complex, could be considered as a separable variant.
104. In addition to the works of Kissinger and Hoffmann already cited, see George Kennan, *American Diplomacy, 1900–1950,* Chicago, 1951; *Memoirs 1925–1950,* Boston, 1967; *Russia and the West Under Lenin and Stalin,* Boston, 1961.

Chapter 2   Cuba II: A First Cut

1. This chapter presents, without editorial commentary, a Model I analyst's explanation of the central puzzles in the missile crisis. The purpose is to illustrate a strong, characteristic classical account. This account is (for the most part) consistent with prevailing explanations of these events — for example, those of Schlesinger, Sorensen, Horelick and Rush, and the Wohlstetters. The character of the analysis in this chapter has benefited most directly from Horelick and Rush.
2. As Myron Horelick and Arnold Rush state in *Strategic Power and Soviet Foreign Policy* (Chicago, 1965, p. 141): "Soviet calculations throughout the Cuban missile crisis can be reconstructed with some degree of confidence, because the confrontation with the United States was so open."
3. This piece of "conventional wisdom" — namely, that the Soviet Union did not station medium-range and long-range nuclear missiles outside the Soviet Union — played an important part in establishing the climate of opinion and consequently the subsequent surprise. See Theodore Sorensen, *Kennedy,* New York, 1965, pp. 670–71, 673. For its importance within the intelligence community, see U.S., Congress, Senate, Committee on Armed Services, Preparedness Investigating Subcommittee, *Interim Report on Cuban Military Build-up,* 88th Congress, 1st Session, 1963, p. 11 (hereafter referred to as *Cuban Military Build-up*). For this line of reasoning in the September 19 estimate, see Roger Hilsman, *To Move a Nation,* New York, 1967, p. 172.
4. *The New York Times,* September 12, 1962. Emphasis added.
5. See Robert F. Kennedy, *Thirteen Days: A Memoir of the Cuban Missile Crisis,* New York, 1969, pp. 24–26.
6. *The New York Times,* September 5, 1962.
7. Sorensen, op. cit., p. 667. At an earlier meeting between Sorensen and Dobrynin the principal topic of conversation had been Berlin. This assurance also made explicit reference to Berlin and suggested that the Chairman might visit the United Nations in the last half of November.

8. Ibid., p. 668.

9. Ibid. See also Arthur Schlesinger, Jr., *A Thousand Days: John F. Kennedy in the White House,* Boston, 1965, p. 820.

10. Roger Hilsman, op. cit., p. 166.

11. *The New York Times,* September 5, 1962.

12. *The New York Times,* September 8, 1962.

13. *The New York Times,* September 14, 1962.

14. See for example Adam B. Ulam, *Expansion and Coexistence,* New York, 1968, p. 671.

15. U.S., Department of State, *Bulletin,* Vol. 47, No. 1220, November 12, 1962, pp. 741–43.

16. *The New York Times,* September 5, 1962.

17. This concept of strategic doctrine in diplomacy is developed by Henry Kissinger, *Nuclear Weapons and Foreign Policy,* New York, 1957, pp. 5 ff. See also Kissinger, *The Necessity for Choice,* New York, 1961, ch. 1.

18. This concept of signaling and commitment is developed by Thomas C. Schelling, *Strategy of Conflict,* New York, 1960, ch. 3. See also Schelling, *Arms and Influence,* New Haven, 1966, chs. 3 and 7.

19. As Hilsman points out (op. cit., p. 189), the U.S. intelligence community expectations were grounded not only in these warnings but in the general proposition that "the opposition is acting in its own best interest." Henry M. Pachter, in *Collision Course: The Cuban Missile Crisis and Coexistence* (New York, 1963, p. 8), explains this estimate in a similar fashion: "The CIA, which must always assume that an opponent is acting rationally and according to his best interest, therefore discarded the most unlikely apprehensions."

20. This document is paraphrased by Hilsman, op. cit., pp. 172–73. As Hilsman emphasizes, the September estimate did hedge 'by "noting that medium or intermediate range missiles in Cuba would significantly increase the Soviet capacity to strike at America's heartland and go far toward altering the strategic balance of power between East and West. It therefore urged the intelligence community to maintain a continuous alert."

21. *The New York Times,* October 23, 1962.

22. *The Washington Post,* October 25, 1962.

23. *The New York Times,* September 12, 1962.

24. Sorensen, op. cit., p. 691.

25. U.S., Department of State, *Bulletin,* Vol. 47, No. 1220, November 12, 1962, pp. 741–43. Emphasis added.

26. U.S., Congress, House of Representatives, Committee on Appropriations, Subcommittee on Department of Defense Appropriations, *Hearings,* 88th Congress, 1st Session, 1963, p. 57 (hereafter referred to as Department of Defense Appropriations, *Hearings*). Though the President's commitment had not

been publicly stated, it was nevertheless widely known around Washington, available to Soviet intelligence with minimum effort. See also Robert F. Kennedy, op. cit., pp. 94–95.

27. Elie Abel, *The Missile Crisis*, Philadelphia, 1966, pp. 189–90; Hilsman, op. cit., pp. 202–03; Joint Committee on Atomic Energy, *Report*, "The Study of U.S. and NATO Nuclear Weapon Arrangement," February 11, 1961. See also U.S., Congress, House of Representatives, Committee on Armed Services, *Hearings on Military Posture*, 88th Congress, 1st Session, 1963, p. 277.

28. Albert and Roberta Wohlstetter, *Controlling the Risks in Cuba*, Adelphi Papers, London, April 1965, p. 13.

29. *Missiles and Rockets*, January 7, 1963, p. 26.

30. Horelick and Rush (op. cit., pp. 128–29) reject this hypothesis by some similar arguments. Leon Lipson, in "Castro on the Chessboard of the Cold War" in *Cuba and the U.S.*, John Plank (ed.), Washington, D.C., 1967, pp. 192–93, argues against this hypothesis with a number of additional — but very weak — arguments. First, he asserts, "the time scales do not match. Removal of missiles from Cuba would have to take place quickly in order to be worth much to the United States. And disruption of the U.S.-Turkish military cooperation or (all the more so) abandonment of a basic, concerted Allied position on Berlin would require long and uncertain consultation." While this assertion would be true in the natural course of events, if the Soviets had demanded a deal and the U.S. had accepted it the Turkish missiles could have been withdrawn immediately. Second, Lipson asserts, "the categories do not match. In the Turkish case the relevant frame of reference is not missiles here versus bases there, but missiles suddenly introduced into Cuba versus bases long established in Turkey and tacitly accepted by the Soviet Union." While these categories may not be ideally "matched," the analogy was, as has been argued, overwhelming.

Another, and somewhat stronger, version of this hypothesis can be formulated by focusing on the political importance of the Turkish bases and the international repercussions of any removal of them under pressure. The Russians would possibly have been willing to trade off their more costly Cuban missile sites for the *political* gain inherent in forcing the Americans to make concessions under pressure. President Kennedy recognized the potential gain for the Russians in such a deal when he unequivocally refused to consider any Turkey-Cuba trade as a way to resolve the crisis.

31. Sorensen (op. cit., p. 677) mentions this stronger version of the hypothesis but then rejects it. Lipson (op. cit., pp. 192–93) argues inconclusively against this hypothesis. Michel Tatu, in *Power in the Kremlin* (New York, 1968), on the other hand, advocates this stronger hypothesis. "The objective of the manoeuver was clearly Berlin" (p. 232). Tatu, however, ignores

. many of the objections to this line of thought already mentioned. His argument in favor of the hypothesis is two-pronged. First, he asserts that Khrushchev moved in Cuba because he "was quite aware that unilateral action on his part in Berlin would be illegal" (p. 233). In fact, however, the Soviet Union had been acting unilaterally in Berlin for some time and hesitation on those grounds seems unlikely. Secondly, Tatu uses to *support* his hypothesis the argument that the American commitment to Berlin was known to be unshakable. Thus, he argues, Khrushchev knew "that the Atlantic camp would regard any violation of freedom of access to West Berlin as a *casus belli*" (p. 233). Therefore, Tatu asserts, a successful Russian move in Cuba would force the West to yield in Berlin. This hypothesis neglects its first assumption, i.e., that the West was firmly committed to Berlin. Pachter (op. cit., pp. 26–27) also supports this hypothesis, and Abel (op. cit., pp. 47–48) seems to lean in this direction.

32. See hypothesis four.

33. Abel, op. cit., p. 102. Invitations to newsmen had been issued prior to any significant developments in Cuba.

34. U.S., Department of State, *Bulletin,* Vol. 47, No. 1220, November 12, 1962, pp. 743–45.

35. "Khrushchev's Report on the International Situation — 1," *The Current Digest of the Soviet Press,* Vol. 14, No. 51, January 16, 1963, pp. 4–5. Published weekly by the Joint Committee on Slavic Studies.

36. Sorensen, op. cit., p. 677.

37. Tatu (op. cit., pp. 230–31) asserts that this hypothesis can be ignored and supports his assertion with the following: "Had Cuba's defense been the main object, it would have been far simpler to extend the Warsaw Pact guarantees to cover the island, or else for the USSR to commit itself to declare war in case of aggression against its ally." But this argument provides no grounds for believing that the Warsaw Pact, geographically a NATO-oriented alliance, could credibly have been extended to Cuba. Indeed, even if such an implausible extension were possible, the other members of the pact might well have had reservations. Similarly, though Khrushchev could have extended a Soviet commitment to Cuba, again the question of credibility arises. If, in the same situation, the United States meant to attack Cuba, would the United States be significantly influenced — or more important, did Castro and Khrushchev have good reason to believe that the United States would be significantly influenced — by such a Soviet commitment? Such a commitment alone, which could be backed only by Soviet willingness to initiate a major war, would hardly constitute a strong deterrent. Moreover, such a commitment could become a source of serious embarrassment or danger if Castro were to provoke a U.S. attack. Lipson (op. cit., p. 190) dismisses this theory with sim-

ilar arguments, though he includes an additional point. The rationale of Cuban defense, he asserts, is based on the premise that the Soviet Union is a nonaggressive power. But Lipson rejects that premise and therefore the rationale.

38. *Pravda,* April 9, 1962.

39. Tatu, op. cit., p. 234.

40. Hilsman, op. cit., p. 161.

41. *Cuban Military Build-up,* pp. 5–6; see also Department of Defense Appropriations, *Hearings,* p. 2.

42. Hilsman, op. cit., p. 161.

43. A number of American analysts have agreed with this interpretation of Soviet intentions and thus of Soviet success. For example, Horelick, in "The Cuban Missile Crisis: An Analysis of Soviet Calculations and Behavior" (*World Politics,* April 1964, pp. 4 ff.), cites Professor Leslie Dewart: "The conclusion appears reasonable that Russia set up missile bases in Cuba in full knowledge or expectation of the consequences." Horelick and Rush (op. cit., p. 13) attempt to discredit the effort to interpret the outcome as a success with the argument that "if deterrence of an attack on Cuba was the sole Soviet objective, however, the plan backfired: the Soviet weapons provoked rather than deterred strong American action." But the logic of this argument is confused. Only if "attack" and "strong American action" are considered as equivalents does their conclusion follow. If Khrushchev's purpose were simply to prevent an American attack on Cuba, his venture can be considered a success, for no American attack on Cuba has occurred and Kennedy did pledge not to invade Cuba. The authors go on to speculate that if Cuban defense had really been the Soviet objective, then Khrushchev would have given control of the weapons to Cuba: "To maximize the effectiveness of - Soviet missiles deployed in Cuba as a deterrent against an American attack on Cuba and to reduce the risk that their employment, in the event of an attack, would bring down United States nuclear retaliation upon the USSR, it might have been desirable for Khrushchev to have the American government believe that the Soviet missiles were at Castro's disposal and under his control" (p. 131). This speculation, however, neglects two critical points. First, if the United States believed that the missiles were controlled by Castro, it would presumably have been even more willing to preemptively attack the missiles — both from fear of Castro's possible use of the missiles and from confidence that there would be no Soviet reprisal. Second, if the Soviets had actually permitted Cuban control of the missiles and the United States chose to insist nevertheless on Russian responsibility for their use (as in fact Kennedy's October 22 statement did: "It shall be the policy of this nation to regard any nuclear missile launched from Cuba against any nation in the Western Hemisphere as an attack by the Soviet Union on the United

States, requiring a full retaliatory response upon the Soviet Union."), then the destiny of the Soviet Union would have been placed in Castro's hands. In fact, the Soviets took extraordinary precautions against any semblance of Cuban control of these missiles and were quick to assure the United States on this point.

44. *The New York Times,* January 26, 1963. Also see U.S., Department of Defense, *Special Cuba Briefing,* by Robert McNamara, February 6, 1963, p. 32.

45. See Morton Halperin, *Limited War in the Nuclear Age,* New York, 1963.

46. *Pravda,* December 14, 1962.

47. Sorensen, op. cit., p. 669. See also Schlesinger, op. cit., pp. 796, 821. As Schlesinger observes, the "too liberal to fight" quotation was Frost's interpretation in a New York press conference of an anecdote cited by Khrushchev from Gorki's memoirs in which Tolstoy described himself as "too weak and infirm to do it but still having the desire." Schlesinger maintains that Frost transposed Khrushchev's application of this anecdote, applied to nations, into a remark about liberals. Also see Franklin Reeve, *Robert Frost in Russia,* Boston, 1964, pp. 115, 120–23.

48. Sorensen, op. cit., p. 677. This hypothesis, though perhaps implied, is not treated separately or in any detail by Horelick and Rush, Tatu, or Lipson.

49. Sorensen (op. cit., p. 683) recalls that the President "was concerned less about the missiles' military implications than with their effect on the global political balance. The Soviet move had been undertaken so swiftly ... and with so much deliberate deception — it was so sudden a departure from Soviet practice — that it represented a provocative change in the delicate status quo."

50. Schlesinger, op. cit., p. 811.

51. *The New York Times,* October 23, 1962.

52. *The Washington Post,* December 18, 1962.

53. Schlesinger, op. cit., p. 796.

54. Sorensen, op. cit., p. 678.

55. The rift between Russia and Cuba would be partially healed. That a small power near the American heartland could convert to Communism and depend on the protection of the Soviet Union would be demonstrated. Expectations in Latin America and elsewhere would be influenced by U.S. failure to act — especially expectations concerning the American will to act. This would be a feather in the Soviet cap in their contest with the Chinese for leadership among the socialist countries.

56. *The New York Times,* September 14, 1962.

57. Horelick and Rush, op. cit., p. 126. Tatu (op. cit., p. 233) argues that while the U.S. commitment to Berlin was demonstrably firm, the Bay of Pigs may have suggested that U.S. will-

ingness to act in the case of Cuba was an entirely different matter.

58. Edward Weintal and Charles Bartlett, *Facing the Brink: An Intimate Study of Crisis Diplomacy,* New York, 1967, p. 56. Weintal and Bartlett, however, suggest perhaps "why not." "The record of American policy toward the Castro regime certainly contained concrete evidences of discrepancy between what the U.S. desired to do and what it dared to do in Cuba. The record was an accumulation of strong words unmatched by strong actions." Horelick also makes the latter line of argument in "The Cuban Missile Crisis: An Analysis of Soviet Calculations and Behavior," *World Politics,* April 1964, p. 38.

59. Claude Julien, *Le Monde,* March 22, 1963. For an excellent discussion of Castro's conflicting statements, see Horelick and Rush, op. cit., pp. 134–35; and the Wohlstetters, op. cit., pp. 3 ff.

60. The Wohlstetters, op. cit., p. 10.

61. Ibid., pp. 10 ff. The Wohlstetters' article is a classic model of the propriety and circumspection required in public discussion of issues the crux of which is classified and quantitative. Failure to recognize the relevance of classified data and the complexities of quantitative calculations has led to numerous facile remarks of the sort they criticize. See for example Roger Hagan and Bart Bernstein, "Military Value of Missiles in Cuba," *Bulletin of Atomic Scientists,* Vol. 19, February 1963.

62. Department of Defense Appropriations, *Hearings,* p. 7. According to the Institute of Strategic Studies estimate, the Soviet Union had no more than seventy-five ICBMs at this time (*The Communist Bloc and the Western Alliance: The Military Balance 1962–63,* London, 1963). According to Oleg Penkovskiy, in *The Penkovskiy Papers* (New York, 1965), the number of operational ICBMs in the Soviet Union was very small: "Right now we have a certain number of missiles with nuclear warheads capable of reaching the United States or South America; but these are single missiles, not in mass production, and they are far from perfect" (p. 340).

63. Horelick and Rush (op. cit.) advocate this hypothesis. Their arguments are similar to those employed here.

64. Schlesinger, op. cit., p. 796. Pachter (op. cit., p. 26) also emphasizes U.S. overall superiority and therefore concludes, "The effect [of the Soviets' placing missiles in Cuba] was psychological and political rather than military."

65. See Horelick and Rush, op. cit., p. 141. Lipson (op. cit., p. 192) dismisses this hypothesis with a somewhat weak argument: "If the Soviet missiles in Cuba were designed to play that role [i.e., to alter the strategic balance], the withdrawal must have come too early for the role to be fulfilled, for it can hardly be maintained that Soviet ICBM capabilities had improved fast enough between the decision to ship the missiles to Cuba and the decision to withdraw them." Actually, all this argument

proves is that if the purpose of putting in the missiles was strategic, it failed. But certainly, the Russians, when formulating their moves, expected them to succeed. Therefore, the fact that they were forced to remove the missiles without altering the strategic balance in no way proves that that was not their original goal. Tatu (op. cit., p. 241) considers hypothesis five but mentions it only as one. of secondary importance — i.e., if the missiles-had not proved valuable as a bargaining counter, Khrushchev "would at least have retained the strategic benefit of his advanced base." Thus, though Tatu recognizes the hypothesis, he does not develop it at length.

66. Schlesinger, op. cit., p. 797.

67. Sorensen, op. cit., p. 673.

68. Ibid., p. 667.

69. Ibid.

70. Tatu, op. cit., pp. 241 ff.

71. Department of Defense Appropriations, *Hearings,* p 12.

72. See Tatu, op. cit., p. 241. He accents this plan but neglects the difficulty.

73. Abel (op. cit., p. 26) points out that in fact American intelligence did note this: "This configuration roused Colonel Wright's suspicion. It resembled the placement of missile installations photographed repeatedly by pilots like Gary Powers over the Soviet Union." See also Department of Defense Appropriations, *Hearings,* p. 71.

74. See Amron Katz's persuasive arguments that the Soviets must have known about U.S. U-2 overflights (*The Soviets and the U-2 Photos,* RM-3584-PR, RAND Corporation, March 1963).

75. *The New York Times,* November 3, 1962. For a quite similar explanation see the Wohlstetters, op. cit.

76. Sorensen, op. cit., p. 674. Also Schlesinger, op. cit., p. 802; Robert F. Kennedy, op. cit., p. 30. Others who sat in on occasional meetings included Vice-President Lyndon Johnson, Special Assistant Kenneth O'Donnell, Deputy Director of the USIA Don Wilson, Dean Acheson, Ambassador to the United Nations Adlai Stevenson, and Robert Lovett. Ambassador to France Charles Bohlen met with the group initially until he departed for France. Deputy Director of the CIA Marshall Carter attended meetings until Director McCone returned to Washington.

77. Sorensen, op. cit., p. 675. Emphasis added.

78. Ibid., p. 679.

79. Ibid. See also Robert F. Kennedy, op. cit., p. 46.

80. Abel, op. cit., p. 144; also Robert F. Kennedy, op. cit., p. 74.

81. Abel, op. cit., p. 102.

82. Sorensen, op. cit., p. 684; also Robert F. Kennedy, op. cit., pp. 48–49.

83. Schlesinger, op. cit., pp. 806–07. See also Robert F. Kennedy,

op. cit., pp. 31, 38–39. Though this was the formulation of the argument, the facts are not strictly accurate. Our tradition against surprise attack was rather younger than 175 years. For example, President Theodore Roosevelt applauded Japan's attack on Russia in 1904.

84. Sorensen, op. cit., p. 685. Pachter (op. cit., p. 27) also rejects this course but does not go into the question of effectiveness and discusses only briefly the considerations of the morality of a surprise attack — the two primary considerations.

85. Abel, op. cit., p. 62. See also *The New York Times,* November 3, 1962. On September 16, 1962, James Reston had assailed administration critics who were calling for a blockade of Cuba with the argument that a blockade was an "act of war."

86. Sorensen, op. cit., p. 688. Pachter (op. cit., p. 27) supports this though he does not go into much detail.

87. *The New York Times,* June 11, 1963; also Robert F. Kennedy, op. cit., p. 126.

88. U.S., Department of State, *Bulletin,* Vol. 47, No. 1220, November 12, 1962, pp. 743–45.

89. For different but equally simple explanations of the Soviet withdrawal see U.S., Congress, Senate, Committee on Armed Services, *Military Procurement Authorization, Fiscal Year 1964,* 88th Congress, 1st Session, 1963; and U.S., Congress, House of Representatives, Committee on Armed Services, *Hearings on Military Posture,* 88th Congress, 1st Session, 1963. Thomas Freeman, in *Crisis in Cuba* (New Haven, Conn., 1963), also presents this military interpretation: "Faced with overwhelming conventional forces poised over Cuba, which could take the island in a matter of days, deterred by an over-all American nuclear superiority, his bases in Cuba still incomplete, Khrushchev's pragmatic mind could see no other course than to back away" (p. 143). Freeman goes on: "Getting the Russian missiles and bombers out of Cuba was a success for American policy, any way it was cut. But what was tragic, particularly with the other side blinking, was that Castro was not removed along with the weapons" (p. 145). Mario Lazzo, in *Dagger in the Heart* (New York, 1968), goes so far as to suggest that the U-2 that had inadvertently strayed over Russia so terrified Khrushchev with the thought of a pending nuclear attack that he withdrew the missiles.

90. Weintal and Bartlett, op. cit., pp. 54–55.

91. Ibid., p. 55.

92. Herman Kahn, *On Escalation,* New York, 1965, pp. 74–82.

93. Schelling, *Arms and Influence,* pp. 80–83. But Schelling also recognizes the "threat of more isolated action."

94. The Wohlstetters, op. cit., p. 16. The Wohlstetters also recognize U.S. willingness to "take the next step if necessary."

95. Ibid., p. 16. Emphasis added.

96. On this incident and the arguments it produced, see Robert F. Kennedy, op. cit., pp. 73–74, 76–77.

97. *The New York Times,* October 27, 1962; see also Robert F. Kennedy, op. cit., p. 82.

98. Department of Defense Appropriations, *Hearings,* p. 13.

99. U.S., Department of State, *Bulletin,* Vol. 47, No. 1220, November 12, 1962, pp. 740–41.

100. Department of Defense Appropriations, *Hearings,* p. 31.

101. *The Washington Post,* October 27, 1962.

102. *The New York Times,* October 28, 1962.

103. Tatu (op. cit., p. 264) goes along with this reasoning. He especially notes the threat of invasion of Cuba, which would be a great blow to Soviet prestige and power, since the only way Russia could prevent such an attack from succeeding would be by using nuclear weapons. No Soviet leader who understood the implications of nuclear war could risk that.

104. *The New York Times,* December 14, 1962. Emphasis added.

105. Ibid.

106. Sorensen, op. cit., p. 715.

107. *John Fitzgerald Kennedy . . . as We Remember Him,* New York, 1965, p. 172.

108. Department of Defense Appropriations, *Hearings,* p. 31. Emphasis added.

Chapter 3   Model II: Organizational Process

1. The "decisionmaking" approach represented by Richard Snyder, H. W. Bruck, and Burton Sapin, in *Foreign Policy Decision-Making* (Glencoe, Ill., 1962), incorporates a number of insights from organization theory.

2. While organization theory as such is a newcomer to the intellectual scene, it is a linear descendent of two older disciplines. The classic study of bureaucracy is, of course, Max Weber's *The Theory of Social and Economic Organizations,* A. M. Henderson (trans.), Talcott Parsons (ed.), Glencoe, Ill., 1947, Weber explores bureaucracy as an "ideal type," emphasizing the impersonal, rationalistic, specialized aspects of bureaucracies. His followers, by pursuing the implications of the "ideal" bureaucracy to the logical end, presented the other side of the case. Merton emphasized the inefficiencies (dysfunctional aspects) of bureaucratic "impersonality" when it crossed the fine line into rigidity. Sleznick, observing large and decentralized bureaucracies, stressed the problem created by divergent subgoals. Gouldner noted the internal effect of impersonal, explicit

rules — that by making known minimum acceptable behavior, might decrease efficiency.

The other parent is Taylorism or "scientific management." Indeed, both organization theory and the "human relations" school of industrial management can be seen as challenges that arose in reaction to the excessive rationalism and formalism of Taylor's philosophy.

3. James March, *Handbook of Organizations,* Chicago, 1965, p. xiii.

4. James March and Herbert Simon, *Organizations,* New York, 1958.

5. Ibid., p. 5. Emphasis added.

6. March, op. cit.

7. Ibid., p. ix.

8. Ibid., p. xiv.

9. Ibid., p. vi.

10. Although not as relevant to our paradigm, other branches have had equal claim on the attention of specialists. In particular, Homans' application of role theory in the small group and Parsons' grander attempt, *Toward a General Theory of Action,* have aroused both interest and controversy. Parsons, who views the organization as a functioning social subsystem of a larger social system, and Homans, who takes the organization as a special group interacting on the basis of both external (societal) and internal norms, have taken the individual actor as the critical unit for analysis.

11. As Herbert Simon states clearly in the Preface to his fascinating collection of essays, *Models of Man* (New York, 1957), "In assembling these sixteen essays in a single volume, together with some analysis of their mutual relations, I make confession that the compliments [for the broad range of my interests] were largely undeserved; that what appeared to be scatteration was really closer to monomania" (p. vii). "The principle of bounded rationality lies at the very core of organization theory, and at the core, as well, of any 'theory of action' that purports to treat of human behavior in complex situations" (p. 200).

12. Ibid., p. 3.

13. This point is derived from C. Barnard, *The Function of the Executive,* Cambridge, Mass., 1938. See March and Simon, op. cit., pp. 190 ff.

14. See Simon, *Models of Man,* pp. 204 ff.; March and Simon, op. cit., pp. 140 ff.

15. Simon, op. cit., pp. 263 ff; March and Simon, op. cit., pp. 48 ff.

16. Simon, op. cit., pp. 204, 219 ff.

17. March and Simon, op. cit., pp. 177 ff.

18. R. Cyert and J. March, *A Behavioral Theory of the Firm,* Englewood Cliffs, N.J., 1963, p. 6.

19. See J. Robinson, *Economics of Imperfect Competition*, London, 1942.

20. K. Rothschild, "Price Theory and Oligopoly," *Economic Journal*, 1947; W. J. Baumol, *Business Behavior, Value and Growth*, New York, 1959. My guide to these critics is Cyert and March, op. cit., pp. 8 ff.

21. G. Katona, *Psychological Analysis of Economic Behavior*, New York, 1951.

22. A. Papandreou, "Some Basic Problems in the Theory of the Firm," in *A Survey of Contemporary Economics*, B. F. Haley (ed.), Homewood, Ill., 1952.

23. R. Gordon, "Short-Period Price Determination," *American Economic Review*, Vol. 38, 1948; J. Margolis, "The Analysis of the Firm: Rationalism, Conventionalism, and Behaviorism," *Journal of Business*, Vol. 31, 1958; H. Simon, "A Behavioral Model of Rational Choice," in Simon, *Models of Man*.

24. March and Simon, op. cit., pp. 48 ff.

25. Cyert and March, op. cit., pp. 26 ff.

26. R. L. Hall and C. J. Hitch, "Price Theory and Business Behavior," *Oxford Economic Papers*, May 1939.

27. W. J. Eiteman, *Price Determination*, Ann Arbor, Mich., 1949.

28. W. W. Cooper, "A Proposal for Extending the Theory of the Firm," *Quarterly Journal of Economics*, Vol. 65, 1951.

29. R. Gordon, op. cit.

30. M. Friedman, "The Methodology of Positive Economics," *Essays in Positive Economics*, Chicago, 1953. See Chapter 1, note 93.

31. Friedman states: "Evidence is extremely hard to document; it is scattered in numerous memorandums, articles, and monographs concerned primarily with specific concrete problems rather than with submitting the hypothesis to test" (ibid.).

32. Cyert and March, op. cit., p. 15.

33. According to Samuelson's razor: "All economic regularities that have no common-sense core that you can explain to your wife will soon fail" ("Problems of Methodology, Discussion," *American Economic Review*, May 1963). The meaning of Samuelson's dictum is not entirely clear. Does it apply solely to the brilliant Mrs. Samuelson or to all wives?

34. Cyert and March, op. cit.

35. Ibid., p. 1.

36. Ibid., pp. 26 ff.

37. Ibid., pp. 117 ff.

38. Ibid., pp. 118–20.

39. Ibid., pp. 120–22.

40. Ibid., pp. 123–25.

41. Ibid., ch. 10. See G. P. Clarkson, *Portfolio Selection: A Simulation of Trust Investments*, Englewood Cliffs, N.J., 1962.

42. Yair Aharoni, *The Foreign Investment Decision Process*, Boston, 1966.

43. John P. Crecine, *Governmental Problem Solving: A Computer Simulation of Municipal Budgeting*, New York, 1969; Aaron Wildavsky, *The Politics of the Budgetary Process*, Boston, 1964. The similarities between Wildavsky's work and Cyert and March's model are most striking when the formalization of Wildavsky's work, O. Davis, M. Demster, and A. Wildavsky, "The Budgetary Process," *American Political Science Review*, September 1966, is compared with Crecine. For interesting points of tangency see W. Sayer and H. Kaufman, *Governing New York City*, New York, 1960; and V. A. Thompson, *The Regulatory Process in OPA Rationing*, New York, 1950. See also H. Simon and C. E. Ridley, *Measuring Municipal Budgets*, Chicago, 1943; H. Simon, "Birth of an Organization: The Economic Cooperation Administration," *Public Administration Review*, 1953; H. Kaufman, *The Forest Ranger*, Baltimore, 1960; R. Chapman et al., "The System Research Laboratory's Air Defense Experiments," *Management Science*, 1959.

44. A number of unpublished memoranda by A. W. Marshall are very instructive in this regard.

45. This formulation's debt both to the orientation and insights of Herbert Simon and the behavioral model of the firm formulated by Richard Cyert and James March is considerable. Here, however, one is forced to grapple with the less routine, less quantifiable activities of the less differentiated elements in government organizations.

46. Theodore Sorensen, "You Get to Walk to Work," *New York Times Magazine*, March 19, 1967.

47. It has been suggested by Charles Wolff, Jr., that a threshold phenomenon may be at work to displace the basic organizational processes from time to time. If the results of organizational processes diverge by more than some value, *a*, from a Model I calculation of expected results, then forces emerge to change the organizational processes. In every case *a* will be large (indeed, how would one measure it?). But the size of this parameter probably depends on factors such as whether there is an active systems analysis staff, whether the President takes a direct interest in the area, whether there is a degree of pluralism in the internal bureaucratic structure, and whether the external environment is favorable.

48. M. S. Eccles, *Beckoning Frontiers*, New York, 1951, p. 336.

49. Arthur Schlesinger, Jr., *A Thousand Days: John F. Kennedy in the White House*, Boston, 1965, p. 406.

50. Roberta Wohlstetter, *Pearl Harbor: Warning and Decision*, Stanford, Calif., 1962.

51. See W. J. Baumol and R. E. Quandt, "Rules of Thumb and Optimally Imperfect Decisions," *American Economic Review*, Vol. 54, March 1964; H. W. Kuhn and W. J. Baumol, "An Ap-

proximative Algorithm for Fixed-Charges Transportation Problem," *Naval Research Logistics Quarterly*, Vol. 9, March 1962; and H. Chernoff, "Rational Selection of Decision Function," *Econometrica*, Vol. 22, October 1964.

52. R. Wohlstetter, op. cit., p. 74; see also p. 67.

53. Ibid. See also p. 27.

54. These propensities have direct analogies for organizational information and organizationally noticed problems.

55. R. Wohlstetter, op. cit., pp. 166 ff.

56. Ibid., p. 36.

57. Ibid., p. 279.

58. Ibid., p. 75.

59. Ibid., p. 290.

60. Ibid., p. 68.

61. Ibid., pp. 13, 104.

62. The order in which organizations attend to inconsistent goals is thus a critical factor.

63. R. Wohlstetter, op. cit., pp. 12–13.

64. Ibid., p. 317.

65. Ibid.

66. Ibid., p. 167.

67. These factors are discussed on pages 98–100.

68. See Horelick and Rush, op. cit., pp. 18 ff; Allen Dulles, *The Craft of Intelligence*, New York, 1963, pp. 162–63; and Robert Kilmarx, *A History of Soviet Air Power*, New York, 1962, pp. 253–54.

69. See Horelick and Rush, op. cit., pp. 45, 50, 83 ff.

70. Institute for Strategic Studies, *The Communist Bloc and the Western Alliances: The Military Balance 1962–63*, London, 1963, pp. 2–3.

71. This is in conflict with Secretary of Defense Laird's interpretation of these developments. He maintained: "The Soviets are going for a first-strike capability, and there's no question about it" (*The New York Times*, March 22, 1969).

72. This information would obviously be very expensive.

73. See Chapter 1.

74. "In May 1891 French and Russian soldiers, leading the way to military convention and alliance, met for discussion in Paris. Their conclusions were presented to the Tsar by the Deputy Chief of the French General Staff, Boisdeffre. Among them were 'that mobilization was the declaration of war; that to mobilize was to force one's neighbor to do the same; . . . that to allow a million men to be mobilized along one's frontiers without doing as much oneself at the same time meant denying oneself all possibility of moving later and placing oneself in a situation of an individual who, with a pistol in his pocket, would allow his

neighbor to put a loaded gun against his forehead without drawing his own.'" With these propositions Alexander III agreed. Alfred Vagts, *Defense and Diplomacy,* New York, 1956, p. 398.

75. Thus opening the crack for A. J. P. Taylor's thesis that railroad timetables caused the war.

Chapter 4   Cuba II: A Second Cut

1. Robert F. Kennedy, *Thirteen Days: A Memoir of the Cuban Missile Crisis,* New York, 1969, p. 95.

2. Ibid., p. 98. Sorensen, *Kennedy,* New York, 1965, p. 685.

3. These sources include U.S., Congress, House of Representatives, Committee on Appropriations, Subcommittee on Department of Defense Appropriations, *Hearings,* 88th Congress, 1st Session, 1963 (hereafter referred to as Department of Defense Appropriations, *Hearings*); Department of Defense, Special Cuba *Briefing,* February 6, 1963; U.S., Congress, Senate, Committee on Armed Services, Preparedness Investigating Subcommittee, *Interim Report on Cuban Military Build-up,* 88th Congress, 1st Session, 1963 (hereafter referred to as *Cuban Military Build-up*). The following account is reconstructed from the preceding sources. Additional references are made where central facts or major pieces of information depend on other sources.

4. For the beginning of Soviet arm shipments to Cuba see the Eisenhower administration announcement, *The New York Times,* November 19, 1960. For the lull see *Briefing,* Roger Hilsman, Director of Intelligence and Research, Department of State, August 24, 1962, summarized in Roger Hilsman, *To Move a Nation,* New York, 1967, p. 170.

5. *Cuban Military Build-up,* pp. 5 ff. See also Hilsman, *Briefing.*

6. Department of Defense Appropriations, *Hearings,* pp. 7, 8.

7. Ibid., pp. 8, 25; Hilsman, op. cit., p. 186; also Elie Abel, *The Missile Crisis,* Philadelphia, 1966, p. 42.

8. Department of Defense Appropriations, *Hearings,* pp. 15–19.

9. *The New York Times,* September 23, 1962.

10. Special Cuba *Briefing,* p. 18; also Sorensen, op. cit., p. 709.

11. Department of Defense Appropriations, *Hearings,* pp. 8–9; also *Cuban Military Build-up,* pp. 7, 12.

12. Roswell Gilpatric discussed this point on ABC's *Issues and Answers,* November 11, 1962: "We never knew how many missiles were brought into Cuba. The Soviets said there were forty-two. We have counted forty-two going out. We saw fewer than forty-two." *Cuban Military Build-up* (p. 7) also mentions this uncertainty: "Photographic reconnaissance was unable to

detect precisely how many ballistic missiles were introduced into Cuba. Prior to the Soviet announcement that 42 missiles would be withdrawn, our photographs had revealed a lesser number. It could not be established, therefore, how many ballistic missiles were, in fact, introduced into Cuba or specifically how many the Soviets planned to introduce."

13. Department of Defense Appropriations, *Hearings,* pp. 7, 9, 11. Also *Cuban Military Build-up,* p. 7; Hilsman, op. cit., p. 185.

14. Department of Defense Appropriations, *Hearings,* pp. 6, 15–16; *Cuban Military Build-up,* p. 7.

15. Department of Defense Appropriations, *Hearings,* pp. 17–18; *Cuban Military Build-up,* pp. 6, 13.

16. Department of Defense Appropriations, *Hearings,* p. 19; *Cuban Military Build-up,* pp. 6, 13.

17. Department of Defense Appropriations, *Hearings,* p. 19; *Cuban Military Build-up,* pp. 6, 13.

18. Department of Defense Appropriations, *Hearings,* pp. 18–19; *Cuban Military Build-up,* pp. 4, 7, 10, 14.

19. Department of Defense Appropriations, *Hearings,* pp. 19–21; *Cuban Military Build-up,* pp. 2–4, 8, 14.

20. Hilsman, op. cit., p. 159.

21. Ibid., p. 159.

22. Amron Katz, *The Soviets and the U-2 Photos — An Heuristic Argument,* RM-3584-PR, Rand Corporation, March 1963, p. v.

23. Hilsman, op. cit., p. 183.

24. Sorensen, op. cit., p. 673. Emphasis added.

25. Hilsman, op. cit., p. 200.

26. Department of Defense Appropriations, *Hearings,* p. 10.

27. Robert F. Kennedy, op. cit., p. 58.

28. The Wohlstetters, op. cit., p. 12.

29. Department of Defense Appropriations, *Hearings,* p. 6.

30. Robert F. Kennedy, op. cit., p. 94.

31. *Cuban Military Build-up,* p. 11; Department of Defense Appropriations, *Hearings,* pp. 44–46; Abel, op. cit., p. 26. Abel quotes the citation from the award of an Oak Leaf Cluster to the Legion of Merit given to Colonel Wright for his identification of the trapezoidal pattern: "He performed a unique service to his country by singlehandedly analyzing a series of intelligence reports concerning the activities of the Soviet Union in Cuba, and, by this analysis, pinpointing the location of the first medium-range ballistic missiles deployed by the USSR in the Western hemisphere. His analysis led him to recommend for immediate coverage by high-altitude reconnaissance aircraft the exact location which was photographed on 14th October, 1962, and revealed the existence of those missiles in Cuba" (p. 29).

32. Department of Defense Appropriations, *Hearings,* p. 11.

33. Ibid., p. 9; also see Hilsman, op. cit., p. 185.

34. Lyman B. Kirkpatrick, "Cold War Operations: The Politics of Communist Confrontation," *Naval War College Review*, Vol. 20, No. 8, March 1968, p. 41.

35. See *Aviation Week and Space Technology* editorial, February 11, 1963.

36. *Cuban Military Build-up*, p. 6.

37. Department of Defense Appropriations, *Hearings*, p. 23.

38. Robert F. Kennedy, op. cit., p. 59.

39. Barton Wahley, *Clandestine Soviet Arms Traffic*, forthcoming monograph.

40. The high Soviet intelligence agent, Kudryavtsev, had been relieved of his post to Cuba after the Escalenté affair and he had probably reinforced natural suspicion of the garrulous, less responsible Latin American "brothers."

41. U.S., Senate, Committee on Government Operations, Subcommittee on National Security Staffing and Operations, *Staffing Procedures and Problems in the Soviet Union*, 88th Congress, 1st Session, 1963, chart 11, pp. 32 ff. See also Institute for Strategic Studies, *The Communist Bloc and the Free World: The Military Balance, 1961–62*, London, 1962, p. 4.

42. Institute for Strategic Studies, *The Communist Bloc and the Free World: The Military Balance, 1961–62*, p. 3. Also see Institute for Strategic Studies, *The Communist Bloc and the Free World: The Military Balance, 1960*, London, 1961, p. 2.

43. Department of Defense Appropriations, *Hearings*, p. 9.

44. Hilsman, op. cit., p. 183.

45. Roman Kolkowicz, *Conflicts in Soviet Party-Military Relations: 1962–63*, RM-3760-PR, Rand Corporation, August 1963, pp. v, vi; also Michel Tatu, *Power in the Kremlin*, New York, 1969, p. 236.

46. Kolkowicz, op. cit., p. 5.

47. Ibid., pp. 6–7.

48. Tatu, op. cit., pp. 236–37.

49. Kolkowicz, op. cit., p. 11.

50. "Khrushchev's Report on the International Situation — 1," *The Current Digest of the Soviet Press*, Vol. 14, No. 51, January 16, 1963, p. 5 (emphasis added). Published weekly by the Joint Committee on Slavic Studies. Similarly, the Army's blatant display of insignias at the camp sites may well have reflected their resistance to efforts to "demilitarize" them (e.g., make them shed their uniforms, etc.).

51. Institute for Strategic Studies, *The Communist Bloc and the Western Alliance: The Military Balance, 1960*.

52. Institute for Strategic Studies, *The Communist Bloc and the Western Alliance: The Military Balance, 1962–63*, London, 1963, pp. 2, 3.

53. *Staffing Procedures and Problems in the Soviet Union,* p. 46.

54. Ibid.

55. Kolkowicz, op. cit., p. 5.

56. For the preparation that went into the sounding of the alarm by Deputy Secretary of Defense Roswell Gilpatrick in a speech of November 1961, see Hilsman, op. cit., pp. 163 ff.

57. This inference is based on the remarkable speed of Soviet missile construction in Cuba. See Department of Defense Appropriations, *Hearings,* p. 6.

58. Tatu, op. cit., p. 236.

59. *The New York Times,* October 23, 1962.

60. Schlesinger, op. cit., p. 803.

61. Sorensen, op. cit., p. 675.

62. *Cuban Military Build-up,* p. 2.

63. H. Baldwin, "The Growing Risks of Bureaucratic Intelligence," *The Reporter,* Vol. 29, August 15, 1963, pp. 48–50.

64. Roberta Wohlstetter, "Cuba and Pearl Harbor," *Foreign Affairs,* July 1965, p. 706.

65. Department of Defense Appropriations, *Hearings,* pp. 25 ff.

66. *Cuban Military Build-up;* Department of Defense Appropriations, *Hearings.* Penkovskiy was apprehended by the Soviets in September 1962.

67. See Roger Hilsman's memorandum to Undersecretary of State Ball, reprinted in Department of Defense Appropriations, *Hearings,* p. 48.

68. Hilsman, op. cit., p. 169.

69. Ibid., pp. 174 ff.

70. Ibid., p. 168.

71. Department of Defense Appropriations, *Hearings,* p. 67; *Cuban Military Build-up,* p. 8.

72. Department of Defense Appropriations, *Hearings,* pp. 1–70; *Cuban Military Build-up,* pp. 6 ff.

73. Hilsman, op. cit., pp. 172–73.

74. Ibid., pp. 175–76. Also Department of Defense Appropriations, *Hearings,* pp. 67 ff; Abel, op. cit., p. 25.

75. Department of Defense Appropriations, *Hearings,* pp. 66–67. Testimony is not entirely consistent on this point. Secretary McNamara asserted that the September 5 flight was the last U-2 flight over the western part of Cuba prior to the flight of October 14. But General Carroll testified: "We already, though, had very current coverage of the western end. . . . I am referring to the flights that were flown subsequent to September 5th." See also Hilsman, op. cit., p. 189.

76. For (1), Hilsman, op. cit., p. 186; for (2), Abel, op. cit., p. 24; for (3), Department of Defense Appropriations, *Hearings,* p.

63; Abel, op. cit., p. 24; for (4), Department of Defense Appropriations, *Hearings*, pp. 67–68.

77. The facts here are not entirely clear. This assertion is based on an inference from Hilsman's statement (op. cit., p. 186): "For what was significant was not only that they had large hatches but the fact that the intelligence reports also routinely noted that they were riding high in the water — indicating that they were carrying 'space-consuming' cargo of low weight and high volume." But see R. Wohlstetter's interpretation ("Cuba and Pearl Harbor," op. cit., p. 700). Wohlstetter perceptively cites Hilsman's earlier published account of the crisis. See Hilsman's partial reply, p. 187.

78. Department of Defense Appropriations, *Hearings*, pp. 63–64.

79. *The New York Times*, September 10, 1962; also Hilsman, op. cit., pp. 174, 190.

80. Hilsman, op. cit., p. 174; Abel, op. cit., pp. 25–26.

81. See McNamara's testimony under pressure, Department of Defense Appropriations, *Hearings*, p. 69.

82. Hilsman, op. cit., pp. 172–73.

83. Testimony of General Carroll, Department of Defense Appropriations, *Hearings*, p. 68. General Carroll testified that this piece of information arrived on September 18.

84. Ibid., p. 64. Also Abel, op. cit., pp. 24–25; Hilsman, op. cit., p. 186.

85. Department of Defense Appropriations, *Hearings*, p. 64.

86. Ibid., pp. 44–45, 71; Abel, op. cit., p. 26.

87. Department of Defense Appropriations, *Hearings*, pp. 44–45, 71.

88. Abel, op. cit., pp. 26 ff.; Hilsman, op. cit., p. 189.

89. Abel, op. cit., pp. 26 ff.; Edward Weintal and Charles Bartlett, *Facing the Brink: An Intimate Study of Crisis Diplomacy*, New York, 1967, pp. 62 ff; *Cuban Military Build-up*, pp. 8–9; James Daniel and John Hubbell, *Strike in the West*, New York, 1963, pp. 15 ff.

90. This account differs from the official report of the Stennis Committee (*Cuban Military Build-up*, p. 9), which found: "There is no evidence whatsoever to suggest that any conflict between CIA and SAC existed or that there was any delay in photographic coverage of the island because of the fact that the U-2 program was being operated by CIA prior to October 14. Likewise there is no evidence whatsoever of any deadlock between the two agencies or any conflict or dispute with respect to the question of by whom the flights should be flown."

91. Schlesinger, op. cit., p. 804; Sorensen, op. cit., pp. 684–87; Robert F. Kennedy, op. cit., pp. 31, 34; Hilsman, op. cit., pp. 203–04.

92. Sorensen, op. cit., pp. 683–84.

93. Robert F. Kennedy, op. cit., p. 31. **Emphasis added.**

94. Sorensen, op. cit., pp. 684 ff.

95. Ibid., p. 697. Also see Robert F. Kennedy, op. cit., pp. 48–49.

96. Sorensen, op. cit., p. 697; Abel, op. cit, pp. 100–01; Robert F. Kennedy, op. cit., pp. 48–49.

97. Sorensen, op. cit., p. 669.

98. Hilsman, op. cit., p. 204.

99. Abel, op. cit., p. 101.

100. Sorensen, op. cit., p. 684.

101. Department of Defense Appropriations, *Hearings,* pp. 8–9; Hilsman, op. cit., p. 185.

102. Ibid.

103. Sorensen, op. cit., pp. 708–10.

104. Ibid., p. 708.

105. The contrast between this operation and Truman's handling of the Korean War is noted by Richard Neustadt, *Presidential Power,* "Afterword: 1964," New York, 1964. But one should also recall Lincoln's willingness to interfere in military operations during the Civil War: "During the first three years of the war, Lincoln performed many of the functions that in a modern command system would be given to the chief of the general staff or to the joint chiefs of staff. He formulated policy, drew up strategic plans, and even devised and directed tactical movements. Judged by modern standards, he did some things that a civilian director of war should not do. Modern critics say that he 'interfered' too much with military operations. He and his contemporaries did not think that he interfered improperly. In the American command system it was traditional for the civilian authority to direct strategy and tactics. The Continental Congress in the Revolution and the president and cabinet in the War of 1812 and the Mexican War had planned extensive and detailed campaigns. Lincoln was acting only as the civil authority had acted in every previous war. He was doing what he and most people thought the commander in chief ought to do in war" (T. Harry Williams, "Lincoln," *The Ultimate Decision: The President as Commander in Chief,* Ernest R. May [ed.], New York, 1960, pp. 83–84).

106. Sorensen, op. cit., p. 710.

107. Ibid., p. 708.

108. Ibid., p. 698.

109. Ibid.

110. Ibid.

111. Abel, op. cit., p. 143.

112. Sorensen, op. cit., p. 708.

113. U.S., Department of State, *Bulletin,* Vol. 47, No. 1220, November 12, 1962, p. 717.

114. *The New York Times,* October 26, 1962; Sorensen, op. cit., p. 710.

115. Robert F. Kennedy, op. cit., pp. 73 ff.; Sorensen, op. cit., p. 710.

116. Statement by the Department of Defense on boarding of the *Marcula,* October 26, 1962, reported in *The New York Times,* October 27, 1962.

117. Sorensen, op. cit., pp. 707 ff.; Robert F. Kennedy, op. cit., pp. 73 ff.

118. Schlesinger, op. cit., p. 818. Also see Robert F. Kennedy, op. cit., p. 67.

119. Schlesinger, op. cit., p. 818.

120. Sorensen, op. cit., p. 710.

121. *The New York Times,* October 27, 1962.

122. Abel, op. cit., p. 171.

123. A tanker proceeding at fifteen to twenty knots per hour would, between 10:30 P.M. Thursday and 7:50 A.M. Friday, travel some 153 to 204 miles. That distance, when added to the point at which the ship was boarded (180 miles from Nassau, which is approximately 200 miles from Cuba), suggests the location of the quarantine line, 500 miles out. Robert Kennedy (op. cit., p. 67) states that the blockade was moved from a point 800 miles out from Cuba to the 500-mile line. But evidence suggests that the original arc drawn by the Navy, and never moved, extended 500 miles out from Cape Maysi, Cuba's easternmost tip. See Abel, op. cit., p. 141.

124. *Facts on File,* Vol. 22, 1962, p. 373.

125. Moreover, the East German passenger ship *Voelkerfrend* seems to have been permitted to pass through the screen on Thursday morning, after merely identifying itself. See Robert F. Kennedy, op. cit., p. 77.

126. This hypothesis would account for the mystery surrounding Kennedy's explosion at the leak of the stopping of the *Bucharest.* See Hilsman, op. cit., p. 45; also Abel, op. cit., p. 159.

127. Abel, op. cit., p. 153; Hilsman, op. cit., p. 215.

128. Hilsman, op. cit., p. 215; Abel, op. cit., p. 154.

129. Abel, op. cit., pp. 154 ff. Brock Bower, "McNamara Seen Now, Full Length," *Life,* Vol. 64, May 10, 1968.

130. Abel, op. cit., p. 155.

131. Ibid., p. 156.

132. Ibid., p. 156. According to Abel, some witnesses say that Anderson "accused McNamara of 'undue interference in naval matters.'" The Admiral, thereafter Ambassador to Portugal, said that this was not his recollection, adding that he was brought up never to say such a thing even if he felt it.

133. U.S., Department of State, *Bulletin,* Vol. 47, No. 1220, November 12, 1962, pp. 743–45.

134. Robert F. Kennedy, op. cit., p. 60. Emphasis added.

135. Letter from Chairman Khrushchev to President Kennedy, October 27, 1962, U.S., Department of State, *Bulletin,* Vol. 47, No. 1220, November 12, 1962, pp. 741–43. Emphasis added.

136. Letter from President Kennedy to Chairman Khrushchev, October 28, 1962, ibid., pp. 745–46. Emphasis added.

137. Robert F. Kennedy, op. cit., p. 87.

138. Roberta Wohlstetter, *Pearl Harbor: Warning and Decision,* Stanford, Calif., 1962. See also "Cuba and Pearl Harbor," *Foreign Affairs,* July 1963.

139. *The New York Times,* September 5, 1962.

140. Hilsman, op. cit., p. 166.

141. Sorensen, op. cit., pp. 690–701; Robert F. Kennedy, op. cit., pp. 40–41.

142. Sorensen, op. cit., p. 675. According to *Cuban Military Build-up* (pp. 8–9), SAC flew seventeen high altitude sorties between October 14 and October 22, as compared with two a month until September and four in the month of September. It is not clear how these facts can be reconciled with Hilsman's assertion (op. cit., p. 194): "From that time [the first meeting of the ExCom] on, there was hardly an hour of daylight that did not see a U-2 over some part of Cuba."

143. Sorensen, op. cit., p. 675.

144. Weintal and Bartlett, op. cit., p. 65; also Robert F. Kennedy, op. cit., p. 30.

145. Abel, op. cit., p. 79.

146. Ibid., pp. 65–66. Major General Sir Kenneth W. D. Strong, Director of the Joint Intelligence Bureau in the British Defense Ministry, happened to be in Washington attending a conference "on intelligence methodology." Noting the beds carried into Pentagon offices of high officials, the late arrivals and early exits of participants at the conference, etc., he became suspicious.

147. Ibid., p. 85.

148. Ibid., pp. 98–99.

149. Ibid., p. 109.

150. Hilsman, op. cit., pp. 166–67.

151. Ibid., p. 183.

152. Robert F. Kennedy, op. cit., p. 96.

153. W. E. Knox, "Close Up of Khrushchev During a Crisis," *New York Times Magazine,* November 18, 1962.

154. Robert F. Kennedy, op. cit., p. 58.

155. *Staffing Procedures and Problems in the Soviet Union,* p. 25. See Zbigniew Brzezinski and Samuel Huntington, *Political Power USA/USSR,* New York, 1963, pp. 200–01.

156. Robert F. Kennedy, op. cit., pp. 69–71.

157. Navy League Banquet, New York, November 9, 1962. Quoted by Abel, op. cit., p. 155.

158. U.S., Congress, House of Representatives, Committee on Armed Services, *Hearings on Military Posture,* 88th Congress, 1st Session, 1963, p. 897.

159. Abel, op. cit., pp. 154–55.

160. Ibid., p. 155.

161. William W. Kaufmann, *The McNamara Strategy,* New York, 1964, p. 271; also Abel, op. cit., p. 114.

162. Sorensen, op. cit., p. 708.

163. Robert F. Kennedy, op. cit., p. 59.

164. Ibid.; also Sorensen, op. cit., p. 708.

165. Robert F. Kennedy, op. cit., p. 86.

166. Hilsman, op. cit., p. 220. For Khrushchev's Saturday letter see U.S., Department of State, *Bulletin,* Vol. 47, No. 1220, November 12, 1962, pp. 741–43.

167. Hilsman, op. cit., p. 220; Abel, op. cit., p. 187.

168. Sorensen, op. cit., pp. 708, 713.

169. Ibid., p. 713.

170. Ibid.

171. For this occurrence see the account by Roger Hilsman, op. cit., pp. 221 ff. Also see "The Cuban Crisis: How Close We Were to War," *Look,* Vol. 28, August 25, 1964.

172. Hilsman, op. cit., p. 221.

173. U.S., Department of State, *Bulletin,* Vol. 47, No. 1220, November 12, 1962, pp. 743–45. The U-2 that strayed over the Soviet Union had been on what the U.S. government called an "air sampling mission." But after a U-2 had strayed over Sakhalin on August 30, Khrushchev said, "These flights are explained by alleging that they have peaceful purposes — they take samples of air, study cloud movement. But today it is still clearly visible what samples they are taking and for what purposes these flights are undertaken" (*Tass,* September 11, 1962; also *The New York Times,* September 12, 1962).

174. Abel, op. cit., pp. 189–90; Hilsman, op. cit., pp. 202–03.

175. According to Secretary McNamara's testimony, the Joint Committee on Atomic Energy's report entitled "The Study of US and NATO Nuclear Arrangements," dated February 11, 1961, states: "Compared with the solid fuel Polaris missiles or the second-generation medium-range ballistic missiles offered by Secretary Herter in his speech before the NATO Council in December 1960, the liquid fuel, fixed Jupiters are obsolete weapons. Since they will not be placed in hardened bases and they will not be mobile, their retaliatory value is highly questionable. In the event of hostilities, assuming NATO will not strike the first blow, the USSR with his ballistic missile capabil-

ities, logically could be expected to take out these bases on the first attack which, undoubtedly, would be a surprise attack. Recommendations: construction should not be permitted to begin on the [deleted] Jupiter sites in Turkey. Instead of placing obsolete [deleted] liquid fuel IRBM's in Turkey, an alternative system such as Polaris submarines should be assigned to NATO." U.S., Senate, Committee on Armed Services, *Military Procurement Authorization, Fiscal Year 1964*, 88th Congress, 1st Session, 1963, p. 7.

176. Abel, op. cit., p. 190.

177. Ibid., p. 190. Hilsman, op. cit., pp. 202–03; Robert F. Kennedy, op. cit., pp. 94–95.

178. Abel, op. cit., pp. 190–91.

179. For a related account, see Robert F. Kennedy, op. cit., p. 98.

Chapter 5   Model III: Governmental Politics

1. Walter Millis (ed.), *Forrestal Diaries*, New York, 1951.

2. Richard Neustadt, *Presidential Power*, New York, 1960.

3. Ibid., p. 33. Emphasis added.

4. Ibid., p. 10. Emphasis added.

5. Richard Neustadt, "Whitehouse and Whitehall," *The Public Interest*, No. 2, Winter 1966, p. 64. Emphasis added.

6. Neustadt, Testimony, U.S., Congress, Senate, Committee on Government Operations, Subcommittee on National Security and International Operations, *Conduct of National Security Policy*, 89th Congress, 1st Session, June 29, 1965, p. 126. Emphasis added.

7. Neustadt, *Presidential Power*, p. 2. Emphasis added.

8. Ibid., p. 184. Emphasis added.

9. Neustadt, Testimony, p. 126. Emphasis added.

10. See Neustadt, Testimony, U.S., Congress, Senate, Committee on Government Operations, Subcommittee on National Security Staffing, *Administration of National Security*, 88th Congress, 1st Session, March 25, 1963; Testimony, 1965; "Afterword: 1964" to *Presidential Power; Alliance Politics*, New York, 1970.

11. Arthur Schlesinger, Jr., *A Thousand Days: John F. Kennedy in the White House*, Boston, 1965, p. 859. Neustadt's *Alliance Politics* contains a brief, summary account of the Skybolt episode.

12. Neustadt, *Presidential Power*, pp. 123 ff.

13. Ibid., p. 124.

14. Memoirs of Harry S. Truman, Vol. 2, *Years of Trial and Hope*,

Garden City, N.Y., 1956, p. 341, quoted by Neustadt in *Presidential Power*, p. 123.

15. Neustadt, *Presidential Power*, p. 126.

16. Ibid., p. 139.

17. Ibid., p. 140.

18. Ibid., p. 144.

19. Ibid.

20. Ibid.

21. Ibid., p. 145.

22. Ibid.

23. Gabriel Almond, *The American People and Foreign Policy*, New York, 1950.

24. Compare, for example, David Truman, *The Governmental Process*, New York, 1951.

25. Charles E. Lindblom, "Bargaining? The Hidden Hand in Government," RM-1434-RC, Rand Corporation, February 22, 1955; "The Science of 'Muddling Through,'" *Public Administration Review*, Vol. 19, Spring 1959; *The Intelligence of Democracy*, New York, 1965. See also Charles E. Lindblom and D. Braybrooke, *A Strategy of Decision*, Glencoe, Ill., 1963.

26. This notion is developed in *The Intelligence of Democracy* as "partisan mutual adjustment." The critical differences between the analysis developed in this essay and that of Lindblom are two. First, whereas Lindblom's focus of attention is the actual process by which policy is *made,* the Governmental Politics Model concentrates on *explanations* of policy outcomes. Second, while Lindblom's examination of the process of partisan mutual adjustment by which policy is made is harnessed with a defense of this process as the best mechanism for making decisions, the Governmental Politics Model is neutral on the merits of the process.

27. Warner Schilling, "The Politics of National Defense: Fiscal 1950," in W. Schilling, P. Hammond, and G. Snyder, *Strategy, Politics, and Defense Budgets*, New York, 1962.

28. Ibid., pp. 21–24.

29. Ibid., pp. 25–26.

30. Ibid., p. 191.

31. Ibid., p. 199.

32. Ibid., pp. 216–22.

33. Samuel Huntington, *The Common Defense*, New York, 1961. See Huntington's earlier statement of this idea, "Strategy and the Political Process," *Foreign Affairs*, Vol. 38, January 1960.

34. Huntington, *The Common Defense*, p. ix.

35. Ibid., p. 146.

36. Ibid.

37. Ibid.

38. Ibid., p. 153.
39. Ibid., p. 128.
40. Ibid., p. 158.
41. Ibid., p. 162.
42. Ibid., p. 163.
43. Ibid., p. 164.
44. Ibid., p. 165.
45. Roger Hilsman, *To Move a Nation*, New York, 1967.
46. R. Hilsman, "Congressional-Executive Relations and the Foreign Policy Consensus," *American Political Science Review*, September 1958; "The Foreign-Policy Consensus: An Interim Research Report," *Journal of Conflict Resolution*, Vol. 3, No. 4, December 1959.
47. Hilsman, *To Move a Nation*, pp. 13, 562.
48. As the title of Hilsman's first chapter asserts, "Policy Making Is Politics" (*To Move a Nation*).
49. Ibid., p. 553.
50. Ibid., p. 554.
51. Ibid., pp. 554–55.
52. Ibid., p. 561.
53. Ibid., p. xviii. Emphasis added.
54. Ibid.
55. Ibid., p. 6.
56. Ibid.
57. Ibid., p. 8. See also Morton Halperin, "The Gaither Committee and the Policy Process," *World Politics*, Vol. 13, April 1961.
58. Hilsman, op. cit., p. 8. This constituted considerably less than a victory in the major battle, since leaked reports rarely make the most powerful ammunition.
59. See, for example, H. Stein (ed.), *American Civil-Military Decisions*, Birmingham, Ala., 1963; H. Stein (ed.), *Public Administration and Policy Development*, New York, 1952; and the Inter-University Case Program. The Institute of War and Peace Studies at Columbia University, and especially William T. R. Fox, have played an important role in developing bureaucratic politics studies.

    In almost every area of foreign policy and international relations reviewed in our earlier characterization of Model I, there are now scholars at work using a version of a Model III perspective. In diplomatic history, see, for example, Ernest R. May, *The World War and American Isolation*, Cambridge, Mass., 1966; "Bombing for Political Effects," unpublished paper; and *The Washington Naval Conference*, forthcoming; Richard H. Ullman, *Anglo-Soviet Relations, 1917–1921*, Princeton, N.J., Vol. 1, 1961, Vol. 2, 1968; Samuel R. Williamson, *The Politics of Grand Strategy*, Cambridge, Mass., 1969.

    For strategy, see Graham Allison and Morton H. Halperin,

"Bureaucratic Politics: A Paradigm and Some Policy Implications," in *World Politics*, special issue, 1971; and A. W. Marshall and Graham Allison, "Strategic Nuclear Deterrence: Do We Understand the Behavior of the Black Box?" forthcoming. For Sovietology, see A. W. Marshall, unpublished papers; and Thomas W. Wolfe, "Policymaking in the Soviet Union: A Statement with Supplementary Comments," P-4131, Rand Corporation, June 1969.

For Sinology, see Allen Whiting, "U.S.-Chinese Political Relations," an unpublished paper presented at the Conference on the Foreign Policy of Communist China, January 4–8, 1970.

For American foreign policy, see Morton H. Halperin and Tang Tsou, "U.S. Policy Toward the Offshore Islands," *Public Policy*, 1966; Morton H. Halperin, *Bureaucratic Politics and Foreign Policy*, forthcoming; and John Steinbruner, *The Mind and the Milieu of Policy Makers*, forthcoming.

60. Paul Hammond, "Directives for the Occupation of Germany," in H. Stein (ed.), *American Civil-Military Decisions.*

61. Ibid., p. 427.

62. Paul Hammond, "Super Carriers and B-36 Bombers," in H. Stein (ed.), op. cit.

63. Paul Hammond, "NSC-68: Prologue to Rearmament," in Schilling, Hammond, Snyder, op. cit.

64. This comparision was noted by N. J. Spykman, *America's Strategy in World Politics*, New York, 1942. See also Roger Hilsman, "The Foreign-Policy Consensus," op. cit., p. 368; and *To Move a Nation;* also Warner Schilling, "The Politics of National Defense: Fiscal 1950." Both Schilling and Hilsman credit William T. R. Fox.

65. On hierarchical bargaining, see Herbert Simon, *Models of Man,* New York, 1957, pp. 66–68; Robert Dahl and Charles Lindblom, *Politics, Economics, and Welfare,* New York, 1953, pp. 341–44; N. E. Long, "Public Policy and Administration," *Public Administration Review,* Winter 1954; Richard Fenno, *The President's Cabinet,* Cambridge, Mass., 1959, ch. 6.

66. Inclusion of the President's Special Assistant for National Security Affairs in the tier of Chiefs rather than among the Staffers involves a debatable choice. In fact he is both super-Staffer and near-Chief. His position has no statutory authority. He is especially dependent on good relations with the President and the Secretaries of Defense and State. Nevertheless, he stands astride a genuine action process. The decision to include this position among the Chiefs reflects my judgment that the function that McGeorge Bundy served is becoming institutionalized.

67. These points are drawn from Neustadt, Testimony, 1963; see especially pp. 82–83.

68. Hilsman, *To Move a Nation,* p. 81.

69. Daniels, *Frontier on the Potomac*, New York, 1946, pp. 31–32.

70. This proposition was formulated by Ernest R. May.

71. This aphorism was stated first, I think, by Don K. Price.
72. P. Hammond, "Super Carriers and B-36 Bombers," op. cit.
73. Neustadt, *Presidential Power*, ch. 3.
74. P. Hammond, "Super Carriers and B-36 Bombers," op. cit.
75. Dean Acheson, "The President and the Secretary of State," in D. Price (ed.), *The Secretary of State*, New York, 1960.
76. Richard Neustadt.
77. Roberta Wohlstetter, *Pearl Harbor: Warning and Decision*, Stanford, Calif., p. 350.

Chapter 6   Cuba II: A Third Cut

1. Robert Kennedy interview quoted by Ronald Steel, *New York Review of Books*, March 13, 1969, p. 22.
2. Robert F. Kennedy, *Thirteen Days: A Memoir of the Cuban Missile Crisis*, New York, 1969, p. 30. Others involved included Charles Bohlen, before leaving for his post as Ambassador to France; Vice-President Lyndon Johnson; Special Assistant Kenneth O'Donnell; Ambassador to the United Nations Adlai Stevenson; and Deputy Director of the United States Information Agency Don Wilson. Just which fourteen Robert Kennedy's remarks refer to is unclear.
3. Ibid., p. 29.
4. Theodore Sorensen, *Kennedy*, New York, 1965, p. 675.
5. Ibid., p. 670.
6. Ibid., p. 669.
7. Ibid., p. 670.
8. Ibid., pp. 669 ff. Also see Roger Hilsman, *To Move a Nation*, New York, 1967, p. 196.
9. *The New York Times*, August and September 1962.
10. *The New York Times*, August 30, 1962.
11. *The New York Times*, September 5, 1962.
12. *The New York Times*, September 14, 1962.
13. *The New York Times*, October 14, 1962.
14. U.S., Congress, House of Representatives, Select Committee on Export Control, *Hearings*, 87th Congress, 2nd Session, 1963, p. 811. For discussion of the accuracy and frankness of these remarks see U.S., Congress, House of Representatives, Department of Defense Appropriations, Subcommittee of the Committee on Appropriations, *Hearings*, 88th Congress, 1st Session, 1963, p. 40 ff. (hereafter referred to as Department of Defense Appropriations, *Hearings*).

15. Cited in Elie Abel, *The Missile Crisis,* Philadelphia, 1966, p. 13. Emphasis added.

16. Hilsman, op. cit., p. 194.

17. *The New York Times,* September 5, 1962.

18. *The New York Times,* September 14, 1962.

19. See Senate Foreign Relations Committee, Senate Armed Services Committee, House Committee on Appropriations, House Select Committee on Export Control.

20. For McCone's role, see Arthur Krock, *Memoirs,* New York, 1968, pp. 378 ff. Also see Sorensen, op. cit., p. 670, and Abel, op. cit., pp. 17–18. As recorded in Krock, McCone told Kennedy: "The only construction I can put on the material going into Cuba is that the Russians are preparing to introduce offensive missiles." See also Edward Weintal and Charles Bartlett, *Facing the Brink: An Intimate Study of Crisis Diplomacy,* New York, pp. 60–61.

21. Krock, op. cit., p. 379.

22. For De Vosjoli's role, see Phillippe Thyraud de Vosjoli, "So Much Has Been Swept Under the Rug," *Life,* April 26, 1968; also Krock, op. cit., pp. 378 ff.

23. De Vosjoli, op. cit., p. 35.

24. Abel, op. cit., p. 23; also Weintal and Bartlett, op. cit., pp. 60–61.

25. Abel, op. cit., p. 23.

26. Weintal and Bartlett, op. cit., p. 62.

27. *The New York Times,* September 10, 1962.

28. Abel, op. cit., pp. 25–26; Hilsman, op. cit., p. 174.

29. Department of Defense Appropriations, *Hearings,* p. 69. This interpretation is supported by Secretary McNamara's reply, when pressed by Congressman William Minshall (Ohio) about the twenty-nine-day gap of coverage of Western Cuba (September 5 to October 14). The Secretary stated: "We were facing surface-to-air missile systems that might be coming into operation." Roberta Wohlstetter seems to draw a similar inference from the Secretary's statement ("Cuba and Pearl Harbor," *Foreign Affairs,* July 1965, p. 697). Roger Hilsman states, "It was agreed that the usual flight pattern should be altered to minimize the risk of a shoot-down" (op. cit., p. 174). Also see Abel, op. cit., p. 25.

30. The United States Intelligence Board is the highest assembly of the American intelligence community. During this period, its membership included the chairman, John McCone, Director of the CIA; General Carter, Deputy Director of the CIA; Roger Hilsman, the Director of Intelligence and Research, Department of State; Lt. Gen. Joseph Carroll, Director of the Defense Intelligence Agency; Maj. Gen. Alva Fitch, Assistant Chief of Staff for Intelligence, Department of Army; Rear Adm. Vernon Lawrence, Assistant Chief of Naval Operations (Intelligence),

Department of the Navy; Maj. Gen. Robert Breitweiser, Assistant Chief of Staff, Intelligence, U.S. Air Force; Lt. Gen. Gordon Blake, Director, National Security Agency; Maj. Gen. Richard Collins, Director for Intelligence, Joint Staff; Harry Traynor, Assistant General Manager for Administration, Atomic Energy Commission; Alan Belmont, Assistant to the Director, FBI. See Department of Defense Appropriations, *Hearings,* p. 51.

31. *Aviation Week and Space Technology,* October 1, 1962.

32. Hilsman, op. cit., pp. 187–88.

33. A basic, but somewhat contradictory, account of parts of this story emerges in Department of Defense Appropriations, *Hearings,* pp. 1–70.

34. Ibid., p. 71. See also Abel, op. cit., pp. 26, 29.

35. Krock, op. cit., p. 380.

36. Abel, op. cit., p. 44.

37. Sorensen, op. cit., pp. 673 ff.

38. See Richard Neustadt, "Afterword: 1964," *Presidential Power,* New York, 1964, p. 187. For an extreme version of this argument see I. F. Stone, "The Brink," review of Elie Abel, *The Missile Crisis,* in *New York Review of Books,* April 14, 1966.

39. See Presidential statements and press conferences, August and September 1962.

40. Sorensen, op. cit., pp. 668 ff.

41. Hilsman, op. cit., p. 197.

42. Sorensen, op. cit., p. 688.

43. Robert F. Kennedy, op. cit., p. 53.

44. Ibid., p. 54.

45. Sorensen, op. cit., p. 702; also Robert F. Kennedy, op. cit., pp. 53–54.

46. As Richard Neustadt argues in *Presidental Power* (pp. 183 ff.), in the President's seat, all these distinctions dissolve.

47. Sorensen, op. cit., p. 683.

48. Robert F. Kennedy, op. cit., p. 67.

49. Hilsman, op. cit., p. 195.

50. Ibid., p. 195.

51. Several forms of diplomatic approach were considered; see Abel, op. cit., pp. 60–61.

52. Walter Lippmann's column of October 25 (*The New York Times*) criticizing the administration for this "suspension of diplomacy" echoed Bundy's arguments.

53. Patrick Anderson, *The President's Men,* New York, 1968, p. 270.

54. Ibid., p. 270.

55. Robert F. Kennedy, op. cit., p. 31.

56. Ibid., pp. 38–39.

57. Sorensen, op. cit., p. 684. See also Dean Acheson, "Homage to Plain Dumb Luck," *Esquire*, February 1969.

58. Sorensen, op. cit., p. 679. This quotation describes Sorensen's account of Robert Kennedy's role. Sorensen also notes that he and Bundy assisted in this enterprise.

59. Ibid., p. 684.

60. General David M. Shoup, the Marine Commandant, a member of the Joint Chiefs of Staff during the missile crisis, has taken issue with the widespread tendency to treat the Joint Chiefs as a single entity in accounts of the crisis. Shoup asserts: "I fought against invasion of Cuba from the start" (*The New York Times*, October 26, 1968).

61. Robert F. Kennedy, op. cit., p. 36.

62. Arthur Schlesinger, Jr., *A Thousand Days: John F. Kennedy in the White House*, Boston, 1965, p. 831.

63. Acheson, op. cit.

64. Ibid.

65. Acheson's published recollection (see note 57) singles this out as the glaring error of Robert Kennedy: "Once this occurred [i.e., the missiles became operational], Cuba would become a combination of porcupine and cobra. My criticism of Senator Kennedy's narrative is that it does not face this possibility — indeed, probability — frankly, it is merely stated and dropped."

66. Ibid.

67. Sorensen, op. cit., p. 682.

68. Abel, op. cit., p. 100.

69. Ibid., p. 127.

70. Sorensen, op. cit., p. 686; Abel, op. cit., pp. 69–70.

71. Sorensen, op. cit., p. 686.

72. Abel, op. cit., p. 70. Schlesinger quotes John Hightower, the Associated Press' State Department reporter, who wrote on August 22, 1965: "Criticism over his role in the missile crisis angered Rusk to the point that he heatedly defended it in talks with newsmen on one or two occasions. He said that the responsibility of the Secretary of State was to advise the President and he did not think he should commit himself before all the facts were in. Therefore he withdrew himself from the argument for several days though Under Secretary of State George Ball, instructed by Rusk to take a free hand, presented the State Department viewpoint" (Schlesinger, op. cit., p. 807). Acheson (op. cit.) comments on the "other duties" which kept Rusk away from early ExCom meetings as follows: "One wonders what those 'other duties and responsibilities' were to have been half so important as those they displaced."

73. This metaphor seems to have been coined by Joseph Alsop and Charles Bartlett in their *Saturday Evening Post* article of December 8, 1962. Also see Abel, op. cit., p. 70.

74. Sorensen, op. cit., p. 680.

75. Ibid., p. 683.
76. Abel, op. cit., pp. 61, 77.
77. Sorensen, op. cit., p. 685.
78. Ibid., p. 676.
79. Abel (op. cit., p. 77) quotes Bundy's recollection that: "It made all the difference — I felt then and have felt since — that the Russians were caught pretending, in a clumsy way, that they had not done what it was clear to the whole world they had in fact done."
80. Sorensen, op. cit., p. 683.
81. Abel, op. cit., p. 49.
82. Sorensen, op. cit., p. 695. Abel (op. cit., p. 49) quotes a Stevenson remark made in March 1965, four months before his death: "I was a little alarmed that Kennedy's first consideration should have been the air strike. I told him that sooner or later we would have to go to the U.N. and it was vitally important we go there with a reasonable case."
83. Robert F. Kennedy, op. cit., p. 34. Also see Abel, op. cit., p. 81.
84. Acheson, op. cit.
85. Ibid.
86. Ibid.
87. Ibid.
88. "Introduction" to Robert F. Kennedy, op. cit., p. 13. The reference of McNamara's statement is considerably wider. As he testified at the time of Robert Kennedy's bid for the Presidential nomination, it was Kennedy, "acting with his brother's consent, who did so much to organize the effort, monitor the results and assure the completion of work on which recommendations to the President were based." And, he went on: "We'd been through a lot of trying experiences together, shared views that were similar, were allies during President Kennedy's administration. There is a bond that it would have been difficult to sever. Other people turned away from me to further their own positions whom I didn't expect would do it, but if he'd done it, if he'd been any different, I'd have been the most shocked person in the world" (quoted by Brock Brower, "McNamara Seen Now, Full Length," *Life,* Vol. 64, May 10, 1968).
89. Sorensen, op. cit., p. 685. For President Kennedy's expectations, see Robert F. Kennedy, op. cit., p. 36. See also note 2 to Chapter 4 for another perspective on this exchange.
90. Robert F. Kennedy, op. cit., p. 34.
91. Sorensen, op. cit., p. 684
92. Ibid.
93. Ibid., p. 691.
94. Ibid.
95. Ibid., pp. 691 ff.
96. Schlesinger, op. cit., p. 296.
97. Acheson, op. cit. Emphasis added.
98. Robert F. Kennedy, op. cit., p. 119. Emphasis added.

99. Ibid., p. 48.

100. Ibid., p. 119.

101. Ibid., p. 46.

102. Abel, op. cit., p. 58.

103. Robert F. Kennedy, op. cit., p. 46.

104. Sorensen, op. cit., p. 679.

105. Ibid.

106. Brower, op. cit.

107. Abel, op. cit., p. 58.

108. Ibid., p. 58. This participant went on to say: "This had a healthy effect in stimulating real discussion. It inhibited the striking of attitudes. Having him there in the conference room was perhaps better, because it was less inhibiting, than having the President there."

109. Robert F. Kennedy, op. cit., p. 47.

110. Sorensen, op. cit., p. 692; see also Abel, op. cit., p. 83.

111. Sorensen, op. cit., p. 692.

112. Ibid.

113. Ibid.; see also Schlesinger, op. cit., p. 806.

114. Sorensen, op. cit., p. 692.

115. Schlesinger, op. cit., p. 806.

116. Sorensen, op. cit., p. 692.

117. Abel, op. cit., p. 89.

118. Sorensen, op. cit., p. 693.

119. Robert F. Kennedy, op. cit., p. 47.

120. Sorensen, op. cit., 693. Abel (op. cit., pp. 106 ff.) asserts incorrectly that the first National Security meeting convened Sunday afternoon.

121. Robert F. Kennedy, op. cit., p. 47.

122. Abel, op. cit., p. 186.

123. Alsop and Bartlett, op. cit.; see also Sorensen, op. cit., p. 693.

124. Ibid., p. 694.

125. Ibid.

126. Ibid.

127. Ibid.

128. Hilsman, op. cit., p. 205.

129. Sorensen, op. cit., p. 695.

130. Ibid., pp. 695–96.

131. Ibid., p. 696. According to Sorensen, Stevenson also "talked of a U.N.-supervised standstill of military activity on both sides — thus leaving the missiles in with no blockade — and of a summit meeting, and of U.N. inspection teams investigating not only Cuba but possible U.S. bases for attacking Cuba."

132. Abel, op. cit., p. 95.

133. Sorensen, op. cit., p. 695.

134. Abel, op. cit., p. 96.

135. Robert F. Kennedy, op. cit., p. 49.

136. Abel, op. cit., pp. 100–01; Hilsman, op. cit., p. 205.

137. Hilsman, op. cit., p. 215.

138. Robert Graves, from *Oxford Address on Poetry,* cited by Abel, op. cit., p. 54.

139. Abel, op. cit., p. 54.

140. Richard Neustadt has developed this point in his "Afterword: 1964" to *Presidential Power,* pp. 188–89.

141. *The Washington Post,* December 18, 1962.

142. Acheson, op. cit.

143. Robert F. Kennedy, op. cit., p. 106.

144. Ibid.

145. Ibid., p. 99.

146. Neustadt, op. cit., p. 189.

147. "Khrushchev's Report on the International Situation — 1," *The Current Digest of the Soviet Press,* Vol. 14, No. 51, January 16, 1963, p. 7. Published weekly by The Joint Committee on Slavic Studies.

148. Robert F. Kennedy, op. cit., p. 89. Emphasis added.

149. Ibid., pp. 89–90. Emphasis added.

150. Ibid., p. 79.

151. Ibid., p. 87.

152. Ibid., p. 81.

153. Ibid. Emphasis added.

154. U.S., Department of State, *Bulletin,* Vol. 47, No. 1220, November 12, 1962, pp. 743–45.

155. Ibid.

156. Sorensen, op. cit., p. 725.

157. Weintal and Bartlett, op. cit., p. 67.

158. Ibid., p. 68.

159. Robert F. Kennedy, op. cit., p. 124.

160. Weintal and Bartlett, op. cit., p. 68.

161. *The New York Times,* June 11, 1963.

162. Robert F. Kennedy, op. cit., p. 62.

163. Schlesinger, op. cit., p. 841.

164. Robert F. Kennedy, op. cit., pp. 126–27.

165. Indeed, during the second week, a number of *ad hoc* subcommittees of the ExCom were formed as a way of getting secondary issues raised and also as a path whereby secondary officials could get into the act.

166. U.S., Congress, Senate, Committee on Government Operations, Subcommittee on National Security Staffing and Operations, *Staffing Procedures and Problems in the Soviet Union,* 88th Congress, 1st Session, 1963, p. 25.

167. Ibid.

168. Robert F. Kennedy, op. cit., p. 73.

169. Ibid., pp. 77–78.

170. Ibid., p. 82; also Abel, op. cit., pp. 158–59.

171. The inadequacy of the private communication channels between the President and the Chairman led, in the aftermath of the crisis, to the establishment of a direct channel of communication between Washington and Moscow. See U.S., Congress, Senate, Committee on Government Operations, Subcommittee on National Security Staffing Operations, *Administration of National Security, Hearings,* 88th Congress, 1st Session, 1963, part 6, pp. 421–27.

172. Sorensen, op. cit., p. 712.

173. Robert F. Kennedy (op. cit.) records several conversations through this channel.

174. Ibid., p. 62.

175. According to a post-mortem on the crisis, written by Walt Rostow and Paul Nitze, as reported by Weintal and Bartlett, op. cit., pp. 54 ff.

176. Ibid.

177. Sorensen, op. cit., p. 711; see also Hilsman, op. cit., p. 206.

178. Robert F. Kennedy, op. cit., p. 83.

179. Ibid., p. 85.

180. For this episode see Hilsman, op. cit., pp. 217 ff.

181. Ibid.

182. Ibid.

183. Ibid., p. 218.

184. Ibid.

185. Abel, op. cit., p. 178.

186. Robert F. Kennedy, op. cit., p. 86

187. This reconstruction is based on Robert F. Kennedy, ibid., pp. 86–90, and Abel, op. cit., pp. 178 ff.

188. Abel, op. cit., p. 182. According to Abel, Acheson argued: "We were too eager to liquidate this thing. So long as we had the thumbscrew on Khrushchev, we should have given it another turn every day."

189. Robert F. Kennedy, op. cit., p. 91.

190. U.S., Department of State, *Bulletin,* Vol. 47, No. 1220, November 12, 1962, pp. 741–43.

191. Abel, op. cit., pp. 188–89.

192. Robert F. Kennedy, op. cit., p. 96.

193. Abel, op. cit., p. 188.

194. For evidence of these differences see Roman Kolkowitz's analysis of differences among the major Soviet newspapers, *Conflicts in Soviet Party-Military Relations: 1962–63,* RM-3760-

PR, Rand Corporation, 1963, pp. 9 ff. In the October 28, 1962, issue of *Izvestia,* while the front page announced Khrushchev's letter to the President proposing a trade of Cuban and Turkish bases, a commentary on an inside page stated: "There are those in the U.S.A. who speculate that in exchange for denying Cuba the ability to repel American aggression, one might 'give up' some American base close to Soviet territory. . . . Such 'proposals,' if you can call them that, merely serve to betray the unclean conscience of the authors."

195. Hilsman, op. cit., p. 220.

196. Robert F. Kennedy, op. cit., p. 94.

197. Sorensen, op. cit., p. 713.

198. Ibid.; see also Hilsman, op. cit., p. 220.

199. Robert F. Kennedy, op. cit., p. 98.

200. Ibid.

201. Ibid., pp. 98–101.

202. Sorensen, op. cit., p. 713.

203. Ibid., p. 714.

204. Robert F. Kennedy, op. cit., p. 94.

205. Ibid., p. 95.

206. Abel, op. cit., p. 189.

207. Ibid.

208. Sorensen, op. cit., p. 714.

209. Ibid., p. 696.

210. Harold Macmillan, "Introduction" to Robert F. Kennedy, op. cit., p. 19.

211. U.S., Department of State, *Bulletin,* Vol. 47, No. 1220, November 12, 1962, p. 741 White House press release dated October 27, 1962.

212. Sorensen, op. cit., p. 714.

213. Robert F. Kennedy, op. cit., pp. 96, 97.

214. Ibid., p. 98.

215. Ibid.

216. Ibid., pp. 101–02.

217. Ibid., p. 102.

218. U.S., Department of State, *Bulletin,* Vol. 47, No. 1220, November 12, 1962, p. 743. White House press release dated October 27, 1962.

219. Sorensen, op. cit., p. 715. Sorensen's account of Robert Kennedy's warning quotes a speech by Robert Kennedy at Columbia, South Carolina; see *The New York Times,* April 26, 1963.

220. Robert F. Kennedy, op. cit., pp. 108–09. In threatening military action unless the Soviet missile construction in Cuba stopped, Robert Kennedy seems to have been bluffing — to some extent. Sorensen records his judgment that the President would not

have moved immediately to an air strike or invasion (op. cit., pp. 715–16).

221. This judgment is contrary to that of many sovietologists; see Horelick and Rush, op. cit., p. 141.

222. Robert F. Kennedy, op. cit., p. 27.

223. Schlesinger, op. cit., p. 802.

224. Sorensen, op. cit., p. 681.

225. For this line of reasoning see Schlesinger, op. cit., p. 796.

226. J. William Fulbright, "Some Reflections upon Recent Events and Continuing Problems," *The Congressional Record,* June 29, 1961, p. 11704.

227. Analysts favorable to a Soviet second-strike capability would have been strongly against the Soviet missile bases in Cuba, which could be used only in a first strike. But this distinction was not well understood in the Soviet Union at the time.

228. Robert F. Kennedy, op. cit., p. 25.

229. Ibid., p. 26.

230. Department of Defense Appropriations, *Hearings,* p. 25; also Hilsman, op. cit., p. 184.

231. Department of Defense Appropriations, *Hearings,* p. 25.

232. For a similar argument see Horelick and Rush, op. cit., p. 146.

233. Kolkowitz, op. cit., pp. v, vi. See also Michel Tatu, *Power in the Kremlin,* New York, 1969, p. 236.

234. Sorensen, op. cit., p. 674. Sorensen develops this point further in another context: "President Kennedy, on the morning of the first of those seven days, sent for copies of all his earlier statements on Cuba . . . on the presence of offensive, as distinguished from defensive, weapons . . . on threats to our vital interests . . . and on our armed intervention in that island. These earlier decisions made it *unlikely that he would respond to the October crisis by doing nothing and unlikely that his first step would be an invasion*" (*Decision-Making in the White House: The Olive Branch and the Arrows,* New York, 1963, pp. 34–35; emphasis added).

235. The Stennis Committee report, *The Cuban Military Build-up,* asserts that "the intelligence community adhered to the view that they [Soviet personnel in Cuba] were military instructors, advisers, and trainers" until after the missiles were discovered (p. 6).

236. *The New York Times,* September 5, 1962.

237. Department of Defense Appropriations, *Hearings,* p. 6.

238. *The New York Times,* September 5, 1962.

239. Abel, op. cit., p. 13. Emphasis added.

240. Ibid., p. 14.

241. Hilsman, op. cit., p. 167.

242. Ibid., p. 181.

243. A number of excellent, suggestive studies are available, includ-

ing Carl A. Linden, *Khrushchev and the Soviet Leadership*, Baltimore, 1966; Roman Kolkowitz, op. cit; and *The Soviet Army and the Communist Party*, R-446-PR, RAND Corporation, 1966. *Staffing Procedures and Problems in the Soviet Union* provides a number of interesting insights into Soviet decision-making processes. Michel Tatu, op. cit., and William Hyland and Richard Shryock, *The Fall of Khrushchev*, New York, 1968, offer very suggestive accounts of this period.

244. *Staffing Procedures and Problems in the Soviet Union*, pp. 24 ff.

245. Ibid., pp. 26–27.

246. Evidence about the role of individual Presidium members during the public weeks of the crisis supports this inference. Ibid., p. 25.

247. *Pravda*, July 10, 1960. Emphasis added.

248. Andres Suarez, *Cuba, Castro and Communism: 1959–1966*, Cambridge, Mass., 1967, pp. 157 ff.

249. Tatu, op. cit., p. 231.

250. Horelick and Rush, op. cit., p. 135.

251. Theodore Draper, *Castro's Revolution: Myths and Realities*, New York, 1962, pp. 201–06.

252. *Staffing Procedures and Problems in the Soviet Union*, pp. 26–27.

253. This announcement was made by Roswell Gilpatric, Deputy Secretary of Defense, in November 1961.

254. Hilsman, op. cit., pp. 163–64.

255. Kolkowitz, op. cit., p. 9.

256. For a similar speculation, see Tatu, op. cit., pp. 236 ff.

257. For Kennedy's comment see Stewart Alsop, "Kennedy's Grand Strategy," *Saturday Evening Post*, March 31, 1962.

258. *Pravda*, May 19, 1962.

259. Tatu, op. cit., pp. 236–37.

260. It should be noted that Walt Rostow delivered a speech in Berlin on October 18, before he had learned of the Soviet missiles in Cuba, analyzing the crisis that Khrushchev then faced and warning that he might make a move against Berlin. Rostow said: "The vision of the world as seen from Moscow has thus substantially changed in the past 2 years. The policies which Khrushchev set in motion after he had acquired leadership of the Soviet Union have failed to achieve a breakthrough; meanwhile, the response of the Western World — plus the corrosive dynamics within the Communist bloc — have intertwined to produce a deep but quiet crisis in the history of communism. Moscow must ask itself: Where do we go from here? In the short run, the answer may well be Berlin. It is possible that Mr. Khrushchev may miscalculate the will and the strength of the Allies and will attempt to precipitate another crisis in this city." See "The Present Stage of the Cold War,"

Address before Ernst Reuter Society at the Free University of Berlin, Berlin, Germany, October 18, 1962, U.S., Department of State, *Bulletin*, Vol. 47, No. 1219, November 5, 1962, p. 680.

261. For an extensive account of these developments, see Thomas Wolfe, *Soviet Power and Europe*, RM-5838-PR, Rand Corporation, 1968, pp. 120 ff.

262. *The New York Times*, November 28, 1958.

263. Tatu, op. cit., p. 232.

264. Oleg Penkovskiy, *The Penkovskiy Papers*, New York, 1965, pp. 207, 220, 244.

265. Ibid., pp. 207–09, 216.

266. Further evidence linking Berlin to the missile move is provided by Gromyko's statement to President Kennedy on October 18, affirming that Moscow would sign a separate German peace treaty if a settlement of the Berlin issues proved impossible in the period after the American elections. See Sorensen, op. cit., p. 690.

267. For an excellent discussion of these developments, see Linden, op. cit., pp. 146 ff.

268. For evidence about this opposition, see Kolkowitz, *Conflicts in Soviet Party-Military Relations*, pp. 16 ff.; and *The Soviet Army and the Communist Party*, pp. 337 ff. This hesitancy by military leaders seems to have been allayed, to some extent, by an argument that even if the United States forced withdrawal of all the Soviet missiles, the Soviet Union could demand withdrawal of U.S. Turkish missiles as a *quid pro quo*. See, for example, Khrushchev's threats against the U.S. missiles in Turkey in May 1962 (around the time when the decision must have been made); *Pravda*, May 17, 1962.

Chapter 7 Conclusion

1. Some Model I analysts go a step further in constructing their explanations: they try to account for a large number of particular characteristics of the action, or to find more subtle reasons for the action. One could imagine a competition among Model I analysts, the point of which would be to construct the most subtle set of objectives that the action maximized. A competition of this sort has developed among economists using a maximizing model to explain the behavior of consumers and firms.

2. For an excellent discussion of the interdependence of facts and theory see Hilary Putnam, "The Analytic and the Synthetic," *Minnesota Studies in the Philosophy of Science*, Vol. 2, 1963.

3. Explanations produced by physical scientists of much more carefully specified *explicanda* are also accompanied by a not fully specified appendix or text that spells out some of the elements of the *ceteris paribus* clause. See P. Bridgman, *The*

Nature of Physical Theory, New York, 1936. Bridgman states (pp. 59–60): "If I set up mathematical theory of a body falling under the action of gravity, I have the equation $dv/dt = g$, but I have to supplement this by a 'text,' saying that v is a number describing a property of the moving body which can be obtained by a certain kind of measurement, which is specified, that t is the time obtained by another kind of measurement, etc. . . . It must also specify the connection between the different symbols in the equation. . . . The text specifies that the s and the t are the distance and time obtained by *simultaneous* measurements. The equation itself has no mechanism for demanding that s and t be simultaneous, and in fact this demand cannot be described in the language of the equation."

See also G. Holton's explication of Galileo's law of projectile motion: "We find in his work a thorough examination of the major limitations involved; for example, he points out that the trajectory will not be parabolic for extremely large ranges because then the acceleration of gravity, being directed toward the center of our round earth, will no longer be parallel for different parts of the paths assumed in our equations. Of course this failure applies, strictly speaking, even to small trajectories, but in such cases it is by theory and test permissible to neglect it for our purposes, just as we have already neglected the effect of air resistance, rotation of the earth, variation of the value of g over the whole path, etc. . . . If we were required to deal with actual motions in which these secondary factors are not negligible, we are confident that we would surely be able to discover the laws guiding those smaller effects, and add them to our calculations" (*Introduction to Concepts and Theories in Physical Science,* New York, 1952, p. 270). For a discussion of texts in the social sciences, see R. Brown, *Explanation in Social Science,* London, 1963, pp. 148 ff.

4. Variants of Model I can be produced by changing the constraints, e.g., by changing the assignment to: make a powerful argument for a more complex national objective function, including both foreign and domestic objectives, that permits the reader to see how he could have chosen that action.

5. For a persuasive argument that this concept underlies our notion of causation, see H. L. A. Hart and A. M. Honoré, *Causation in the Law,* Oxford, 1959, and S. Hampshire, *Thought and Action,* London, 1959. Primitive man tends to explain natural phenomena in similar terms: by reference to the goals and purposes of spirits, or the *telos* of an object. See R. G. Collingwood, *The Philosophy of History,* New York, 1946.

6. Herbert Simon developed the concept of "bounded rationality" for individual actors, stressing bounds such as costs of information and calculation. An analogous concept could be developed for governments, though in this case the central problems would be identification of the governmental actor's goals, perceptions, etc.

7. Steinbruner's Model IV emphasizes cognitive processes of individuals. It can therefore be understood as a gloss on Model III or Model II. See his forthcoming study, *The Mind and the Milieu of Policy Makers.*

8. To make Model I ask questions about determinants requires some translation.

9. Perhaps the focal concepts of Model I permit explanation of the quadrant in which action is taken.

10. Though the explanations produced by analysts relying predominantly on different models reflect differences in emphasis, focus, and collateral purpose, can one satisfactorily account for the seeming conflicts among explanations by noting that different models address somewhat different questions? Is this not analogous to some physicists' attempts to explain the differences between wave and quantum theories of light? Certainly this does not relieve the suspicion that at some level there is a conflict between President Kennedy's explanation of the U.S. imposition of the blockade as the only rational strategic choice and the Model III analyst's explanation of the blockade as the result of a struggle in which the majority of the ExCom's first choice was eliminated by the believed (but inaccurate) assertion that a surgical air strike could not be chosen with high confidence of success. The difficulty in coming to grips with the complementarity or contradiction between explanations produced by different models stems from the problem of unraveling the central propositions implied by these explanations. What basic propositions are entailed by the Rational Actor Model's explanation of the presence of missiles in Cuba by reference to the Soviet Union's objectives? Is this compatible with a diversity of objectives on the part of central Soviet leaders? Must all have subscribed to the same objective? Diplomatic historians often attribute objectives to nations, though they would allow that no one in the nation at the time appreciated the fact that this was the nation's objective. Proper attention to the question of whether these models simply present partial, alternate, complementary stories (as Gilbert Ryle's philosophical equivalent suggests) or rather permit contradictions will require much more careful definition of the propositions employed and entailed by explanations according to each model. See Gilbert Ryle, *Dilemmas,* Cambridge, England, 1954.

11. Edward Weintal and Charles Bartlett, *Facing the Brink: An Intimate Study of Crisis Diplomacy,* New York, 1967, pp. 54–55.

12. This paper, delivered at the September 1968 meetings of the American Political Science Association in Washington, D.C., was reproduced by the Rand Corporation as P-3919, August 1968. The discussion is heavily indebted to Ernest R. May.

13. Richard Snyder, *Deterrence and Defense,* Princeton, N.J., 1961. p. 11. For a more general presentation of a similar position see Paul Kecskemeti, *Strategic Surrender,* New York, 1964.

Index